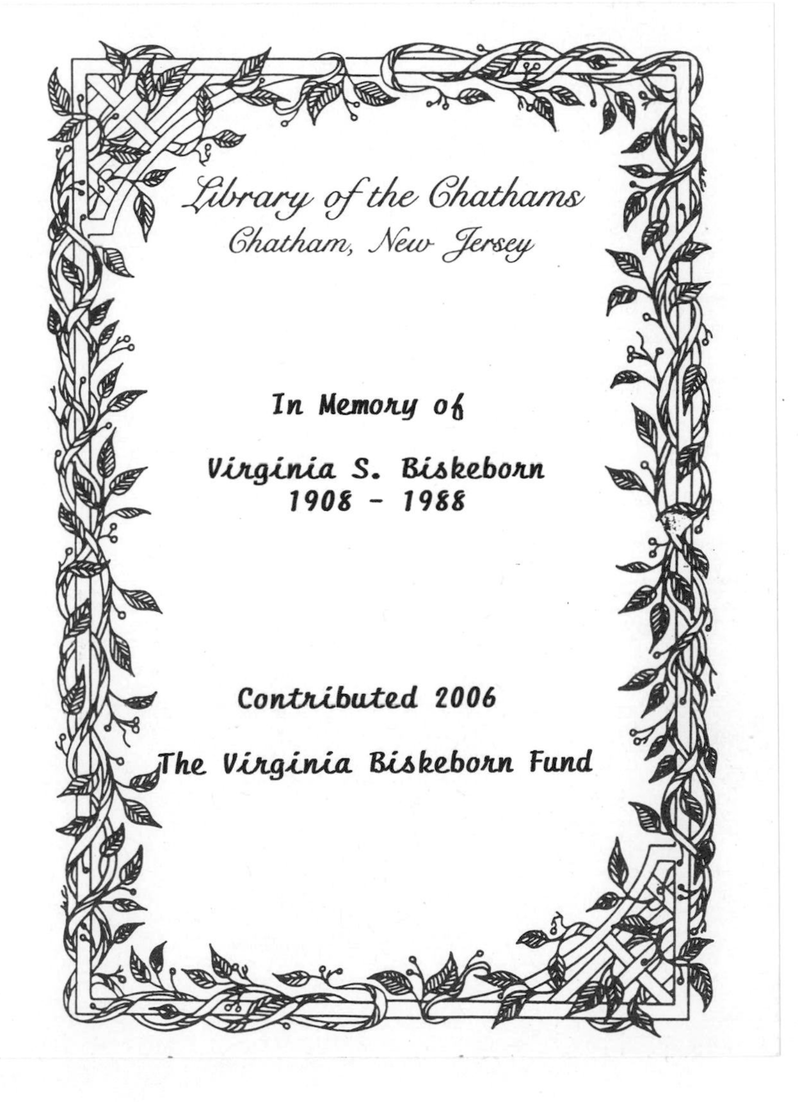

FOR THE PREVENTION OF CRUELTY

DIANE L. BEERS

FOR THE PREVENTION OF CRUELTY

The History and Legacy of Animal Rights Activism in the United States

Swallow Press / Ohio University Press Athens

Swallow Press / Ohio University Press, Athens, Ohio 45701
www.ohio.edu/oupress

Printed in the United States of America

Swallow Press / Ohio University Press books are printed on acid-free paper ∞ ™

Cover image: Street-cab horses drinking from half-barrel of water provided by the ASPCA. Courtesy Library of Congress, reproduction number LC-USZ62-49241.

13 12 11 10 09 08 07 06 5 4 3 2 1

Library of Congress Cataloging-in-Publication Data
Beers, Diane L.
For the prevention of cruelty : the history and legacy of animal rights activism in the United States / Diane L. Beers.
p. cm.
Includes bibliographical references and index.
ISBN 0-8040-1086-2 (cloth : alk. paper)—ISBN 0-8040-1087-0 (pbk. : alk. paper) 1. Animal rights movement—United States—History. 2. Animal welfare—United States—History. 3. Animal rights—United States—History. I. Title.

HV4764.B44 2006
179'.30973–dc22

2006004294

For Chance

Contents

Illustrations

Acknowledgments

In the journey of writing this book, I have encountered along the way many wonderful people who have helped immeasurably in its creation. And although I alone claim responsibility for any shortcomings, its strengths can be attributed in great part to those who guided and encouraged me. My appreciation begins where my journey began, with my dissertation committee. Adele Lindenmeyr, Bettye Collier-Thomas, and Margaret Marsh all provided unparalleled support in those early years of research and writing, and their suggestions greatly improved my own thinking about the subject of animal advocacy. Without question, the person to whom I owe the greatest intellectual debt is my mentor and adviser, Kenneth Kusmer. I still vividly recollect that day when a nervous and unsure graduate student met that demanding and accomplished professor. I remember wondering if I would meet his unwaveringly high standards and expectations, but what I discovered was that behind that somewhat intimidating exterior was my staunchest ally. His support never diminished, and without his faith in my work and his persistent nudging, *For the Prevention of Cruelty* would still be a dusty dissertation on an equally dusty shelf.

Several colleagues and friends read the entire manuscript and offered invaluable feedback on both my writing and my interpretations. Early in its evolution, Daniel Richter graciously read a burdensomely long dissertation and showed a novice writer how to better present her ideas. More recently, Glenda Riley's helpful critique shaped the manuscript's final revisions and brought it down to a reasonable (and readable) length. Special gratitude goes to friend and writer extraordinaire Deborah Carlin for her detailed reading, crucial input, and ongoing support of this project. Various other friends and colleagues have read chapters over the years, and many of their ideas were woven into my revisions. As the project neared completion, Holyoke Community College and particularly

Lisa Wyatt-Ganson offered enthusiastic encouragement and generous support.

In my research travels, I visited organizations large and small and always found welcoming staff members willing to sacrifice their precious time to assist me in digging through piles and files of archival material. Those organizations include, among others, the Argus Archives, the Animals' Agenda, the Women's Humane Society, the American Anti-Vivisection Society, the Animal Welfare Institute, the Humane Society of the United States, the International Society for Animal Rights, and the People for the Ethical Treatment of Animals. I also spent time at the Animal Welfare Information Center at the National Agricultural Library. When I could not visit organizations in person, I corresponded by mail and telephone and experienced the generosity of the dozens of groups that sent me scores of helpful documents. More specifically, I would like to thank Kim Stallwood, who opened up his offices and his home to me on more than one occasion. His activism and kindness epitomize the animal advocacy movement. Several humanitarians, including John Kullberg, Virginia Woolf, Elliot Katz, Helen Jones, and Esther Mechler, granted interviews that significantly enhanced my understanding of the post-1945 movement. Sadly, some of those who assisted me on my journey have since passed away. I honor the lives and memories of Tina Nelson, Ron Scott, Helen Jones, and Christine Stevens; this book would not have been possible without them. Finally, I would like to thank the Culture and Animals Foundation and Tom Regan for the research grant that made some of my trips possible.

Special thanks to Rick Huard and Gillian Berchowitz at Swallow Press / Ohio University Press, both of whom strike the perfect balance between offering guidance and fostering independence, rare and commendable virtues.

And lastly, I would like to recognize those who inspired me in more personal ways. Some say writing is a lonely task, and perhaps that is true in part, but my life is so blessed by the wonderful people who surround me that I never felt alone in the evolution of my work. Without doubt, I would not even be a writer or professor today without the faith and support of early mentors Barb Hetrick, Gerald McKnight, Roger Reitman, and Len Latkovski. In my other life as a professor, my students continually remind me of what really matters in education; their intellectual curiosity and enthusiasm make my job a pleasure each day. Moreover, my teaching partner and close friend Deborah Fairman has taught me how to be a better writer, instructor, and person; she is the other element of joy in my career. I would also like to thank my family members for never giving up on me, even in those moments when they surely wondered at my career choice. Similarly, I could not now imagine my life without the Butterworth Road "family": Frederick, Allen, Celt, Jerry, Rob, Chris, Buddy, Dean, and Kathleen all bring much happiness into my life. I also cannot adequately express my appreciation to Tammi Nell for always being there through even the most trying years and to Karen Butler for being the most loyal friend anyone could ask for. My eternal gratitude to Catherine for showing me that one's journey must enrich the soul. Finally, I would be remiss if I did not mention my deepest affection and appreciation for the companion animals that grace my life and those of my friends. Their spirits light every page. This book is their voice.

Abbreviations

AAVS	American Anti-Vivisection Society
ABC	American Broadcasting Company
ACP	Animal Care Panel
AHA	American Humane Association
AHES	American Humane Education Society
AMA	American Medical Association
API	Animal Protection Institute
ASPCA	American Society for the Prevention of Cruelty to Animals
AWI	Animal Welfare Institute
BBS	Bureau of the Biological Survey
CDMR	Council on Defense of Medical Research
CITES	Convention on International Trade in Endangered Species
CLP	Council for Livestock Protection
ESA	Endangered Species Act
FFA	Fund for Animals
FoA	Friends of Animals
FoE	Friends of the Earth
HSUS	Humane Society of the United States
IDA	In Defense of Animals
ILAR	Institute of Laboratory Animal Resources
LAWA	Laboratory Animal Welfare Act, later amended as the Animal Welfare Act
MMP	Marine Mammal Protection (act)
MSPCA	Massachusetts Society for the Prevention of Cruelty to Animals
NAVS	National Anti-Vivisection Society

NCSAW	National Catholic Society for Animal Welfare, renamed Society for Animal Rights and subsequently International Society for Animal Rights
NEAVS	New England Anti-Vivisection Society
NHES	National Humane Education Society
NIH	National Institutes of Health
NRA	National Rifle Association
NSMR	National Society for Medical Research
NWF	National Wildlife Federation
PETA	People for the Ethical Treatment of Animals
PSPCA	Pennsylvania Society for the Prevention of Cruelty to Animals
PTA	Parent Teacher Association
RSPCA	Royal Society for the Prevention of Cruelty to Animals
SAPL	Society for Animal Protective Legislation
SAR	Society for Animal Rights
SPCA	Society for the Prevention of Cruelty to Animals
UAA	United Action for Animals
USDA	U.S. Department of Agriculture
UNESCO	United Nations Educational, Scientific, and Cultural Organization
WARDS	Working for Animals Used in Research, Drugs, and Surgery
WCTU	Women's Christian Temperance Union
WPSPCA	Women's Branch of the Pennsylvania Society for the Prevention of Cruelty to Animals (previously the Women's Branch of the PSPCA), also known as the Women's Humane Society
YWCA	Young Women's Christian Association

CHAPTER 1

Resurrecting the Voice

Animal Advocacy in History

> A Robin Redbreast in a cage
> Puts all Heaven in a Rage.
>
> —William Blake

During an unusual warm spell early last year, I shed some of the many layers of clothes required to survive a New England winter and ventured out for a stroll in a nearby town. I eventually migrated to the local bookshop in search of something to read during the inevitable return and last stand of the winter season. As row after row of magazines tempted me with discourses on everything from rock "grrrls" to literary criticism, a rather striking cover drew my eye toward the nature section. A chimpanzee with hand tucked under chin stared back at me as though contemplating some weighty issue of the world. The bold, multicolored headline next to the philosophical primate asked "Should Animals Have Legal Rights?" Since I had spent many of my self-absorbed graduate school years researching the historical issues and people surrounding this very question, I quickly flipped to the relevant pages behind the provocative cover.

The article satisfied the casual reader within me but disappointed the social historian. The author adeptly maneuvered through many of the current and hotly contested issues related to animal rights, including animal intelligence, the ability of various species to feel pain, the prevalent use of animals in medical experiments, and dissection in schools, among others. Furthermore, he persuasively argued that there had been a recent, discernible shift in public attitudes toward a greater concern for the rights of animals, citing public opinion polls, numerous legislative initiatives (mostly at the state level), and legal victories since 1990 to reform, regulate, or ban everything from steel traps to factory farms, cock- and dogfighting, greyhound racing, and puppy mills. All of this was fascinating. What disappointed me was the painfully brief foray into past debates over the ethical consideration for nonhumans (or lack thereof, according to the author) and what amounted to a cursory, one-sentence nod to the contributions of the post–Civil War antivivisection movement. Furthering my dismay, the article focused primarily on what the author characterized as a "new movement" to "afford some genuine legal rights for animals."[1]

But neither the movement for "genuine" legal recognition of nonhumans nor any one of the current issues detailed in that article is a new phenomenon. Granted, the author's intent was not to study the past, but the article's ahistorical perspective exemplifies a broader trend of omission that extends from popular conceptions to academia. When it comes to the animal advocacy movement, a historical amnesia effectively erases the significant legacies today's animal activists and society as a whole have inherited from their mostly forgotten predecessors. As we stumble uncertainly into the twenty-first century, this intriguing social justice cause marks nearly 140 years of persistent and diverse activism. In April 1866, Henry Bergh, buttressed by the support of a prominent group of New York men and women, chartered the American Society for the Prevention of Cruelty to Animals (ASPCA). At the end of the society's first meeting, he proudly declared that the verdict had been rendered: "The blood-red hand of cruelty shall no longer torture dumb beasts with impunity."[2] His prediction was a bit overconfident, but his organization heralded the genesis of a definable, organized animal advocacy movement in the United States. Since then, the cause has grown steadily and attracted an enthusiastic following. By the turn of the twentieth century, nearly seven hundred organizations, most molded in the image of Bergh's ASPCA, combated cruelty across the country.[3] Changes in post–World War II society provided fertile ground for greater growth, and by 1967, the number ballooned to one thousand groups, with a collective membership in the millions.[4] After the 1975 publication of Peter Singer's seminal treatise, *Animal Liberation*, the movement experienced a veritable organizational explosion. Currently, over seven thousand organizations, representing well over ten million members, lobby, agitate, and educate on issues concerning the rights and treatment of nonhumans.[5]

Historically, this expansive movement has embraced people who have variously called themselves animal welfarists, protectionists, zoophilists, humanitarians, rightists, and, most recently, liberationists. The multitudes who have supported the cause over the years probably fall somewhere on the continuum between the two most common terms, welfarists and rightists, depending on the issue at hand. In general, welfarists oppose cruelty to animals but not the humane use of them for purposes such as food or clothing. This faction asserts human superiority and accepts the socially constructed hierarchies that rank all species but always place *Homo sapiens* at the top of the pyramid. Moreover, welfarists believe all animals that interact with humans deserve ethical consideration—but some more so than others. The family companion animal, they contend, unquestionably earns a higher place on the pyramid than a cow or pig. In contrast, rightists raise fundamental questions about those human-imposed hierarchies. This faction perceives scant difference between the artificial boundaries we use to rationalize away rights for animals exploited for our purposes and those used to justify the subjugation and legal exclusion of other races or groups of people. Rightists believe that all sentient creatures, human and otherwise, are entitled inherently to certain legal and social rights, and they argue that in denying these rights, society commits a grave moral injustice. Liberation ideology emerged mostly after 1975 and thus falls beyond the scope of this study, but it simply presents the most radical, uncompromising articulation of animal rights by demanding an immediate end to the speciesism (a concept similar to racism and sexism but applied to animals) perpetuated by humans.

Clear distinctions exist between the most pragmatic welfarist and the most radical rightist, of course, but from 1870 on, activists of all stripes have embraced a diversity of terms—and often used them interchangeably—in describing their own views and activities. Few scholars familiar with Henry Bergh would characterize him as a champion of animal rights. However, he frequently employed that more provocative term in his propaganda, and under the auspices of his organization, he initiated what was probably the first court case for animals' substantive legal rights just a few years after the ASPCA's founding.[6] A few decades later, prominent activist Caroline Earle White commented that "now, nearly all agree that the lower animals have certain rights, as inalienable as those of man to life, liberty and the pursuit of happiness."[7] Although White's understanding of rights would align more closely with what modern advocates assert, she, too, frequently blurred the distinction between terms. More recently, Helen Jones played an integral role in founding several prominent animal welfare organizations, including the Humane Society of the United States (HSUS) in 1954, but she nonetheless characterized her lifelong activism as unwaveringly rightist.[8] Terms and identities became even more muddled with the publication of *Animal Liberation*. Responding to both the book and an increasing public receptiveness to the arguments contained within it, the movement shifted slightly toward the more radical end of the ideological continuum. Some ideological differences have certainly hardened between factions, but currently, even the most conservative animal welfare groups have appropriated elements of the language and more popular campaigns of the rightist factions. In the present study, I frequently employ the term *animal advocacy* to encompass this continuum of identities and the commonalities of ethical concern for animals, yet I also recognize the complex and evolving differences and make clear distinctions where it is important to do so. Although the various branches of the movement are often united by a common outrage, significant tensions and divisions between them have, at times, undermined the unity and success of their cause.

Despite animal advocacy's complex nature, long history, and impressive numbers, surprisingly few scholars, especially historians, have studied either the movement itself or the broader issues surrounding our historical and often contradictory relationship with animals. Several works have carved significant inroads into the European experience, but far fewer explore developments in the United States. Those that do broach the subject typically emphasize intellectual history or recent sociological aspects of the American movement. Rare older studies tend to simply recount the creation of organizations and document legislative initiatives without providing any context or analysis. Limited in scope and depth, much of the existing scholarship incorrectly concludes that early organizations suffered from a narrow agenda that attacked only a few highly publicized issues, such as beasts of burden or humane education. Most concede there was a more vigorous and expansive movement after 1945, but only a few endeavor to explain the forces driving the postwar activism. Nearly all downplay the American movement's overall success and broader historical significance.[9]

Limitations aside, these studies certainly add to our general understanding of animal advocacy. Yet there is a clear need for research that resurrects the movement's influence and locates it within a social and environmental history framework as well as in the context of larger social changes. In particular, the relatively new field of environmental history offers a useful way to understand this important chapter in the national narrative. Environmental historians offer fresh insights into diverse issues and events by studying the interaction between natural environments, cultural values, and socioeconomic factors over time. Certainly, the relationship between humans and animals represents one aspect of the environment that is particularly relevant to the study of social change. Wild and domestic animals—whether used as food (approximately six to nine billion animals are slaughtered each year in the United States alone), clothing, scientific subjects, entertainment, or companions—are an integral part of our aesthetic, emotional, and consumer lives.[10]

Given the complex nature of this relationship, situating animal advocacy within a broader environmental and social history paradigm will perhaps best reveal the heretofore ignored dynamics and impact of this movement as it evolved in American society.

My hope is that this book will begin the process of new discoveries and revised interpretations, but I emphasize that my research represents only small beginnings. Much of this study, for example, explores organizations located in the eastern and mid-Atlantic regions of the United States, where the majority of animal advocacy activities occurred. Although midwestern and western humane groups are mentioned occasionally, I do acknowledge a great need for future research in these areas. I do not claim to be comprehensive or complete. Rather, this work is a first step into a vast territory, and I hope others will venture into it to further broaden our understanding of this fascinating topic. Those scholars should recognize, however, that the research limitations are frustrating and pervasive. The records of many organizations are scattered and unorganized at best; at worst, they were long ago tossed into the trash bin. Those small grassroots organizations that preserved records of past activities could ill afford the time or money to create anything resembling an archive. Consequently, I spent many a research day in the broom closet or storage room (but always made comfortable by welcoming, apologetic staffers), sifting through dusty boxes that contained a mishmash of artifacts in no particular chronological order. Photographs from 1910 mingled with cruelty reports from 1870, fund-raising invitations from 1920 stuck to journals from 1942, and personal correspondence from 1954 lay atop newspaper clippings from 1973. The larger, national organizations were often more organized, but few had even a rudimentary archive at the time I conducted my research. Fortunately, the situation is changing. A growing number of activists and organizations (such as the Massachusetts Society for the Prevention of Cruelty to Animals [MSPCA]) recognize the historical significance of their work and have started the process of systematically preserving materials. In no way is my digression into the tribulations of research an attempt to rationalize any shortcomings of this book; rather, it is intended to further illustrate the untapped potential this movement offers for historical research on a topic that deserves greater attention. No longer should we scholars ignore a movement that not only unearthed and chopped at the roots of entrenched notions of human superiority but also actually succeeded in changing people's views—sometimes subtly, sometimes dramatically—about those very notions.

Broom closet days behind me, I offer the following study of the U.S. animal advocacy movement from 1865 to 1975, the year when Peter Singer's book signaled a shift in the cause toward liberation ideology. Rejecting many of the accepted interpretations, I contend that this cause has been far more successful historically and has had a far greater impact on society than previously suggested. Admittedly, there were periods during the movement's history—like that of any social movement—when victories were fewer and battles tougher. Those opposed to animal experimentation (known as antivivisectionists), for example, won few legal concessions to restrict or end the practice between World War I and World War II, but the impetus and the determination behind the cause never faltered. More so, antivivisectionists handed researchers legal defeats on many related issues, such as the forced seizure of pound animals for research and dissection in schools. Whatever the issue, persistence and commitment were evident during the movement's entire history, and such dedication reaped dividends. Although variously ridiculed and applauded by society, the "voice of the voiceless" nonetheless succeeded in making certain aspects of its agenda more palatable to growing numbers of Americans. Evolving within and responding to the larger context of a shift from an industrial to a postindustrial society, the movement shaped and fostered a growing public compassion that, in turn, facilitated concrete legal recognition and victories. In many ways, the time was ripe for this broader ethical consideration of the nonhuman world. The message of humanitarians resonated strongly with people's concerns about broader forces such as unchecked capitalism and consumption, urban-industrial problems, the destruction of nature, and the ethical and moral state of American society. Activists forged their diverse agenda from a critique of these forces and offered a viable solution—striking a better balance between our destructive behaviors and our humane compassion for other species. Through cumulative and persistent efforts, this stubborn little movement has altered both beliefs and actions regarding such varied issues as trapping, sport hunting, dog- and cockfights, wearing fur, strays, scientific experiments, slaughter, and more. Few Americans today perceive either the companionship or the consumption of animals in the same manner that earlier generations did, but because of the lack of any historical narrative, even fewer understand the roots of such changes.

Historical neglect obscures much more than the movement's successes. Today's animal activists have inherited many legacies—both rich and troubling—from their predecessors. I call them the connecting threads of the movement. Without an awareness of them, our understanding of current events can reflect only incomplete shadows of the past, as demonstrated in the magazine article I found in the bookstore. By shedding light on these shadowy connections, however, we can begin to see the bonds that tie Henry Bergh to the People for the Ethical Treatment of Animals (PETA). Broadly, the links between animal advocacy organizations past and present include continuity in membership demographics; a diverse agenda and consistent strategies; disruptive, long-standing internal divisions; and similar opponents with familiar arguments. Who joined this movement? What did they fight for, and how did they fight? What were the internal disputes, and who were the external enemies? By rediscovering these connecting threads, we reconstruct the historical cornerstones of today's movement.

When I began my research, the ancestors of today's movement were indeed shadowy figures. Who were those committed to such a difficult and controversial cause? Partly a result of the middle- and upper-class backgrounds of its founders, the early movement recruited members and leaders from a very circumscribed demographic. Records for pre–World War II organizations indicate that predominantly white, male, urban elites led groups, while a middle- and upper-class constituency dominated by women supplied the rank and file. Certainly, all contributions were welcomed regardless of someone's socioeconomic standing, but the relatively high cost of membership dues effectively excluded any organizational voice from the lower classes. Interestingly, some studies point to the movement's early elitism as evidence of activists' underlying status anxieties and their consequent desire to control the lower classes. Skeptical scholars suggest that animal defenders fretted more about the actions of the so-called dangerous classes than about animal sentience. Yet other social control theorists argue that status anxieties led participants to subordinate human suffering to a misguided concern with animals.[11]

However, when applied to animal advocates, such theories fail to account for the diversity of motivations and activism. Humanitarians responded to larger social forces in the industrial and postindustrial world based on their impact on the human-animal relationship, not class anxieties. Bergh and many of his peers railed not against working-class anarchy but against the inordinate financial and political power of those industries most notorious in their exploitation of both society and animals. Capitalists might have desired greater control of the working class, but humanitarians urged greater control of the capitalists. Moreover, throughout the movement's history, activists aggressively condemned cruelties inflicted by the wealthy and the poor alike. (Campaigns against pigeon shoots, foxhunting, and medical experiments, for instance, all targeted the upper classes.) Lastly, many of those dedicated to animal issues were also actively involved with more than one human reform initiative, including abolition, woman's rights, urban reform, worker reform, and civil rights. Such a wide spectrum of social justice interests effectively smashes the image of the myopic, misanthropic animal lover. In short, social control proponents ignore the complexity and depth of the ideology and motivations behind animal advocates. Like many reform movements, this cause attracted middle- and upper-class men and women not so much because they had misguided obsessions or an overwhelming desire to socially control poor people but rather because they had the time and disposable income to support the diverse reforms they believed would uplift all humanity and protect nonhuman species.

Women in particular subscribed to the movement's ideology, and demographically, they provided the backbone of animal advocacy. During the early decades, traditional gender expectations usually undermined women's attempts to assume leadership positions, and some women, such as Caroline Earle White, expended a great deal of time, personal finances, and energy to form groups they would never lead.[12] An active Philadelphia clubwoman, White helped create and launch the Pennsylvania Society for the Prevention of Cruelty to Animals (PSPCA) in 1867, but her male cofounders denied her any leadership role and relegated her to a subordinate women's auxiliary branch. An outspoken advocate of woman's rights, White never completely acquiesced to the organizational rule of men, and in 1883, she founded and presided over one of the most radical early groups, the American Anti-Vivisection Society (AAVS).[13] But White was the exception. Before 1945, most women asserted their voice through their impressive financial support and extensive volunteerism as members, not leaders. They were both the financiers and the foot soldiers of animal advocacy, and they often justified their actions in gendered terms. Drawing connections between animal cruelty and human domestic abuse, early female activists convincingly reasoned that protecting animals was crucial for the preservation of future families and future generations of children.[14] In addition, like many female reformers, they claimed that their domestic knowledge and maternal instincts best suited them to minister to the needs of these violated innocents. The predominance of female members in both child welfare and animal advocacy societies during the early twentieth century not only shaped the ideology of the movement but also ensured its very survival.

Unlike their earlier counterparts, women of the post-1945 movement increasingly attained leadership roles, often taking the helm of groups they founded. Concentrated in smaller grassroots organizations, this feminization of animal advocacy's leadership originated in part from brewing tensions between society's perceptions of women's roles and socioeconomic realities. Even as the consensus society of the cold war era stressed women's responsibilities as wives and mothers, rising numbers of those family caretakers ventured into the job market to supplement the family consumer income. Likewise, acceptable notions of women serving in Parent-Teacher Associations (PTAs) quickly led to mothers volunteering in charities, political organizations, and animal groups.[15] Larger trends toward greater equality for women certainly facilitated more opportunities for leadership and public activism than during the previous century, but this change sometimes collided with the lingering domestic rationale behind much of women's volunteerism. Environmentalist and author Rachel Carson, for example, frequently couched her arguments in appropriately gendered language, vividly describing how environmental abuses threatened home and family. Her work dramatically impacted Americans' views of nature, yet her efforts to maneuver between her very public environmental activism and more traditional expectations of proper female behavior often put her in the crosshairs of conservative critics. Carson's most vitriolic detractors used gender stereotypes to simultaneously question her femininity and discredit her as a hysterical, overly sensitive female.[16] A decade after her death, a more radical wave of feminism would upend the old rationales, but Carson's experience was not unique. Despite such attacks, however, women continued to represent the spiritual, financial, and physical vanguard of the struggle after 1945.

Historically, the movement may have lacked demographic diversity, but most organizations, whatever their original focus or mission, have always maintained a diverse agenda of issues and campaigns. Driven by their radical ethics and their perceptions of pervasive cruelty, activists launched battles on multiple fronts: abused workhorses, seal hunts, inhumane slaughter, trapping, hunting, strays, performing animals, feathered hats and fur coats, wildlife extinction, and vivisection. Such a far-reaching and ambitious approach might have developed into a weakness for the movement, stretching resources too thin and sapping organizational strength. Instead, a broad agenda emerged as a strength that activists nurtured through successive generations. The diversity potentially offered something for everyone and thus appealed to a much wider audience despite the generally controversial nature of the cause. Wider socioeconomic changes simply dictated which issues garnered the most attention. As machines increasingly replaced workhorses, groups redirected the thrust of their activity toward the next relevant cause, such as strays, wild animals, the mistreatment of performing animals, or animal experimentation. As existing studies accurately suggest, the movement expanded and further diversified its agenda after World War II because larger postwar trends simultaneously intensified human exploitation of animals (cold war militarism, biomedicine, consumer product testing) while engendering greater respect for them (ecology, leisure time, and environmental recreation).

Success also shaped and reshaped goals and priorities. During the early years, those who spoke for animals had to shout to be heard above the cacophony of their many contemptuous opponents. But as the advocates, the voice of the voiceless, increasingly gained respect and acceptance, their message edged toward the mainstream, and they pursued goals that appealed to the interests of that more receptive public. Even so, most organizations complemented their headline campaigns with numerous and varied smaller campaigns. From the large MSPCA of the 1900s to the much smaller Friends of Animals (FoA) of the 1970s, the organizations consistently addressed multiple issues. Perhaps their tendency to headline certain campaigns has led scholars to erroneously assume they had a myopic agenda, but as this book clearly reveals, the extensive, ambitious agenda of today's animal rights groups is a direct and important legacy from past activists.

Although it is a great start, a popular smorgasbord agenda is not a guarantee of success. Audience appeal and interest can quickly dissipate without substantive victories. Effective strategies are crucial, and in this respect, the connections between past and present in animal advocacy are less surprising and unique. Most social movements borrow and build on the successful tactics of their predecessors and contemporaries. Animal advocacy did just that, and since many humanitarians participated in several social movements, the activists did not have to look far for ideas. To achieve their wide-ranging goals, they borrowed and reworked the strategies of their abolitionist, feminist, environmental, and civil rights counterparts: (1) public protest and intervention, (2) prosecution, (3) legislation, (4) economic boycotts, (5) organizational networking, and (6) public education and awareness. Most groups combined more than one tactic to enhance the visibility and potential success of a campaign. Typically, they first worked to enact stronger laws to protect animals and then demanded enforcement through arrests and litigation. At the same time, a humane education blitz recruited supporters and chipped away at entrenched attitudes about the human-animal relationship. Keenly aware, however, of humans' reluctance to concede their superiority to other species, activists made sure that some of their initiatives coupled ethical concerns about animals with more self-centered human concerns. The early campaign to enact more-humane slaughter methods, for example, attached cruelty concerns to decidedly anthropocentric concerns about tainted meat and human health.

But victory depended on widespread publicity and media attention even more than on humane education and legal maneuvering. Sometimes, activists staged outrageous public spectacles or protests to attract media attention, whether positive or negative. Many people are familiar with stories of PETA activists throwing blood on fur coats, but few know of the traffic jams caused by Henry Bergh's headline-grabbing bravado during his urban workhorse protests in New York City. Most humanitarians eschewed such extreme tactics, which could evoke a public backlash, yet they nonetheless recognized the public relations value of using some sort of shock tactic. The dusty boxes I explored on my research trips invariably disclosed disturbing, if not horrific, images and lurid descriptions of animal abuse through the ages—an emaciated, dying workhorse; a burned and beaten kitten; a macabre experiment that grafted the head of a puppy to its mother. As abolitionists had done before them, animal advocates devoted significant organizational resources to countless publications, photographs, and lectures that emphasized the visual and often shocking aspects of cruelty. They knew that sympathetic media coverage of the gruesome and the dramatic sometimes reaped significant public and political support and generated the momentum needed for change. Such momentum might then attract the support of prominent figures and further enhance the issue's visibility and credibility. Whether Mark Twain or Jack London of previous generations or Paul McCartney and Kirsten Dunst today, celebrities are powerful and inspirational motivators for the public's involvement in other tactics, such as petitions, marches, and economic boycotts. Star power, prosecution, legislation, education, and boycotts all contributed to a campaign's success, but the real key was using these strategies in conjunction with organizational networking. When groups came together, the combination of strategies and sheer numbers of activists worked like a battering ram to break down more than a few of society's worst abuses of nonhumans.

Early successes, however, also sparked the problematic internal disagreements that have persistently haunted the movement. In particular, as humane arguments slowly but successfully permeated American culture, some organizations modified their strategies and goals to more closely mirror the attitudes and expectations of the general public. Not wanting to alienate their swelling constituency, these groups increasingly pursued modest or even conservative reforms that promoted cooperation rather than confrontation with the perpetuators of animal abuse and exploitation. Dropping more aggressive strategies, moderates such as the American Humane Association (AHA) instead proffered subdued humane education programs and bestowed honorary awards on former enemies that promised self-regulation and voluntary reforms. According to this emerging view within the cause, slowly building a foundation of smaller, feasible gains within the halls of power would ultimately reap greater long-term benefits for both animals and the movement.[17] More-militant factions, represented by groups such as the AAVS, rejected the new approach as naive and accused groups such as the AHA of undermining and betraying the principles and integrity of the struggle for animals. Moderates lashed back that radical groups' unrealistic demands threatened the very existence and future of the cause.[18]

Both sides expressed valid points, but these early divisions soon infected the movement's agenda, and they troubled national campaigns over the next century of activism. The expanded regulatory role of the federal government after World War II inspired the politically connected moderates to lobby hard for federal reforms for some of the most egregious practices in both meat production and laboratory research.

Radicals initially expressed interest in the campaign, but the ideological and strategic antagonisms between the two sides had so deepened that the factions reached an impasse over the reform bills' contents and language. The conservative branch ultimately prevailed, and through its own organizational networking, the Humane Slaughter Act (1958) and Laboratory Animal Welfare Act (1966, 1970) were both passed by Congress. Militants resented that the more conservative wing co-opted the cause and denounced the new laws as "sellouts" that betrayed animals by perpetuating cruelty.[19] As the social context of the 1960s and 1970s slowly nudged the movement as a whole into more controversial terrain (such as antifur protests), radicals often aided the cause. However, during much of the postwar period, they remained outside the action, embittered and alienated. Their star would not rise again until after 1975.

As it struggled with internal divisions, the movement also experienced difficulty forging external alliances, particularly with nature advocates. Early on, animal activists included wildlife in their agenda, but when they criticized sporting clubs for their hunting activities, they antagonized a nascent but increasingly powerful conservation movement.[20] Conservationists viewed nature as a resource to be efficiently managed by humans, and they strongly rejected humanitarians' sentimental view of animals, wild or domestic.[21] For their part, humanitarians disliked conservationists' apparent insensitivity to cruelty and also distrusted their endorsement or ambivalence about hunting and trapping. During rare moments, the two movements confronted related issues and recognized the formidable strength of their united voices. During the late nineteenth century, one of their most successful joint campaigns ended the wanton slaughter of exotic birds for use in women's feathered hats.

More often, however, they clashed, and their early disagreements were the historical antecedents to the post-1945 tensions that arose when the two movements cautiously united once again to stem the tide of wildlife destruction. As before, they rarely felt comfortable in each other's company, and the ideological schisms remained. Biocentric thinking supplanted traditional conservationism, but whereas modern environmentalists grounded their activism in ecological systems, humanitarians still focused primarily on animal suffering. Nonetheless, they forged a reluctant alliance that effectively used both ecological and cruelty arguments and culminated in the most significant legal recognition for wild animals to that point—the Endangered Species Act (1969, 1973) and the Marine Mammal Protection Act (1972). In the aftermath of these triumphs, both movements again acknowledged the enormous potential of their unity, but they stubbornly traveled separate roads of activism and ideology. In recent years, activists have talked again of tearing down the barriers, but beyond sporadic, fleeting unions, nature and animal advocates still founder in their attempts to construct an enduring bond that valorizes a passion for both the individual animal and natural systems.

Undoubtedly, infighting and strained alliances inhibited development of the unified front needed to combat the power and responses of numerous oppositional forces. Over the years, animal advocacy's diverse agenda has spawned many enemies, including railroads, meatpackers, carriage and omnibus companies, circuses, hunters, trappers, the fashion industry, zoos, factory farms, biomedical interests, multinational corporations, the casual carnivore, local municipalities, state governments, and even the federal government. But in the first years of the movement, few of those targeted took the threat seriously. In fact, most dismissed animal advocates with a derisive chuckle and predicted the rapid demise of such a strange fringe element. In their view, no intelligent person would support the preposterous notion that, ethically, animals deserved rights. However, as animal defenders racked up successful prosecutions and public opinion shifted toward the humane cause, the early flippancy quickly faded, and opponents coalesced into their own groups. Adversaries of the movement sometimes worked together, and sometimes they did not, but all constructed and reconstructed persuasive criticisms. In particular, the biomedical interests and corporations were most effective in distilling their scorn into manifestations of what I dub the animal rights "bogeyman"—a devious monster that threatened the very welfare of human society. Depending on the social context and the interest being attacked, the bogeyman assumed various and often interrelated guises. As bogeyman 1, 2, or 3, the animal advocate was depicted as antiprogress, antiscience, or unpatriotic, respectively—someone who would sacrifice inventions, product safety, or even national security for the sake of a suffering rabbit. As bogeyman 4, the advocate was portrayed as antihuman—a misanthrope who would rather save a dog than a sick child. All of these allegations were repeatedly tied to bogeyman 5, the animal advocate as a fanatic and probably mentally unstable individual. Early provivisectionists found this particular manifestation so appealing that several late nineteenth-century physicians concocted a diagnosable form of mental illness to explain such bizarre behavior. Sadly, they pronounced, these misguided souls suffered from "zoophil-psychosis." With so many women in the movement, the doctors further concluded that the weaker sex was particularly susceptible to the malady. Coming from men who were increasingly viewed as sociocultural role models, such charges undermined antivivisection's credibility.[22] Later critics dropped the archaic terminology, but they retained the idea and still manipulated gender politics. Think about the charges leveled against Rachel Carson as a hysterical female: they echoed the old zoophil-psychosis diagnosis. In short, critics continued to finesse the essential bogeyman archetypes because they worked—and worked more than once. Positing such threats and charges effectively manipulated the entrenched belief systems that subjugated other species to humans and women to men.

For all its limitations and problems, the early animal advocacy movement laid the foundation for the more radical activism of the post-1975 period. Certainly, many of its accomplishments only modestly improved exploitive practices and abuses and left large elements of cruelty very much intact. Still, over generations, society did change its attitudes and behavior toward animals in important ways, and the boundaries of ethics for nonhumans expanded outward. The American animal advocacy movement planted a firm foot in society. And by 1975, humanitarians had constructed an impressive framework of legal and cultural precedents on which the next generation of radicals would build animal liberation.

And so, my thoughts circle back to the chimp on the magazine cover—and the question that was posed there. Does that primate possess certain rights long denied by humans? Does the dog in the laboratory, the hawk flying high overhead, or the cow facing slaughter? This book does not answer such questions: the debate on the issue of animal rights will surely persist and evolve. But by studying the advocacy movement and resurrecting its place in our broader history, we surely enrich our understanding of that moral and philosophical discussion. Equally important, we humans gain meaningful insight into who we are in terms of our beliefs and the impact of our actions on the natural world. The victims that animal advocates represent possess no socioeconomic power, no political clout, no voice to express their torment, and no means to participate in their own movement. They also do not possess the capacity to assert their historical significance to our society. And they are significant. Whether or not we believe they have rights, animals are central to our lives, past and present. Our collective historical neglect, born of our own power and arrogance, effectively obscures a remarkable and fundamental chapter in our nation's narrative. The pages that follow begin the process of reclaiming the story.

CHAPTER 2

A Movement Takes Shape

The Origins of Animal Advocacy

92. No man shall exercise any Tirranny or Crueltie towards any bruite Creature which are usuallie kept for man's use.
93. If any man shall have occasion to leade or drive Cattel from place to place that is far of, so that they be weary, or hungry, or fall sick, or lambe, It shall be lawful to rest or refresh them, for a competent time, in any open place that is not Corne, meadow, or in-closed for some peculiar use.

—"Body of Liberties,"
Massachusetts Bay Colony, 1641[1]

Were there Puritans for animal rights? I suspect that few historians, myself included, would go so far as to make that claim, but nonetheless, our journey into the historical context of this unique movement must necessarily begin in early New England. Adopted by the General Court of Massachusetts in 1641, "The Body of Liberties" outlined one hundred statutes regarding both proper behavior and rights within the colony, including Liberties 92 and 93, excerpted here, which specifically addressed the welfare "Off the Bruite Creature." In doing so, the Massachusetts Bay Colony enacted the earliest known law in this part of the world to afford some sort of legal protection to animals. An important precedent was set, but not surprisingly, those first laws sparked little similar activity elsewhere. The larger societal forces that would give rise to an actual movement were not in place in 1641 or even 1741. The situation would change, however, by the middle of the next century, when dynamic social and cultural shifts facilitated the emergence of a more broadly based animal advocacy movement. Specifically, the model of the Royal Society for the Prevention of Cruelty to Animals (RSPCA) in Britain, the ideological and strategic inspiration of abolition, the revolutionary ideas of Charles Darwin, and the sometimes troubling manifestations of industrialization combined to transform a nascent and at best sporadic impulse for greater compassion for animals into a viable movement—a movement that would change history.

Liberties 92 and 93 unquestionably established a significant legal precedent for animals, but the motivating principles behind them, property and religion, underscored decidedly human interests. The statutes mirrored Puritan concerns with human charity, virtue, discipline, and predestined salvation. Animal abuse contradicted those ideals and, thus, the achievement of a model Christian commonwealth on earth, namely, leader John Winthrop's "City upon a Hill." In a broader cultural sense, Puritans and society as a whole at that time generally accepted the notion that domesticated animals were the property of humans. In part, then, outlawing cruelty was simply an attempt to protect an individual's property, particularly from potential attacks by other humans. Humans could exercise nearly complete control over the welfare of the nonhumans in their service. Although many people may have privately abhorred the beating of a cow, most also believed that the cow belonged to its owner and that the owner alone should control its existence.

For nearly two centuries after "The Body of Liberties," humane attitudes in what became the United States evolved little. When change occurred, it arose from several sources, but one of the early inspirations for the American animal welfare movement was the well-heeled, well-organized, and relatively successful British movement for animals. In part, the growing popularity of the philosophy of natural rights for humans, successful British efforts to abolish slavery, anxieties about the more destructive effects of industrialization, and romanticism's appreciation of nature opened the door in eighteenth-century England for the ethical consideration of nonhumans. As early as 1749, articles appeared in British newspapers and magazines protesting blood sports such as cockfights.[2] A few decades later, during the turbulent year of 1776, Rev. Dr. Humphrey Primatt published *A Dissertation on the Duty of Mercy and Sin of Cruelty to Brute Animals,* which combined traditional views of animal subservience with a theological defense of kindness.[3] However, it was the 1789 treatise *An Introduction to the Principles of Morals and Legislation* by philosopher Jeremy Bentham that directly applied the concept of rights to animals. Building on contemporary criticisms of human slavery, Bentham rejected traditional notions of animals as unthinking and undeserving automatons, an idea first proposed by philosopher and mathematician René Descartes. Instead, he argued that the criteria for the legal consideration and protection of nonhumans should be derived from the answer to the following query: "The question is not, Can they *reason?* nor, Can they *talk?* but, Can they *suffer?*"[4] These eloquent words became the rallying cry of reformers and heralded a new era of debate concerning humans' relationship and obligation to other sentient creatures.

In particular, many English abolitionists and suffragists supported Bentham's perspective and pointed to the ethical similarities between oppressing slaves or women and abusing sentient animals. During the first decades of the nineteenth century, many social reformers rallied to the new cause and regarded it as the next logical step in civilization's progress toward greater humanity. They pressed their case in 1800 and again in 1802 by introducing bills in Parliament outlawing the popular blood sport of bull baiting (in which the animal was tethered and then attacked by trained dogs). Opponents defeated both initiatives by narrow margins.[5] Their legislative attempts faltered yet again in 1809 when Bentham's close friend Lord Thomas Erskine could not convince his fellow parliamentarians to pass a sweeping anticruelty law that proclaimed domestic animals' "rights, subservient as they are, ought to be as sacred as our own."[6] It was not until 1822 that Richard Martin, nicknamed "Humanity Dick" by his contemporaries, successfully persuaded legislators to enact a law protecting only cattle, horses, sheep, and mules from excessive cruelty.[7] What became known as Martin's Act was an emasculated, vaguely worded shell of the previous bill, but its significance lies less in the specific protections it provided than in the legal and philosophical precedent it established. As reformer Henry Salt mused, "It is scarcely possible . . . to maintain that 'rights' are a privilege with which none but human beings can be invested; for if some animals are already included within the pale of protection, why should not more and more be so included in the future?"[8]

Jubilation over the act's passage quickly turned to frustration. Legislative success does not always translate into enforcement, and few in the English legal system rushed to farm and field to carry out the mandate of Martin's Act. Undaunted, Martin assembled a group of notable humanitarians, including abolitionist William Wilberforce and Anglican clergyman Arthur Broome, and proposed the formation of an organization specifically designed to investigate and prosecute animal abuse and awaken public sympathy to the cause. On June 16, 1824, the Society for the Prevention of Cruelty to Animals (SPCA) was born.[9] Attracting primarily members of the middle and upper classes, the SPCA grew and eventually achieved a degree of political influence that silenced some skeptics. In 1833, 1835, 1849, and 1854, the society successfully lobbied to revise Martin's Act to define cruelty offenses more specifically and expand the law's coverage. The new amendments covered all domesticated animals, including dogs, chickens, pigs, and cats, and outlawed a variety of activities, including the baiting and fighting of animals, cropping dog's ears, and dehorning cattle.[10] During those first decades, the SPCA also secured hundreds of cruelty convictions; distributed hundreds of thousands of humane publications; and established veterinary hospitals, ambulance services, and shelters for stray dogs and cats.[11] These accomplishments eventually caught the eye and admiration of Queen Victoria, and with her patronage, the organization became the Royal SPCA in 1840.[12]

During the 1860s, the RSPCA hit troubled times when it became embroiled in what continues to be one of the most contentious and controversial issues on either side of the Atlantic—experimentation on live animals. Vivisection divided English humanitarians into two combative camps, those who endorsed the methods of modern medicine and wanted only to regulate the most odious aspects of vivisection and those who adamantly opposed all forms of animal experimentation and demanded an immediate end to the practice. The leaders of the RSPCA chose the more conservative path, and in the 1870s, the organization successfully lobbied for a law to regulate but not outlaw vivisection. On paper, the Cruelty to Animals Act of 1876 monitored all researchers through an annual licensing program; outlawed the common and highly criticized practice of performing multiple experiments on the same, unanesthetized animal; and authorized the government to establish acceptable parameters for particularly painful experiments. In reality, well-organized efforts by the medical community weakened the bill so much that even the moderate RSPCA expressed disappointment with the end result.[13] More radical activists, such as suffragist and journalist Frances P. Cobbe, were less diplomatic and derisively rechristened the bill as the "Vivisector's Charter."[14] Although the 1876 law set another historic legal precedent, the vivisection issue exposed both the opposition's determination to defeat such initiatives and the emerging ideological dissension among animal advocates.

Despite its problems, the English movement continued its work through the ensuing decades. The rest of that tale is fascinating, but I will leave the telling of it to others. For our present purposes, what is important is that those early decades of the British animal advocacy movement served as an inspiration and a model for American reformers. Equally important, the fight over vivisection portended similar troubles for humanitarians in the United States. Even so, as the publicized activities of the English movement reached U.S. shores, several state legislatures took up cruelty issues. First New York (in 1828) and subsequently Massachusetts (in 1835) passed laws defining wanton cruelty toward a domestic animal as a misdemeanor, punishable by a small fine and/or a few days in jail. Other states quickly followed suit, and by the time an organized animal advocacy movement emerged in the United States in 1866, fourteen states and six territories had established legal punishment for those who abused domestic animals.[15] Like the early Puritan statutes, however, many of these laws reflected a greater concern for upholding human social morality, and most perpetuated the entrenched view of animals as property. Furthermore, few of them were effectively enforced.[16] Nonetheless, these early reforms demonstrated a slow, plodding shift toward the opinion that, notwithstanding their status as property, animals possessed some right to kind treatment at the hands of their owners. From the 1830s through much of the 1850s, newspapers increasingly carried articles reporting acts of cruelty and editorials denouncing them, and a smattering of respected ministers, physicians, and politicians publicly exhorted people to be kind to "brutes."[17]

Still, the emergence of a definable American movement lagged over four decades behind its English counterpart. A number of contextual factors were responsible for the delay. Unlike England, the United States was a relatively new nation still undergoing the growing pains of territorial expansion and government formation. Some of the larger sociocultural forces that facilitated the ethical consideration of animals across the Atlantic—the philosophy of natural rights, abolition and other reform movements, industrialization, and urbanization—did not thoroughly root themselves in the United States until the middle of the nineteenth century. Once they did, however, the American struggle for animal rights began. Although details are sketchy, the record shows that sometime around 1860, two prominent Philadelphians, Caroline Earle White and S. Morris Waln, acting separately and apparently unbeknownst to each other, initiated discussions among family and friends to gauge interest in the formation of an American organization modeled on the RSPCA.[18] But another force would delay the formation of any organization yet again. Fate intervened at Fort Sumter in the spring of 1861.

Paradoxically, although the Civil War delayed the movement, it also indirectly inspired it. Although sown of many seeds, the war erupted in large part because of the question of slavery. With the South's defeat in 1865, the U.S. government discarded laws defining slaves as property and constitutionally granted them legal rights. At the very heart of this long struggle and the ultimate victory, the abolition movement spawned a monumental shift in race relations and civil rights. For those interested in animal protection, the victory inaugurated hopeful discussions among some reformers that perhaps society would consider an even broader definition and application of natural rights that would include other species as well.[19]

One of the nation's earliest reform initiatives, abolitionism bequeathed many legacies to subsequent social justice movements. It served as a

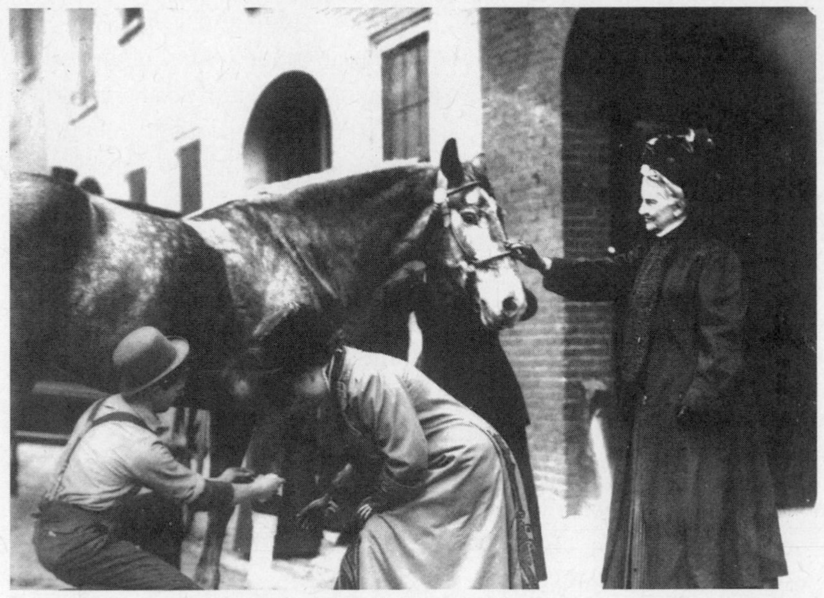

Figure 2.1. As a child, Caroline Earle White could not bear to see the overworked and sometimes abused horses on Philadelphia's streets. As an adult, she, along with other animal advocates, made workhorse reform a headline campaign. *Reproduced with permission of the American Anti-Vivisection Society.*

wellspring for both the leaders and the followers of efforts to secure woman's rights, prison reform, sanitation, civil rights, and, eventually, animal protection, with many activists dividing their time among several issues. More specifically, it provided the ideological and strategic underpinnings for animal advocacy. Converts to the new movement such as Harriet Beecher Stowe and Caroline Earle White perceived many common threads between the institutionalized oppression of a specific group of humans and the institutionalized oppression of nearly all nonhumans. Slavery had denied moral, social, and legal status to African Americans. Likewise, human society deemed animals unfit for such recognition. Few whites believed that owning African Americans, who were widely regarded as biologically subhuman, constituted any injustice: slaves were simply property. Humans applied a similar reasoning to animals, arguing that biological inferiority predestined them for servitude. As an economic institution, slavery exploited African Americans for the financial gains of white society. Humans abused and exploited animals on a massive scale for food, sport, profit, fashion, and entertainment. Slaves and animals were simply objects to be purchased, used, and sold at will. The murder of either a slave or an animal usually resulted in no greater punishment than providing financial compensation for the loss of property.[20]

Radical abolitionists had dared to suggest that regardless of established opinion, laws, or court rulings, slaves deserved ethical and legal consideration not as property but as human beings. Later, animal rights proponents such as Henry Salt challenged society to once again acknowledge its moral hypocrisy and realize that "the present condition of . . . animals is [in] many ways very analogous to that of the negro slaves . . . look back, and you will find in their case precisely the same exclusion from the common pale of humanity; the same hypocritical fallacies, to justify that exclusion; and, as a consequence, the same deliberate stubborn denial of their social rights."[21] Astutely aware of the emotional power of Salt's analogy, both American reformers and the reporters covering movement activities frequently drew explicit comparisons between human and animal slavery. In 1879, an early and highly sympathetic retrospective on ASPCA founder Henry Bergh appeared in the popular magazine *Scribner's Monthly.* The author not only described animals as "sentient chattels" but dramatically concluded by comparing Bergh's fight for "the principles of humanity" to that of the martyred Abraham Lincoln.[22] In addition, animal advocates peppered their own polemics with similar allusions that depicted the use of the "lash" and "branding iron" on enslaved animals as akin to the "torture of human beings" once trapped in servitude.[23] Activists found the vivisection controversy particularly conducive to slavery analogies, comparing muzzled dogs strapped to the operating table to human slaves subjected to physical restraints and punishments.[24] The American movement for animals could even boast its own version of *Uncle Tom's Cabin* when humane educator George T. Angell published the first U.S. edition of Anna Sewell's *Black Beauty* in 1890. The American Humane Education Society distributed over two million free copies with the expressed hope that Sewell's book—a sometimes harrowing tale of abuse told from the perspective of a victimized horse—"shall have as widespread and powerful influence in abolishing cruelty to horses as *Uncle Tom's Cabin* had on the abolition of human slavery."[25] Although the notion was still unfathomable to many Americans, the new humanitarians devoutly believed that the emancipation of slaves should and would inevitably lead to the emancipation of animals.

In addition to adopting abolitionism's moral ideology, animal advocates borrowed some of the earlier movement's strategies. Like their antislavery predecessors, early animal proponents proposed that touching the moral nerve of society by exposing the ugly realities of an injustice was the best way to lure potential converts to their cause. "Moral suasion" soon became the linchpin of early organizations' efforts.[26] What human possessing even a modicum of decency, they reasoned, would not be outraged by the detailed atrocities of kittens tortured, pigs skinned alive, or horses beaten and starved to death? The strategy took hold, and most early groups established humane education departments that dispatched lecturers to public schools and churches, organized humane youth clubs, published newsletters, and distributed hundreds of thousands of pamphlets.[27] When their efforts bore fruit in the form of greater public awareness and expanded newspaper coverage, activists—again taking their cue from the abolition experience—moved their cause into the political and legislative arenas. Although the various groups typically worked independently on local issues, leaders quickly recognized the importance of nationwide organizational networks when campaigning for federal laws. As subsequent chapters will show, early campaigns often relied on the combined tactics of persuasion and political pressure. By first arousing the public's moral outrage and then channeling that anger toward Congress, animal advocates periodically achieved notable legislative victories.

But as happened with abolition, the strategic move into politics facilitated a split in the movement. Even the most effective lobbying frequently culminated in only weak or piecemeal reforms. Though most reformers initially supported regulatory legislation, some—such as Caroline Earle White and fellow Pennsylvania activist Mary Lovell—increasingly criticized the weaknesses of such laws, arguing that leaving any element of cruelty intact undermined the movement's long-term goal of emancipation for animals.[28] Just as some antislavery activists understood that an inherently evil institution could not be improved on through legislative reform, a vocal minority of animal advocates insisted that the vile nature of animal exploitation required eradication, not regulation: no law could ameliorate the immorality, for example, of dissecting live animals. These radical humanitarians gravitated toward an abolitionist stance on several significant issues and became a persistent thorn in the side of conservative animal welfarists. The internal fractures, sparked in part by the antislavery model, have continued to plague the movement to this day.

Traveling an ideological path similar to the abolitionists' also meant encountering a similarly determined opposition. Both movements denounced deeply held societal beliefs, and consequently, both faced strong resistance and ridicule. Slavery was a complex socioeconomic institution designed to keep millions in bondage. Many nineteenth-century Americans ascribed to the belief system undergirding that institution and disparaged abolitionists as "fanatics" espousing "mischievous and unfounded" opinions.[29] Likewise, the domination of animals and nature is a long-held and deeply embedded belief in human social structures.[30] Historically, since most people accepted and willingly participated in nonhuman subjugation, suggestions of animal rights seemed downright absurd. Like abolitionists, animal advocates became a popular target for editorial parody. Many a Victorian reader probably chuckled in agreement as one particularly caustic journalist, Rupert Hughes, surmised that if society permitted proselytizing animal lovers to advance their cause to its logical conclusion, they would assign souls to vegetables, rights to microbes, and suffrage to all creatures. Feigning conversion, Hughes facetiously proposed that if animals were to be emancipated, then humans should aid them through "a little education, a little night-school training, [and] a few newspapers printed in their language."[31] The abusive barrage did not stop with the printed media. Reminiscent of the abolitionist experience, early antivivisectionist lectures frequently descended into mayhem as medical students and researchers crowded meeting halls and generated enough cacophony to force the cancellation of these events.[32]

Unfortunately, derision sometimes escalated into physical assault. Henry Bergh and his agents suffered repeated threats and periodic beatings during the movement's early years, and in 1888, a cruelty agent for the Women's Branch of the Pennsylvania Society for the Prevention of Cruelty to Animals (WPSPCA) was "severely beaten while attempting to arrest a carter."[33] Refusing to be intimidated, activists maintained an unwavering commitment to and belief in the righteousness of their cause. As another frequent victim of assault, the abolitionist William Lloyd Garrison, declared, "I will be heard," animal advocates such as Ella Wilcox Wheeler, heralded by some as the "poet laureate of humanity," vowed that her movement would agitate "till the deaf world's ear be made to hear."[34] When skeptics chided them, animal advocates retorted by pointing to the abolitionists. Despite the tremendous unpopularity of their cause, those opposed to slavery had proven that a small, resilient minority could destroy an entrenched injustice and profoundly transform society in the process.

The two movements shared many common threads both in beliefs and barriers, but there were important distinctions as well. By 1870, abolitionism prevailed as the Thirteenth, Fourteenth, and Fifteenth Amendments were added to the Constitution. In contrast, the animal advocacy movement, from its inception to the present day, has secured some important victories but no comprehensive social or legal recognition of all animals' rights. Society persisted in its unwillingness to apply human rights to a diverse group of creatures that, unlike slaves, possessed no physical ability to communicate as humans and could not participate in their own liberation movement. Many early animal advocates countered that language alone should not be a prerequisite for social and legal protection. Increasingly in the United States, the mentally ill and the physically handicapped received some ethical and legal consideration despite their inability at times to speak on their own behalf. Activists insisted that animals simply communicated through different means, not unlike those of handicapped humans. Henry Childs Merwin reasoned that animals translated the "logic of feelings into the logic of signs; and so far as this particular action is concerned, it is psychologically indistinguishable from that which is performed by the deaf mute."[35] Merwin and others boldly suggested that differences between the language, needs, and affections of humans and those of animals represented differences of degree, not kind. Just as proslavery adherents mistakenly justified their institution by characterizing African Americans as biologically different and inferior, they contended, humans now repeated the error by denying any discernible kinship with nonhumans. Many nineteenth-century social commentators scoffed at the mere suggestion of any affinity between humans and the brute creation, but one man's trip to the Galapagos Islands in 1831 would throw traditional notions of the human-animal relationship into disarray.

As the details of Charles Darwin's theory of evolution reached an incredulous public, animal advocates felt both empowered and vindicated by science. Darwin's research, articulated first in *The Origin of Species* (1859) and subsequently in *The Descent of Man* (1871), effectively challenged social constructions of human superiority. Until Darwin, most people readily accepted Descartes's conclusion that animals, void of "thinking souls," existed and functioned only as "natural automata" incapable of pleasure or pain, unlike superior humans.[36] Designed to serve the needs of dominant humans, these so-called living machines could not logically be endowed with rights. Darwin, however, upended many such traditional views of nature, arguing instead that all life, composed of diverse organisms, had evolved in an interconnected manner through the process of natural selection. In *The Descent of Man,* he further elaborated his theory by provocatively declaring that "man bears in his bodily structure clear traces of his descent from some lower form."[37] Although a discomforting thought for many, some sort of primeval relative(s) inextricably linked humans to nonhumans.

Most animal advocates were elated. As one antivivisectionist exclaimed, Darwin "put into our hands the most formidable weapon ever forged for combating prejudice and superstition."[38] Indeed, the larger social implications of his theory were explosive. Darwin not only knocked humans from their allegedly preordained pedestal but also dared to suggest they were the evolutionary progeny of everything from amoebas to monkeys. In this revolutionary science, humans existed simply as a branch of a tree of life, not, as previously assumed, above that tree.[39] Furthermore, biological affinities meant that humans and nonhumans shared many physical, emotional, and mental traits. Darwin himself said it best: "The senses and intuitions, the various emotions and faculties, such as love, memory, attention and curiosity, imitation, reason, etc., of which man boasts, may be found in an incipient, or even sometimes in a well-developed condition, in the lower animals."[40] For movement advocates, evolution validated the rights of animals. Although those who were the voice of the voiceless still relied on moral and emotional arguments to promote the ethical consideration of animals, Darwin's concept of the tree of life cloaked such positions with the prestige and authority of science.

Evolution certainly encouraged a reassessment of the human-nonhuman relationship, but participants on both sides of the debate often detached Darwin's ideas from their scientific moorings and inappropriately applied them to just about any topic that furthered their own perspective. Those opposed to animal rights constructed an ominous social interpretation of Darwin's theory. Dismissing humanitarians' sentimental portrayal of animals, this faction insisted that evolution revealed the violence of nature and nonhumans. Biology had endowed both the wild lion and the domesticated dog with necessarily brutal survival instincts. In turn, if

Homo sapiens were simply an evolutionary extension of other species, then no matter how advanced civilization appeared on the surface, our natural savagery would always lurk just below any semblance of order.[41] Evolution proved that both humans and animals would never escape their natural proclivities for violence and competition. Similar to social Darwinism's concept of the survival of the fittest in human society, these critics contended that humans, in their domination and use of nonhumans, simply displayed their superior evolutionary skills for survival.[42] Whether human or nonhuman, the strong savage naturally dominated the weak savage.

Animal advocates rallied immediately to discredit this anthropocentric interpretation and its supporters. The outspoken Henry Salt retaliated that it was no coincidence that those most likely "to disallow the rights of others, and argue that suffering and subjection are the natural lot of all living things, are usually themselves exempt from the operation of this beneficent law, and . . . profit most largely at the expense of their fellow creatures."[43] Parading the image of a universe regulated by "internecine competition," it was argued, maintained the status quo of power relations. Salt disputed social Darwinist claims that human evolutionary progress emerged solely from savagery and competition, asserting instead that a sense of equal justice and compassion also governed modern society.[44] Still other humanitarians endeavored to soften the unsympathetic depiction of animals as violence incarnate. Further manipulating Darwin's evidence of biological kinship, animal defenders endowed nonhumans with only the most positive of human faculties. Writers such as E. P. Evans and Allen Pringle published numerous detailed observations of animals' complex reasoning processes and advanced intellect.[45] Naturalist Samuel Lockwood concluded from his own observations that animals expressed a sense of humor in their daily lives.[46] Yet others published more thoroughly humanized and emotion-laden accounts of their subjects. Anna Sewell's famous horse, Black Beauty, not only endured tribulation with dignity but communicated, reasoned, mourned, remembered, and celebrated the events of his life.[47] Sewell's story also exemplified the increasingly popular tactic of contrasting admirable virtues of animals with ignoble human behavior. Radical activists loved that approach. Physician and untiring critic of vivisection Albert Leffingwell would frequently contrast disturbing human actions—such as a New Jersey researcher dropping 141 dogs from a height of twenty-five feet in order to observe traumatic spinal cord injuries—with those of the animal victims, in this case, the dogs' piteous attempts, despite paralyzing injuries, to "greet their master with extravagant expressions of joy" when the experimenter approached them.[48] Although Leffingwell conceded that wild animals and even the loyal family dog sometimes committed savage acts, he countered that the biological necessity to survive justified such actions. In contrast, he said, humans could rarely defend their own violence, since motivations other than survival, such as power, love, revenge, and greed, frequently distinguished it. The human capacity for savagery was unique in its potential for unjustifiable evil, and for humanitarians, few acts illustrated this truth better than the reprehensible, unprovoked abuse of animals.

But according to humanitarians, we humans were redeemable. And again, evolution held the key. In 1898, animal rightist Rosa Abbot suggested that Darwin's revelations presaged positive changes for animals because, though the process might take time, the biological evolution of humans entailed their spiritual evolution as well. Human civilization was "passing out of the physical-intellectual stage of evolution into the intellectual-spiritual phase," a new moral level at which humans would experience an "awakening of conscience, compassion, and sympathy for the weak."[49] Humans, it was said, necessarily had to harness their power not to subordinate other species but rather to establish a new evolutionary model in which humane behavior would supplant competition and violence. And the way to achieve this new moral state was, not surprisingly, humane education, particularly for children. In a Darwinian sense, focusing on future generations ensured that human inclinations for violence would ultimately be eliminated from the social evolutionary process. And humane education promoters could boast of support from none other than Charles Darwin himself. In *The Descent of Man*, the scientist whose ideas sparked so much controversy pointedly stated that "love for all living creatures is the most noble attribute" and that such virtues could be disseminated "through instruction and example to the young, and eventually become incorporated into public opinion."[50] For the apostles of teaching kindness, if society failed to heed Darwin's words, then humans would languish "but half emerged from savagery."[51]

Although Darwin certainly supported humane schooling and considered himself an animal lover, he was often dismayed by adulterations of his ideas to serve either side in the debates over animal or human rights.

He periodically reminded the public that his theory simply offered a scientific explanation for biological diversity and indicated nothing definitive about the inevitability of hierarchies, human progress, or social survival skills.[52] In terms of specific animal advocacy issues, Darwin expressed decidedly humane but centrist views. He contributed often to the RSPCA but publicly supported animal experimentation and testified in its favor before a royal commission in 1875. He could never bring himself to experiment on animals, and he strongly advocated laws requiring the anesthetizing of all vivisected subjects, yet Darwin fully subscribed to the right of free scientific inquiry.[53] In 1881, he wrote, "I know that physiology cannot possibly progress except by means of experiments on living animals, and I feel the deepest conviction that he who retards the progress of physiology commits a crime against mankind."[54] In the end, Darwin and his discoveries impacted the humanitarian movement in contradictory ways. Scientific proof of the biological affinity between species bolstered the case for greater recognition of animals' inherent rights, but divergent interpretations of natural selection, competition, and the role of science sometimes strengthened entrenched attitudes of human superiority.

Charles Darwin's intellectual struggle between humanitarian ethics and the goals of modern science symbolized larger social anxieties felt on both sides of the Atlantic. Darwin was a product of his time. The nineteenth-century Victorian world sped at what must have seemed a dizzying pace toward an uncertain twentieth-century industrial urban order, and the consequent changes were probably the catalysts for the ambivalence of many a Victorian. Although the process of industrialization began in the United States prior to the outbreak of hostilities, the Civil War dramatically stimulated the unprecedented mass production of goods. Afterward, industrial expansion continued as new technologies further streamlined processes, allowing factories to manufacture even cheaper goods for an even more voracious consuming public. Businesses grew—and then grew more. Managers expanded their control over workers. Mass-market advertising for those mass-market goods created a societal homogenization as Americans increasingly consumed similar goods. Trains crisscrossed the nation to further integrate society socially, culturally, politically, and economically.[55] For some, the distinct mark of industrialization signaled a very modern version of the "City upon a Hill."

But, of course, not everyone interpreted the dramatic social changes in optimistic terms. Critics commented that so-called progress was fraught with discomforting contradictions.[56] Big business might stimulate general economic growth, but many companies used ruthless and unethical tactics to destroy competition and exploit the American worker. Furthermore, industrialization's insatiable demand for cheap labor drew millions of immigrants into urban centers that were ill prepared to confront the ensuing eruptions of congestion, crime, pollution, and poverty. A growing class of poor, ethnically diverse workers inundated the cities. In response, many economically prosperous families fled into the suburbs, and consequently, geography hardened class divisions and antagonisms.[57] To critical observers, the country appeared caught between two diametrically opposed yet inextricably bound worlds: one characterized by prosperity, culture, and consumption and the other replete with slums, malnourished children, and despair.

For romantics, conservationists, and animal advocates, the very heart of the anxiety rested in modern society's victimization of nature. In the unending quest for more resources, industrialization required the destruction of natural areas. Likewise, the closing of the western frontier in the late nineteenth century seemed only to confirm that the last vestiges of nature had fallen under human control. But the damage went beyond the physical and touched the spiritual.[58] The processes under way permanently shifted society away from its rural, agrarian roots. The lives of more and more Americans revolved around urban streets, not cow pastures. Food came from grocers and eateries, not hunting. Though still numerous, even animals in the urban setting were being replaced by machines. Society had indeed changed. The rise of an urban-industrial society had removed people from their once-intimate relationship with nature. Admittedly, the naysayers of industrialization came from the middle and upper classes; few workers had the time or the money to contemplate such issues. Still, the critique reached a wide audience and sparked a nostalgic desire to repair those tattered bonds with nature and, in turn, with animals.

The "back–to-nature" movement of the late nineteenth and early twentieth centuries found its philosophical hero in a previously obscure, romantic nature lover, Henry David Thoreau.[59] His writings, particularly *Walden*, eloquently and passionately praised nature's inspirational serenity while decrying the intrusions of industry. For many Victorians,

Thoreau, perhaps better than anyone, grasped the physical and spiritual implications of the new urban order: "The whistle of the locomotive penetrates my woods. . . . Here come your groceries, country; your rations, countrymen! Nor is there any man so independent on his farm that he can say them nay. . . . All the Indian Huckleberry hills are stripped, all the cranberry meadows are raked into the city. Up comes the cotton, down goes the woven cloth; up comes the silk; down goes the woolen; up come the books, but down goes the wit that writes them."[60] But what were people to do? Responses varied. Some left the city and muddied their boots in the woods to see those huckleberry hills firsthand. Other, less-ambitious nature lovers simply picked up the popular new nature books and embarked on imaginary wilderness treks: summering in the Sierra with John Muir, exploring the desert with Mary Austin, or observing the forests and farms of New York with Susan Fenimore Cooper.[61] In urban areas, Frederick Law Olmstead and other planners designed new green spaces—Central Park being perhaps the most famous example—so that those without the resources to travel to places such as Yosemite could contemplate "natural scenes of an impressive character."[62] Whatever form the movement assumed, it boded well for animal advocates. Any definition of nature and thus of a nature lover necessarily included nonhuman species, and that heralded real opportunities to get a message out to a more receptive audience. If people could love a majestic hawk, then why not the gentle cow?

In theory, humanitarians were on to something, but the reality proved to be far more complex. To be sure, people demonstrated genuine affection for some animals and wanted to protect them—but not if protection meant sacrificing their health, their hats, or their prime rib. Most Americans were stubbornly reluctant to restrict their level of consumption in order to preserve either nature in general or animals in particular. Thoreau's train whistles continued to split the air of field and forest. Trees fell, land was developed, factories spewed their wastes into air and water, and rampant consumerism of various stripes exploited, commodified, and killed animals on a massive, unprecedented scale. Consumer demands for fashion, for instance, exacted an incredible toll on animal populations. Broadly speaking, mass production had democratized fashion by making clothing more affordable and accessible to all classes. Now, the rank-and-file American could imitate the elite lifestyle by simply visiting that new icon of mass culture known as the department store.

However, dressing like the rich meant making the requisite adjustments to the latest styles. By using the influential force of mass-market advertising, manufacturers increasingly manipulated public tastes and generated a perpetual demand for new products.[63] During the latter half of the nineteenth century, the mass consumption of two particularly popular symbols of upper-class fashion, fur coats and women's feathered hats, resulted in the wholesale extermination of seals and exotic birds. Shockingly, just one New York plumage dealer reported killing forty thousand terns during their mating season.[64] Likewise, a comparable annual slaughter of baby harp seals fulfilled consumers' demands for articles composed of or trimmed in their fashionable fur.[65] Between 1850 and 1900, Norwegian and Newfoundland sealers slaughtered, on average, over eight hundred thousand harp seals each year.[66] Meanwhile, through their advertising, manufacturers maintained a formidable control over consumer tastes. Animal advocates would have to initiate aggressive public relations campaigns designed to make the wearing of feathers or furs decidedly unfashionable.

But the industry that was probably responsible for sending more animals to their deaths than any other was the meat industry, and in this regard, the first big business in the United States—the railroads—played an integral role in amplifying the exploitation of food animals. The capability to transport livestock and slaughterhouse products more efficiently to more distant markets ensured the rise of several innovative entrepreneurs (among them Gustavus Swift and Philip Danforth Armour) who stepped in early to take advantage of the urban meat market. Their large operations modernized the industry through technological and managerial innovations, and soon, major companies such as theirs suffocated the small beef farms characteristic of the eighteenth century. By 1903, six companies controlled approximately 90 percent of the industry.[67] The most significant boost to the industry came with the introduction of the refrigerated railcar. Now, more Americans than ever developed a penchant for a flesh-based diet, and with the persuasive reinforcement of advertising, most came to believe in the necessity of consuming such a diet daily.[68] Demand and consequently production of slaughter products soared. Historian James Barrett estimates that between 1870 and 1890, the Chicago stockyards experienced an astronomical growth rate of 900 percent.[69]

In response, the major packing companies redoubled efforts to streamline the production process. Many in the industry increased production by introducing limited assembly-line methods, which, in turn, exerted greater control over labor.[70] In Chicago, Swift integrated the numerous elements and stages of production. In addition to amassing his own fleet of refrigerated cars and delivery wagons, he put together an extensive network of refrigerated storage facilities and employed a veritable army of purchasers and sales professionals. Swift and others could further augment their profits by successfully developing and marketing goods derived from animal by-products, such as glue, fertilizer, soap, and gelatin.[71] As a result, industry production soared; between 1865 and 1900, four hundred million animals became dinner (and various other consumer items), and by 1900, the figure approached one billion per year.[72] Importantly, these figures do not include those animals that never made it to the killing floor. Estimates suggest that 20 percent or more of the feed animals perished due to starvation or physical injuries sustained in transit.[73] Yet even with such losses, profits remained high, and the ever-increasing consumer demand guaranteed that Gustavus Swift's stockyards of the late nineteenth century would evolve into the immense and exploitive factory farm feedlots of today.

The rapid and extraordinary growth of the U.S. meat industry exemplified the complex and truly daunting obstacles confronting the new humanitarians. With the rise of an industrial society, many Americans became caught between two conflicting desires—the desire to consume, which necessitated the exploitation of nature and animals, and the desire to save and restore an intimacy with both. We are still caught in that dilemma today. But animal activists in that era believed (just as their successors do) that through protest, reform, and education, they could free people from that trap or at the very least make the situation less destructive. But could they? Some scholars have suggested that once the animal movement emerged, it provoked little threat to established belief systems and political or economic structures; instead, it simply provided an acceptable and nonthreatening outlet for emerging "humanitarian impulses."[74] In reality, however, this movement threatened many of the deeply held beliefs that shaped human behaviors. Few Americans perceived any inherent ideological or ethical contradiction between lavishing affection on one creature defined as the family pet while dining on another. Those who defended the rights of other species exposed the contradiction. Building on the iconoclastic work of abolitionists and Darwin, movement advocates challenged humans to recognize their anthropocentrism and reevaluate entrenched notions of progress, property, and rights. They raised unpopular and disturbing issues about the human-animal relationship that jarred the very bedrock of society—the notion of human superiority.

CHAPTER 3

Leaders and Followers

The New Humanitarians

> The vast majority of the race, whether savage or civilized, are secretly kindhearted and shrink from inflicting pain, but in the presence of the aggressive and pitiless minority they don't dare to assert themselves. . . . Some day a handful will rise up on the other side and make the most noise . . . and a determined front will do it.
>
> —Mark Twain,
> *The Mysterious Stranger*

> I and my daughters and husband have been regarded as almost fanatical in our care of animals wherever we have been, and in Florida we have seen much to affect us. . . . I for my part am ready to do anything that can benefit the cause. I am glad of this opportunity to say with what wholehearted delight we have watched your noble course, in pleading for the dumb and helping the helpless. May God Bless you.
>
> —Harriet Beecher Stowe to
> Henry Bergh, November 6, 1877

By the second half of the nineteenth century, the larger societal forces necessary for the rise of both an animal advocacy movement and a more receptive audience had taken root. Within a few short years of the founding of the first animal protection group in 1866 (New York's ASPCA), animal activists had chartered societies in Philadelphia, Boston, Washington, D.C., Providence (Rhode Island), San Francisco, and St. Louis, as well as twenty other locations.[1] At first, much of the public disparaged those who championed animal rights, but over the next several decades, the message of compassion for animals resonated with an ever-widening audience. But who were these voices of the voiceless? For the most part, they were people who already believed fervently in various social justice issues and already participated in other reform movements. Like many reformers of the time, they tended to be financially comfortable urbanites from the East Coast. Women reformers in particular gravitated to the cause, and they represented the majority of the membership of most organizations. In fact, the very survival, growth, and success of this movement hinged on their participation. By putting flesh on the bones of these early founders, leaders, and followers, we can see more clearly some of the legacies bequeathed to today's movement. Although animal rights groups in the twenty-first century have certainly expanded well beyond the East Coast, they remain primarily white, middle-class, and female demographically. The individuals described in this chapter determined the fundamental ideology, goals, and tactics that would shape and guide the movement throughout its history.

In the decade before the formation of the ASPCA, the idea for some sort of anticruelty society germinated in several locations, but Philadelphia—a city with a reformist tradition—seemed to be the hotbed for protomovement activities. Shortly after his marriage in 1854, Philadelphia attorney Richard P. White learned that his young wife, Caroline, emphatically cared about animals and deplored their suffering. He told her of an English humane group he had heard of called the Royal Society for the Prevention of Cruelty to Animals and suggested that she join. Unaware of its existence, she was delighted at the news and immediately expressed a desire to establish a similar group in Philadelphia.[2] Just a few years later, in 1860, Philadelphian S. Morris Waln, not knowing of White's interest in the English movement, sent a letter to the RSPCA detailing his own plans to replicate the group in the United

States and requesting advice on how to do so. Just after the Civil War, yet another resident of the City of Brotherly Love, M. Richards Muckle, solicited his circle of friends to start an SPCA, but when his idea met little enthusiasm, he abandoned it.[3] Muckle, Waln, and White would all subsequently play integral roles in founding Pennsylvania's first animal advocacy group. Farther north, Boston attorney George T. Angell recollected that, even as a young man, he had abhorred cruelty toward any living creature and on more than one occasion had intervened to stop such behavior. In 1864 (two years prior to the formation of the ASPCA), he demonstrated the sincerity of his commitment to animal welfare by drafting a will dictating that a significant portion of his estate should fund educational materials designed to "impress upon the minds of youth their duty towards those domestic animals which God may make dependent upon them."[4] Each of these individuals helped to ferment an idea and subsequently contributed much to the organized movement, but history necessarily accords official credit to the person responsible for the first tangible manifestation of that idea. That distinction goes to a wealthy New Yorker, Henry Bergh.

In contrast to other early leaders, Henry Bergh's interest in the cause of animal abuse blossomed later in life. Born in New York City in 1813, he spent his early years enjoying the leisurely lifestyle made possible by the success of his shipbuilder father, Christian Bergh.[5] Much to his parents' chagrin, Bergh dropped out of Columbia University after attending only a few courses and traveled to Europe to make his mark as a literary figure. He composed and occasionally published a smattering of obscure plays and poems, most of which critics resoundingly panned. When he complained to a publisher about the bad reviews, a friend purportedly cautioned him that criticism might be preferable to obscurity.[6] The young writer would remember that advice years later when he became an activist. Conceding the question of his talent, he abandoned his literary ambitions sometime around 1839, returned to New York, and married Matilda Taylor, the daughter of a wealthy Englishman. The newlyweds then caught a steamship to Europe, and for the next several years, they casually toured Europe and Asia.[7] To that point, little in Bergh's life suggested that he would one day become the dynamo of American animal advocacy, but interestingly, his life of leisurely excursions led him not so much to exotic destinations as to the world of activism that would be the focus of the rest of his life.

Figure 3.1. Henry Bergh, founder of the ASPCA, recognized the power of publicity—even bad publicity—to awaken the public to animal welfare issues. *Copyright © 2005 The American Society for the Prevention of Cruelty to Animals (ASPCA). Reprinted with permission of the ASPCA. All rights reserved.*

Although Europe certainly held no monopoly on animal cruelty, Bergh's travels awakened him to both the pervasiveness of abuse and the public's apathy toward the issue. He observed carriage drivers routinely beating their horses in the face and farmers transporting calves and other livestock to market by simply binding their legs and piling them haphazardly in carts. While visiting Spain, he attended a bullfight during which twenty-five horses and eight bulls died in the name of a day's sport. The event so appalled Bergh that he wrote an editorial about his experience and sent it to a New York newspaper, which published it in the late 1840s.[8] The brief editorial on bullfights, like his literary efforts, brought no accolades and soon faded into obscurity, but it marked the onset of Henry Bergh's transformation from a complacent, anonymous member of the moneyed elite to a controversial crusader.

In 1863, he accepted President Lincoln's offer—largely a result of Bergh's friendship with Secretary of State William Seward—of a diplomatic appointment as secretary of the U.S. legation in Saint Petersburg. Russia's severe climate so affected his health that he resigned the post after only one year, but he described his brief stay as the final stage in his conversion to animal advocacy.[9] According to Bergh, animal abuse was so rampant and severe in Russia that he felt morally sickened and compelled to act. On one occasion, he happened on a driver severely whipping an overworked and exhausted donkey; he stepped in and ordered the man to stop. Much to his surprise, the driver obeyed. Although sympathetic biographers embellished the story with dramatic and unsubstantiated details over the years, the incident did occur, and it convinced Bergh that direct action could stop abuse.[10] On their way back to the United States in 1864, he and his wife made a brief stopover in England to consult with the Earl of Harrowby and John Colam, the president and secretary, respectively, of the RSPCA.[11]

When they landed in New York in the autumn of 1864, Bergh initiated the process of introducing an SPCA to the United States. He canvassed the wealthy New York neighborhoods so familiar to him and elicited promises of financial support as well as seventy signatures for a document entitled the "Declaration of the Rights of Animals." Bergh confidently predicted that posterity would compare his declaration to that composed by Thomas Jefferson.[12] He was wrong, of course, but nevertheless, his document was unprecedented in both the statement it made and the prestigious support it garnered. Signatories included *New York Tribune* owner and editor Horace Greeley, city mayor John Hoffman, industrialist and philanthropist Peter Cooper, historian George Bancroft, Unitarian minister Henry Bellows, and statesman Hamilton Fish.[13] The involvement of such prominent citizens invariably caught the attention of several newspapers, and soon, many middle- and upper-class New Yorkers knew of Bergh's plan. Riding the wave of publicity, he announced that he would lecture to the public on the subject of animal cruelty on February 8, 1866. He hoped his words would kindle within the people such an overwhelming humanitarian spirit that they would enthusiastically join the ranks of his new society. Despite cold and inclement weather, "a good sized audience" of men and women gathered in Clinton Hall to hear Bergh's appeal.[14]

As his voice filled the hall that February night, it became clear that his plea for animals arose not from any sentimental attachment to them but rather from the moral teachings of his religion, Unitarianism. Throughout his life, he demonstrated no personal affection toward those species he championed, and he never shared his house with any companion animals. His detractors relished lampooning him as a fanatical animal lover, but for Henry Bergh, the ethical recognition of nonhumans involved no emotion, no complex theories, and no extraordinary intellect.[15] It was a simple moral struggle between right and wrong. As he concluded on that icy February night, "This is a matter purely of conscience. It has no perplexing side issues. No, it is a moral question in all its aspects . . . it is a solemn recognition of the greatest attribute of the Almighty Ruler of the Universe, mercy."[16] This theological justification for animal protection probably resonated well with a Victorian society that promoted one's moral and religious duty generally. But the crowd that night in Clinton Hall was primed for Bergh's message in ways already mentioned: Darwinian questions, urban-industrial anxieties, and the spirit of previous reform movements all helped shape the reception Bergh received. The time for American animal advocacy had arrived.

Bolstered by the substantial and supportive crowd that night, Bergh tucked his "Declaration of the Rights of Animals" under his arm and journeyed to Albany to submit an official SPCA charter for legislative approval.[17] Several lawmakers immediately opposed any act that brought nonhumans within the pale of legal rights, but Bergh used his political connections to persuade a majority to enact a measure that, on April 10, 1866, legally recognized and incorporated North America's first animal advocacy organization.[18] Acting quickly, he then enlisted yet another prominent citizen—businessman, state legislator, and university founder Ezra Cornell—to assist him in sponsoring a bill to replace the ineffective 1828 anticruelty statute. The unprecedented law that passed on April 19, 1866, specifically stipulated that the state had to classify and prosecute any act of cruelty toward any animal as a misdemeanor offense, regardless of issues of ownership.[19] Although it rectified few of the previous law's deficiencies, the new measure differed dramatically in that it existed in conjunction with a group endowed with the right to enforce it. Three days later, the founding members met and approved a constitution that specifically directed the ASPCA "to provide effective means for the prevention of cruelty to animals throughout the United States, to enforce all laws which are now or may hereafter be enacted for the protection of animals and to secure, by lawful means, the arrest and conviction of all persons violating such laws."[20] The wording reflected Bergh's ambitious vision for his anticruelty cause. The ASPCA was to be not just a New York organization but a national one. On the constitution's approval, Bergh was unanimously elected the organization's first president, a position he held until his death in 1888.

As word of the new humane society spread through the nation's largest newspapers, the organization received scores of letters requesting information on how to launch similar groups.[21] Caroline Earle White wrote one of those letters. She, like Bergh, grew up in a wealthy family, but the two shared few additional similarities in their formative years. Born in 1833, White was encouraged by her Quaker parents to partake in diverse intellectual and reformist pursuits. White's father, Thomas Earle, a successful Philadelphia lawyer, devoted considerable time to the abolition cause. Her mother, a cousin to Lucretia Mott, was both an abolitionist and a suffragist. The political ideology and activism of the Earle household greatly influenced Caroline, and while still a young girl, she, too, adopted abolitionist views, supporting the Female Anti-Slavery Society. She was intellectually curious, and her family's wealth afforded her educational opportunities not available to many young women at that time. She studied Latin; fluently spoke and wrote German, French, Italian, and Spanish; and mastered astronomy. Although her upbringing may not have been typical, she did accept one traditional gender expectation for women. In the mid-1850s, she married attorney Richard White and converted to his religion, Catholicism.[22]

After her marriage, a variety of intellectual and reformist activities occupied her time. Like Bergh, White wrote and published. She composed several travel guides, short stories, and novels, but unlike Bergh, she received critical acclaim for her work.[23] Along with many middle- and upper-class women during the second half of the nineteenth century, she was an active clubwoman. After her religious conversion, she became president of the St. Vincent's Aid Society, a group that donated medical services and supplies to poor and orphaned children. She also chaired the Ladies Auxiliary of the American Catholic Historical Society and served on the board and as vice president for the Browning Society, a local women's literary club. At the national level, she joined the Women's Christian Temperance Union, submitted several articles to the publication *Women's Progress*, and ardently endorsed woman suffrage.[24] Even before her controversial activism for animals, she was well known among many contemporaries and particularly among fellow female reformers.

Figure 3.2. Although Caroline Earle White played a key role in the creation of the PSPCA in 1868, as a woman, she was not permitted to serve as one of its leaders or board members. In 1883, she founded the AAVS, but again a man served as president. *Reproduced with permission of the American Anti-Vivisection Society.*

When she died in 1916, a woman eulogized her as "one of the most justly famous women of the country."[25]

But even though she divided her energies among many activities, White's greatest lifetime commitment and her major contributions were to animal rights, and in sharp contrast to Bergh, her motivations were moral and personal. As a child, she had frequently witnessed the physical abuse many drivers inflicted on the fatigued draft animals that pulled heavy freight down Philadelphia's Market Street. She later recounted that such scenes so traumatized and depressed her that for days afterward, she loathed returning to that street. A self-described animal lover, she personally rescued and adopted numerous homeless animals throughout her life.[26] Moreover, as her involvement in the movement intensified over the years, she subscribed to an increasingly radical animal advocacy philosophy. By 1894, she expressed these views explicitly, insisting that "animals have certain rights, as inalienable as those of man to life, liberty and the pursuit of happiness."[27] She questioned what she saw as the artificial, human-imposed hierarchies of the various species and eventually applied her principles to her personal lifestyle by becoming a vegetarian (Bergh enjoyed steak) and boycotting animal-based commodities such as fur coats and feathered hats.[28] Like most Americans, Bergh emotionally and ideologically detached the cow from the steak. For Caroline Earle White, however, the struggle for animal rights meant that the two could not be separated.

Their views differed, but these two early leaders shared many common goals, so much so that sometime during the late spring or early summer of 1866, White visited Bergh. He counseled her to begin her advocacy efforts as he did, by securing the patronage of the city's most prominent residents. Invigorated by Bergh's enthusiasm, she returned to Philadelphia and drafted the following petition: "We the Undersigned citizens of Philadelphia cordially approve of the formation and incorporation of the Society for the Prevention of Cruelty to Animals, and promise to support it by every means in our power."[29] Throughout the fall of 1866, she called on many a wealthy Philadelphia family, persuasively stated her intentions, and secured dozens of signatures and pledges of monetary aid. Around the same time, M. Richards Muckle and S. Morris Waln also read of New York's ASPCA and revived their efforts to develop a similar society for Pennsylvania. As he had done in 1860, Muckle placed advertisements in the *Philadelphia Evening Bulletin*, asking those interested in animal welfare to contact him. Waln publicly announced that he would provide the new organization with an initial financial infusion of several thousand dollars.[30]

Surprisingly, all written accounts of the Pennsylvania society's formation suggest that Muckle, Waln, and White acted independently and completely unaware of each other's activities until Bergh brought them all happily together. This version of events seems suspect. All three traveled in the same social circles, and if each knew of the ASPCA's successful formation, then they undoubtedly kept informed of current events through the city's newspapers. Furthermore, in canvassing Philadelphia's upper-class neighborhoods, they probably would have encountered each other personally or visited the same supporters. An equally plausible scenario, albeit conjecture, is that Muckle, Waln, and White were indeed aware of each other's initiatives but wanted to create and control independent organizations that reflected their own idiosyncratic views on animal welfare. White perhaps had the most to lose by joining forces with the male Philadelphians. Since few possibilities existed for women in public spheres dominated by men, she certainly realized that a joint effort meant her exclusion from any position of power. Perhaps early movement hagiographers constructed a more harmonious story line to cover conflicting egos, ideologies, or gender discrimination. Whatever the historical truth, Bergh did successfully unite Philadelphia's activists, and on June 21, 1868, the Pennsylvania Society for the Prevention of Cruelty to Animals came into existence. In the same year, the state legislature granted the society's charter and incorporation, and in 1869, members elected Waln to the presidency. White held no official position, but her husband served on the board of managers and spoke for her.[31] Like its New York counterpart, the PSPCA captured the interest of many middle- and upper-class Pennsylvanians, and by 1870, its membership roster surpassed six hundred.[32]

Fewer mysteries surround the origins of what quickly emerged as one of the largest of the early groups, the Massachusetts Society for the Prevention of Cruelty to Animals. Two individuals, George T. Angell and Emily Appleton, initiated animal protection in New England. In contrast to most of his peers in the movement, Angell was born to a poor family, in 1823. His father, a Baptist minister, died early in his childhood, and his mother worked as a teacher, eking out a meager existence for her family. On more than one occasion, financial destitution forced his mother to send Angell to stay with relatives. During his teenage years, he did odd jobs, and by 1842, he somehow had saved enough money to enter Dartmouth. After graduation, he accepted a teaching position in Boston's public schools and studied law at a wealthy relative's Salem practice. A member of the bar by the age of twenty-eight, Angell partnered with abolitionist Samuel Sewell for fourteen years and, like White, became an ardent opponent of slavery. With time, his legal practice thrived, and in 1875, he retired a wealthy man.[33]

We know significantly less about Emily Appleton. A member of Boston's upper class, she may have inherited her concern for animals from her father, John Collins Warren, a respected physician who occasionally lectured on kindness toward beasts of burden.[34] She married wealthy Boston merchant William Appleton, but for the years until 1867, additional details of her life remained shrouded in obscurity. After writing Henry Bergh sometime during the latter months of 1867, Appleton took his often-repeated advice and began gathering signatures of support (her petition had ninety signatures by 1868), and she submitted a charter for an SPCA to the Massachusetts legislature. State politicians cautioned her that the legislature would likely reject her proposal because there was little public sentiment in favor of such a group. Prospects for establishing a Massachusetts SPCA looked grim, but then, a fateful event catalyzed public support and brought Emily Appleton to George Angell's door.[35]

Early in 1868, four men rode two horses (two riders astride each) in a forty-mile endurance race between Brighton and Worcester, Massachusetts. The riders forced the animals to traverse the entire distance of rough terrain at a full gallop, with no rest or water. Both horses subsequently died. When Angell read of the tragic event, he immediately fired off an angry editorial to the local paper denouncing the despicable consequences of a so-called human sport. Within hours of its publication, an equally outraged Appleton entered Angell's office. In the discussion that followed, they discovered that they shared a deep and lifelong affection for animals as well as an equally strong belief that their exploitation constituted a grave moral injustice. Appleton, perhaps realizing that a man would wield greater influence socially and legislatively, suggested that Angell assume the public spotlight and captain the cause she had worked so hard to launch. She faded once again into the shadows—but not before committing several thousand dollars to the enterprise.

The charter eventually passed the legislature, and on March 31, 1868, the MSPCA met and elected Angell as its first president. He retained the office until his death in 1909. Reminiscent of White's experience, Emily Appleton received no formal recognition except vicariously through her husband, who sat on the board of directors.[36] Due in large part to Angell's aggressive promotion of the society, the MSPCA experienced a meteoric growth that outshone even Bergh's organization. Angell constantly conjured up new and innovative ways to reach the public and potential members. In one of his more creative schemes, he asked a prominent friend in the Boston police force if he could "borrow" nearly two dozen officers to canvass the city's middle-class neighborhoods and recruit new members for the MSPCA. Imagine opening the door to one

Figure 3.3. Like many humanitarians, the founder of the MSPCA, George Angell, divided his time among several social justice issues including abolition, child welfare, and penal code reform. *Courtesy of the MSPCA-Angell, www.mspca.org.*

of Boston's finest soliciting for animal welfare! It seemed an unusual tactic, but within months of the campaign, the dues and contributions of sixteen hundred new members augmented the organization's treasury by a hefty $13,000.[37]

Together, Angell, Appelton, White, and Bergh built the foundation of a new movement. They shared a common goal—ensuring compassion and legal protection for animals—and a common faith in the power of reform generally. Interestingly, critics and some historians accuse these founders and many subsequent animal activists of being blatantly antihuman. This charge proved particularly explosive and effective during certain debates, such as those on animal experimentation, in which human interests directly clashed with animal rights. Proponents of research juxtaposed the images of a sick child and a dog and suggested that antivivisectionists cared more about the dog than the child. On the whole, however, these allegations are inaccurate. Looking at the careers of activists throughout the history of this movement reveals that numerous individuals fought for a wide spectrum of reforms.[38] Nearly all organization founders and many of their supporters divided their time between diverse reforms, and most were decidedly human in their focus. Bergh, for example, spoke out on behalf of rights for women, temperance, and urban reforms.[39] Moreover, detractors often ignore his central role in the formation of the Society for the Prevention of Cruelty to Children in 1874.[40] One of Bergh's most vocal promoters, Horace Greeley, often used his *New York Tribune* to publicize and support many causes, including abolition and child welfare.[41] Similarly, Harriet Beecher Stowe, famous for penning the powerful antislavery novel *Uncle Tom's Cabin*, and her brother Henry Ward Beecher lent their support to Bergh's crusade.[42] White, attributing her lifelong interest in social reform to her Quaker parents, fought for woman suffrage, legal protections for children, and temperance.[43] Throughout his life, Angell advocated abolition, penal code reform, crime prevention through education, and pure food laws.[44] And nearly every issue of the MSPCA's primary publication included articles by prominent reformers such as Julia Ward Howe and Harriet Beecher Stowe that addressed a host of social justice concerns, among them woman suffrage, pacifism, the rights of workers, and child welfare.[45]

Since many reforms and reformers originated in the urban Northeast, it is not surprising that animal advocacy advanced most rapidly in that area. But though the stronghold was the East, interest in the cause arose in some of the more developed regions of the Midwest and the West as well, including San Francisco (SPCA, 1868), Illinois (SPCA, 1869), and Minnesota (SPCA, 1869), to name a few.[46] Humanitarians had a much harder time in the South and largely rural regions, where organizational activity lagged nearly two decades behind the rest of the movement. In part, many of the sweeping societal forces that had given rise to the growing concern for animals foundered in the South, but equally important, people in rural regions had very different relationships to the nonhuman world. Animals were often an intimate and critical part of daily human work and survival; there was no back-to-nature movement among the farmers of Pennsylvania or Alabama. When groups did form, they frequently struggled to recruit members and consequently suffered financially. The earliest known southern SPCA, the Humane Society of

Charleston, South Carolina, was founded in 1880, followed by those in Alabama (Mobile SPCA, 1885), Tennessee (Knox City Humane Society, 1885), and North Carolina (North Carolina SPCA, 1887). But by the 1890s, the South Carolina, Alabama, and North Carolina chapters existed primarily on paper, and they were not reactivated until the 1940s.[47] Other southern states, such as Mississippi, reported no animal advocacy organizations as late as the 1920s. In rural regions throughout other parts of the country, the situation was just as bleak. In 1919, for example, no known animal advocacy societies of any kind existed in the fifty-seven rural counties of Pennsylvania.[48]

But where the movement thrived, membership grew rapidly. Although the new organizations reflected the idiosyncratic beliefs of their founders, their constitutions and early legislative initiatives typically replicated the model established by Bergh. Furthermore, whether visiting an SPCA in Boston, Chicago, or San Francisco, one would immediately notice distinct similarities in terms of the gender, class, and race of members. Most organizations' recruiting efforts effectively ignored anyone outside the white middle and upper classes, and they portrayed humanitarianism as a "fashionable" trend among the more socially attuned. One observer noted the leaders' shrewd ability to manipulate middle- and upper-class status concerns through their publications and annual reports, which consisted of "a few pages of statistics, several half-tone cuts, and a copy of the Social Register."[49] The MSPCA, for instance, finessed its prestige by advertising the support of celebrities such as Ralph Waldo Emerson.[50] Annual dues further limited membership. Some groups, among them the ASPCA, charged the expensive rate of $10 per year for men and $5 for women,[51] and lifetime memberships frequently required a one-time outlay of over $100. Other societies established more reasonable rates, ranging from $1 to $5 each year, but even so, most working-class families could ill afford to sacrifice such precious dollars.[52] Likewise, few African Americans contributed their money and time to the cause. Economics surely played a role for some, but most blacks probably believed that there was a much larger and more relevant battle for them to wage—that of their own civil rights. This reality may explain what happened in 1903 when the Women's Pennsylvania Society for the Prevention of Cruelty to Animals proposed introducing humane society programs specifically in African American communities. Although initially enthusiastic, leaders aborted the effort for unspecified reasons, and no future records or publications mentioned the idea.[53] In all likelihood, the WPSPCA effort represented an exceptional case. No evidence indicates the intentional exclusion of African Americans from humane organizations, but leaders probably ignored them as much as they did the poor as a whole.

Some historians and critics have jumped on evidence of this type and concluded that leaders such as Bergh were "snob[s]" and early animal advocacy as a whole was so concerned with its "respectable image" that it "did not welcome the common man."[54] Though it is important to acknowledge the obvious elitism of the organizations in that era, such criticisms incorrectly single out this movement and neglect to mention that much of the general reform impetus of the late nineteenth century originated among the middle and upper levels of society. Few organizations—whether fighting for workers, women, children, or animals—refused donations or bequests from the working class or African Americans, but most routinely and of necessity filled their coffers with contributions from well-known and the well-to-do citizens. Early animal protectionists were hardly unique in seeking favor from a particular segment of society.

Of all the membership demographics, gender is perhaps the most significant, as large numbers of women joined the movement. Men, however, controlled most groups, and they relegated women to member, benefactor, or volunteer status. White and Appleton endured such discrimination firsthand; they neither shared the power with men nor received proper recognition for their efforts. Commenting on the role of women, one early movement historian noted in 1924 that "social convention prevented her from taking a lead in public affairs . . . though it was frequently her generous and devoted spirit that enabled success to be attained."[55] *Social convention* is the key phrase of this quote. The experiences of female humanitarians must be understood within the wider context of societal gender roles. The nineteenth-century woman's world revolved around a highly gendered division of public and private space. Whereas men dominated the public sphere of politics, business, and organizations, women maintained the private realm of family and home.

The boundaries were, in theory, rigid: career men and caretaker women. But middle-class women in particular renegotiated those boundaries to create new opportunities for themselves in the other sphere. They justified their entry into the very public world of reform by using traditional gender stereotypes to their advantage. Specifically, they argued that if biology bestowed women with the nurturing ability required to instruct their families in the virtues of kindness, gentleness, sobriety, and chastity, then this "deep-seated instinct for right and justice" logically made them the ideal candidates to take up civilizing reform initiatives such as child welfare, urban reform, conservation, and kindness to animals.[56] But the issue was fraught with contradictions and tensions. Women reformers' acceptance of separate spheres philosophically provided both the justification that freed them to enter the public sphere as well as a reaffirmation of the domestic roles that subordinated them. Around the same time, other changes—including new economic opportunities under industrialization and the expanding suffrage movement—more directly challenged the very notion of separate spheres.[57] As a result, women found themselves upholding certain traditional notions in order to move into some public roles while contesting others in order to achieve greater rights generally. Middle-class women reformers struggled to find their place between the worlds of tradition and change.

Women in animal advocacy also carved out a niche between those two worlds, and the majority of early SPCAs quickly formed women's auxiliaries to address those "certain special fields" of humane work.[58] These branch societies slowly appropriated control from men on "feminine" issues—humane education, animal refuges, water fountains for horses, parades to honor workhorses, and so forth. Despite the limitations of their position, these women achieved notable successes, and their considerable participation ensured not only the movement's survival but also its notoriety and its prosperity.[59] In just one case, the ASPCA auxiliary organized New York City's first workhorse parade, spearheaded the construction of two animal shelters (located in the Bronx and on the Lower East Side of Manhattan, these shelters received nearly five thousand animals during their inaugural year of 1908), built and administered the city's first low-cost animal clinic, erected numerous elegant watering fountains for horses and strays, and dispensed thousands of nonslip chain shoes for horses. By 1909, in furtherance of humane education, the group enrolled thousands of children in a humane youth club (the Young Defenders' League), distributed tens of thousands of pamphlets, and sponsored an extensive series of lectures at five settlement houses.[60] As the auxiliaries expanded their role and public visibility within the movement, at least one national, male-dominated organization felt obligated to officially recognize their contributions. The

American Humane Association, founded in 1877, appointed several women's auxiliary leaders to positions as directors of national humane education departments in the late nineteenth century.[61] In many ways, these auxiliaries were important stepping-stones to greater power for women within the movement because they gave them control over significant elements of the agenda and created a path into the hierarchy of previously exclusive organizations.

But the tension between tradition and change persisted, for most women's branches remained firmly under the financial and organizational authority of the parent SPCA's male leadership. Eventually, a small number of female activists found this relationship too constrictive and responded by breaking away and forming independent societies. Only four years after its birth, the ASPCA women's auxiliary completely severed ties with its parent and renamed itself the New York Women's League for Animals.[62] The Women's Branch of the PSPCA, which White created in 1869 after her male cofounders excluded her from any official position in their hierarchy, broke ranks in 1897 and rechristened itself the Women's PSPCA, also known as the Women's Humane Society.[63] Those who declared independence reaped many pragmatic benefits, including control over their organization's administration, guiding philosophy, tactics, and finances. In particular, financial independence enabled them to more adequately fund and aggressively pursue the diverse agenda many believed necessary to combat equally diverse cruelty. In doing so, women again redefined the boundaries of acceptable roles within their movement.

A small number of other female-led groups soon emerged. Perhaps inspired by White's activism, Philadelphia women in particular transformed their city into a hotbed of anticruelty activity. Since 1858, Elizabeth Morris had used her personal finances and home to provide an informal shelter for the city's strays. Systematically walking the city's streets with her friend Annie Waln, she gathered up the abandoned animals and either placed them into adoptive homes or chloroformed them. In 1874, the Women's Branch of the PSPCA raised enough money for Morris to open the country's first official animal shelter, the Morris Refuge Association for Homeless and Suffering Animals (the directors shortened the name to the Morris Animal Refuge in 1907).[64] The Morris shelter, in turn, inspired several other female-run animal rescue leagues in the city, including the nation's first retirement farm and infirmary for workhorses—the Ryerss Infirmary, which started with a $70,000 donation from Lydia Ryerss in 1889.[65] The unprecedented work in Philadelphia then served as a model for activists in New York and Boston. Anna Harris Smith chartered the Animal Rescue League of Boston in 1899; Harriet Bird presided over the opening of the Red Acre Farm for Horses in 1903 in Stow, Massachusetts; and New York City's Flora D'auby Jenkins Kibbe designed, funded, and administered the nation's first known "no-kill" animal shelter in 1903.[66]

A very few bold women spearheaded organizations that more directly challenged notions of acceptable behavior within the movement. In 1899, a small group of wealthy Chicago women encroached on the movement's "masculine" territory when they created the city's first broad-based humane society, the Anti-Cruelty Society, and more shockingly, they elected a woman as its first president.[67] But the movement's most radical women gravitated toward the vivisection controversy, which presented yet another opportunity to expand their public role in animal advocacy by directly confronting the male-dominated medical profession. Caroline Earle White once again set the organizational precedent with the establishment of the American Anti-Vivisection Society in 1883.[68] This highly visible and vocal organization not only inspired similar antivivisection groups in nearly every state but also generated interest in the cause among other women's reform groups, such as the Women's Christian Temperance Union (WCTU).[69] AAVS officer and WCTU member Mary Lovell convinced temperance leaders to launch a special committee, the Department of Mercy, in 1891 to work primarily on antivivisection issues, but the mission of the department was quickly enlarged to embrace a wide variety of animal welfare reforms.[70] A coalition with the powerful WCTU demonstrated both the growing popularity of animal advocacy among female reformers and the pragmatic recognition that, as a united force, women could more effectively promote their own brand of social change. Although few completely rescinded their membership in the male-led groups, they undoubtedly perceived their own groups as a means for empowerment in a movement that sometimes stifled their voice for the voiceless.

Women's animal protection organizations rarely suffered from anemic membership numbers or financial hardship. Indicative of many, the Women's Humane Society prospered both before and after its separation from the PSPCA. During its first few months in 1869, over four hundred women paid the annual dues of $1 and volunteered their time.[71] Notably, the relatively inexpensive membership costs did not undercut the group's financial development. At the end of their first year, their treasury boasted $7,000, and by 1883, it reached an impressive $14,000. When the group filed for a separate incorporation, their accounts swelled to over $50,000.[72] In large part, White's charisma and leadership skills fostered such impressive success. Her shrewd investment of donations and bequests guaranteed future assets, and her ability to evoke a seemingly untiring devotion among her followers netted significant financial returns for the operating budget.[73] During just one citywide fund-raising bazaar in 1886, Women's Humane Society volunteers collected $3,000 (about the equivalent of the cost of a middle-class home at the time).[74] White even recruited her aging mother, who single-handedly raised the money necessary for the organization's first salaried cruelty agent. Soon after, two more officers were added to the payroll, and together, these three men formed the city's first patrols to prevent and punish cruelty toward animals.[75] Ultimately, the Women's Humane Society achieved such a level of success that it effectively eclipsed the PSPCA in terms of money, publicity, and achievement.

Many women's organizations replicated the WPSPCA's success, but gender discrimination both within and beyond the movement constantly jeopardized the credibility and, thus, the effectiveness of their reform efforts. In the WPSPCA's first year, White felt compelled to rebuke male critics in the press for their "misrepresentation and ridicule" of the women's activism on behalf of animals. One particularly acerbic attack accused WPSPCA members of an unnatural desire to devote their lives as "nurses" to abandoned and abused animals rather than to their human families. Although White countered such slander with detailed discussions of the numerous benefits of women's humane work, the attacks were unrelenting throughout her life.[76] The fact that early sympathetic accounts of White's life specifically and repeatedly addressed the issue of "proper" gender roles reveals just how damaging some perceived the "ridicule" and "slander" directed at White to be.[77] These supporters carefully juxtaposed her public sphere achievements with reassurances that despite her activism, "she found time to make her home a beautiful sanctuary."[78] White and her peers could not escape society's insistence that they prove they had not neglected their homes or families. During the twentieth century, strides toward greater gender equality eased some of the tensions between tradition and change, but even so, the women of the nineteenth century bequeathed to succeeding generations of female activists an ideological legacy to be used as they likewise struggled to construct their own gendered rationale for participation in the modern animal advocacy movement.

On the whole, however, gender issues and elitism did little to slow the movement's pronounced organizational growth. But though thousands of middle- and upper-class urbanites proclaimed their support for one or more animal protection groups, a more generalized public affection remained elusive in the early days. When the nation's first animal advocates enthusiastically carried their crusade to the people, many initially regarded them as misanthropic zealots or, worse yet, as crazed disciples of St. Francis of Assisi. The suggestion that animals possessed any rights akin to humans' seemed as alien as notions about giving the vote to women. But that, too, would change; animal advocacy was an idea whose time had arrived. The movement flourished because it confronted issues relevant to people's anxieties over larger societal changes. The motivating ideas behind humanitarianism meshed with a general concern about society's moral and ethical advancement as well as more specific worries about the destruction of nature, rampant capitalism, and the ramifications of modern science. Furthermore, as will be discussed, early leaders necessarily established a highly diverse agenda designed to expose the countless ways in which an industrial, technological, consumer society exploited nonhumans. Campaigns in that period protested a wide range of abuses involving, among other things, the treatment of workhorses, slaughter methods, the transport of livestock, milk production, poultry production, the extermination of the buffalo, vivisection, pet theft, pigeon shoots, foxhunts, seal hunts, the wearing of feathered hats, circus acts, dogfights, cockfights, bear baiting, rat baiting, and strays. With nearly something for everyone, the movement attained a wide popular appeal that brought even more new recruits into its ranks. The rising trends in organization and membership numbers rightfully dismayed adversaries, who responded by starting their own groups and initiating a more concerted effort to discredit the movement. However, when one trend more than any other caused the opposition to shift uncomfortably in their fur coats, the American animal advocacy movement tasted success.

CHAPTER 4

"The Voice of the Voiceless"

Early Campaigns, 1866–1915

I am the voice of the voiceless;
Through me the dumb shall speak,
Till the deaf world's ear be made to hear
The wrongs of the wordless weak.

From street, from cage, and from kennel,
From stable and zoo, the wail
Of my tortured kin proclaims the sin
Of the mighty against the frail.

And I am my brother's keeper,
And I will fight his fight,
And speak the word for beast and bird,
Till the world shall set things right.

—Ella Wheeler Wilcox (1850–1919)

Urban workhorses, Chicago slaughter yards, Pribilof seal hunts, back-alley cockfights, upper-class pigeon shoots—modern "progress," epitomized by industrialization, mass consumption, and increasing leisure time, stimulated a seemingly ravenous appetite for both wild and domestic animals. The first generation of defenders of the so-called brute creation firmly believed that the pervasive nature of society's cruelty necessitated an agenda that would speak for *all* victims of that voiceless population. From its inception, the cause used a variety of tactics to achieve many different goals. Along the way, problems arose; radical humanitarians broke ideological ranks with their peers, and those opposed to animal welfare issues increasingly found their own voice and a receptive audience. Nonetheless, early activists, motivated by a crusading spirit, never flagged in either their determination or their commitment to a diverse agenda. Although not always successful, their early campaigns generated a new public awareness of animal protection and established a vibrant and rich tradition of reform that post-1945 activists would inherit and carry forward.

Early reformers knew that before they could justify or effectively implement an expansive agenda, they needed a substantive victory. After their inception, most SPCAs immediately lobbied their state legislatures for more-stringent anticruelty statutes, and in general, they succeeded. But the new ordinances frequently said nothing about who would enforce such laws (New York was the exception, conferring that power to the ASPCA). Consequently, most early groups decided that they would be the ones to put teeth into the new codes. And so, the nation's first humane officers set to work. Movement founder Henry Bergh was among them. He donned his coat and trademark top hat and stepped onto the street as New York's first official cruelty agent. Since he had a legislative mandate, he naively assumed that citizens would heed his authority, just as they obeyed any law-enforcement official. At Fifth Avenue and 22nd Street, he came on his first case, a carriage driver beating a lame horse with the handle of his whip. Bergh intervened, identified himself, and told the offender to cease under threat of arrest. As he recalled later, the man momentarily looked befuddled, then burst into laughter and resumed whipping his horse. The deflated crusader went home. The next day, he bypassed polite intercession and opted for the more direct tactic of arrest. This time, he targeted a man inhumanely transporting his livestock, but when Bergh escorted the man into court, an amused judge questioned the validity of the new statute and dismissed the case.[1] Bergh's experiences were not exceptional. The first humane officers in nearly every major city discovered that moral suasion reformed few abusers, and even in the most appalling cases, prosecution rarely culminated in convictions.[2]

Skeptical judges persistently hindered efforts, but Bergh eventually reached an important milestone when he successfully prosecuted a case against a butcher in late April 1866. In the first recorded cruelty conviction in the United States, the court fined the defendant $10 for the cruel mishandling of livestock. Reaping the benefits of the precedent, Bergh secured another conviction the next day. This time, the incredulous offender paid $10 and spent one day in prison. Judicial resistance to such cases eased somewhat, and by the end of its first year, the ASPCA had prosecuted 119 cases, resulting in 66 convictions.[3] Initially, Bergh supervised and prosecuted each case, but the growing caseload soon convinced him to hire legal aid, and in 1870, he employed attorney Elbridge Gerry as the organization's official counsel.[4] By 1879, the society had racked up 6,000 prosecutions, and by the time of Bergh's death nine years later, agents had handled 12,000 cases.[5]

Similar developments transpired in other cities. Between 1867 and 1921, PSPCA agents investigated an astounding 1,192,203 cases and procured 17,826 convictions.[6] During 1871, just one agent for the WPSPCA arrested 75 people, 54 of whom the courts subsequently fined.[7] And by 1896, MSPCA case files detailed 102,523 incidents and 4,716 convictions.[8] Though the conviction rates may not seem impressive, they, too, represented a victory of sorts. Despite some more-receptive judges, many on the bench steadfastly refused to legally consider animals as anything but human property. Furthermore, most anticruelty laws did not empower any individual or group to enforce them. Considering that the humane agents often acted with no official authority before hostile judges, their conviction rates take on greater import. Ultimately, many states amended their laws and granted specific animal protection groups the powers of investigation and prosecution.[9] This move also signaled a turning point for animal advocacy, as the humane organization became a permanent and accepted fixture in policing society's abuse of nonhumans.

Prosecution cases improved animal advocacy's reputation and accelerated its growth. Still, during the movement's infancy, public attitudes vacillated wildly, inclining occasionally toward praise but often falling somewhere between apathy and derision. Such skepticism found expression in the print media. In New York, several prominent papers, such as Greeley's *Tribune*, championed Bergh, but others sarcastically labeled him a "crank," a "fanatic," and the "Moses" of animals.[10] One particularly contemptuous writer parodied the ASPCA by proposing the formation of a society for the *promotion* of cruelty to animals as a countervailing force to the sentimental extremism of animal lovers.[11] In Philadelphia, the city press initially responded in much the same fashion. In 1869, when the Women's Branch of the PSPCA voiced concern about the plight of the city's sizable population of strays and resolved to raise funds for a humane shelter, the local press mocked the refuge "as an old age home for dogs."[12] Certainly, such attitudes frustrated many leaders during those first trying years. But most also grudgingly acknowledged that they preferred publicity of any stripe—even ridicule—over apathy and no publicity at all. Perhaps recalling his friend's admonishment years earlier that criticism was preferable to obscurity, Bergh argued that activists should not wait for the media's attention but rather hijack it through provocative direct actions that highlighted their agenda. He fast became famous (and infamous) for instigating daylong traffic jams on the city's busiest thoroughfares as he ordered freight drivers to unhitch weary horses and passengers to dismount from overloaded omnibuses. In another part of town, he arrested an entire ship's crew for the cruel transport of a shipment of sea turtles destined for New York restaurants. The judge threw the case out on the grounds that turtles were fish, not animals, but Bergh never expected to win the case. Instead, he wanted to incite the media. His plan worked. Nearly every city newspaper carried the story, and the *New York Herald* featured such an amusing satire of the case, complete with testimonials for the turtles from supportive animals, that it was reprinted throughout the country within days, reaching an estimated half million people. ASPCA membership and donations soared.[13]

Determined to "invoke the potent influence of the Press," Bergh mastered the art of public spectacle and propelled the ASPCA into the national spotlight.[14] While many skeptics remained antagonistic and continued to stereotype the new humanitarians as "maniacal" sentimentalists, a growing body of favorable public opinion increasingly offset the derision.[15] By the late 1870s, the movement's reputation had improved. Fewer people questioned the authority of cruelty agents, and judges who presided over the cases treated them with greater respect. Visibility was the key. Whether in Philadelphia, San Francisco, or New York, dispatching cruelty agents throughout the metropolis to meticulously examine a workhorse's load or inspect the transport of sheep made the movement's beliefs and goals comprehensible to the public. As these patrols became more commonplace, people increasingly accepted the agents and indeed expected them to uphold the new doctrines of animal protection. And by publicizing the details of the most dreadful cases through the newspapers, organizations further turned public opinion in their favor. Publicized prosecution cases of fellow humans pitchforking horses, torturing dogs, severing a horse's jaw, or dashing kittens against a wall seemingly confirmed activists' assertions that animal cruelty was a serious societal problem.[16] Arrest and conviction rates steadily rose each year, and newspapers, including the *New York Herald*, retired their Bergh caricatures and began to publish increasingly sympathetic portrayals of the man and the cause. During the early 1870s, for example, opponents introduced a bill into the New York Assembly to abolish the ASPCA. Newspapers rallied to the society's defense and generated enough public protest to ensure the bill's defeat.[17] When Caroline Earle White formed her second animal advocacy group in 1883, she witnessed a similar transformation in the Philadelphia press. In sharp contrast to the public mockery inflicted on the Women's Branch of the PSPCA in 1869, "several prominent newspapers and magazines" clamored to patronize the American Anti-Vivisection Society.[18]

"CHEAPER THAN OATS": WORKHORSES

As public opinion shifted, humanitarians initiated a more ambitious agenda—one that targeted not just individual cases of cruelty but also what reformers perceived as endemic societal abuse. At the top of their list for early campaigns was the nation's ubiquitous laborer, the horse. Before the advent of motorized vehicles, horses transported nearly everything that moved within a city, including goods, railcars, municipal waste, and people. Horses were plentiful, relatively cheap, and considered expendable; as one manager of a horse-railroad company remarked, "horses are cheaper than oats."[19] Residents of any city could readily witness the consequences of such attitudes. On one street, they might see a driver whipping a team of horses as they strained to pull a freight wagon heaped high with heavy goods (companies compensated teamsters who hauled goods according to the size and weight of the load as well as the speed of delivery).[20] On another street, they might hop onto an omnibus meant to carry thirty or forty passengers but struggling instead with double that number.[21] These buslike wagons, the country's first form of mass urban transit, were typically pulled by two horses. On nearly any street, the carcasses of horses were in plain view. During the late nineteenth century, approximately twenty-five thousand streetcar horses died from overwork annually in the nation's largest cities.[22] Typically, a driver would simply unhitch the dead animal and deposit the body along the curb. For humanitarians, workhorse abuse epitomized one of the most troubling ills of the industrial order, the pernicious quest for profit at any cost. By headlining the issue, they hoped to secure not only legal protection for beasts of burden but also the moral reform of another animal, *Homo sapiens.*

At first, workhorse campaigns typically concentrated on the most blatant purveyors of abuse—operators of omnibuses and freight wagons—and integrated several strategies, including physical intervention, prosecution, public awareness efforts, boycotts, and legislation. Following Bergh's lead, SPCA agents in large cities repeatedly stopped overloaded vehicles and either removed debilitated horses from service or demanded that drivers lighten the animals' burdens. If the offenders refused, agents arrested them.[23] Some transport companies aggressively fought the charges in court, and one company attempted unsuccessfully to have Bergh arrested for obstructing traffic. Most, however, acquiesced in order to avoid prosecution and costly legal battles. By 1879, the ASPCA had removed an estimated seventeen thousand horses and mules from service in New York City without coercion or arrest.[24]

Companies also gave in because they recognized the power of bad publicity. Animal protection groups actively encouraged the public to berate cruel drivers. Caroline Earle White called on Philadelphia women to actually intervene and make citizen's arrests of abusers, although she cautioned them not to engage in any activity "which is not within the legitimate province of woman."[25] White and others also asked citizens to reevaluate their consumer behavior and boycott those companies that mistreated their equine workers. Evoking both sympathy and guilt, pamphlets reminded transit riders that, all too frequently, while omnibus horses suffered great cruelty, passengers remained "so callous and indifferent, so unmindful of the sufferings of the poor brutes as to remain quietly in their places and show no desire to afford them even temporary relief by dismounting from the car."[26] The strategies worked. Fearing the potentially disastrous financial consequences of rider boycotts, the owners of several large companies in Philadelphia and New York publicly pledged to institute more humane standards. The owner of one of the largest transport firms in Philadelphia even invited a delegation from the WPSPCA to personally inspect the reformed conditions of his business.[27]

With this success in hand, activists next added legislative reform to their multipronged attack. The women of the Philadelphia society, together with other Pennsylvania humanitarians, secured legislation in 1909 that prohibited the sale or purchase of disabled workhorses.[28] In Massachusetts, the campaign strove to regulate the labor of workhorses and also to protect them from other dangers, such as stable fires. After a decades-long struggle, the state legislature approved the nation's first fire code for company stables during the early 1900s.[29] Notably, however, opponents in nearly every state defeated repeated attempts to enact legislation specifically limiting the amount of load or passengers carried by freight wagons and omnibuses. By characterizing the restrictions as antibusiness, they managed to prevent a complete victory.[30] Even so, the first stage of the workhorse campaign successfully changed the views and actions of many urban dwellers.

Such success prodded leaders to broaden the campaign, and again, they accomplished much of what they set out to do. During the late 1870s, for example, ASPCA officers investigated the mysterious deaths of dozens of seemingly healthy New York City workhorses. Autopsies revealed odd, marblelike stones in their stomachs. Obviously suspecting the feed, Bergh staked out the local gristmill and uncovered a scheme devised by its owner and the local plaster company to pad profits by adulterating horse feed with marble dust. During the ensuing sensational exposé—which Bergh, of course, personally coordinated—agents arrested the owners, terminated the operation, and reaped glowing accolades from the press.[31] The society earned even more praise when it waged a successful campaign to ban the check rein, a bridle modified with spikes or nails that caused carriage horses to "prance" and thus attract more customers.[32]

Yet other programs benefited horses and publicized the cause without prosecution. The rutted terrain of many urban streets caused serious injuries to the thousands of horses that stumbled over them each year. Advertising the benefits of smooth streets for both beast and human, the

PSPCA and the Women's Branch persuaded Philadelphia leaders in 1872 to resurface the streets with a new process (an early form of pavement) developed by John Louden McAdam.[33] Using a similar argument, advocates in several cities proposed the construction of public water stations for thirsty animals. By appealing to aesthetic and artistic benefits, activists received generous public sponsorship to erect many of the permanent fountains that still grace cities today.[34] Another creative innovation that emerged from the basic needs of workhorses was the large-animal ambulance. Interestingly, round-the-clock ambulance service for horses predated ambulance transport for humans. The service was first introduced in 1869 or 1870, and nearly every organization soon had a specially designed wagon to convey injured or exhausted horses to one of the growing number of animal hospitals, dispensaries, or rest farms.[35] Lastly, beginning in 1903, groups organized workhorse parades to elevate the status of equines, encourage their proper care, and educate the public on kindness toward all creatures. As the proudly and colorfully decorated animals marched down the street, judges awarded prizes to the healthiest, best-maintained entries. Advertised as good, wholesome recreation for the family, the parades remained popular through the 1920s, with an estimated fifty-four major cities staging such an event each year.[36]

But technology soon changed everything, for it was not long before the combustion motor consigned workhorse protests to the movement's back burners. Still, the historical significance of animal advocacy's first major agenda issue should not likewise get pushed to the shadows. Prosecution cases, economic boycotts, and civil disobedience established important movement precedents legally and achieved discernible reforms for nonhumans. Furthermore, although parades, dispensaries, and rest farms succeeded in great part because they posed no serious social or economic threat to oppositional interests, they, too, nurtured the cause through publicity. The horse campaigns accomplished much more than physical or legal reforms: their victories spawned new opportunities for protest.

FROM SLAUGHTER TO SWILL MILK: LIVESTOCK

As horses labored for the humans involved in the industrial machine, livestock fed them. Animal advocates reasoned that if people could change

Figure 4.1. The ASPCA created the first known horse ambulance in 1867 to transport injured equines. In 1902, the society introduced a motorized version.

their views of work animals, then why could they not change their views of food animals as well? In those years of unregulated capitalism, cattle, sheep, and pigs represented nothing more than animated dollar signs, and corporations had little regard for their well-being during transport or slaughter. Railroads indiscriminately crowded all types of livestock into cars, with the inevitable result that larger animals trampled smaller ones and horned animals gored anything within proximity. In this way, they traveled day after day and, according to one livestock official, languished "without food, water, or possibility of lying down."[37] Some estimates placed the average steer's weight "shrinkage" during transport at 120 pounds.[38] Sometimes, entire shipments perished before reaching the slaughterhouse. On arriving at the slaughterhouse, the dead or dying animals were tossed into a pile, and the rest were herded toward the killing floors.

Conditions inside were no better. As the disoriented animals entered the plants, workers swung large poleaxes at the animals' heads to stun them prior to the killing process. The mallet man had to deliver a precise blow and penetrate the frontal bone of the skull, but unfortunately, the general state of confusion among the animals as well as the rapid pace of production rendered proper execution of the task nearly impossible.[39] One American Humane Association investigator described the macabre scene that was repeated with only slight variation thousands of times each day: the man with the ax "struck the first animal three blows before he could even drop him to his knees. The first blow dropped the second one. The third one he struck twice. . . . The first one got to his feet again. Already struck with three blows . . . a final blow was struck which threw him on his knees."[40] The imperfect stunning technique resulted in pigs being skinned alive and calves being hung fully conscious on meat hooks for hours. In addition, the leg chains that hoisted the wailing animals upside down above the killing floor usually dislocated or snapped hipbones.[41] The process continued as each animal was "jerked up . . . and carried, thus suspended, by an overhead device to where the sticker stands. As rapidly as he can thrust his knife into the throat he does his work. On they swing down the line, the blood pouring over the face and eyes in blinding flood while they slowly bleed to death."[42] Putting meat on American plates was a primitive, brutal business. As a senator from New Jersey declared, the livestock industry was "one long and uninterrupted line of suffering from the West to the East."[43]

Groups first directed their protests where the long road to slaughter began, at the railroads. Ideally, they wanted regulatory legislation through which they could then initiate prosecution cases, but to effectively battle the powerful railroad and meatpacking trusts, they needed public support. The dilemma was how to convince consumers that something terribly wrong occurred in the production of their beloved meat. As with workhorse cruelty, humanitarians opted to use a variety of arguments and strategies. They elicited compassion for the animals by publicizing shocking details, such as those just quoted, of their mistreatment at the hands of heartless big businesses. Certainly, these accounts upended the blissful stereotype of the quaint family farm and replaced it with sordid images of agony, barbarity, and greed, and some activists, such as Bergh, eagerly pursued the cruel "capitalists run amuck" angle.[44] But even though this approach was persuasive, appeals to public health concerns about tainted meat generated the greatest response. This tactic was still very much a capitalists-run-amuck approach, but it incorporated a human focus that many activists knew would incite a more forceful outcry. Decades before the publication of Upton Sinclair's *The Jungle* in 1906, animal protectionists sickened Americans with vivid descriptions of "decomposing carcasses converted into human food" and equally disturbing cases of preslaughter livestock suffering from tuberculosis, "hog cholera," and "putrid, malignant tumors," as well as "infected wounds."[45] By manipulating the public's fear of disease and linking it to cruelty, the campaign effectively demonstrated the need for transport and slaughter reform.

In 1871, with the repulsed public's support, the nation's humane societies—including the ASPCA, PSPCA, WPSPCA, MSPCA, San Francisco SPCA, and Washington Humane Society, to name a few—united to push Congress to act. White, Angell, and others testified, and after two years of impassioned debate, Congress passed the nation's first federal cruelty statute, the Twenty-eight Hour Law.[46] The law stipulated that railroads provide facilities along their lines where animals could be fed, watered, and rested every twenty-eight hours.[47] Without delay, animal protection groups prosecuted companies that failed to fully comply. The WPSPCA deployed agents to railroad junctures throughout the Pennsylvania and prosecuted several companies, including the prominent Reading Railroad in 1896. The company was charged with transporting a shipment of horses for fifty-two hours without food or water, and the courts decided in favor of the WPSPCA and fined Reading officials $200. Appellate courts upheld the verdict.[48] It was a significant precedent, but the outcomes of cases in other states varied widely. Local organizations struggled with the costs of both patrolling miles of track and tangling with resource-rich corporate attorneys in protracted court proceedings.[49]

Other enforcement issues further undermined campaign efforts. Perhaps most problematic, railroad lobbyists had successfully cajoled key legislators into amending and thus weakening the central provisions of the original bill. In its final version, the law failed to specify rest stop designs. The omission allowed railroads to construct shoddy facilities that often exacerbated problems by exposing the animals to inclement weather, forcing them to "rest" in mire and consume hay covered with mud.[50] Companies could also easily circumvent the twenty-eight hour directive by simply requesting a time extension or proving the impossibility of a stop due to "accidental or unavoidable causes."[51] As a result, most simply ignored the law, and attempts to strengthen it culminated in an equally inadequate revision in 1906.[52] Passed largely in conjunction with the Pure Food and Drug Act, the revised law promised greater enforcement and prosecution through the Bureau of Animal Industry (created in 1884 as an agency within the U.S. Department of Agriculture) but extended the time in which animals could be transported without provisions to thirty-six hours. The amended law also lacked adequate funding; in the end, the rates of inspection and prosecution rose only slightly, and most officials readily conceded that an untold number of serious violations went undetected.[53]

Disappointed humanitarians decided to explore alternative routes of activism. John G. Shortall, leader of the Illinois Humane Society (headquartered in the heart of meatpacking territory), proposed that the scores of state organizations struggling individually against corporate powers should come together and form a national congress of humane societies. If the loose, temporary alliance of a few years earlier had produced the unprecedented Twenty-eight Hour Law, then a permanent network might wield even more influence. In October 1877, the American Humane Association convened its first meeting, and the early conventions drew a diverse membership.[54] Conservative elements, however, soon commandeered the group and inaugurated a new brand of activism, one that championed collaboration rather than altercation. Suggesting that humanitarians should diplomatically engage in "conciliatory negotiations with livestock interests," the AHA invited railroad and stockyard executives to its annual conventions. Together, the parties carved out a safe, noncontroversial balance between profits and protection. In particular, AHA officials consulted with shippers on plans for a more humane cattle car, and beginning in 1880, they awarded prizes for the best designs.[55] In 1910, the Pennsylvania Railroad unveiled what corporate and AHA representatives hailed as a state-of-the-art innovation, a car with internal feed and water troughs.[56] Unfortunately, the design failed to account for the persistent overcrowding of cars that turned the troughs into useless repositories of animal wastes.[57] In another joint program initiated during the early twentieth century, the national society sponsored humane training courses for railroad employees, suggesting that the problem of mistreatment resided with the workers and not the owners.[58] Once the AHA cemented its rapport with the railroads, it formed a similar alliance with meatpacking executives, focusing again on the humane education of slaughterhouse employees and the sponsorship of contests for improved stunning and killing devices.[59]

More-militant animal advocates accused the AHA of both conspiring with the enemy and scheming to position itself as the controlling force within the movement. In 1899, White's *Journal of Zoophily* condemned the AHA leaders for their "caution and conservatism" and characterized their strategies as a "serious barrier" to genuine progress toward animal rights.[60] In part, evidence supported the charges. As the national organization's reputation and influence as a political insider spread, its policies increasingly reflected the interests of the opponents, and conventions increasingly ousted radical delegations.[61] Furthermore, industrialists generously funded the association, and that patronage created inherent limitations for campaign strategies and reforms.[62] More-radical groups might simultaneously publish explicit exposés, prosecute companies for violations, admonish consumers for eating cruelly produced meat, and even endorse vegetarianism, but the AHA carefully avoided any tactics that would antagonize its proindustry beneficiaries.[63]

The AHA defended its cooperative strategies as a pragmatic response to the political and economic environment of the laissez-faire era. Moreover, the group's proponents insisted that moderation frequently benefited the entire movement. In 1884, the association solicited enough funds from its supporters to launch the "first nationwide advertising campaign" for the humane cause, with entreaties for reform appearing in "newspapers of every political party; also in the leading religious magazines, besides those known as agricultural, railroad, stock, etc."[64] In the AHA's view, diplomacy had gained it entry to the halls of power, and entry enabled it to acquire national respectability, visibility, and thus reform. Association leaders contended that radical sermonizing about fanciful abolitionist goals such as vegetarianism and unreasonable regulations alienated the public and harmed the cause by making it susceptible to charges of fanaticism.[65] The battle lines thus drawn between the conservative and radical elements, the movement visibly cracked. Although conflicts probably would have surfaced anyway, it is ironic that the organization created to bring a movement together facilitated a rupture instead. As animal advocacy's agenda expanded, the division between abolitionist and restrictionist, radical and conservative sometimes grew to troubling proportions.

Even as the national food animal campaign drifted toward conservatism and division, local groups' efforts remained more aggressive and often more effective as members of these organizations expanded their work into diverse areas of food animal production. The WPSPCA conducted extensive raids on local poultry dealers who housed their birds in filthy, overcrowded conditions.[66] The MSPCA, under the leadership of its second president, Francis Rowley (George Angell died in 1909), halted illegal shipments of "bob veal" (unweaned infant calves) and persuaded state officials to grant MSPCA agents the authority to inspect Massachusetts slaughterhouses.[67] Perhaps one of the most sensational local issues involved urban dairies in New York and Philadelphia. Metropolitan dairies advertised their milk as wholesome and pure, but a visit to the typically underground facilities uncovered a jarring reality. Void of fresh air and sunlight, cellar operations confined hundreds of cows in small stalls that workers rarely cleaned. Manure accumulated and festered around the animals' legs, causing sores and infections. Many cows also contracted tuberculosis and brucellosis. In some cases, "the animals were so diseased that they had to be supported by belts from the ceiling."[68] To make matters worse, owners fed the cows a diet of garbage and "distillery slops." In a period before systematic sterilization, the milk produced within these facilities sickened large numbers of people, most of them poor.[69]

Focusing again on issues of human health, SPCAs in both New York and Philadelphia exposed what came to be known as the swill milk or garbage milk scandal. At first, some municipal leaders denied the activists' allegations and insinuated that Bergh and others had fabricated the story about the abysmal dairy conditions to garner publicity. Not easily intimidated, the ASPCA president arranged for members of the New York Board of Health and several prominent reporters to accompany him on an unannounced tour of the dairies. The visits confirmed the allegations and shamed health officials into closing the most negligent businesses and inspecting the rest.[70] In Philadelphia, the PSPCA and the Women's Branch publicized case after case of swill milk incidents during the 1880s and collected specific data on twenty-two of the worst instances. Public anger grew, and in 1889, city officials hired a milk inspector to correct the problem.[71] As evidenced by the successful swill milk campaign, such local initiatives often obtained more substantive reforms as well as more favorable publicity than the early national campaigns.

"ORPHANS IN THE STORM": STRAYS AND SHELTERS

Early animal defenders were not unusually preoccupied with larger domestic animals, as their opponents sometimes portrayed them. Rather, the abuse of horses and livestock was simply the most obvious example of modern society's cruelty toward nonhumans. And for advocates, their work with these animals served as a gateway to numerous other issues and campaigns. One such campaign featured much smaller urban animals: the all-too-common stray cats and dogs. Rarely could one walk the streets without seeing these roaming, hungry animals or the often violent methods used to dispose of them in the name of public health. Thousands were clubbed to death each year, but large cities such as New York used a more efficient method—a large cage that was repeatedly filled with dozens of homeless animals and lowered into a local river. Nearly all humanitarians denounced the practice, but interestingly, Henry Bergh refused to intervene on this issue.[72] His critics called him a hypocrite, but he countered that the miserable life of a stray constituted the real cruelty. "It is more a question of death than cruelty," he stated, "and I am free to confess that I am not quite satisfied in my own mind whether life or speedy dissolution is most to be coveted." Bergh also believed that animal control fell outside the mission of the ASPCA, and until his death in 1888, he supported the municipal authority's handling of the detestable task.[73]

Caroline Earle White took a very different approach, spearheading the creation of the nation's first public animal shelters. Almost certainly, her inspiration came from two fellow Philadelphians, Elizabeth Morris and Annie Waln (see chapter 3), whose efforts during the 1850s to house and humanely kill strays predated any organized animal advocacy movement. White and the Women's Branch of the PSPCA initially supported Morris and Waln, but within its first year, the WPSPCA established its own shelter that likewise temporarily housed strays, returned lost pets to owners, searched for adoptive homes, and "mercifully killed" those remaining.[74] In 1870, with the mayor's support, White petitioned the city to allow the WPSPCA to assume complete control of the problem. Officials agreed and allotted $2,500 to defray shelter expenses. Four years later, Elizabeth Morris established her own public shelter and allied it with the Women's Branch. The affiliation lasted fourteen years, but in 1888, the Morris Association for the Relief and Protection of Animals became an independent shelter.[75]

The successful work in Philadelphia started a national trend, and by the turn of the twentieth century, dozens of SPCAs and humane societies had opened similar facilities. But since most animal advocacy groups undertook a broad-based agenda of humane reform, they typically allotted only a small percentage of their resources to shelter construction and maintenance.[76] To fill the void, concerned citizens in several states chartered organizations devoted solely to dealing with the overpopulation of strays. Most notably, Anna Harris Smith and a group of like-minded benefactors funded what would soon become one of the nation's largest and most prosperous shelters, the Animal Rescue League of Boston. By 1920, thirty-six organizations in the United States defined themselves exclusively as animal rescue leagues.[77] The plight of strays generated a widespread support that translated into both favorable publicity and donations. Activists correctly realized that even though many people could emotionally distance themselves from food animals, few could ignore the connections between the animals sharing their homes and those fending for themselves in cold alleys. By the 1890s, the intense public interest convinced a number of groups, including the ASPCA, to assume control of city pounds and become the urban dogcatchers.[78]

Initially, most shelters functioned primarily as killing centers. During 1871, the Women's Branch captured 2,748 dogs and destroyed 1,864; in 1893, workers killed 4,797 of the 5,471 dogs that arrived at the shelter.[79] According to Anna Harris Smith, the primary mission of her facility was the rapid processing of strays so as to "release . . . from suffering" as many animals as possible. Her rescue league kept dogs no longer than five days and destroyed all but twenty or thirty of the best kittens and cats during any period.[80] By today's standards, such views might seem incongruous with the image of animal advocacy, but they must be located within the historical context of the movement and its ideology. Few women involved in the campaign considered themselves or their task callous or hypocritical. The crucial issue for Smith, White, and others was not so much the destruction of unwanted animals but rather the *method* of destruction and its implications for humans and nonhumans alike. Looking back on her shelter's first year, White wrote of the campaign's central motivation: "The system heretofore in vogue was not only most cruel to the animals upon whom it was practiced but brutalizing in the extreme to those who were made the instruments of carrying it out and demoralizing to those who were witness of it."[81] For them, the campaigns nurtured not only greater kindness toward animals but also greater kindness within humans.

The women also frequently described their work in gendered terms that evoked appropriately maternal images. Shelters were frequently called "homes" or "refuges," strays were referred to as "orphans in the storm," and those lucky enough to find new homes were said to have been "adopted."[82] The shelter represented the safe, domestic refuge, whereas the city street was the cruel, public space. But though the language sounded homey, shelters faced a grim dilemma: how to humanely kill thousands of dogs and cats each year. The search for methods of cruelty-free killing occupied considerable attention in animal welfare publications, and inventions designed to accomplish the task ranged from the logical to the bizarre. Early on, sulfurous gas replaced chloroform, but during the 1880s, many shelters experimented with carbonic acid gas. The recommended procedure entailed carefully redirecting a woodstove chimney to a sealed chamber filled with dogs or cats. Theoretically, the plan seemed sensible, but many shelters discovered that if workers excessively stoked the fire, they inadvertently cooked the dogs and cats. In 1911, Smith unveiled what she considered the greatest innovation in humane killing, the electrified cage. However, that device sometimes took too long to kill the animal, with obviously unsettling results. And so, the quest for a better means to inflict death went on.[83]

In 1903, however, a new voice in the movement spawned the first protest to the general practice of killing strays. While traveling in France, Flora Kibbe stumbled on a "no-kill" shelter that stressed saving strays, not destroying them. She transplanted the idea to New York City and launched her pioneering Bide-a-Wee Home Association, with a strict policy that no animal taken in would be killed unless it was hopelessly ill. The shelter instead started an aggressive and quite successful adoption program.[84] But Kibbe was far ahead of her time, and most shelters persisted in their singular humane killing approach. Still, Bide-a-Wee harkened a change. During the twentieth century, pets snuggled their way into an even more hallowed cultural niche, and eventually, shelters increasingly boasted of the number of animals saved, not humanely destroyed.

BLOOD SPORTS

For some organizations, shelter responsibilities eventually became overwhelming, absorbing a disproportionate share of their finances and constricting their agendas. Most, however, continued to pursue a wide-ranging attack on cruelty, conducting several campaigns at the same time.

While fostering public sympathy for the plight of strays, advocates simultaneously led people into a much darker realm of abuse where cats, dogs, and many other animals died. Collectively termed blood sports, this broad array of so-called leisure activities included dogfights, cockfights, animal baiting (which typically involved tethering anything from a bull to a rat and then inciting other animals to attack it), rabbit coursing (hunting hares with greyhounds), gander pulling (wherein riders on horseback endeavored to decapitate a greased, suspended bird), pigeon shoots, and foxhunts. For reformers, these events exemplified the human capacity for senseless evil, particularly since participants rationalized their actions under the guise of recreation. But blood sports enjoyed an immense popularity that crossed class lines, so combating them meant confronting an opposition ranging from the notorious underworld figures of animal fight rackets to the millionaire members of the Hempstead Coursing Club on Long Island, New York.[85]

Societies first targeted the fight rings with the proven strategies of prosecution and prohibitive legislation. Starting in the late 1860s, the WPSPCA, MSPCA, San Francisco SPCA, Rhode Island SPCA, and ASPCA all conducted "vigorous" raids on the popular back-alley contests.[86] Such forays required agents of steely disposition. On a typical ASPCA raid, Bergh led a mere three to five humane officers against upwards of two hundred rowdy, intoxicated spectators (most with outstanding bets) and ordered them to cease under threat of arrest. Mayhem usually erupted as participants pummeled humane officers and each other. The danger did not end with the last raid and morning light but continued throughout the entire campaign, for underworld thugs trailed agents on rounds and harassed people outside SPCA headquarters. Eventually, the nightly stream of arrests undercut the events' popularity, and Bergh's men even nabbed several notorious figures, including Kit Burns, who ran the city's largest dogfighting ring.

Whether in New York or San Francisco, the campaign's inherent danger and intrigue made for sensational journalism, and again, the press gave a supportive voice to the struggle.[87] Politicians took note, and in numerous states, SPCA-sponsored legislation eventually banned all staged animal fights. By the first decades of the twentieth century, only seven states refused to criminalize dog- and cockfights, but even they conceded to better regulating the events.[88] In addition, the AHA led the efforts that ended gander pulling in several western states and defeated repeated attempts to legalize bullfighting.[89] The movement crippled back-alley blood sports, both legislatively and in terms of social acceptability. Although a smaller number of rings continued to operate in nearly every state, fight enthusiasts moved deeper underground; today, such fights are conducted as nomadic operations to evade detection.

Lower-class blood sports fell relatively quickly under the legislative ax, but lawmakers often sanctioned and even participated in the foxhunts, pigeon shoots, and rabbit coursing of upper-class gun and hunt clubs. When newspapers published lurid details of East End (New York City) dogfights, many wealthy Victorians were aghast. But most of the same readers saw nothing wrong with the sporting challenge of running down a tame fox. Humanitarians viewed the situation somewhat differently. They typically judged cruelty not by class but according to their perceptions of the pain inflicted on innocent creatures by deviant humans. As Henry Salt explained, "All such barbarities, whether practised by rich or poor, are alike condemned by any conceivable principle of justice and humaneness."[90] Reformers assailed upper-class blood sports with just as much zeal as they did Kit Burns, and many societies, such as the WPSPCA, began prosecuting pigeon shoot and foxhunt participants during their charter year.[91]

But elites could bring considerable influence and resources to bear on such protests, and they often quashed attempts to outlaw their sports. In 1889, for example, the WPSPCA won an unprecedented victory when a judge convicted the Philadelphia Hunt Club of cruelty to foxes, but with the best lawyers in town counted among the club's members, the decision was overturned on appeal. Foxhunts and rabbit coursing remained legal in many states well into the twentieth century.[92] Similarly, pigeon shoot protests culminated in prohibitive laws in only a handful of states, including Rhode Island (1874) and Massachusetts (early 1870s).[93] In Pennsylvania, White introduced bills every year, only to watch them go down to overwhelming defeat. By the 1890s, the WPSPCA abandoned the legislative route and instead tried prosecuting live animal shoots under the general cruelty statute, but again, the group met with little success.[94] ASPCA attempts to stop the shoots also frequently failed. During one notable confrontation, the publicity-hungry Bergh boldly placed himself between the shooters and their live targets and ordered the contestants to go home. The participants then trained their guns on Bergh, who wisely stepped aside and allowed the shoot to proceed.[95]

During the 1870s, New York sporting clubs handed the ASPCA a demoralizing defeat when they successfully maneuvered their own law through the legislature to legalize pigeon shoots. Activists eventually secured the law's repeal, in 1901, and persistent agitation on the issue did inspire a new and ultimately popular invention, the glass or clay pigeon.[96] But these were less-than-decisive victories, and eventually, early leaders decided, as White put it, to "bide our time and wait until public opinion has become more enlightened in this commonwealth."[97]

Although they never completely disappeared, pigeon shoots did slowly fall from the good graces of an increasingly compassionate public. The mixed results of the campaign against the shoots can be traced to two factors: the considerable power wielded by the elite opposition and the fact that the controversy pitted issues of individual animal suffering against emerging issues of conservation management. Animal defenders stressed the birds' pain, whereas sportsmen and sportswomen insisted that effective management of natural resources necessitated the elimination of large numbers of so-called problem species (pigeons, rabbits, predatory foxes) so as to conserve more-desirable wild resources (especially those desirable to hunters). Throughout the controversy, middle- and upper-class participants in the sport waged a relatively effective public relations drive in which they contrasted themselves as conscientious stewards of nature with what they perceived as overly sentimental animal lovers.[98] Certainly, not all conservationists agreed with pigeon shoots, and some, among them Theodore Roosevelt, sided with the humanitarians.[99] Nonetheless, the debate over the fate of the cooing birds generated a sometimes implacable animosity between the animal advocacy movement and the evolving conservation movement.

That animosity erupted again over the issue of sport hunting. Many animal advocates judged killing for fun as "the most wanton and indefensible" example of the unjust infliction of pain on nonhumans, but they converted few conservationists or preservationists to their position.[100] Sierra Club founder John Muir eventually came out against recreational hunting, but he never officially aligned himself with any humanitarian groups.[101] The immensely popular nature writer Ernest Thompson Seton did affiliate with the humanitarian protests, and in 1901, he published *Lives of the Hunted*, an unabashedly sympathetic portrayal of the victims of the hunt.[102] But for the most part, nature advocates avoided the issue. Many of them despised the indiscriminate slaughter of game animals by unethical gunners, yet most hunted themselves and balked at any bans that might inadvertently impact them. Instead, they supported laws that punished poachers and created game commissions to enforce them.[103] Animal protectionists rejected those same laws; for them, hunting for any reason other than survival debased the individual as well as society's common moral fabric.

Humanitarians appealed to the public, but here again, the hunting lobby found greater favor. When George T. Angell denounced Teddy Roosevelt's highly publicized big-game hunting trips, the irascible president retaliated by ordering Washington, D.C., schools to purge all issues of the MSPCA magazine from their collections.[104] Roosevelt, who glorified hunting as the ultimate expression of masculinity, viewed Angell's attack as sentimental rubbish.[105] And even though some attitudes toward animals were changing, many Americans agreed with Roosevelt. They believed nature and animals were subordinate, utilitarian aspects of a human-dominated world. For them, hunting simply reflected that philosophy in action.[106] Moreover, many felt that hunting fostered a greater respect for and connection with nature. In other words, humanitarians could not escape the sociocultural reality that most Americans still considered spending a day in the woods with a gun as a healthy pastime. The two sides so thoroughly antagonized one another that when issues of common concern brought the two movements together in later years, these historical and ideological disagreements sometimes threatened to undermine a campaign's success.

BERGH AND BARNUM: CIRCUSES

The two movements diverged when advocates confronted yet another issue involving wild animals—those caged in zoos and performing in circuses. The nineteenth-century effort to improve the lot of animals in zoos and circuses brought fresh challenges, for these popular entertainment venues often proved impervious to protest and resistant to reform.[107] They drew large crowds for several reasons. Like hunting, visiting a zoo or attending a circus was considered a healthy pastime by most people. Moreover, zoos and circuses were relatively cheap entertainment, and they allowed urbanites to reconnect with nature. They also offered everyone a chance to witness some of the world's most exotic animals being tamed by the most dominant of all of Darwin's species, humans.

In circuses—unlike in blood sports—the most egregious acts of animal exploitation and abuse occurred out of sight of the paying customers, which posed a real problem for reformers. How could they convince the enthusiastic crowds at these venues that beyond the big top was a world where lion tamers liberally administered clubs and whips and hot irons, where zoo collectors slaughtered mature animals to capture their young, and where trainers cut the tendons of elephants to drop them to their knees?[108] Circuses masked their darker secrets behind smiling, costumed figures, and they enhanced the onlookers' experience with everything from bands to warm peanuts. The facade exasperated activists, and they realized that popular opinion often worked against them; furthermore, the public's skepticism about their efforts was fueled by media-savvy circus owners who portrayed themselves as victims of the activists' extremism. As a result, only a few organizations mounted serious anticircus/antizoo initiatives, and perhaps not surprisingly, the ASPCA was in the forefront of the campaign. What transpired was a dramatic and contentious exchange between two masterful manipulators of the public—Henry Bergh and the world-famous showman P. T. Barnum.

In 1867, Bergh struck first, criticizing both Barnum's caged menageries and his trained animal acts. The ASPCA president accused the showman of removing animals from their native environments; caging them in small, damp, unventilated pens; and forcing them to perform humiliating acts to "have peanuts and tobacco thrown at them by gaping crowds."[109] Barnum defended his New York complex, known as Barnum's American Museum, and declared that he loved his animals and provided them comfortable, safe facilities far superior to the dangerous, unpredictable conditions of the wild. In an era when environmental ethics held little sway with the public, many sided with Barnum, and even some humanitarians accepted the showman's explanation.[110] In 1868, however, a fast-moving fire destroyed the building Barnum had deemed safe (a first building had burned in 1865), and scores of trapped animals died. Seeing an opportunity, Bergh renewed his attack and prosecuted Barnum for subjecting animals to conditions that caused them to be "roasted alive." The courts disagreed and acquitted Barnum of any malicious intent. The showman went on to establish new venues of entertainment, including a traveling circus, and attendance figures at what came to be known as "The Greatest Show on Earth" steadily rose.[111]

Bergh kept trying, but Barnum always prevailed. During the late 1860s, the humane crusader criticized the circus for permitting the public to watch (for a fee, of course) zookeepers toss live pigeons and rabbits to the resident boa constrictors. Bergh first argued against the immorality of such a public spectacle, and if he had stopped there, he might have bested Barnum. But instead, he opened himself to criticism by questioning, in a letter to Barnum, whether boas required live prey at all.[112] For Bergh, like many humanitarians, issues of pain and morality guided his activism, and in this case, such concerns blinded him to the biological needs of a boa constrictor. Barnum saw his chance and offered for public consumption an affidavit from Harvard naturalist Louis Agassiz that confirmed the fact that constrictors required live prey. The choice of expert was a shrewd one, since Agassiz frequently supported the ASPCA and sometimes testified for the group in legal cases.[113] Barnum then published Bergh's letter, Agassiz's statement, and his own editorial in the *New York World*.[114] The incident cast the city's leading animal advocate as a scientific dolt, and a normally sympathetic press turned against Bergh. Although the two sides ultimately compromised, with museum officials agreeing to feed the snakes only after closing, the damage to the campaign's legitimacy was done.[115]

A vexed Bergh tried one more time before his death to prosecute his old nemesis. In 1880, the circus proudly announced a new performer, Salamander the Fire Horse. In his act, the equine jumped through a series of flaming hoops, and sometimes, spectators observed what appeared to be burns on Salamander's mane and tail. Bergh sent agents to halt the performance, but once again, Barnum was ready. As the officers dramatically entered the tent to arrest the flamboyant owner, Barnum backed away, proclaimed to the crowd his commitment to humane conditions, and then proceeded to casually stroll through each of the fiery hoops. When he emerged unscathed, ASPCA agents left in humiliation, and the performance proceeded before an ecstatic crowd. The press again reprimanded Bergh for his extremism, and the incident thoroughly discredited the anticircus campaign.[116] Not until decades later would a new generation of activists and a more conducive environment reinvigorate the initiative.

FEATHERS AND FURS: WILDLIFE

As the popularity of circuses and zoos demonstrated, human recreational interests often took precedence over the welfare of animals, particularly wild ones. Furthermore, many Americans balked at the contention that wild beasts deserved protection at all. In part, larger societal forces explain such misgivings. Historically, the country's white settlers had viewed much of the native fauna, particularly predators, as expendable and/or worthless, and that perception persisted well into the twentieth century. And although the nation sped rapidly away from its rural past and toward its urban future, many Americans felt that abundant natural areas still existed to provide ample sanctuary for wildlife.[117] Still, early advocates (despite their sometimes misguided views about the eating habits of certain wild creatures) reasoned that an ethical consideration of animals must necessarily embrace wildlife concerns. A few even attempted to raise public awareness about species destruction beyond the continental United States; White, for instance, informed her members of the dire situation of the cuckoo and the African elephant.[118] More commonly, humanitarians concentrated on familiar North American wildlife, such as the buffalo. During the early 1870s, animal protection groups and conservationists briefly put aside their feud and pressured Congress to save the rapidly vanishing prairie behemoths. In 1874, the Committee on Territories reported favorably on a bill to "prevent the useless slaughter of buffaloes," but with little public or, for that matter, political support, the bill died.[119] The few bison that survived the onslaught of the railroads, government-hired guns, and sport hunters did so only because they wandered onto the protected lands of Yellowstone Park.[120]

Before World War I, conservationists and animal advocates uncomfortably joined ranks twice more to defend wildlife, specifically furbearers and birds. Fur was a truly ubiquitous fashion item at the time, adorning the heads, bodies, hands, and even feet of many nineteenth-century Americans. To meet the market demand, trappers culled millions of beavers, minks, otters, raccoons, martens, and seals. Some species, such as beavers, were driven to the verge of extinction along much of the East Coast.[121] The introduction of the steel leghold trap in 1823 drastically accelerated the rate of extermination of all furbearers. Designed to ensnare and incapacitate an animal, the leghold freed trappers from their most laborious and time-consuming task, hunting.[122] Instead, they simply set multiple lines, each consisting of dozens of traps, and returned periodically to collect their spoils. As furbearer populations fell, trappers struggled to keep up with consumer demands, and the industry searched for alternative sources. U.S. sealers traveled to distant lands, such as the Falklands, where they herded hundreds of seals to shore each day to be bludgeoned to death. By 1824, only a few seals remained there. In 1867, the United States obtained a new, lucrative source of seal fur when it purchased the Alaskan territory from Russia. The deal included the Pribilof Islands, a breeding ground for a herd estimated at five million. But again, hunting reduced the number of seals precipitously, to around 124,000 by 1912.[123]

Such indiscriminate slaughter in the name of consumption incensed animal advocates and conservationists alike. As she often did, Caroline Earle White set her pen to the cause, and in a series of articles beginning in the 1890s and continuing until her death in 1916, she shocked readers with explicit descriptions of the seal hunter's clubbing methods, of pups skinned while still alive, of wailing mother animals, and of the bloodied shores left in the aftermath of the slaughter. Once she had sufficiently sickened her readers, she implored them to boycott fur products and write letters of protests to every country that participated in the hunts.[124] Several respected conservationists, including William T. Hornaday, director of the New York Zoological Park, echoed her call for action, warning that if such commercial hunting continued, certain species would surely vanish.[125] Organizations representing both movements petitioned the international community, and in 1912, the United States, Britain, Russia, and Japan signed an international agreement to end the offshore seal hunts around the Pribilof Islands.[126]

But closer to home, the unregulated killing and trapping of other furbearers continued. Several regional SPCAs coordinated efforts with conservation groups, such as the Boone and Crockett Club, and worked to outlaw the worst fur-trapping abuses. As with the seal hunts, this coalition was somewhat influential, and two states, Maine (1907) and Massachusetts (1913), enacted some of the first laws regulating trapping practices. The laws did nothing to stop the trade, but they did lessen cruelty by requiring trappers, under threat of fine, to check their lines every twenty-four hours.[127] Clearly, animal protectionists had won a victory, but it fell far short of their real goal—a trapping ban. They resolved to continue the fight and placed the antifur platform on their permanent agenda. Conservationists, by contrast, were elated. For them, the laws struck a perfect balance between the rights of sportsmen and sportswomen and appropriate ethical restrictions on those rights.

Given the profur context of the era, humanitarians could not expect much more, and even limited wildlife reforms testified to both the coalition's muscle and the public's slowly shifting attitudes. And though no angry consumer backlash rattled the fur industry during the 1890s, as it would a century later, White's boycott strategy was not necessarily premature. Even during the early movement, leaders understood that the consumption of a product often depended on an artificial, advertising-induced need. By explicitly connecting that act of consumption with willful cruelty, activists hoped to wrest away marketers' influence over consumers. Moreover, White's call to action specifically targeted her female supporters. It was a smart move on two levels: first, because women made up a majority of the movement, and second and equally important, because their "proper" role as household managers meant they exerted considerable power in the marketplace. Through that power, surmised White, women's boycotts of cruel industries would lay the foundation for more humane and moral families in the future. In the end, the fur boycott never materialized; women were not the only consumers of that item. But White was on the right track.

A feathered hat, not a fur, was the vulnerable target. Marketed exclusively to middle- and upper-class women, plumaged headwear was wildly popular during the second half of the nineteenth century. On a Sunday stroll through Central Park or just about anywhere else, even the most casual observer could admire the many women wearing everything from a few decorative gull feathers jutting from a bonnet to an entire nest—complete with posed, stuffed birds—perched precariously on a wide-brimmed hat. To meet the market demands of this unique fashion trend, the millinery industry killed millions of wild birds, particularly migratory shorebirds. Equally gruesome were the methods used to procure the feathers. During the spring nesting season—when large flocks of birds congregated and their protective instincts kept them stubbornly close to the nest—hundreds of workers would descend on the birds, grab the parents, and tear the wings (considered premium) from their bodies. The adults would slowly die, which invariably doomed the young to starvation.[128] Here, then, was a potent opportunity to structure a boycott on the gendered rationale White proposed. Furthermore, the issue would have wide appeal, drawing support from humanitarians, conservationists, preservationists, bird-watchers, and diverse women's clubs. These groups consolidated their resources into a powerful force against what they vilified as "murderous millinery," and in the end, they changed the way nearly every woman in the country perceived her attire.[129]

Despite some claims to the contrary, animal advocates were not the first to raise the alarm against the market hunters' plunder of wildfowl.[130] During the early 1880s, the American Ornithologists Union initially publicized the issue, and in 1886, conservationist George B. Grinnell (publisher of *Forest and Stream* magazine) organized the nation's first Audubon Society to promote the protection of wild birds. Women nature advocates played a key role in the organization's early success. While still a student at Smith College, Florence Merriam (who later married another naturalist, Vernon Bailey) organized a campus chapter of the new group and enlisted fellow students to help her distribute ten thousand circulars protesting the slaughter. She would dedicate the rest of her life to writing about birds and advocating their protection. Interest in the cause spread quickly and attracted tens of thousands of women like her. New members signed a pledge to abstain from and protest three acts: the killing of nongame birds, the destruction of wild bird nests, and the wearing of any feathered apparel. Soon, other conservation groups, such as the Boone and Crockett Club, the Campfire Club of America, and the League of American Sportsmen, dedicated resources to the cause.[131]

Around the same time, several animal advocacy groups, including the MSPCA, the WPSPCA, and the AAVS, signed on and added wild bird protection to their respective agendas.[132] White in particular used the joint publication of her two societies, the *Journal of Zoophily*, to raise public awareness and urge action. Asking women to consider their roles as reformers, caretakers, and consumers, she beseeched them to renounce their feathered hats.[133] As the initiative grew, national women's clubs such as the Women's Christian Temperance Union (WCTU) and the General Federation of Women's Clubs endorsed the boycott. In 1899, the WCTU's Department of Mercy circulated appeals in eighteen states endorsing the action, and delegates at the club's annual convention overwhelmingly approved a resolution asking Congress to ban plumage sales.[134] Women took charge of the campaign, and as the boycott developed and tightened its grip on the feather industry, hat sales plummeted.

The effect of the boycott rippled into the halls of political power. Between 1886 and the 1920s, fourteen states banned plumage sales and numerous others enacted "Audubon laws," which specifically protected song and insectivorous birds.[135] During the 1880s, White and Angell led the effort in Massachusetts that outlawed the hunting of seagulls prior to the end of their nesting season.[136] At the federal level, the campaign achieved a landmark victory in 1900 when Congress passed the Lacey Act, which restricted the importation of foreign birds and mammals and authorized the U.S. Department of Agriculture to safeguard and reestablish wild bird populations.[137] Other federal actions soon followed. In 1903, President Roosevelt established the nation's first wildlife refuge, in this case for birds, at Pelican Island, Florida. Three years later, disturbing birds on government reserves became a federal offense.[138] The 1913 Underwood Tariff included a provision that prevented the importation of any wild bird feathers and even compelled many an incensed woman arriving from Europe to relinquish her plumed bonnet.[139] A few years after that, the United States and Canada signed an agreement to preserve certain migratory birds.

The antifeather campaign achieved unmitigated success economically, legislatively, and, perhaps most important, culturally. By the second decade of the twentieth century, seventy-two government and fifty Audubon Society sanctuaries provided safe harbor for millions of birds.[140] Audubon organized approximately two million youths into bird study clubs and annually published "about three million colored pictures of birds and twelve million pages of literature."[141] Bird-watching emerged as one of the country's most beloved hobbies. Admiring and protecting birds had gone mainstream, and that, more than any law, was the campaign's greatest accomplishment. By transforming something once considered a stunning fashion statement into a repulsive symbol of cruel selfishness, nature advocates and their humanitarian allies effectively altered both public attitudes and private behavior.

THE POWER OF KNOWLEDGE: HUMANE EDUCATION

Educating women about feathered hats had liberated them from their ignorance and spared millions of birds from a miserable fate as head ornaments. Knowledge had awakened these women. Right from the start, animal advocates extolled humane education as a pivotal weapon in protests, and almost immediately, education evolved into its own campaign. Activists believed that by teaching adults and especially children the core values of their cause, they would cultivate a more compassionate society for everyone: children who treated animals with respect matured into adults who treated all beings with benevolence. Some took this thinking a step further and argued that, over time, humane education could even curtail certain societal ills. When he lectured, Angell frequently pointed to the connections between childhood animal abuse and adult criminal behavior.[142] White similarly declared that "cruelty to animals, unchecked, leads to commission of the most revolting crimes." Temperance reformers tied alcohol abuse to domestic violence, and humanitarians, particularly women, contended that the man who beat his horse would surely commit equal atrocities on his family and others.[143] But, as White concluded, "to teach children . . . that animals have certain rights . . . creates in their minds a respect and regard for life *per se* and there is little danger that a child brought up in this manner will ever become a murderer."[144] The solution seemed deceptively simple and enticing: teach the children, and the children would rise to heal the world.

Many movement historians laud George Angell as the father of humane education, but the task of implementing such programs fell primarily to women. After all, who was better suited to teach children kindness and virtue than members of the inherently nurturing sex? The women set to work, and the first stage of the campaign entailed introducing voluntary humane education into schools. Through cooperative initiatives with officials, activists distributed millions of publications and sponsored thousands of lectures and essay contests in elementary, secondary, and even undergraduate institutions. During 1869, the WPSPCA printed and issued to city schools 5,000 "little books" entitled *Early Lessons in Kindness* and 7,000 "slips" inscribed with "The Horse's Petition" and "Take Not the Life You Cannot Give." By 1899, 15,000 schoolchildren in the Philadelphia area had received the organization's propaganda.[145] Other sympathetic organizations replicated these efforts. In 1899, for example, the WCTU published 256 articles on humane education subjects, and in 1903, it distributed over 280,000 pages of such literature.[146] Emboldened by the success of the voluntary initiative, humane organizations in nearly every state, along with the AHA and the WCTU, then converged on state legislatures and demanded "humane education under law for every child."[147] Several states enacted such laws in the early 1900s, but since most provided few funds and failed to specify how schools should integrate the topic, implementation was sporadic at best.[148]

Perhaps more than any others, the MSPCA's female members, led by Angell, threw themselves into the campaign with nearly evangelical zeal. In 1889, Angell founded the American Humane Education Society (AHES) to specifically administer the dissemination of materials and coordinate hundreds of lectures each year, delivered to school groups, church congregations, legislators, police officers, judges, grangers, prisoners, and anyone else who would listen. He also created the nation's first humane magazine, *Our Dumb Animals*; with the assistance of the Boston police, two hundred thousand area homes received the first edition in 1868 free of charge.[149] The success of the magazine (each member of Congress also received a complimentary subscription) inspired other societies to create journals of their own, and by the early twentieth century, people could educate themselves through a hodgepodge of periodicals, including *National Humane Review* (AHA), the *Animal Kingdom* (ASPCA), *Animal Protection* (ASPCA), *Our Four Footed Friends* (Animal Rescue League), *Our Animals* (San Francisco SPCA), *The Humane Advocate* (Illinois Humane Society), and the *Journal of Zoophily* (WPSPCA and AAVS).

Publications targeted all age groups, but humane educators remained, above all, committed to the instruction of children, and they constantly searched for new, creative means to capture their attention. Clubs—political, literary, and social—were popular during the nineteenth century, and so humanitarians incorporated the club concept in their campaigns. Although Angell is typically credited with starting the first youth humane club, WPSPCA records clearly show that White actually started the first club of that type in Philadelphia in 1874. The Juvenile Society for the Protection of Animals exclusively recruited boys because, according to White, their biology and socialization made them more prone to cruelty. Assigning each affiliate a color—for example, designating them the "Blue Banner Boys" or the "Rose Banner Boys"—the WPSPCA hoped to foster positive peer reinforcement by offering free outings, lectures, books, and the not-so-subtle bribes of prizes and badges. When Angell later organized his youth group, the Bands of Mercy, in 1882, White merged her local clubs with the national organization.[150]

Modeled on an English society of the same name, the American Bands of Mercy grew rapidly, and nearly every humane society and the WCTU established branches. In 1883, ten thousand young people belonged to ninety-three bands, but by the 1890s, the figure rose to over eleven thousand groups and nearly half a million members who pledged "kindness and justice to all living creatures."[151] The bands traversed geographic and even racial lines. Bands could be found across the South, and Booker T. Washington organized a branch at the Hampton Institute in 1883.[152] In 1914, hoping to build on the momentum created by the bands, MSPCA president Francis Rowley convinced AHA members to sponsor a national, week-long event to celebrate the work of both these youth groups and adult humanitarians. A proud culmination of early humane education efforts, the third week of May 1915 marked the first "Be Kind to Animals Week," during which state organizations posted exhibits, held gatherings, and awarded medals commemorating the event.[153] Today, long after the bands were replaced by other groups and activities, Be Kind to Animals Week (usually held sometime in May) continues to remind us all of one of the movement's fundamental values.

Figure 4.2. Early Be Kind to Animals Week posters such as these reflect a core philosophy of humane education: the future of the ethical consideration of animals and, thus, the future of the movement depended on getting the message to children. *Copyright © American Humane Association. Reproduced with permission. Be Kind to Animals Week® is a registered trademark of the American Humane Association.*

Despite the popularity of humane education and several successful campaigns, no cruelty-free, utopian society materialized. Animal advocates' efforts competed with other, often more powerful sociocultural influences such as industrialization, mass consumption, and entrenched values of human supremacy. Humanitarians jockeyed against these forces in hopes they could dilute what they perceived as their inhumane consequences. This was a daunting task in itself, and the movement also struggled with its own nascent conflicts over ideological directions and alliances—troubles that would pursue the cause into the next century. Still, early activists made great strides toward reforming some of the country's most blatant cruelties toward nonhumans, and even when the legislatures and judiciaries handed them defeat, they garnered small sociocultural victories by familiarizing growing numbers of people with humane ideals. By the first decades of the twentieth century, animal protection had achieved a level of respect that attracted the endorsement of numerous celebrities, including dancer Irene Castle, actress Minnie Maddern Fiske, Mark Twain, Ellen Glasgow, Thomas Edison, William Dean Howells, and Clarence Darrow.[154] As the nation approached and then moved into the new century, White reflected back on the previous thirty-four years and aptly declared that "the progress of our movement seems really marvelous when we remember the condition of the public mind at the time it was first begun."[155] She was right, but as society continued to modernize and change, yet new challenges would surface to test the movement's resolve.

CHAPTER 5

Reaching Out to the Mainstream

Animal Advocacy Evolves, 1915–45

> I suggest that all men and women, and boys and girls . . . should become members of, and ally themselves with, the local and national organizations of humane societies and societies for the prevention of cruelty to animals.
>
> —Jack London, foreword to *Michael, Brother of Jerry*

By the early twentieth century, animal advocacy had undeniably experienced both success and growth. Some movement scholars, however, suggest that following an initial burst of activity and a few victories, the cause noticeably declined after 1915. Variously characterizing it as "ossified" or in "suspended animation," this interpretation proposes that both the deaths of charismatic founders and the international crisis of World War I sent the movement into hibernation. But scholars also suggest that other intriguing forces were at work. In particular, they argue that the extremist position of the more radical activists and the well-publicized failures of some antivivisection campaigns (to be discussed in chapter 6) ultimately discredited nearly all other animal protection initiatives. At the same time, the more moderate organizations redirected their energy solely toward the popular but noncontroversial issue of strays, accepting their role as municipal dogcatchers. The movement, according to this view, thus lapsed into a period of relative inactivity in which once-vigorous societies abandoned their diverse agendas and instead rounded up homeless dogs and cats.[1]

At least one of the studies mixes in yet another factor: animal advocacy receded because the impetus behind it receded. It is argued that the initial concern for nonhumans emanated from people's anxieties over the emerging urban/industrial order and a consequent desire to alleviate some of those anxieties. Since few outlets for urban reform existed early on, some funneled these desires into a sentimental concern for animals. However, by the early twentieth century, both the shock of change had eased and a new outlet for reform had emerged, namely the Progressive movement. Tackling everything from temperance to education to sanitation, Progressivism sapped the very life from an already weakened humane movement as reformers generally focused more on the plight of humans rather than nonhumans.[2] Work on behalf of animals waned and remained dormant until other, larger forces reinvigorated it after 1945.

I have no debate with those who suggest that animal advocacy changed between 1915 and 1945. But I would propose that the historical record offers an alternative interpretation for exactly *how* the movement changed. Progressivism, for example, did not stifle the movement's momentum but rather fed it. As noted earlier, most animal defenders devoted time to multiple social justice issues, so the new surge of reform simply meant that many humanitarians also called themselves Progressives. But the reverse is also true. Progressives, particularly women, were attracted to animal advocacy and incorporated it into their own wide-ranging agenda. As historians of this large movement have so expertly demonstrated, reformers believed that some societal ills begot other societal ills, which, in turn, weakened the entire moral fabric of society. Abuse was one of those ills, and few Progressives drew sharp distinctions between animal abuse, child abuse, and domestic abuse, believing instead that each fed on and perpetuated the other: they were elements of the same battle.[3] Animal protection organizations began investigating and publicizing child cruelty early on, specifically the ASPCA in 1874 and the AHA in 1885. By 1922, approximately three hundred animal advocacy groups in the United States had integrated activism on behalf of animals and children. Conversely, many Progressive Era child protection societies prosecuted animal cruelty.[4] Animal defenders had long perceived such connections, and during the early twentieth century, their activism meshed well with the larger Progressive program of reform.

The opposite also seems to have been true for the impact of radical factions on the general movement. Rather than stigmatize or dampen the vitality of the movement, these more strident and uncompromising advocates may have inadvertently boosted the credibility, popularity, and general acceptance of those less confrontational, less doctrinaire humanitarians. As this chapter unfolds in the pages that follow, what becomes clear is that the conservative branch of animal advocacy became ascendant between 1915 and 1945. Moderate activists had finally permeated mainstream culture, and that success altered both the movement and the type of attention it received. Perhaps this change has led to interpretations of decline. Like many social justice movements, when animal advocacy began, it was a novel and sensational phenomenon that attracted a great deal of public attention (mostly hostile). But as organizations proliferated and campaigns succeeded, the notion of animal rights, albeit a very incomplete notion, seeped slowly into the general culture. The movement was no longer the edgy, raging, headline controversy but rather the weekly feature on the radio. Millions of Americans received solicitations from organizations; more than ever sent money back. And more celebrities than ever aligned with the cause (new converts included Jack London, Albert Einstein, Thomas Edison, Gertrude Stein, Albert Schweitzer, and Presidents Warren Harding and Calvin Coolidge).[5] Ironically, early radical activists contributed mightily to many of the movement's achievements, and those achievements moved animal advocacy into the mainstream.

Admittedly, success created new issues and difficulties. Humanitarians necessarily grappled with the inherent dilemmas of their own conservatism and successes. Acceptance entailed more cultural, political, and economic power, but that power was circumscribed by public expectations of moderation and compromise. In turn, the movement's radicals were further alienated, maintaining that compromise served to entrench cruelty by obscuring only its most viscerally objectionable features. As in the antislavery fight, they contended, there could be no compromise for something so thoroughly wrong. In many ways, they were correct, but moderate victories, flawed as they were, limited radicals' power and voice within the movement. For the time being, that force rested with the conservatives, but just because the movement shifted in that direction does not mean that total complacency ensued.

Nor did society's acclimation to an urban/industrial environment necessarily undercut protests against institutionalized cruelties. The general movement remained active, diverse in its agenda, and ever evolving within a larger social milieu characterized by consumption, leisure, science, and war. The nation experienced significant socioeconomic and cultural changes, and activists responded to the changes by adapting their ideology and shifting their agenda priorities. As horses faded from the urban scene and feathers fell from fashion grace, humane activists addressed new issues, such as animal abuse in the film industry, and revitalized older campaigns that acquired renewed relevance, such as circuses and trapping. Similarly, as the scientific community's discussion of ecology filtered to the public, the movement embraced the perspective and stepped up protests against the destruction and exploitation of wildlife. When the United States went to war, animal advocacy followed, and as more Americans gave their hearts to pets, animal advocates nurtured the relationship.

And they did so with a flourish. Aiding stray dogs and cats had always held a revered place on the movement agenda, but by the beginning of the twentieth century, a growing number of organizations expanded this work by taking on the official dog-licensing and impoundment duties of their regions. Adding shelter responsibilities did not necessarily signify a waning concern about other institutional cruelties; rather, it was a logical extension of the groups' established reform ideology and a response to the public's increasingly close bond with companion animals. Most city-owned pounds were cruelty nightmares, and most Americans endorsed efforts to reform them.[6] To ignore the mistreatment of the nation's homeless dogs and cats would have been antithetical to the very spirit of animal advocacy. But did sheltering activities overburden those groups and usurp resources from other campaigns? In a few cases, the answer is yes. A number of humane societies across the nation, particularly those with smaller budgets, struggled financially to maintain adequate pound facilities and gradually withdrew from unrelated campaigns. In New York City, the seemingly endless stream of strays—hundreds of thousands of them—pushed the nation's oldest animal advocacy society to its financial and physical limits. Henry Bergh's wariness about the issue years earlier proved prophetic.[7] But despite the strain, the ASPCA did not completely divorce itself from other cruelty issues. Equally important, the difficulties that some groups encountered did not represent the situation of the entire movement. Many organizations—the MSPCA, WPSPCA, the San Francisco SPCA, the AHA, the Animal Rescue League of Boston, and the Chicago Anti-Cruelty Society, to name a few—assumed pound duties without suffering financially (in fact, some thrived) or losing a sense of their broader purpose.[8]

Indicative of the shelter campaign's popular support, many groups extended their services and constructed larger, more elaborate (and expensive) shelters. During the 1920s, the AHA spent over $200,000 to build an impressive, modern facility in New York. Likewise, Anti-Cruelty Society board member Irene Castle presided over the ground breaking for the sizable and costly Orphans of the Storm shelter in northeast Illinois in 1928. The Animal Rescue League of Boston expanded its shelter service to the beaches of Cape Cod, where the problem of abandoned animals reached critical proportions at the end of each tourist season as vacationers intentionally or inadvertently left pets behind. The demand for shelters even penetrated the rural South, where animal advocacy counted far fewer supporters, and new organizations such as the Kentucky Rescue League emerged to fill the void. Although nearly all shelters still euthanized large numbers of strays, the public relations emphasis clearly shifted toward adoption, and many of the new buildings reflected the trend in their welcoming, less institutional designs. Both the Animal Rescue League (1933) and the Anti-Cruelty Society (1936) erected large auditoriums or welcome centers to lure more visitors to their facilities.[9]

Shelters drew even more people to their doors by offering related practical services that appealed to many pet lovers. During this period, on-site clinics and hospitals proliferated as nearly every large shelter and a multitude of smaller ones entered the business of animal health care. Some of the earliest include the MSPCA's Angell Memorial Hospital (1915), the San Francisco SPCA Hospital (1920), the PSPCA's Rutherford Memorial Hospital (1927), and the Missouri Humane Society Hospital (1930s). Many institutions, including the Anti-Cruelty Society, the Animal Rescue League, and the WPSPCA, founded low-cost or free clinics in their respective cities. During the Depression, the Caroline Earle White Dispensary in Philadelphia treated approximately eleven thousand animals, and the caseload for the free clinic of the Anti-Cruelty Society tripled each year for the six years following the stock market crash of 1929.[10] Whether for profit or charity, ministering to sick animals led the way in what many activists viewed as the next logical and pragmatic application of movement goals. Veterinarians and staffers endeavored not only to heal the animal but also to heal the cultural ill of cruelty by teaching people the proper care of the nonhumans sharing their lives.[11]

Pet health care and the campaign for strays corresponded perfectly with another traditional headline initiative, humane education. This effort was universally popular among activists: existing groups expanded their programs, and several notable new groups arose to specifically promote humane education, including the Latham Foundation (1918), the William O. Stillman Fund of the AHA (1925), and the Eve Meyer Fund (1929).[12] Although these developments could be interpreted as a safe, decidedly conservative response in a decidedly more conservative era, it is important to remember that the women and men of animal advocacy possessed an abiding faith in the transformative power of knowledge. Even the most radical organizations allotted significant resources to education. Moreover, the campaign evolved in an interesting manner, and in this regard, Progressivism left an indelible mark. Progressives were early sociologists. To conclusively demonstrate the need for reform, whether in housing codes or temperance laws, they conducted exhaustive studies of urban conditions. They crawled through dark corridors and documented dangerous, unsanitary buildings. They collected data to prove their point and convince legislators to act.[13] Proponents of humane instruction loved the sociological approach and quickly adapted it to their cause. Beginning in the 1920s, humanitarians encouraged the study, discussion, and publicity of cruelty's causes ("ignorance, poverty, viciousness, indifference," among others) as a means to silence critics, facilitate new legislation, and further enhance public support for cruelty's cures ("education, kindness and understanding, warning, prosecution"). But humane educators also hoped such efforts would touch people on a much more personal level. If the man who raised a hand against a child and the teenager who beat a dog could be shown both the forces driving their violence and the remedy, then perhaps those abusers would understand the unjust nature of cruelty and reform their ways.[14]

Above all, the campaign directed much of that faith in the transformative power of knowledge toward children. As one group's literature put it, the animal advocate who knelt down to talk to a child today would be rewarded by tomorrow's "higher and nobler grade of citizenship."[15] Many of the earlier strategies used to reach the nation's youth evolved and achieved new vigor during the period. Humanitarians renewed their attempts to establish compulsory humane education in every state, and by 1924, twenty-three states had approved such laws. But unlike earlier efforts, the campaign now possessed the power to make sure states followed through with action. When New York State's Department of Education delayed implementing its new statute, activists mounted protests against the agency until it created the required program. Organizations also worked to strengthen existing laws; the AHA, for instance, collaborated with schools and state legislatures to clarify measures that contained vague language, ensure adequate funding, and generate detailed curricula.[16] A testament to the public's growing endorsement of the cause, many school districts voluntarily invited humane educators from local societies to their classrooms or sponsored field trips to one of those new, impressive animal care facilities. During the 1920s, for example, staffers from the New York Women's League for Animals and the ASPCA regularly visited the schools to educate children about the overpopulation of strays. And as a class project, students helped ASPCA agents round up and dispose of fifteen thousand strays![17]

And so, the doors of thousands of schools opened to animal advocates—a dream come true—and they marched right in. With a captive audience numbering in the millions, the advocates skillfully extended their influence and expanded their activities. They encouraged students to form their own humane clubs or join existing ones. By 1930, most of the Bands of Mercy had changed their names, becoming Junior Humane

Leagues. Still under the auspices of the American Humane Education Society (of the MSPCA), these leagues numbered an astounding one hundred and forty thousand, with a membership of an even more astounding four million children. The momentum spread further as these children then carried their interest in humane principles to yet other youth groups, such as the Boy Scouts and Girl Scouts. The Girl Scouts' rule 6 promised kindness to animals, and Boy Scouts pledged kindness and received merit badges for proficiency in animal first aid.[18] Consider the potential impact of all these extraordinary educational efforts. For the first time in U.S. history, an entire generation of schoolchildren listened to the message of animal advocacy. They heard sad tales of abuse, but they also heard inspiring stories of reform and activism. Above all, they learned that they, too, could make a difference. In a true snowball effect, millions of children in small towns and large cities alike served as enthusiastic little ambassadors for the humanitarian cause. One wonders how many of these young people grew up to become the vanguard of the post-1945 advocacy movement.

But the effort did not end in the classroom or with the local youth group. Each year, humanitarians channeled that enthusiasm and idealism into the annual national event known as Be Kind to Animals Week. The inaugural event in 1915 drew a considerable audience, but it paled next to the celebrations in subsequent years. With the help of supportive press, radio broadcasts, and those millions of youths, the event grew every year from 1915 through 1945. Mayors and governors issued official proclamations, and humane organizations and clubs distributed literature, solicited funds, and sponsored myriad activities, including shelter tours, wildlife exhibits, radio addresses, poster contests, and medal ceremonies to recognize humane deeds. Philadelphia's 1939 celebration exemplified the pervasive acclaim of the event; the mayor granted the women of the WPSPCA permission to hang a large neon sign on City Hall that flashed "Be Kind to Animals Week" for the duration of the holiday. The week typically ended on an introspective note with Humane Sunday. On this day, religious leaders structured their sermons around the themes of kindness and compassion for all.[19] Be Kind to Animals Week was a public relations coup that, in the words of one animal advocate, created a very "favorable attitude on the part of the public."[20] And although it was not a traffic-stopping event, the publicity-minded Henry Bergh would have been eminently pleased with a holiday for animals.

Figure 5.1. The impact of Be Kind to Animals Week on the movement was immediate. In 1916, the ASPCA initiated formalized humane education programs for children. Here a class receives humane education certificates. *Copyright © 2005 The American Society for the Prevention of Cruelty to Animals (ASPCA). Reprinted with permission of the ASPCA. All rights reserved.*

Children were the hope of the campaign, and Be Kind to Animals Week stressed that hope. But humane education did not ignore the rest of the population. Adults, not children, committed most acts of cruelty, and activists searched for ways to appeal specifically to them. Radio entertained and informed nearly everyone, and humane educators extensively used the medium to advertise causes or stimulate general interest through programs such as the Anti-cruelty Society's *Animals in the News*, which first aired in 1936 and continued through the 1950s. Some of the wealthier organizations, including the MSPCA, produced film shorts for distribution to movie theaters and churches.[21] And sometimes, humane educators went to unusual lengths to change minds. In 1919, a wealthy benefactor offered to donate $5,000 to the AHA if it would present an evangelical-style educational tour. The association agreed, and over the next five years, a humane "revivalist" crisscrossed the nation and preached the message of animal advocacy. In particular, the tour concentrated on predominately rural areas as well as the South, where the cause garnered less support. Somewhat comical images might come to mind when one tries to envision a tent revival for the cause somewhere in 1920s

Georgia, but the tactic exemplified the movement's greatest strengths—persistence, adaptation, and flexibility. Activists refused to give up on those regions that were resistant to their message, and this particular strategy was designed to mimic the Christian revivals that were popular in such areas. Importantly, the unique effort produced converts, as several new societies appeared in Iowa, South Carolina, and Florida.[22]

As the tent revival demonstrated, the long life and success of animal advocacy derived in large part from the aforementioned strengths. But times of severe crisis can test the abilities of any social justice movement. War is one of those tests, but paradoxically, the world wars, particularly World War I, brought yet another public relations windfall for the cause. Certainly, it was not all good news. For a few SPCAs, wartime inflation and a downturn in donations ultimately proved fatal; AHA records note that several smaller societies ceased operations during 1918. But such cases were the exception, not the rule.[23] Instead, the war offered an unprecedented opportunity to knit together the nation's intense patriotic fervor and animal advocacy issues. Though it is often described as the first modern war, World War I required tens of thousands of horses and a corps of trained dogs. Most countries dispatched some variation of veterinary care to the fronts, but the services proved sorely inadequate as fighting engulfed Europe. Caught literally in the cross fire of armies, the animals frequently went without any medical care. In response to what they viewed as a humane crisis, animal defenders put forward a novel proposal in 1916. As the United States edged closer to entering the war, the member organizations of the AHA would sponsor their own version of the American Red Cross. Modeled on a similar English creation, the relief organization would assist the U.S. Veterinary Corps in providing both emergency and general care for animals serving abroad and on the home front. But would the War Department agree to such an ambitious plan? The answer came in the form of an enthusiastic yes from Secretary of War Newton Baker. The American Red Star was born.[24]

Within months, efforts were in full swing. Rhode Island activists organized the first branch, but soon, many groups throughout the nation boasted an auxiliary that collected funds and coordinated the distribution of veterinary supplies for military bases within their region.[25] Women in the movement devoted considerable energy to the campaign, and several raised so much money that the U.S. Army bestowed honorary military rank on them. Notably, however, the women of the WPSPCA very publicly withheld their support for Red Star until the government agreed to stop selling old or disabled horse "veterans" to rendering plants. Justifiably worried about a groundswell of bad press, Washington acceded to the demand and sent the horses to rest farms instead. Elated, the WPSPCA members became avid fund-raisers for the relief program.[26] The money raised for Red Star accomplished much in a few short years. The ASPCA auxiliary sent staffers to lecture soldiers on animal first aid, and the national Red Star produced a medical guidebook that the army issued to one hundred and fifty thousand soldiers who worked with animals. Within its first year, the coalition funded eleven motorized horse ambulances (costing approximately $60,000) and donated them to the American Expeditionary Force. Subsequently, the Red Star purchased cars and motorcycles for the small number of military veterinarians who traversed great distances. Gen. John "Black Jack" Pershing sent a personal note of thanks.[27]

Like the humane education campaign, the American Red Star cast the movement in a very favorable public light. Accolades such as Pershing's translated into donations that helped many smaller humane groups avert greater financial difficulty during the war. When people reached into their pockets to aid the Red Star, they sometimes joined the local sponsoring organization or contributed money to its general fund. When the war ended in the fall of 1918, the AHA transformed the finely tuned structure of the Red Star into a peacetime disaster-response agency capable of addressing "conditions of suffering that exist on too large a scale to be handled successfully by local anti-cruelty societies."[28] In 1941, Red Star auxiliaries remobilized for World War II, but the need for a large voluntary effort had subsided as armies increasingly supplanted draft animals with machines.[29] Moreover, although the Department of War continued to enlist thousands of other animals, ranging from pigeons to camels, the U.S. Veterinary Corps had dramatically improved its capabilities. Thirty years after its inception, the Red Star was a shadow of its former self, redirecting its energies toward rescuing animals after bombing raids and publicizing the heroic exploits of the military's "dogs for defense."[30]

Between the wars, the American Red Star rushed supplies and medical aid to the animal victims of floods, fires, and other natural disasters. But perhaps most interestingly, the AHA activated its relief organization for its ongoing battle for livestock reform, an action that clearly demonstrated the conservative shift of the movement. The thriving meat industry required a constant supply of cattle, and in an effort to satisfy demand, reduce costs, and turn a larger profit, many ranchers gambled with their herds. Releasing them onto large expanses of public and/or private land, they left the animals to survive without external care. A mild winter and plentiful grass guaranteed low mortality and high profit at slaughter time. But if the rains came sporadically and then winter snows repeatedly blanketed the ground, few cattle lived to go on to the meat plants; those that did came off the range emaciated. The practice of letting the animals fend for themselves was so common in the plains and mountain states that some lawmakers specifically excluded the intentional starvation of livestock from their cruelty statutes.[31] But they need not have worried because the AHA never pursued criminal prosecution or laws mandating the proper treatment of range herds. Instead, the national society negotiated an agreement that allowed Red Star auxiliaries to care for the cattle during inclement conditions. In exchange, livestock associations and agricultural colleges agreed to encourage more humane care of herds. Industry representatives offered gestures of good faith and happily consented to having the Red Star incur the cost of feeding their herds.[32] In the end, AHA diplomacy only minimally improved conditions for these animals, and cruelties involving range stock would only disappear when ranchers began sending their cattle to the more questionable factory feedlots of post-1945 agribusinesses.

Conservatism also undercut ongoing efforts to reform two of the livestock campaign's most recalcitrant adversaries, railroads and slaughterhouses. The Twenty-eight Hour Law corrected few cruelties in transport, and as trucks replaced trains in moving livestock, the act's provisions no longer protected most animals. The AHA called for new regulations and industry cooperation, but nothing changed in the legislative arena. Activists did, however, thwart repeated attempts by the railroads to further lengthen the time animals could legally go without nourishment.[33] Only the grassroots efforts of several regional organizations yielded a substantive, albeit small, victory. During the 1920s and 1930s, meat companies sold animals that were injured or crippled in transit to local butchers for a reduced rate. In several states, unscrupulous dealers resorted to criminal behavior to increase the percentage of cheap animals. When shipments arrived, these dealers clandestinely sent workers into the yards to break the legs of healthy livestock. Investigations by SPCAs in Massachusetts, New York, Illinois, Missouri, and California exposed the abuse and, with the cooperation of railroads, eradicated the practice.[34]

At processing plants, the killing floors of twentieth-century slaughterhouses looked very much like those of the nineteenth. Mallet men still swung at the heads of bellowing cows and screaming pigs, and chains still flipped them upside down to prepare them for the knife. But one difference stood out to animal advocates: the sheer volume of animals entering plant gates soared during the interwar period, which caused conditions within to dramatically worsen. Numerous AHA, MSPCA, and ASPCA investigations during the 1920s and 1930s revealed that the rapid pace of the processing lines often pushed the mallet men beyond their physical capabilities, meaning that fewer of their blows struck their mark. Consequently, thousands of animals were fully conscious when they went to the killing floor.[35] Animal protection groups across the nation clamored for reform, and the potential for a political coalition like that of 1873 hung menacingly over the meatpacking industry. Once again, however, the organization created in 1877 to empower such campaigns through a national coalition weakened the initiative. The AHA directed the national livestock initiative and stubbornly refused to deviate from its established strategy of cooperation. The aggregate of political might never materialized, and the movement drafted no proposals for legal reform. Instead, the campaign sponsored programs similar to those of the previous century, such as worker education classes and contests that awarded cash prizes for the development of more humane killing devices. Industry officials acknowledged the movement's efforts, expressed an appreciation for its concern, and sent ever-greater numbers of beasts through the chutes to the mallet men.[36]

Generally speaking, the livestock campaign of this period primarily succeeded in garnering publicity and preventing future abuse through education. The targeted industries repelled any comprehensive reforms, and the AHA's cautious approach hindered more combative protests, even those that had the potential to overcome the opposition. Yet the fire behind the livestock campaign never died. It stayed at the forefront of animal advocates' fight against institutional cruelties and drew together an increasingly diverse coalition of activists. For radicals, however, the piecemeal results confirmed their allegations that pursuing a moderate approach was like putting a Band-Aid on a gaping wound. The AHA leaders countered that their perspective came closer to many

Americans' views on animal protection. By slowly chipping away at livestock cruelty with education, volunteerism, and, yes, even flawed legislation, their work fostered a level of public acceptance that at least created the possibility for greater change in years to come.

The internal debate over strategy only grew more pronounced as animal advocates struggled to combat cruelty in an ever-changing society. In particular, the growing forces of consumption and leisure were the primary culprits behind many activities that exploited or abused nonhumans. As the industrial workday shortened and the standard of living rose during the 1920s, more people than ever purchased nonessential goods, picnicked in parks, frequented circuses and zoos, and enjoyed the movies. The nation's ballooning interest in buying merchandise and entertaining itself boded ill for some species as consumption-driven humans forced them to perform tricks, eliminated them from parks and public lands, and skinned them for their fur. Humanitarians did not shy away from the colossal fight, and in the case of circuses, a more radical approach brought the owners of the nation's premier big-top show to their knees—a feat even the confrontational Henry Bergh could not accomplish. However, during most campaigns, such as those directed at Hollywood or trapping, conservative factions again ruled the day.

Watching motion pictures quickly became one of the nation's favorite pastimes, and as Hollywood brought more and more stories to the screen, some of them inevitably involved animals. A few states, such as Maine, passed laws protecting animals in movies as early as 1921, but the issue gained national prominence during the filming of the 1939 motion picture *Jesse James*. A chase scene described in the script ended with a dramatic tumble over a cliff. Wishing to sustain the excitement and realism of the plot, filmmakers decided to drive a horse over the cliff and film it as it fell forty feet to its death in a small pool of water.[37] The public outcry that resulted was so great that the major film studios arranged a meeting with the AHA. In the subsequent agreement, the Motion Picture Association of America acknowledged the AHA as the "official watchdog for animals in the film industry" and granted the organization the right to set guidelines for actor animals and monitor their treatment on all movie sets. In 1940, the AHA opened an office of humane consultants for animals in film in Hollywood. Those small scrolling words of AHA approval on films today are the legacy of a 1939 animal advocacy protest.[38]

Hollywood's use of animals continually expanded, but the great majority of wild and domestic animal performers lived under the big top. Dozens of circuses, large and small, roamed the nation offering millions of Americans a relatively cheap visit to the exotic. But like Henry Bergh before them, the activists of the 1920s wanted nothing more than to rip away the facade of dancing elephants and prancing bears and show the crowds the less pleasant realities behind the performance. The campaign, however, began haltingly. The distinctly more radical AAVS publicized circus abuses and called for boycotts when the shows stopped in Philadelphia, but no mass protest occurred.[39] A smattering of other groups added their voices to the AAVS protests, but the interwar circus campaign seemed destined for a fate similar to that of Bergh's efforts. The situation changed, though, when a self-described "hard head, inured to hardship, cruelty, and brutality" stepped forward to fight for circus animals' rights.[40] That hard head was none other than Jack London, and the famous writer's outrage over trained animal acts sparked a reaction that reverberated all the way to the tents of the Ringling–Barnum and Bailey Circus.

Intrigued by wild animals' performances, London ventured behind the tents to watch them train. His curiosity turned to horror as he witnessed some of the methods used to transform lions, tigers, elephants, and bears into prancing, chair-sitting, obedient performers. Dancing bears danced because trainers burned the pads of their feet; horses pranced because their saddles were spiked; lions sat quietly on chairs only after the tamer beat, whipped, and pitchforked them; and the famous Dumbo strolled quietly around the big top arena because he had spent twenty years in martingales (fetters running from tusk to foot).[41] Circus animals lived truncated lives, often dying from disease, in train wrecks, or from unknown causes after just a few years with the shows. In 1913, an industry magazine praised the Sells-Floto Circus for the humane care given to its animals, noting that although most circus orangutans lived only two years in captivity, Sells-Floto's orangutan was a venerable three.[42]

London funneled his shock and anger into his writing, and in 1916 and 1917, respectively, he released two related novels, *Jerry of the Islands* and *Michael, Brother of Jerry*.[43] Told from the perspective of their title characters, both of whom are trained dogs, the novels depicted the sad lives of various performing animals. The training of the Indian tiger Ben Bolt was typical. Fresh from the jungle, the large cat was restrained by large ropes, beaten on the nose, and jabbed in the ribs until he was exhausted and fearful. Then he was ready to learn a trick:

> Mulcachy tapped the chair sharply with the butt of the whip to draw the animal's attention to it, then flicked the whip-lash sharply on his nose. At the same moment, an attendant, through the bars behind, drove an iron fork into his ribs to force him away from the bars and toward the chair. He crouched forward, then shrank back against the side-bars. Again the chair was rapped, his nose was lashed, his ribs were jabbed, and he was forced by pain toward the chair. This went on interminably—for a quarter of an hour, for half an hour, for an hour; for the men-animals had the patience of gods.[44]

Using the same foreword for both books, London explained his motivations for writing the story of Ben and other circus animals. For him, the world of trained animal acts was a double nightmare. Foremost, he hated circuses for their "cold-blooded, conscious, deliberate cruelty. . . . Cruelty as a fine art has attained its perfect flower in the trained animal world."[45] But he equally blamed the happy, applauding crowds that condoned the acts and even gleaned enjoyment from them. Forcing animals to perform for human entertainment degraded not only the animals but also the humans who participated in any way in the event. Expressing hope that such misguided pleasure resulted from ignorance rather than maliciousness, London implored people to educate themselves on the issue of circus cruelty and join any of the organizations working to end it.[46] Then, toward the end of his statement, he appealed to the reader to do something more intrepid: he urged civil disobedience. He asked circus patrons to simply leave the performance for the duration of trained animal acts, for he believed that such a dramatic show of consumer disapproval would surely persuade owners to drop those acts.[47] Sadly, London died shortly before the publication of *Michael, Brother of Jerry*, so he never saw the furor caused by his words.

The novels caught the attention of MSPCA president Francis Rowley, who decided to transform London's plea into a campaign. In 1918, the MSPCA and AHES jointly created the first Jack London Club. Honoring the author's vision of a protest free of organizational hierarchy or financial obligation, the club required no annual dues and elected no officers. Instead, this unique animal advocacy group required "members" to (1) pledge their opposition to trained animal acts, (2) distribute anticruelty literature outside the entrances of circuses, (3) write letters of protest to the shows' managers and the local press when such engagements came to their towns, (4) send the names and addresses of those who sympathized with the cause to the MSPCA, and, most important, (5) express their disapproval of such acts by hissing or leaving during the performance. The AHES also distributed free copies of London's books to all members.[48] Although the author could no longer personally speak for the cause, Rowley hoped that his words and his fame would propel the protest and that his rugged image would silence critics who derided humanitarians as sentimental animal lovers. Rowley's hopes were realized. Within a few years, the club boasted over 175,000 supporters, and by the mid-1920s, the number approached a jaw-dropping (even by today's standards) 750,000.[49] And then came victory. In 1925, the nation's most prominent circus, Ringling–Barnum and Bailey, bowed to the overwhelming public criticism generated by the Jack London Club and withdrew all trained animal acts from its schedule.[50] The MSPCA had proven that direct action and confrontation could sometimes more effectively defeat cruelty than the AHA strategy of cooperation and compromise.

But the triumph was fleeting. Just five years later, Charles Ringling announced that his show would once again include trained big cats. Shortly thereafter, renowned lion tamer Clyde Beatty entered the ring at Madison Square Garden with whip in hand and twenty-eight imposing lions and tigers standing before him.[51] In part, circus protests weakened because of the industry's response: in 1926, owners and employees of Ringling–Barnum and Bailey formed their own public relations group, the Circus Fans Association of America, which vigorously promoted their business as a healthy, inexpensive, all-American pastime.[52] But industry efforts alone did not dismantle the Jack London Club. Instead, it was a larger, unrelated force that drained the momentum from the campaign. The national economic catastrophe known as the Great Depression understandably preoccupied many Americans after 1929, as worries about jobs, housing, and food superseded concerns about circus animals. Protests faltered, and without an organizational structure or budget, there was little supporters could do to save the club. Sensing the campaign's weakness and acutely aware that their own economic survival depended on drawing large crowds, circus owners restored the exotic animal performances. It was a shrewd move, as millions seeking a cheap escape from the misery of their times plopped down their change and entered the big tents of circuses. The once-powerful and popular Jack London Club receded into obscurity, and during the 1930s, the only victory the enfeebled circus initiative could muster was a WPSPCA-sponsored bill to regulate conditions at all roadside menageries in Pennsylvania, which passed in 1936.[53]

The forgotten phenomenon of the Jack London Club is significant not only because it represented a divergence from the broader movement's moderation but also because it mirrored a shift in societal attitudes about nature. London's writings as well as the popular nature stories of his friend Mary Austin (*The Land of Little Rain*, 1903) and literary contemporaries James Oliver Curwood (*The Grizzly King*, 1918) and Ernest Thompson Seton (*Lives of the Hunted*, 1901) celebrated the wild spirit inherent in nature and animals (especially the much-maligned predator species) and defended the right of both to exist without human interference.[54] Although they sometimes overly humanized their bears, lions, wolves, and coyotes, these writers gave literary voice to an emerging vein of thought within the population—the ethical consideration of nature. London stirred up that nascent concern with his plea for captive wild animals, and through the circus campaign, Americans tried to give form to what was at the time a nebulous desire to strike a balance between exploitive consumption activities and a blossoming appreciation of the natural world.

But people's ambivalence about the natural world also stemmed partly from an ideological tension between Progressive conservation policies and the ecological thought that germinated before World War I and slowly trickled down to the general public. During the nineteenth century, with its smokestacks and tenements, a nostalgia for nature arose, but romancing the wild was insufficient to stem the often destructive impact that consumption had on the environment. With the rise of Progressivism, more Americans learned to respect nature but primarily as a valuable resource to be conserved for future consumption; conservation was for the most part a government-led, anthropocentric, and utilitarian movement. Nature was for human use, whether that use entailed logging, hiking, hunting, camping, mining, or grazing. When animals interfered with human interests, many conservationists advocated and initiated their eradication. Predators were perceived as problematic because they killed the game humans hunted and the livestock humans raised and consumed. Moreover, large carnivores such as bears, mountain lions, and wolves allegedly threatened the safety of the multitudes of people recreating in parks.[55] This point is in no way meant to belittle the monumental achievements of conservationists and conservation-minded administrations, from Theodore Roosevelt's to Franklin Delano Roosevelt's.[56] Their hard work saved millions of acres of land and significantly expanded the national parks system. At the same time, however, those ancestors of today's nature advocates destroyed untold numbers of species that fell outside their definition of usefulness.

In part, the ranchers of the West instigated conservation's involvement in the destruction of wild animals. During the early 1900s, they began complaining to government officials about coyotes killing livestock on public grazing lands. Ranchers claimed that since they paid for grazing privileges, the federal government should assume responsibility for the safety of their herds. In 1915, Congress appropriated $125,000 for a predator control program to be administered under the Bureau of the Biological Survey (BBS) of the USDA. The program steadily expanded, and by 1931, under the Animal Damage Control Act, the government was exterminating predators and nuisance animals such as prairie dogs on an unprecedented scale.[57] Between 1915 and 1947, BBS employees shot, trapped, poisoned, or set afire nearly two million coyotes.[58] By 1929, so few wolves remained in the wild that federal reports rarely mentioned them. Other species suffered a similar fate as agents killed 7,000 to 10,000 bobcats, 100 to 200 mountain lions, and 300 to 600 bears *each year* from 1937 to 1945.[59] The National Parks Service also participated in the program, and between its founding in 1916 and the 1930s, it culled thousands of predators from park environs to make the locations more suitable for visitors.[60]

The conservation effort's efficient elimination of certain wild animals continued throughout much of the period prior to World War II, but a changing attitude was in the wind. The predator control program had produced unintended, unexpected, and sometimes environmentally disastrous results. The populations of those animals that predators once hunted exploded, causing massive starvation in deer herds and rodent and rabbit infestations in some towns.[61] In the first decades of the twentieth century, a small number of government-employed conservationists and independent scientists began to reevaluate and even rebel against the logic of such actions. Charles Adams, Charles Elton, Olaus Murie, Liberty Hyde Bailey, and Arthur Tansley examined the consequences of the "gospel of efficiency" and generated new ideas about the value and functions of nature. As early as 1915, Bailey, a horticulturist, used the term *biocentric* to describe nature's interdependence.[62] At the 1924 meeting of the American Society of Mammalogists, Adams lectured on "The Conservation of Predatory Mammals," and in 1929, BBS scientist Murie criticized his employer for disrupting the natural balance of the wild. The pace of change quickened in 1927 when Elton introduced the term *food chain* and argued that if one part of the chain was disrupted, the entire chain would suffer.[63] And in a 1935 article in the journal *Ecology*, Tansley added the term *ecosystem* to the brewing scientific mixture.[64]

Then came arguably one of the most influential and eloquent spokespeople for ecological thinking, Aldo Leopold. Leopold had spent much of his early career believing in and carrying out predator extermination for the U.S. Forest Service. But by the mid-1930s, he had begun to question the policy and propose alternatives. He first attempted to distill his ruminations in a 1933 article in the *Journal of Forestry*, but the posthumously published *Sand County Almanac* best expressed his evolving "conservation ethic" or "land ethic." An enthusiastic disciple of the new ecology, Leopold criticized humans for failing to understand our place in nature. Historically, he said, we have perceived ourselves as civilized, superior, and separate from nature. We have deemed ourselves the conquerors and owners of nature and believed that animals and land exist for our benefit. Not so, declared Leopold. *Homo sapiens* are simply another member of the biotic community, much like the trees or the wolves or the soil. As such, we must extend the same ethical consideration to the land and its nonhuman inhabitants as we do to each other. We must stop thinking like a conqueror and start "thinking like a mountain." Only then, concluded Leopold, will we understand that the "opportunity to see geese is more important than television."[65]

Leopold, Bailey, Tansley, and the other skeptics of the scientific status quo brought forth a new understanding of nature. And although conservation-driven predator control continued, the massive wave of destruction slowly ebbed; by 1936, the National Parks Service had abolished its program.[66] Just as important, changes in the scientific community filtered through to popular culture, where a new generation of nature writers exalted and perpetuated the incipient environmental values. Composing in the tradition of London, Martin, Seton, and Curwood, these new authors enjoyed a popularity reminiscent of the earlier back-to-nature movement. Berg Bengt's motherless bear, Henry Williamson's otter Tarka, Rachel Carson's sea creatures, Donald C. Peattie's almanac of the wild, and Cherry Keaton's island of seals and penguins all beckoned the people of an expanding urban society into the mysterious intricacies of wilderness ecosystems and the animals that lived there. While traveling the pages of such tales, readers often confronted the ethical and ecological issues arising from humans' harmful actions.[67] Influenced by both stories and science, public opinion noticeably shifted toward a new environmental outlook. A recent historical study of public attitudes about animals indicated that during the 1920s and 1930s, Americans demonstrated a significantly greater interest in and appreciation for wild animals.[68] But a contradiction remained. In a culture and economy of consumption, the new attitude all too frequently clashed with actions that were detrimental to nature. More Americans visited parks and natural areas, but they typically did so in one of the 30 million polluting automobiles that were on the road by 1930.[69] Americans increasingly loved nature, but they loved materialism more.

The surge in ecological ideas and the related shift in perceptions of wildlife noticeably affected the direction of animal advocacy. Biocentric thinking nicely complemented the movement's broad ethical consideration of animals, and for humanitarians, one man best elaborated this marriage of ideas. Albert Schweitzer, one of the most widely read and admired personalities of the period, based his famous "reverence for life" philosophy on ecological principles. Observing that "nature compels us to recognize the fact of mutual dependence, each life necessarily helping the other lives which are linked to it," the European philosopher espoused an ethic of kindness toward all creatures. Animal defenders frequently quoted Schweitzer and incorporated his ideas into their activism, but organizations' specific wildlife campaigns varied widely.[70] When an unusually harsh winter in 1920 prevented Yellowstone's elk from effectively foraging for food, the AHA's Red Star rushed large shipments of hay to the herd to prevent widespread starvation. The more radical AAVS revitalized its campaign against the excesses and cruelties of sport hunting, and the MSPCA raised the issue of wildlife extinction and called for national and international laws to protect certain threatened species.[71]

The resurrection of one issue united all these groups and many more. For a great number of animal advocates, the campaign against trapping offered the best means by which to work the new ecological interests into their established framework. Trapping made a mockery of both Schweitzer's reverence for life and Leopold's conservation ethic. Trappers killed millions of wild predators and furbearers each year, which, in turn, triggered the disruption or even destruction of entire ecosystems. According to its own reports, the U.S. fur industry processed and sold 107,689,927 animal pelts between 1919 and 1921. The harvest represented over 125 species, including 9 million American opossums and 4 million Australian opossums, 23 million moles, nearly 7 million skunks, 14 million muskrats, 14 million European squirrels, nearly 2 million raccoons, and over 200,000 Australian koalas. Highly valued martens, beavers, and fishers were trapped to extinction in many regions of North America.[72] In Alaska, the prize catch was the handsome and plentiful arctic fox, but within a few short years, it, too, was pushed toward extinction.[73]

Moreover, trapping devices inflicted considerable and intentional pain in the name of selfish economic pursuits and frivolous consumerism. Through their purchases, people condoned the use of these cruel implements, and such ignorant disregard rankled humanitarians. As World War I ended, the nation entered a decade affectionately dubbed the Roaring Twenties. Whether the decade roared for most Americans is debatable, but for the fur industry, the term is apt. The combination of postwar spending, the mass production of cheaper furs, and abundant advertising generated an unprecedented demand for animal pelts, particularly among women. In 1922, a woman could purchase a fur muff, complete with the deceased animal's head, feet, and tail, for as little as $4.98. The skins of squirrels, foxes, beavers, minks, martens, and myriad other creatures adorned the body of the stylish 1920s woman. The industry also catered to men, though they were a less lucrative market; the fashionable man of the times would surely sport a full-length raccoon coat.[74] Demand for fur eased during the Depression, but the industry had rebounded by 1940, and fur sales accelerated so rapidly that a number of resourceful entrepreneurs began captive-breeding farms for the more valuable species.[75] With fur's widespread popularity, activists faced a tough sell for their campaign, but they were determined to intertwine the issues of cruelty, consumerism, and ecology.

All of the major humane groups participated in the campaign, but the cause was led by a new type of organization that specifically integrated humane and wildlife issues. During a trip to Nova Scotia, diplomat and naturalist Edward Breck witnessed a black bear's slow death between the spiked jaws of a forty-pound trap. He returned to the states committed to reforming the fur trade and founded the Anti-Steel Trap League in 1925.[76] Breck died a few years later, but author and former teacher Lucy Furman became both the group's and the general campaign's guiding force. Furman's strategy was to conduct a massive publicity campaign to educate people on the cruel process behind the production of a fur coat.[77] A 1928 *Atlantic Monthly* article by Furman typified the campaign's approach. She prefaced her case by noting that the nervous systems of furbearers made them, like humans, quite capable of feeling pain. She then described the powerful snap and painful hold of traps, the desperate attempts by their sentient victims to free themselves by gnawing off their own limbs (referred to as "wring off" by trappers), and the slow starvation of some animals due to neglectful trappers.[78] In the slim chance that these scenarios left the reader unmoved, Furman and other activists also recounted tales of innumerable unintended victims of traps, including songbirds, bears, eagles, skunks, hawks, rabbits, and even beloved family pets.[79] Some animal advocacy reports suggested that for every furbearer caught, trappers discarded three nontarget catches. Although such numbers are nearly impossible to confirm, a 1943 *Journal of Wildlife Management* report on predator control admitted that in addition to snaring 325 coyotes, just one trapper killed 473 additional animals, domesticated and wild.[80]

Such articles were intended to shock and educate everyone, but the campaign applied its greatest pressure to women. Hoping to replicate the success of the antifeather initiative, organizations frequently circulated appeals that entreated women to reconsider the purchase of a commodity produced through needless cruelty.[81] The specific format varied widely. In the following poem, "A Paradox," published by the Anti-Steel Trap League, two powerful images—tortured animals and Christ—are juxtaposed:

> *Tis strange how women kneel in church and pray to God above,*
> *Confess small sins and chant a praise and sing that He is love;*
> *While coats of softly furred things upon their shoulders lie—*
> *Of timid things, of tortured things, that take so long to die.*[82]

In another appeal, Charlotte Perkins Gilman, a writer and supporter of trapping reform, used an even more unsettling image to expose the human hypocrisy of assigning some animals status as companions while reducing others to the status of items: "If one woman hung up or fastened down hundreds of kittens each by one paw in her backyard in winter weather, to struggle and dangle and freeze, to cry in anguish and terror that she might 'trim' something with their collected skins . . . she would be considered a monster."[83] The guilt-laden messages urged women to do more than rectify their own ignorance and renounce their own acts of cruelty; propaganda also reminded them that as mothers and reformers, they nurtured the next generation and shaped the country's future society. Activists asked, Would America's women through their own actions teach cruelty and the destruction of nature, or would they foster benevolence and "reverence for life"?[84] Moreover, they warned that if women failed in their duties as humane educators and role models, others stood ready to replace them and corrupt the minds of the young. As evidence, humanitarians pointed to publicized incidents of Boy Scout leaders promoting trapping to the same scouts who pledged kindness to animals, as well as adult male trappers initiating their sons to the trade.[85]

But a national boycott on the scale of the feathered hat effort never happened. Unlike feathered hats, fur had a much longer tradition as both a garment and a status symbol. In addition, only women purchased the decorative hats, but fur coats were popular with both sexes. Equally problematic for any potential fur boycott, the U.S. consumer culture was much more entrenched by the 1920s than it was in 1890. Although Furman and others privately abhorred the wearing of fur and would have preferred to end that practice and trapping as well, they publicly fought for reforms they felt could realistically be achieved given the difficult context of their efforts. And so, even though the campaign strongly suggested that women should shun fur fashions, activists never initiated the kind of uncompromising and systematic boycott that characterized the feathered hat actions. Only the AAVS, true to its radical heritage, asked its members and the public to completely boycott real fur and instead wear fake fur.[86]

Most groups opted to appeal to women to support state legislative initiatives to ban leghold traps; require trappers to check their lines more frequently; establish trapping seasons; or compel companies to design humane, instant-kill devices. Others advertised humane alternatives for fur consumers, recommending that women who insisted on filling their closets with fur should buy only items crafted from farm-raised animals. In doing so, they would eliminate the "lingering suffering" caused by traps and lessen the devastation of wild animal populations (interestingly, few humanitarians initially raised questions about the sometimes deplorable conditions on those farms or the farmers' use of electrocution to kill the animals).[87] Such moderate reforms freed Americans of any guilt they might have about that skin adorning their bodies. Animal advocacy had provided them with what are now called cruelty-free alternatives. As a result, the campaign attracted widespread public support.

By World War II, thirty-seven states had enacted humane trapping laws that conformed to many of the movement's demands.[88] Most laws required trappers to check all traplines every twenty-four to forty-eight hours, depending on the terrain of a particular region. Some states shortened trapping seasons for the most hunted furbearers, such as beavers, but continued to sanction year-round trapping of other species, such as the lynx and bobcat. Still fewer, among them Massachusetts, South Carolina, and Kentucky, outlawed specific devices such as the steel leghold trap.[89] The battle in New England resembled many others, as the MSPCA waged a campaign for nearly five years before successfully placing a referendum against use of the leghold on the 1930 ballot. The measure passed, but like so many animal advocacy victories during that period, the Depression changed everything.[90] In Massachusetts, hunters claimed that trapping offered a viable source of income when few jobs existed. By 1935, amendments had so weakened the 1930 ban that humanitarians considered it dead.[91] As the Depression tightened its grip on the nation and people complained of little opportunity and hungry families, numerous other states similarly repealed their statutes.[92]

Struggling to preserve the thin line of protection for furbearers, animal defenders received little assistance from the conservationists who had championed trapping reforms as ethical sportsmanship earlier in the century. Conservationists did not participate in the new campaign, and they gave only tacit endorsement to selected reforms such as shorter trapping seasons and mandatory trapline checks. Their apathy originated largely from their professional collaboration in the state and federal predator control programs that frequently used traps; comprehensive bans or restrictions of trap usage would impede the work of the conservationist stronghold, the BBS.[93] Incensed by what they viewed as complicity with the enemy, animal advocates turned away from traditional conservationists and nurtured a much friendlier rapport with ecologically minded nature advocates. But if humanitarians believed that the nascent environmental movement would more closely match their own ideology and activism, they were somewhat mistaken. Environmentalists clearly loved animals and nature, but they also valued ecological diversity, and sometimes, that issue overshadowed concern for individual animals. Just as ideological differences drove a wedge between humanitarians and conservationists, disputes between the new allies kept them at arm's length during several crucial post-1945 campaigns.

Moreover, moderation was both the key to success and the Achilles' heel of the trapping campaign, and the same can be said of animal advocacy in general during the interwar period. The movement veered toward middle America, and the shift yielded both similar bounty and similar problems. A more moderate posture generated considerable public favor and culminated in promising, moderate victories. At the same time, mediocre reforms left troubling remnants of cruelty intact and typically fell easily against winds of opposition. Equally significant, as the larger movement endeared more Americans, it increasingly estranged its more confrontational siblings, such as the AAVS. Although ties between radical and conservative activists were never completely severed, the simmering tensions periodically flared and separated the two factions during significant campaigns after World War II.

Despite the pitfalls, animal advocacy's move toward the mainstream did not cause it to "ossify" or descend into "suspended animation." Scholars who argue otherwise are perhaps looking for the same kind of activism and strategies during the interwar period that occurred early in movement history. However, as society changed and developed what one twentieth-century observer called a more "kindly spirit," the struggle for nonhumans similarly progressed in its strategies and agenda.[94] Moderation did not mean that animal protection stopped challenging or combating diverse forms of cruelty. It did mean that those efforts were reflective of a more conservative public mind-set. Nonetheless, the campaigns and supplications of activists continued to remind humans of their connections and ethical responsibilities to the nonhuman world. During this period, humanitarians simply carried the movement to a different level, seeking to reach a wider audience and, in turn, extend the cause's social, cultural, and political influence. In many senses, that approach worked. The public's attitude toward both the cause and animals improved. Fewer people chuckled at the notion of Be Kind to Animals Week or scoffed at concern for the decimation of wildlife. Instead, many nodded their heads approvingly. Scouts pledged kindness, people boycotted circuses, and the clergy sermonized mercy. Animal advocacy had moved next door. As the United States emerged from World War II and gravitated from an industrial to a postindustrial world, public support and the movement's ability to adapt and evolve would prove crucial.

CHAPTER 6

"Our Most Strenuous Protest"

Antivivisection before 1945

Non facias MALUM ut inde fiat BONUM
(You cannot do EVIL that GOOD may result)

—American Anti-Vivisection Society motto

Animal advocacy embarked on numerous campaigns, but perhaps more than any other, the fight over animal experimentation best illustrates both the strengths of the movement and the formidable challenges, internal and external, that often threatened it. A subject replete with charged images of lobotomized dogs and amputee monkeys, vivisection illuminated some of humanitarians' most persuasive arguments, including issues of morality, the undue infliction of pain, human versus nonhumans rights, and anxieties over modernization (in this case, science). Activists effectively coalesced their positions into flexible and diverse strategies that kept the medical and research communities constantly on the defensive. And much to the dismay of their critics, antivivisectionists were dogged in their attacks throughout the first half of the new century. But unlike previous opponents, the provivisection community marshaled its own strengths to launch a powerful counteroffensive. The provivisectionists had resources that typically dwarfed those of the animal advocates, but equally important, they expertly used the bogeyman arguments mentioned earlier to discredit antivivisectionists, variously castigating them as antihuman, antiprogress, antiscience, and even mentally unstable. The medical and scientific fields also shrewdly exploited their own rising prestige and professionalism. Pointing to the growing number of biomedical breakthroughs beneficial to humans, they positioned themselves as modern heroes and fostered public acceptance of experimentation. For the most part, activists could not dislodge them from their new cultural throne. The antivivisection effort weathered the onslaught, but the difficulties compounded disputes between radicals and conservatives within the broader movement. Those tensions linger today.

Translated literally as the "cutting up of life," the word *vivisection* excited emotions on both sides of the Atlantic. The debate over animal experimentation raged with particular ferocity first in England, and in many ways, activities there inspired American radicals to take action. But whether in England or in the United States, the contexts that gave rise to the controversy were markedly similar. Vivisection echoed Victorian anxieties about modernization. Specifically, advances in science and medicine created a tension between an admiration for progress and a fear of some of its more ominous ramifications. On the one side was the symbolic Dr. Jekyll, a highly educated, prestigious professional who conquered the mysterious subject of human disease. Certainly, people applauded the cures of modern medicine, but they also surely noticed that the good doctor's discipline increasingly became as mysterious as some diseases. During the latter part of the nineteenth century, medicine (and, thus, medical research) molded itself into a profession that mandated more-stringent requirements for admittance to its ranks and endorsed self-regulation. Self-regulation, in turn, insulated professionals from public scrutiny and further enshrouded research within a cloud of intellectual elusiveness.[1] By 1894, New York physician Albert Leffingwell observed that his discipline's accessibility to the public had perceptibly diminished and that most research now unfolded in "comparative secrecy, behind locked doors."[2]

But periodically, those doors swung open, and researchers unveiled another breakthrough destined to save lives and improve human welfare. As smallpox, rabies, diphtheria, malaria, and other illnesses fell to diligent inquiry, the public's respect and awe grew, and a new and prestigious culture of science arose. In a society increasingly enthralled with notions of progress, successful scientific experiments elevated medicine—once saddled with a dubious and much-maligned reputation—to hallowed distinction.[3] In the name of yet another cure for yet another ailment, more and more people in England and the United States supported the profession's insistence on having freedom of scientific study. Moreover, some of the discoveries involved vivisection, and vivisection, too, became associated with both the profession and progress. In 1880, many doctors studied and practiced medicine without ever cutting open an animal, but by the twentieth century, animal experimentation had become a mandatory part of the physician's education and career.

Nonhumans became the preferred subjects of biomedical research, but early on, few laboratories existed to offer full-time careers in the field. Paris had the Pasteur Institute and Berlin boasted the Koch—both excellent research facilities; but the best job opportunity for an American researcher was probably within a U.S. government agency such as the Bureau of Animal Industry or the Marine Hygienic Laboratory, where one might be able to pursue a research agenda incidental to one's other duties. In 1901, however, that situation changed when John D. Rockefeller generously endowed the Rockefeller Institute for Medical Research.[4] The institute enlivened American research, and related industries such as pharmaceuticals soon followed. By the first decades of the twentieth century, Merck, Sharp and Dohme, Parke-Davis, and Eli Lilly marketed the products that resulted from scientific inquiry, and many soon installed their own laboratories.[5] As the American research machine churned faster and faster, it demanded more and more animals, and specialized breeding farms arose to meet the need for subjects.[6] In many respects, the mass production of research animals represented the culmination of Dr. Jekyll's rise in society.

But skulking in the shadows was the symbolic and much more sinister Mr. Hyde. Through unethical experimentation, he transformed himself into an immoral monster. Like Hyde's experiments, vivisection tested society's belief in modern civilization's "moral" progress.[7] Few were immune to the sensational news reports of researchers cutting the tracheas of unanesthetized dogs in order to stifle their cries. Such tales, founded on both fact and fiction, fueled questions about the proper role of modern science and its potential for fostering a twisted, Machiavellian attitude. Furthermore, experiments on dogs and cats raised the ire of a public increasingly enamored with pet-keeping.[8] Some, such as English animal advocate Henry Salt, wondered at the moral hypocrisy of forming sentimental and intimate relationships with some animals while sacrificing others to science.[9] Vivisection had opened more wounds than those on the operating table. It symbolized Victorians' social angst as they experienced the many changes and conflicts wrought by modernization. Furthermore, this medical controversy amplified the ideological struggle between traditional views of human superiority and a growing, pervasive uneasiness that such views just might be wrong.

In England, the first decades of the ethical and legislative debate over animal experimentation culminated in the much-disparaged 1876 Cruelty to Animals Act (see chapter 2).[10] But hostilities in the United States did not erupt until the late 1860s when Dr. John C. Dalton introduced the use of vivisection to the New York College of Physicians and Surgeons. Around the same time, Dr. Austin Flint conducted similar studies at Bellevue Hospital.[11] When Harvard approved Dr. Henry Bowditch's proposed physiology laboratory in 1871, the use of animals for demonstration and research became a staple of progressive training in medical schools.[12] By the 1880s, one physician pronounced vivisection "in vogue in our medical schools," and by the turn of the century, Yale, Princeton, Amherst, Cornell, and Stanford wooed prospective students with lavish descriptions of their modern physiology laboratories.[13]

The first rumblings of opposition occurred in New York and Philadelphia during the late 1860s. Replicating research made famous by François

Magendie in Europe, Flint and Dalton proctored procedures in which students first exposed and then irritated the sensory nerves of rabbits in order to examine pain responses. The scientists publicly acknowledged that they performed the demonstrations repeatedly and, necessarily, without anesthesia.[14] Bergh learned of the studies, and needless to say, the ASPCA became embroiled in the issue. However, Bergh did not, as some scholars contend, oppose all experiments on animals but only those that rejected the use of anesthesia.[15] A few years later, in Philadelphia in 1871, a local physician, S. Weir Mitchell, wrote Caroline Earle White at the WPSPCA to ask if his research hospital could negotiate a deal to purchase unwanted dogs from the organization's shelter. Appalled by the proposition, White quickly convened the organization's Executive Committee, which unanimously passed a resolution affirming its "most strenuous protest against vivisection."[16] The incident passed, but it deeply impressed White. During the 1870s, she traveled to England to seek counsel from that nation's most notable animal advocate, Frances Power Cobbe. The doyenne of English activism encouraged her new friend to form a society, warning that if animal defenders in the United States failed to establish their bulwark against vivisection, the Mitchells of the world would prevail.[17] In 1883, White organized the American Anti-Vivisection Society. Although its perspective was primarily abolitionist, favoring a complete halt to vivisection, the AAVS often pursued a more flexible restrictionist strategy in its early years, in hopes of at least restricting the practice.[18] Whatever their stance, leading humanitarians dropped the gauntlet at the feet of the medical and scientific communities, challenging their protocol and their very morality.

A more radical, female-dominated AAVS set the tone for much of the antivivisection campaign. Women organized or participated in the formation of many of the subsequent groups that emerged, including the Illinois Anti-Vivisection Society (1893), the New England Anti-Vivisection Society (NEAVS, 1895), the California Animal Defense and Anti-Vivisection Society (1902), the Vivisection Investigation League of New York (1910), and the New York Anti-Vivisection Society (1910), to name a few. The WCTU's Department of Mercy also frequently canvassed for the cause.[19] Unquestionably, as this campaign unfolded, a distinct majority of women led, followed, and financed organizations and initiatives. Typical of many groups, AAVS records reveal that from 1893 to 1919, women contributed between 69 percent and 73 percent of the organization's finances. And although membership numbers remained small relative to the more conservative humane societies, antivivisection groups quickly amassed enviable bank accounts. By 1912, for example, White's group reported impressive permanent assets of nearly $100,000.[20]

As noted in earlier chapters, animal advocacy attracted a disproportionate number of women, but what was it about animal experimentation that so roused their ire and galvanized their activism? One explanation might be found by integrating a gendered context into the broader Victorian anxieties about medicine. In modern, male-dominated medicine, women exerted little power over their own bodies, not unlike the rabbits in Flint's laboratory. For some, vivisection was about cultural domination over certain of society's most powerless: animals, the indigent, and women. The accusation may contain some truth. As a number of historians have demonstrated, men's gender beliefs impacted the social construction of Victorian medicine and imbued it with a misogynistic attitude about women's health. Many doctors believed, for instance, that a woman's mental health was inextricably bound to her reproductive organs, and they commonly prescribed ovariectomies and hysterectomies for such vague maladies as female "hysteria" and melancholia.[21] For some Victorian women, images of the vivisected animal strapped to a table bore an uncanny and frightening resemblance to the gynecologically vivisected woman.[22] As women agitated for greater rights, this analogy of shared oppression linking themselves and animals provided a powerful motivation for their critique of the dark side of a decidedly patriarchal profession.

Such gendered arguments, however, rarely leached into organizations' public statements against the practice. Instead, antivivisectionists constructed their position to mirror both their own concerns and societal ones. Foremost for them, animal experimentation reeked of immorality and moral hypocrisy. Doctors and scientists were supposed to be society's model elite—"cultivated men" (few women were in their ranks) who nobly and compassionately attended to the needs of the ill.[23] Furthermore, as educators, they shouldered, according to one physician, an "infinite responsibility for the moral impetus for the next generation."[24] But the use of vivisection shattered that cherished ideal. Researchers practiced and perpetuated calculated cruelty in laboratories that critics called a collective "moral sewer."[25] For physician Albert Leffingwell, an outspoken but relatively moderate antivivisectionist, witnessing or performing what amounted to deliberate torture inevitably "deadens one's humanity and begets indifference."[26] And most assuredly, the argument went, indifference for the suffering of animals led to a similar disregard for human lives: for proof, one had to look no further than the shocking incidents of human experimentation that periodically were exposed in the press. In 1910, for example, the AAVS unearthed a local experiment in which doctors injected tuberculosis into the eyes of orphans. In the ensuing media blitz, the AAVS cleverly manipulated the fears of a public still unsure about the methods of modern science and medicine.[27] In doing so, it turned the secrecy that researchers themselves often promoted against them by dangling frightening possibilities before the public eye. Look sharp, it warned, for Mr. Hyde, weaned on tortured dogs, has reappeared in the United States and leers over its sick.

Fears of moral degeneration unsettled many a Victorian, but for antivivisectionists, angst was not enough. They wanted people to get downright queasy, and so they broadened their discussion of moral implications to encompass animal pain and suffering. Harkening back to some of Darwin's conclusions about affinities between the species, they insisted that, like humans, animals writhed in agony from the cut of a knife. To prove their allegation, activists rolled out example after example of dogs howling in pain as researchers variously crushed spines, burned paws, and removed stomachs and brains and other sundry body parts.[28] A Philadelphia reporter's description of a case in 1893 at a "local university" was typical. Accompanied by antivivisectionists, the journalist recoiled at the sight of a filthy cage containing "a fine, large dog with one of its ears gone, the brains on that side of its head having been removed. It lay there in its darkened cage, making a continual distressing, moaning sound."[29] For anyone even remotely fond of animals, such images were distressing, and antivivisectionists knew it. Some, such as White, further fueled the outrage by alleging that experimenters knew they administered undue torment and conspired to veil it from the public. An avid reader of scientific journals, White claimed that editors, prior to publication, carefully omitted any explicit references to pain and replaced them with more innocuous language. Animals no longer "cried out" but rather "vocalized." Some editors did alter language, and for animal defenders, this deception proved their point.[30] Animals suffered and suffered intensely, and vivisectors knowingly bartered sentient creatures for their own selfish gains. Because animals clearly felt pain, antivivisectionists insisted that the only viable response was to grant nonhumans the ethical recognition they deserved.

Even with such cogent reasoning, the call for ethical recognition ran smack into a rather imposing wall: the much-touted benefits of medical research. Here, antivivisectionists tried to fight fire with fire by impugning the science. As White explained, "Owing to the difference in construction," animal subjects were unreliable models for studies relating to human conditions, and the scientific journals abounded with the flawed conclusions to prove the advocates' indictment. They noted that despite the fact that experimenters had discovered that dogs and rabbits rarely contracted peritonitis, many continued to experiment on them to investigate that very problem in humans. Brain surgeons operating on monkeys and dogs often reached contradictory conclusions.[31] And even the famed Robert Koch repeatedly tried and failed to introduce cholera to nonhumans and ultimately drew his conclusions about the disease from observing ill people.[32] They also frequently quoted the small faction of disillusioned researchers, among them the surgeon Charles Bell, who concluded "that the opening of living animals has done more to perpetuate error than to enforce the just views taken from anatomy and the natural sciences."[33]

But antivivisectionists did not stop with the faulty nature of certain experiments. Some jumped to a much more brazen and heretical conclusion: they boldly pronounced that vivisection contributed only minimally to the overall advancement of knowledge. Clinical observation, not cutting up animals, led to some of the most famous medical breakthroughs, and they argued that scientists vivisected simply to illustrate and confirm existing information.[34] And, they deduced, even if some remedy did derive from the vivisector's scalpel, humans paid too high a moral and ethical price for their own well-being. Animals possessed certain rights regardless of human benefit. This assertion, perhaps more than any other, posed the most explicit ideological challenge to that point to entrenched notions of human superiority, and it was the historical root of the animal liberationist philosophy that emerged a century later.

Offended by what they considered slanderous attacks, researchers retaliated with their own provocative evidence. The provivisection faction also introduced and largely perfected the bogeyman defense. First, they painted their detractors as both antiscience and scientifically ignorant. Although antivivisectionists correctly challenged claims of vivisection's role in certain medical discoveries and raised valid questions about the value of using animals, they also made mistakes. Opponents pounced on the errors. They noted, for example, that antivivisectionists prematurely criticized the germ theory as a fleeting "fashion of thinking" and serums and vaccinations as "filthy inoculations of poison into healthy blood and tissue." Both White and Angell denounced the treatments for rabies and diphtheria as unwarranted or dangerous, only to be discredited by additional scientific confirmation of the shots' effectiveness.[35] And in 1890, White completely rejected the utility of any brain surgery.[36] Leaders of the provivisection faction, including Philadelphia professor and surgeon W. W. Keen and Harvard professor and surgeon W. B. Cannon, enthusiastically exposed the errors and dismissed their nemeses as incompetent and "wholly indifferent to . . . facts."[37]

They used a similar logic to address the issue of pain, claiming that ignorance and emotionalism led antivivisectionists to draw erroneous conclusions about the amount of pain animals endured during experiments. Some leading medical minds completely rebuffed the pain issue, asserting that, physiologically, animals felt injuries much less intensely than humans and that the unenlightened observer erroneously interpreted their reactions and sounds as signs of distress.[38] Others took a very different approach by reassuring the public that scientists detested pain as much as anyone and executed every conceivable measure during an experiment to lessen their subjects' discomfort. Most preferred the use of chloroform, and Keen avowed that the lobotomized dogs of his experiments received postoperative care comparable to that afforded his human patients.[39] Keen and others admitted that a few renegade researchers unnecessarily harmed their subjects but argued their numbers were so miniscule that the profession effectively censured and eliminated such aberrations.[40] Self-regulation, the liberal use of chloroform, and animals' differing sensitivities demonstrated conclusively, they asserted, that antivivisectionists founded their contentious claims on what Cannon termed "imagined horrors."[41] Perhaps, vivisection advocates proposed, their opponents should instead divert their "humanitarian energy" toward more legitimate instances of cruelty and cease their persecution of those who conquered disease.[42]

Surely, they continued, any reasonably intelligent person could see that nearly every major medical advance owed an invaluable debt to vivisection.[43] Medical luminaries such as Keen, Cannon, and Johns Hopkins professor William Henry Welch trumpeted that view in both professional and popular periodicals, detailing how vivisection directly aided Louis Pasteur's work on hydrophobia (the original scientific term for rabies), Joseph Lister's investigation of germ theory, and even Robert Koch's quest for the cause of cholera. Animal experiments generated the insights that led to the treatment for syphilis; improved surgical techniques; and enhanced current knowledge of tumors, abscesses, disorders of the brain, and a litany of additional illnesses.[44] Observing patients could never have accomplished so much, for, as physician H. C. Wood noted, "the vivisector working in the laboratory lays the foundation on which the clinician working in the hospital builds."[45] Yes, they conceded, biological discrepancies between humans and animals complicated and sometimes invalidated investigations, but the medical wisdom accrued outweighed any risks or errors. That wisdom ultimately benefited all species, a fact that led some proponents of experimentation to wonder aloud how those so attached to animals could logically oppose research that often bettered the health of domesticated animals.[46] Vivisection equaled progress for all creatures, and how, queried its supporters, could anyone find fault with that?

Obviously, it was a rhetorical question designed to draw the conclusion that antivivisectionist were antiprogress and even antihuman. Hysteria and emotion rather than objectivity and intellect motivated them, and their twisted reform spirit made them cruel to humankind. Early in the debate, researchers exposed and exploited animal advocates' greatest vulnerability, their disavowal of human predominance over nature. At nearly every legislative hearing on antivivisection bills during the late nineteenth and early twentieth centuries, prominent figures from the medical community testified that if any state caved in to antivivisection pressure, then children would needlessly die. Any impediment to experimentation sacrificed human lives, but children in particular became the rallying cry, and doctors and scientists referred to case after case of youngsters cured because of knowledge gained through vivisection.[47] Paradoxically, by brandishing images of sick children, vivisectors baited their science with the same emotionalism for which they disparaged their adversaries. But in doing so, they repositioned themselves as modern bedside saviors, while depicting animal defenders as extremists who would gladly snatch a cure from a child to save a dog's life.[48] American Medical Association (AMA) president William Henry Welch perhaps best expressed his profession's opinion at the group's 1910 gathering: "Agitation for the prohibition of experiments on animals, conducted under the guise of an humane purpose, is fundamentally inhuman, for if it were to succeed the best hopes of humanity for further escape from physical suffering and disease would be destroyed."[49] According to these men, the public needed only to strip away the facade of the radicals' propaganda to find the real threat lurking at the beside of the American patient.

In 1909, the medical community added an ingenious twist, certainly the most vicious of all, to their depiction of antivivisectionists as fanatics. In an article appearing in the *Medical Record*, respected Cornell neurologist Charles L. Dana determined that the antivivisectionist' illogical challenges to human supremacy and scientific progress were the symptomatic manifestations of a new form of mental illness—zoophil-psychosis.[50] Dana defined the condition as a psychotic love of animals and believed that it resulted from the inability of some individuals to adjust to the stress and complexities of a modern, urban/industrial society. Feeling overwhelmed, zoophilists (the word means "animal lovers" and was a term animal advocates often applied to themselves) sometimes lapsed into a state in which they lacked the "power to handle the problems of life, and to see things in their right proportion." Sufferers ultimately succumbed to distorted "obsessive insanities." If this behavior went untreated or, worse yet, was encouraged, it could, Dana warned, deteriorate into other debilitating or more dangerous forms of obsessive or psychopathic behavior.[51]

According to Dana, all animal advocates were susceptible to zoophil-psychosis, but the minority of men who exhibited the disease responded well to therapeutic consultation. However, women, because of their weaker constitution, disproportionately fell victim to the malady, and radical female antivivisectionists nearly always suffered from it. It is worth quoting at length his professional opinion of a female patient brought to him by an exasperated husband. With palpable disdain, he described her as "about 40 years old, married but . . . not desirous of children," belonging to "some kind of zoophilic society," and obsessed over cats:

> She could not bear to have a cat suffer. She made her home a hospital for stray cats, and the house was always full of them. If she heard a "meowing" at night she was unhappy and would

> wake her husband and make him go out and catch the animal. . . . The man's life was made utterly wretched by this condition of affairs, and I was consulted. The patient herself was a woman in good general health, fairly intelligent, but unsocial, [and] unsexual. . . . She was of a very jealous and exacting disposition, ruling the situation by her selfish querulence. . . . She did not . . . have any "insight" or appreciation of her lack of consideration for the human side of her household, or of the real folly of her point of view. . . . It would be difficult to imagine a more morbid household.[52]

Dana considered this case nearly hopeless but suggested that a gynecological operation might offer some relief for the woman and more so for her husband. Only surgery could correct her "perversion of instinct."[53]

Dana's gendered analysis bristled with both the enmity for antivivisectionists shared by many of his peers and the misogyny of Victorian medicine. Antivivisectionists tried to disparage the study as a laughable attempt to divert attention away from the real issues, yet the accusation harbored potentially devastating repercussions for female activists.[54] Donning the respectable cloak of a neurologist, Dana imbued the women of the cause with traits antithetical to the standards of the separate-spheres ideology of the nineteenth-century. He embedded within his science social ideals that glorified traditional notions of domesticity and vilified the public, political woman. As he portrayed it, his patient's affection for felines subverted her proper role as a nurturing wife and potential mother. Instead, she slipped into a kind of pitiful madness within which she became asexual, disinterested in childbearing, selfish, jealous, and foolish. The irony of his own conclusions eluded Dana, for though he speculated that zoophil-psychosis occurred most commonly in those people who were unable to accept modernization, his own view of women rejected the gender roles emerging in a modern United States in the early years of the twentieth century. Nonetheless, in 1909, allegations of inappropriate gender conduct could irreparably tarnish the reputation of female activists and the movement as whole.

As word of Dana's diagnosis spread through the medical community, researchers and then their supporters eagerly seized on the findings and immediately used them to their advantage.[55] By reducing antivivisectionists to a clinical phenomenon, Dana potentially undermined both the legitimacy of cruelty issues and the credibility of those who gave voice to them. Such activists were not to be taken seriously but rather treated medically, and the insinuation was easily applied to the entire movement. Now armed with "scientific" criticism, anyone opposed to the struggle on behalf of animals could dangle images of zoophil-psychotics wholly incapable of understanding the modern world. And they did so often. *New York Times* editorials praised the diagnosis, and provivisectionist groups incorporated it into most of their propaganda. In fact, one historian has concluded that in the early twentieth century, zoophil-psychosis "became a standard charge levied against the anti-vivisectionists."[56] Exactly how much damage the indictment of mental illness caused the campaign or the larger movement remains unclear. It failed to deliver the deathblow some hoped for, but given the loaded implications, zoophil-psychosis almost certainly dissuaded a number of individuals from joining the movement.

Ideological sparring started the vivisection wars, but both sides quickly adopted more creative and confrontational maneuvers. For the most part, antivivisectionists appropriated strategies learned from their experiences in other animal advocacy campaigns. They mustered celebrity support to their cause, and notable actresses (Minnie Maddern Fiske and Clara Morris) and politicians (William Jennings Bryan) and writers (Mark Twain) entreated the public to oppose vivisection and demand its criminalization.[57] They also aggressively solicited medical professionals who voiced reservations about animal experimentation. Employing an innovative strategy aimed at both widening existing divisions within the profession as well as enhancing their own scientific credibility, organizations added scores of physicians and scientists to their membership ranks by 1900. And during its first decades, the AAVS Board of Managers primarily elected physicians to the post of president.[58] Although the outspoken W. W. Keen wrote off the naysayers as few in number and "little known," some were actually quite famous, including Harvard's Henry Bigelow; the nation's first female physician, Elizabeth Blackwell; and psychologist and philosopher William James.[59] These prominent supporters, medical and otherwise, elevated the campaign's reputation, and though no opinion poll exists to gauge the impact of such endorsements, the frustration expressed by some vivisectors suggests that, at least for a time, the strategy had an impact. In 1906, one scientist angrily vented in a *New York Times* article that the favorable endorsements such individuals gave to the antivivisection cause had so thoroughly inflamed public opinion that he could no longer freely experiment without fear of a backlash.[60]

Inflaming public opinion was a forte of antivivisection groups, and they employed diverse methods to do so. Some purchased billboards. Many sponsored traveling exhibits about the horrors of animal experimentation, displays that traversed nearly every state and major city during the late nineteenth and early twentieth centuries. Antivivisectionists even secured exhibition space at both the 1893 Chicago World's Fair and the 1904 St. Louis World's Fair.[61] They also spread the word by distributing millions of pamphlets that vividly recounted the most outrageous experiments (such as one in which researchers sewed two puppies together) and aggressively publicized what they considered two of the most scandalous consequences of vivisection—the theft of pets to supply the laboratories and the sometimes deplorable conditions within the kennels housing the animals.[62] Typical of many organizations, NEAVS records for 1901 indicate that in that year alone, members stood on city streets and pressed over fifty thousand publications into the hands of passersby.[63] Better-known activists published book-length investigations about the most gruesome experiments. Albert Leffingwell's *An Ethical Problem* (1914) captured the public interest with descriptions of scenes such as the following, in which researchers, in an effort to study the correlation between pain and blood pressure, conducted multiple procedures on a small dog: "Sometimes it was accomplished by skinning the animal alive, a part of the body at a time, and then roughly 'sponging' the denuded surface. Sometimes it was secured by crushing the dog's paws, first one and then the other. Now and then the dog's feet were burnt, or the intestines exposed and roughly manipulated, the tail crushed, the limbs amputated, the stomach cut out . . . until . . . death came to the creature's relief."[64] Antivivisectionists understood that they had to combat researchers' loaded images of sick children with equally potent scenes of tortured dogs stolen from those children.

These combined efforts reached many, but the campaign touched thousands more through submissions to major magazines and newspapers. The *New York Herald*, *Life*, the *Nation*, and *Vogue* supported the antivivisection cause and regularly featured sympathetic articles or editorials.[65] More often, the popular press carried views from both sides, but activists did not shrink from the challenge or the debate; they used any available forum to highlight their most explosive and persuasive points. Typical of many articles, Henry Childs Merwin's "Vivisection" in the *Atlantic Monthly* interspersed moral and scientific arguments with the essential dose of morbid experiments.[66] Antivivisectionists also frequently used paid advertisements, and in them, they made the issue much more personal by specifically playing on people's love for their pets. In such announcements, the AAVS and other groups warned of pet theft rings that would snatch a canine or feline friend and sell it for 25¢ to 50¢ to the researchers who vigorously encouraged the practice. That beloved companion, the notice concluded, inevitably died a torturous death.[67] The publicity was designed to shock people into awareness. In the spirit of their antislavery predecessors, antivivisectionists were sure that revealing the evils of the institution they condemned would ultimately persuade the public of its immorality.

Some antivivisectionists proposed a more sophisticated form of publicity that would potentially convert an even wider audience. Fearing that an unending diet of gore might alienate some, they suggested linking the tragedy of vivisection with a more palatable story. Anna Sewell's majestic novel *Black Beauty* had embedded a message about horse abuse in entertaining fiction, and antivivisectionists realized their cause needed a good read. Two authors, both celebrated during their lifetimes, accepted the challenge. New England novelist Elizabeth Stuart Phelps (1844–1911) generously supported groups such as the AAVS and delivered numerous addresses on their behalf, including several to the Massachusetts legislature.[68] Her opposition stemmed from personal affection for her companion animals and abhorrence for "the infliction of avoidable torture."[69] She frequently used her writing to champion causes, and during the first decade of the twentieth century, she published a full-length novel (*Trixy*, 1904) and two short stories ("Tammyshanty," 1909, and "Fee," 1910) about animal experimentation.[70] One of the most interesting elements of *Trixy* is Phelps's use of antivivisectionism's gendered perspective. In the story, a researcher (and vivisector) courts the heroine, and as the plot unfolds, the woman increasingly feels as "caged" and vivisected as his laboratory animals.[71] But Phelps's literary efforts on behalf of the campaign were short on plot and exhaustive in their plea. All three failed to impress critics (then or now) or dramatically expand the pool of antivivisectionist supporters.[72]

The second author achieved a very different result. An avid supporter of animal advocacy, Mark Twain added his voice to the antivivisection campaign. When asked his opinion on the subject, he replied, "I am not interested to know whether Vivisection produces results that are profitable to the human race . . . the pains which it inflicts upon unconsenting animals is the basis of my enmity towards it."[73] In 1903, he published the short story "A Dog's Tale" in the Christmas edition of *Harper's Monthly Magazine.*[74] Despite the brevity of the work, the plot is filled with pathos. Written from a female dog's perspective, the story follows her tragic life as she is sold and separated from her mother and beaten by her new owner. More poignant, the owner, a "renowned" scientist, blinds and kills her puppy in the name of medical progress.[75] As the story closes, Twain contrasts the image of the mother licking her dying, whimpering puppy with the callous humans who cheer the scientist: "You've proved your theory, and suffering humanity owes you a great debt from henceforth."[76] The puppy is nonchalantly discarded and buried. The grief-stricken mother stands vigil at the grave until she starves to death.[77] Unlike Phelps's pleading and preaching, Twain's deceptively simple little tale gave a powerful voice to the voiceless and laid bare human cruelty and arrogance. The story received public and critical acclaim, and the following year, Harper and Brothers released it in book format. Although overshadowed by more famous works in Twain's prolific career, "A Dog's Tale" is to this day a persuasive literary weapon for animal advocacy.

When the antivivisectionists' publicity barrage first started, few researchers responded to the charges, but as the campaign found public favor, the provivisection camp came alive. Leaders of small, regional, or specialized scientific societies banded together to form politically and economically powerful national coalitions. The first such alliance took shape during the early 1890s, when diverse associations including the American Physiological Society, the American Anatomical Society, the American Society of Naturalists, the American Society of Physicians, and the American Society of Surgeons united to issue "A Statement on Behalf of Science"; in it, the groups resolved to protect scientific inquiry from externally imposed restrictions.[78] By far the most influential and permanent effort originated in 1908 when the American Medical Association spearheaded the creation of the Council on Defense of Medical Research (CDMR). W. B. Cannon chaired the council, and for the next eighteen years, he played a critical role in directing the entire biomedical community's defense of vivisection. As one biographer remarked, "Few physicians or scientists in the country knew more than he did about the anti-vivisectionists and few had as much experience defending medical research." Cannon swiftly assembled and coordinated representatives in every state in which the antivivisection campaign exerted even a minimal influence.[79] The vanguard of numerous subsequent proresearch organizations, the CDMR formulated a blueprint of action to neutralize many of the more serious allegations raised by critics.

One way to neutralize the antivivisectionists was to eliminate one of their raisons d'être. During its first year, the council authorized a review of animal care at research laboratories throughout the nation.[80] In the findings, Cannon noted that most laboratories had already instituted rules governing the proper treatment of animals but that they were often inconsistent, unpublicized, and/or haphazardly enforced.[81] In response, the CDMR composed the profession's first formal "Guidelines for Laboratory Animal Care," and dozens of medical schools and laboratories officially and very publicly adopted and posted the new recommendations. An unprecedented counteroffensive and in many ways a turning point in the controversy, the guidelines pledged many reforms, including implementing a system for monitoring the purchase of strays, maintaining sanitary kennels, adopting an approval process for all experiments, using anesthesia (with only approved exceptions), and providing humane euthanasia for all subjects at an experiment's conclusion. The power of words was not lost on the council members, and they intentionally inserted phrases that compared conditions for animals in their facilities to those in "a hospital for human beings."[82] These guidelines represented both victory and defeat for the protesters. Antivivisection agitation had influenced public opinion enough to force the research community not only to acknowledge but also to accede to some of the protesters' demands. Conversely, by addressing certain of the more contentious issues, such as animal abduction, pain, and unsanitary kennels, the CDMR essentially pulled the rug out from under the detractors.

The adoption of the guidelines was a serious blow for the antivivisectionists, but they refused to back down. For them, self-regulation was a ploy designed to hide the fact that the fox still guarded the henhouse. Their attacks were unrelenting, and in response, the council expanded its campaign. Beginning in 1909 and continuing throughout much of the next decade, the CDMR produced a series of articles and pamphlets penned by the nation's leading medical authorities that specifically elucidated the innumerable ways in which society benefited from animal experimentation. Cannon himself contributed over thirty publications during his tenure on the council, variously defending vivisection and criticizing its opponents' credibility.[83] The coalition sent the tracts to newspapers and popular magazines and also mailed them to general practitioners across the nation in order to enlist them to the cause.[84] Cannon surmised that the move would dampen dissension within the profession. More important, rather than having just a few famous physicians singing the praises of research, the CDMR wanted the multitude of small-town family doctors explaining to their patients how vivisection led to the vaccines that saved their children from possible death.

Closing ranks was a CDMR priority, and it next recommended the purging of disloyal laboratory and kennel employees. From the onset of the controversy, antivivisectionists' undercover investigations of laboratory abuse generated sensational headlines and damaging publicity for researchers. By 1915, with the council's support, most facilities implemented a stringent employee-screening process to weed out any potential whistle-blowers and prevent future leaks.[85] In 1914, Cannon vowed to purge yet one more problem from the profession. Corresponding with the editors of major medical journals, he requested that they do just what antivivisectionists accused them of doing—soften the terminology in vivisection articles. Within a few years, professional publications, including the Rockefeller Institute's *Journal of Experimental Medicine*, adopted guidelines that downplayed the numbers of animals used in experiments, deleted descriptions of preoperative or postoperative discomfort, omitted explicit photographs of procedures, and substituted words such as *fasting* for *starving*, *intoxicant* for *poison*, and *hemorrhaging* for *bleeding*.[86] Cannon was convinced that creating a nearly impenetrable, unified front would essentially defuse the controversy, ensure legislative victories, and knock the protesters off balance.

Cannon's unified front proved critical during the heated legal and legislative clashes that raged before World War I. In what amounted to a nasty political chess match, antivivisectionists moved for the restriction or outright abolition of vivisection, organized medicine pushed for pound seizure laws requiring shelters to surrender unclaimed animals, and each group simultaneously worked to defeat the other's legislation. The earliest attack came from Henry Bergh in 1867 and 1868, when ASPCA spies confirmed that doctors at New York's Bellevue Hospital performed vivisections. During nearly every legislative session after 1868, Bergh introduced bills to ban or restrict vivisection within the state, but the medical community consistently prevented their passage. In 1886, he achieved his only victory, with the passage of a vague statute that confined vivisection demonstrations to authorized medical colleges but stated nothing about the nature of particular experiments.[87] Other early initiatives by animal advocacy groups in Massachusetts (1869) and Pennsylvania (1870) also failed, but the rise of antivivisection organizations, particularly the AAVS, heralded a new period of intense political wrangling in dozens of states and even at the federal level.[88]

From the late 1890s through the early 1900s, several states, Massachusetts and Pennsylvania particularly, experienced messy legislative eruptions over the antivivisection issue. In 1894, prior to the CDMR's formation, Angell's MSPCA and the AAVS waged a successful campaign on behalf of a law to bar vivisection in all Massachusetts elementary and secondary schools. Since the law said nothing about animal studies in research laboratories and medical colleges, few researchers expressed concern. The situation changed between 1896 and 1903 when antivivisectionists attempted to capitalize on the precedent by proposing bills that more broadly restricted vivisection and authorized SPCAs to inspect state research facilities. Equally worrisome for the scientific and medical community, the AHA and the newly chartered NEAVS joined the fray, and during legislative hearings, several medical experts and writer Elizabeth Stuart Phelps testified in favor of the bills. But New England's provivisectionists marshaled their own forces and specifically called on Harvard president Charles W. Eliot to speak before the legislature. Eliot knew the power of the bogeyman arguments, and in his testimony, he simply waved the trump card of sick children. Both bills failed.[89]

Around the same time, the controversy landed on the steps of the U.S. Congress. In 1896, despite their varying views on the issue, animal advocates including SPCAs, the WCTU, and nearly every antivivisection group joined ranks in an impressive union to converge on the nation's capital; there, they present a bill before the U.S. Senate that sought to establish a nonmedical commission to strictly regulate and inspect facilities within the District of Columbia. It was an ambitious plan, but activists reasoned that if they could get any federal mandate on the issue, they would significantly improve their chances at the state level. The hearings drew national media attention, and six Supreme Court justices endorsed the bill in the press. Prospects for passage looked promising.[90]

And then, as happens so often in history, larger events interceded. In 1898, the Spanish-American War diverted the nation's attention and stalled the antivivisection momentum. Provivisectionists regrouped. Guided by Welch and Keen, members of the medical community amassed volumes of evidence in support of animal experimentation and scheduled a wide array of experts to testify when hearings reconvened in 1900. And through the *Journal of the American Medical Association,* Keen urged his colleagues to write their representatives. Letters poured in to the capital. Underestimating its opposition, the animal advocacy coalition faltered and offered much the same evidence as in 1896. The antivivisectionists lost the campaign.[91] But vivisectors had come perilously close to defeat in the nation's capital, and that scare, in part, inspired the formation of the CDMR.

The controversy fell back to the states, and by the early twentieth century, dozens of legislatures from New York to California considered antivivisection. Doctors and scientists had some of their toughest confrontations in Pennsylvania, where the Philadelphia-based AAVS stirred up host of protest activities. Although the state's physicians easily crushed the group's first restrictionist bill in 1885, the AAVS had grown more influential in the Keystone State by 1900.[92] Respecting their opposition's power, researchers applied the lessons learned in the D.C. campaign and pooled their resources. The Pennsylvania Medical Society allied itself with the state's medical colleges and a group specifically formed to confront the AAVS—the Pennsylvania Society for the Protection of Scientific Research. This medical front thwarted antivivisection bills in 1907, 1909, 1911, and 1913.[93]

Buoyed by its wins, the alliance introduced its own bills first in 1913 and then in subsequent years, which authorized research laboratories to seize unwanted animals from local shelters. In this instance, the antivivisectionists prevailed on every proposed pound seizure law.[94] The AAVS then tried a different legal tactic; in the busy year of 1913, the organization, along with the WPSPCA, astounded the state's biomedical profession by securing indictments against five University of Pennsylvania faculty members, charging them under the state's general anticruelty law. The prosecution's key witness, a kennel worker, testified that researchers provided no postoperative care to nearly twenty dogs with intentionally crushed spines. The jury deliberated at length but then deadlocked. The judge eventually dismissed the case.[95] It was yet another disappointment for the antivivisection movement but hardly a rout for animal research.

By 1914, both sides had suffered losses, yet they persevered. Several states passed bills ending experimentation in public elementary and secondary schools, including Massachusetts (1894, revised in 1902), Oklahoma (1908), Illinois (1909), South Dakota (1903), Washington (1897, revised in 1903), and Pennsylvania (1905), and between 1896 and 1897, Washington forbade vivisection in all public schools and colleges, exempting only medical and dental schools.[96] Moreover, antivivisectionists soundly trounced all attempts by researchers to secure pound seizure laws before World War I.[97] Scholars who study the movement typically ignore these victories or discount them as marginal, but for antivivisectionists, they were a vital step in an admittedly long journey toward a humane society.[98] In particular, by prohibiting vivisection in elementary and high schools while simultaneously promoting humane education there, activists trusted that future generations would raise a more pervasive and more productive voice against the authority of biomedicine. Like all animal advocates, they viewed children as the linchpin in their struggle's triumph. Historians must not lose sight of or neglect that element of the story.

At the same time, it must also be acknowledged that in those years, proponents of animal experimentation secured the largest and most enduring victories. The absence of any substantive state or federal antivivisection law signified both the power of the research lobby and the public's support for their position. But another factor disabled antivivisectionism from within. More than other animal advocacy campaigns, antivivisection efforts strained the already touchy relationship between conservatives and radicals. The differences frequently played out in public between the campaign's two most respected leaders, Albert Leffingwell and Caroline White. Leffingwell praised the knowledge accrued through research. White questioned it. Leffingwell was willing to work with the scientific and medical communities. White wanted to prosecute them. Leffingwell advocated external restrictions. White, though willing to pursue restrictions, leaned toward abolition.[99] Sometimes, the squabbles threw initiatives off kilter, and by the 1890s, the situation had become dire enough that the two factions took their dispute to the national AHA for resolution.

Although theoretically an umbrella organization for all animal advocates, the AHA was controlled by the conservative wing, and Leffingwell's restrictionist platform triumphed at the 1892 and 1899 conventions (his position was surely helped by his brief service as the group's president). Numerous humane organizations across the nation adopted the resolution as their own. The AHA ideologically disowned radical antivivisectionists, and though the two sides tried several times to work together (as in the Massachusetts campaigns), dissension undermined their success.[100] Rather than mend the split, the AHA resolution had exacerbated it, and at times, the troubled relationship disintegrated into open hostility. When the AAVS prosecuted the University of Pennsylvania professors in 1913, several animal protection groups publicly reproached White for her extremism. Even the ASPCA, where American antivivisection protests had begun, adopted a more conservative stance. When Bergh died, his successor, namesake, and nephew, Henry Bergh Jr., migrated away from his uncle's radicalism and steadily withdrew the group from specific political forays over the issue.[101] Disillusioned by such moves, radical antivivisectionists vowed to carry forward their less compromising agenda with or without the assistance of other humane organizations.

The obvious difficulties and numerous legislative defeats endured by antivivisectionists has led some of the same scholars who see a general weakening of animal advocacy to likewise characterize this particular campaign as "crushed," "fallow," "contained," or "enfeebled" by 1915.[102] Their analyses present four persuasive arguments to bolster the thesis, some of which logically echo their assertions about the larger movement: (1) internal ideological strife and disputes with more conservative animal advocacy organizations subverted organizational and thus strategic cohesiveness; (2) the deaths of charismatic and often uncompromising leaders such as White and Bergh extinguished the vitality and spirit of antivivisectionism; (3) science and medicine rose as the new secular icons, and society increasingly ostracized critics of those icons; and (4) with the death knell of the campaign sounding, World War I absorbed the nation's energies.[103] These scholars suggest that antivivisection protests ultimately succumbed to these overwhelming pressures and essentially fell apart.

To be sure, it looked like a rout on the surface, and some evidence certainly suggests that the aforementioned forces sapped the campaign's strength. But the historical evidence from organizations, archives, libraries, journals, annual reports, magazines, and newspapers suggests a different interpretation. It seems that reports of antivivisectionism's demise during those interwar years were somewhat exaggerated. The cause against animal experimentation did not go fallow in the face of extreme hardship. It not only weathered the onslaught but persisted and even modestly grew during those years between two terrible wars.

The first indication that something was amiss with the prevailing story appeared in some assessments of vivisection written during the 1920s and 1930s. A 1924 report by the AHA (a group hardly enamored with the vivisection controversy) on the status of the animal advocacy movement found numerous "strong societies" supporting the antivivisection program and summarized them as representative of a cause with "considerable impetus."[104] During the same year, a Columbia University study discerned "vigorous growth" in the campaign and credited antivivisectionists "with having aroused great interest in a subject previously ignored." Moreover, it noted that "since the war the anti-vivisection movement has gained strength in the West."[105] A decade later, the editor of *Modern Medicine* responded to news of antivivisection legislation in thirty-two states and grumbled that "the anti-vivisectionists are again hoisting the banners . . . they are apparently indefatigable."[106]

This material was intriguing but hardly definitive, so I dug deeper and found further proof. During the interwar years, new antivivisection groups proliferated throughout the country, but as the Columbia study stated, the cause enjoyed remarkable popularity west of the Mississippi. New groups included the Minnesota Anti-Vivisection League (1918), the California Federation of Anti-Vivisection Societies (organized in 1919, it united the California Anti-Vivisection Society of Los Angeles, the San Francisco Anti-Vivisection Society, and the Alameda County Anti-Vivisection Society), the Washington Humane Education and Anti-Vivisection Society (1921), and the National Anti-Vivisection Society (1929) in Chicago.[107] On the East Coast, established groups expanded membership and financially prospered. By World War II, the NEAVS counted members in every state, and the AAVS financial records showed permanent assets totaling over $250,000, no small sum for the time.[108] Cooperative national efforts likewise flourished. In 1911, twenty-six antivivisection groups formed their own umbrella organization, the Interstate Conference for the Investigation of Vivisection. By the end of the 1920s, the conference, which met three times a year, had welcomed a dozen new members. The organization also sponsored and participated in the International Anti-Vivisection and Animal Protection Congress, held first in Washington, D.C., in 1913 and subsequently in Philadelphia, in 1926.[109]

Cooperation and growth also extended to antivivisectionism's relationship with the broader animal advocacy campaign. Fundamental differences between the two remained, but antivivisectionists were neither totally ostracized nor isolated from the larger movement. At national animal protection conferences and a litany of smaller gatherings, abolitionists, restrictionists, radicals, and conservatives mingled, commiserated, shared ideas, and no doubt argued a lot. Nonetheless, the meetings were earnest attempts to achieve reconciliation and greater strategic cohesion on issues of mutual interest. The diverse participants attended sessions on everything from slaughter reform, vegetarianism, stolen pets, trapping, and, yes, vivisection.[110] The exchanges bore fruit. When they went home, members of more moderate animal advocacy groups championed certain antivivisection initiatives, particularly the headline protest of the 1920s and 1930s—mandatory pound seizure.[111] And antivivisectionists occasionally supplemented their agenda with a variety of concerns unrelated to experimentation, including trapping, slaughter, sport hunting, and even the destruction of the redwoods.[112] In the prevailing interpretation, irreconcilable differences sent antivivisectionism on a path separate from the rest of the animal advocacy movement. But the divisions were not as rigid as the scholars suggest. The factions did not travel away from each other; rather, they recognized that they had to work together, albeit often uncomfortably and not always successfully, in the name of ending all forms of animal cruelty.

Above all, during those supposedly dormant years, antivivisectionists still publicized, still legislated, and still fought for their cause. They were, as that frustrated *Modern Medicine* editor said, indefatigable. They kept the public spotlight focused on the issue, relying on both proven methods and new ones. They continued to send articles and receive extensive coverage in sympathetic newspapers and magazines, particularly the publications of William Randolph Hearst (an ardent supporter), the *Christian Science Monitor*, and the *Washington Times-Herald*.[113] Antivivisectionism continued to boast its own cadre of luminaries from stage, screen, literature, and politics. Franklin Delano Roosevelt spoke favorably of the cause. Alice Stone Blackwell (daughter of the famed suffragist

Lucy Stone) donated generously to the NEAVS. Actor George Arliss and dancer Irene Castle appeared frequently at well-publicized dinners, concerts, conferences, and ceremonial events.[114] At the request of the AAVS, writer Fannie Hurst presided over the society's Animal Protection Day at the 1941 New York World's Fair.[115] And despite the CDMR's best efforts to quell dissension within the medical profession, a significant minority of physicians and scientists continued to criticize animal experimentation.[116]

As times changed, the antivivisection campaign adapted. During World War I, the AAVS reinstituted its traveling exhibit but added a theme appropriate for wartime—heroism. Displaying a series of photographs beginning with a family dog saving a child's life and ending with the dog's abduction and painful death at the hand of a vivisector, the exhibit posed the following question: "Do we as a nation endorse this treatment of our dog heroes?"[117] During World War II, groups such as the NEAVS sent complimentary copies of their journals to men and women in the service. Supplementing the requisite criticisms of animal experimentation, the war journals incorporated articles relevant to combat life, including tales of heroism by canine recruits in Normandy and the Philippines, and instructional advice under the heading "Care of Pets in an Air Raid."[118]

As modern society bred new technologies and a mass culture, the movement added pertinent strategies to its repertoire. With the rise of radio, antivivisectionists took to the airwaves to broadcast their messages. One of the most active celebrities for the cause, Irene Castle, delivered the NEAVS's first radio address, "The Evils of Vivisection," in 1938.[119] In 1941, the AAVS introduced an innovative educational and financial tactic destined to become a staple of modern animal advocacy—the direct-mail campaign. The society sent informational packets that cautioned Pennsylvanians about an active pet theft ring in the Harrisburg area and then solicited contributions to sustain the "great effort . . . being made by our society to stop the dog dealers' traffic to research laboratories."[120]

And as they did before 1914, antivivisectionists conducted an unremitting legislative drive between 1915 and 1945. In 1915, they prevailed when California legislators approved a law requiring inspections for all state research facilities that conducted vivisection. But CDMR lobbyists and lawyers convinced the governor not to sign the measure, and it died by pocket veto. Refusing to concede defeat, activists submitted bills and/or secured voter referenda in the state nearly every year thereafter.[121] In Alabama, the movement snatched a rare victory when legislators ended vivisection in all public schools in 1919. Throughout the 1920s, New York, Pennsylvania, Maryland, Minnesota, Louisiana, and Colorado experienced periodic eruptions over the antivivisection debate as activists fought for prohibitive laws, and as mentioned earlier, between 1933 and 1934, antivivisection bills were pending in thirty-two states. Most failed.[122] At the federal level, the activists placed bills ending all experiments on dogs on the congressional docket in 1919, 1920, 1926, 1930, 1931, 1938, and 1943. None, however, passed.[123]

Even in the face of these defeats, the campaign's vigor never faltered. Moreover, activists could claim decisive victories when it came to one vivisection issue–pound seizures. When the research enterprise significantly expanded in the United States during the 1920s, experimenters realized that animal breeding farms (a business that was still in its infancy) and private animal dealers (who collected strays, bought unwanted dogs from private owners, or, if less scrupulous, stole pets) were inadequate sources. Confident that rational lawmakers would agree, the CDMR renewed its legal claims to unwanted strays. Events in Missouri in 1921 seemingly confirmed the council members' optimism when legislators ordered the state humane society to sell all unclaimed dogs to medical schools for 75¢ each or face misdemeanor charges.[124] But that triumph would be an isolated victory in a much larger sea of defeat. In any state, each time a pound seizure bill surfaced, antivivisection groups, SPCAs, and a cadre of celebrities united and flooded legislators and citizens with testimony and literature that described a dreadful end for their lost pets. States consistently rejected such laws before 1945.[125]

In part, protests against the use of pound animals succeeded because the antivivisection campaign joined with more mainstream and, in some senses, more politically influential SPCAs. But the results also reflected the ambivalent attitudes of the public. Most Americans were enthusiastic about modern medicine, and images of anonymously vivisected dogs failed to dampen that supportive spirit. However, when people were confronted with the unsettling image of their lost pets arriving safely at the pound only to be sold, strapped to a table, and vivisected, their enthusiasm came unhinged, and the public drew a line. Researchers sorely underestimated the sacred place pets occupied in the country's collective heart. And though antivivisectionists bemoaned the hypocrisy of feeling concern for dogs with names but indifference for those without, they counted their victories and set out to change more minds.

Antivivisectionism kept evolving within the changing socioeconomic and political environment, but the struggle must have seemed particularly difficult to some activists as the decades passed from the 1920s to the 1940s. During the 1920s, provivisection forces resurrected the zoophil-psychosis bugaboo in a decidedly pernicious article penned by Ernest Baynes in the popular *Woman's Home Companion.* "The Truth about Vivisection" shrewdly targeted those in the demographic most likely to join the cause and warned them not to fall prey to such fanaticism.[126] Then, during the economic cataclysm of the 1930s, membership in most antivivisection groups declined and contributions dwindled. In turn, leaders dipped into permanent funds, selected their initiatives more judiciously, and printed shorter journals.[127] A few groups did not weather the economic crisis, and at least one, the NAVS, had come perilously close to bankruptcy by 1943.[128] But most organizations survived and maintained enough assets and support to keep their opponents both wary and on the defensive.

Perhaps most disconcerting, few activists could discount their opponents' growing power even during the nation's economic disaster. As new medical wonders such as insulin, vitamins, and infection-fighting sulfa drugs emerged from that secretive world of medical research, spokespeople hailed the value of vivisection. The cultural sentiment that sanctified the profession's authority and autonomy grew more pronounced, and money flowed from varied sources into the coffers of scientific research centers.[129] Pharmaceutical corporations played a crucial role in the research and development of many of these advances and reaped huge financial returns in marketing them as products. Then, in 1930, the federal government expanded and reorganized the Marine Hygienic Laboratory, subsequently renaming it the National Institutes of Health (NIH). The NIH began awarding research grants to laboratories and universities, and although the initial funding was quite small, the government's support for experimental studies grew and provided the medical profession with a new level of political influence and financial support.[130] The die was cast as the interwar years spawned the lucrative research projects that would become the engine of post-1945 science and vivisection.

In such a context, the antivivisection cause certainly seems to have been faltering and inconsequential. But difficulty and defeat do not necessarily equal demise—or even containment. And in reviewing the history of antivivisectionism (or of animal advocacy as a whole, for that matter), it is important to remember the long and arduous struggles of other social movements. During the late nineteenth and early twentieth centuries, for example, institutionalized racism suffocated most civil rights initiatives, including repeated attempts to pass any kind of antilynching law. Yet even in the face of constant defeat, dedicated individuals, black and white, unceasingly agitated for change through campaigns and organizations such as the National Association of Colored Women (1896) and the National Association for the Advancement of Colored People (1909). Although rarely achieving an unmitigated success, participants in the early civil rights movement cleared a path of activism and set the small legal precedents that would facilitate the monumental shifts witnessed after World War II. Likewise, in the antivivisection battles before 1945, the research community certainly captured the largest victories, but in no way did they win the war, nor did their detractors surrender. The struggle against animal experimentation grew rather than withered, attacked rather than retreated. Like those early civil rights activists, antivivisectionists learned the hard lessons and established a foundation of small gains on which post-1945 activists would stand.

In the clashes over experimentation after 1945, some dynamics of the earlier years remained very much intact. The two adversaries confronted each other in the media and the legislatures and employed similar strategies. Researchers persisted in charging that the antivivisection campaign harbored antihuman, antiprogress radicals, and though they dropped the term *zoophil-psychosis,* they still insinuated insanity. Antivivisectionists continued to decry the immorality of animal experimentation, challenge society's attitudes toward nonhumans, attack the science, and above all expose the most sensitive cultural nerve—the visceral image of animals in excruciating pain. But one dynamic did change after 1945: animal defenders would win significant legislative concessions. When Caroline Earle White first proclaimed her "most strenuous protest" against vivisection in 1871, she embodied the determined spirit that would, a century later, achieve the nation's first federally mandated act to protect the welfare of laboratory animals.

CHAPTER 7

The Road to Liberation

The Rise of the Postwar Movement and the Era of Legislation, 1945–75

We stand now where two roads diverge. But unlike the roads in Robert Frost's familiar poem, they are not equally fair. The road we have long been traveling is deceptively easy, a smooth superhighway on which we progress with great speed, but at its end lies disaster. The other fork of the road—the one "less traveled by"—offers our last, our only chance to reach a destination that assures the preservation of our earth.

The choice, after all, is ours to make.

—Rachel Carson, *Silent Spring*

By 1945, organized animal advocacy had existed in the United States for nearly eighty years. The crusade experienced both disheartening defeats and notable victories, while constantly evolving within broader social, cultural, economic, and political contexts. In every state, anticruelty ordinances now afforded animals some degree of legal protection from abuse, and even the federal government occasionally bowed to the movement. Of equal importance was the larger cultural triumph that emerged from the long, trying decades of activism. Through their persistence, flexibility, and diverse strategies, activists challenged entrenched notions about animals and nurtured Americans' burgeoning compassion for them. They handed their successors a strong legacy of both activism and success.

After 1945, the social context shifted again, and in the same social furnace that shaped the nation's postwar society, modern animal advocacy forged its agenda. Larger societal tensions related to consumption, science, and leisure invigorated the movement, and a new generation of activists, some the progeny of pre-1945 humane education programs, founded and led the multitude of groups that arose during this period.[1] For the first time, women figured prominently in the leadership positions of the postwar groups, and this trend became a new legacy for modern animal rights activists. These changes signaled impressive growth and power, but troubling legacies from the past also trailed the movement. The internal schisms that had long vexed animal protection efforts worsened as radical activists grew increasingly disillusioned and vocal about their movement's drift toward moderation, and new groups emerged to give greater voice to that anger. Ideological quarrels also continued to plague coalitions between animal and nature advocates as the two sides tried to jointly capitalize on the public's heightened interest in humanitarian and environmental issues. Yet despite such difficulties, the period from 1945 to 1975 was a crucial juncture for the movement in terms of its monumental legislative achievements as well as the doors those achievements opened for the subsequent and decidedly more radical generation of activists that would follow.

THE CONTEXT

As the preceding chapters have suggested, an understanding of animal advocacy depends, in turn, on an understanding of the larger social context in which it evolved. Interestingly, however, the existing books on this most recent ancestor of the animal rights movement contain little discussion or interpretation of the broader circumstances that so clearly shaped campaigns and attitudes. Ultimately, I did locate a few sources that served as the wellspring for my own emerging interpretation of this crucial juncture on the road to liberation. The greatest insights came not from animal rights scholars but from two respected environmental historians with two very different views. First, I gleaned much from the work of Roderick Nash, who argues persuasively that the rampant consumerism of post-1945 society eclipsed ethical regard for wild or domesticated animals. People in this period were much more interested in buying material goods than safeguarding animals or nature. That situation would not significantly change, according to Nash, until the human liberation movements of the 1960s pushed environmental issues to the forefront of society's conscience.[2] Samuel Hays's more nuanced view is also quite provocative. He proposes that the consumer economy actually facilitated rather than impeded public concern for the nonhuman world. Though not disputing Nash's contention that Americans relished a day at the shopping mall, he contends that a general rise in the standard of living spurred an unprecedented preoccupation with quality-of-life issues. And for many middle-class Americans, quality of life meant a comfortable home situated in a tree-lined suburb and leisure time spent recreating outdoors. These consumption trends connected people with nature, and for Hays, that, rather than the purchase of televisions or hula hoops, shaped the nation's opinion of bears and mountains alike. Traditional conservation values gave way to a more pervasive belief that nature and animals possessed an aesthetic and intrinsic value.[3]

In part, the social justice initiatives of the 1960s moved animal advocacy toward a greater focus on animal rights. Just as the abolition and suffrage movements of the nineteenth century created precedents for the ethical consideration of all creatures, the civil rights and feminist struggles of the late twentieth century blazed a trail of liberation ideology that animal defenders inevitably walked. Groups organized during the tumultuous sixties, such as the Fund for Animals (FFA, 1967), more commonly used the term *rights* in their literature and campaigns, and a few established groups formally changed their names to reflect the ideological shifts occurring around them. Activist Helen Jones, for example, specifically cited the civil rights movement as one of the inspirations for changing the name of her organization in 1972 from the National Catholic Society for Animal Welfare (NCSAW) to the Society for Animal Rights (SAR).[4] But the notion of animal rights already existed within the movement. To view modern animal rights as solely the by-product of 1960s radicalism neglects animal advocacy's rich legacy of activism and evolving ideology. From the voices resurrected thus far in the present volume, it is clear that such beliefs did not just bubble forth from one source; in fact, the framework in which they developed can be traced far back to those first activists. When Helen Jones renamed her society, she did so in the spirit of the indomitable Henry Bergh's controversial protests and Caroline Earle White's principled radicalism.

The debate over consumption, however, is perplexing at first. Both Hays and Nash submit credible evidence for their positions, but who is right? Actually, both are correct. Each provides pieces of the same puzzle, which together create a better rendering of the complex story of society's uses and perceptions of nonhumans after 1945. Some consumer behaviors inspired greater reverence for nature and animals; others led to destruction and disregard. Americans were pulled in two directions, resulting in a tension remarkably similar to that which troubled nineteenth-century Victorians. And as occurred in the previous century, the strain resulted from an uneasy, often contradictory relationship between and within the larger related forces of consumption, leisure, and science. After World War II, the churning and chugging of industrial factories gave way to retail sales and fast-food emporiums as the country transitioned to a service economy, characterized by prosperity and extraordinary levels of consumption. In the decades following the war, personal incomes, discretionary funds, and consumer spending all jumped by double digits or more. Depression-weary and war-weary folks went on a buying spree, and three sectors dominated spending trends after 1945: automobiles, homes, and recreation.[5] Federal policies further stimulated consumerism through the GI Bill (1944), which guaranteed veterans job assistance and low-interest home loans, and the Federal-Aid Highway Act of 1956, which assumed 90 percent of the construction costs for forty-one thousand miles of interstate highways.[6]

The new ribbons of roads carried families in new cars to their new suburban homes, and clearly, these consumer behaviors harmed nature and wildlife. The many millions of automobiles polluted the air with exhaust and contaminated the water with petroleum products and discarded tires. Highway construction ripped up trees and paved over land. Some critics estimated that each mile of a modern freeway obliterated the equivalent of a fifty-acre park. New housing similarly sacrificed hundreds of thousands of acres of wildlife habitat.[7] Presumably, few of the people moving into the new houses stopped to consider the environmental damage the whole process entailed. But Hays shows us another side to this story. The quest to reside in greener suburbs reflected a growing desire to be closer to nature and spend more time in it. A prosperous society offered so much more than nifty consumer gadgets; it offered a shorter workweek and more leisure time.[8] And that, in turn, allowed many more people to venture into natural areas to relax. Outdoor activities ranged widely, from the sedate barbecue in the park to the more adventurous family camping trip. Others went boating, fishing, hiking, or even hunting.[9] In 1956, for instance, 2.5 million Americans visited the Great Smoky Mountains National Park, and two years later, that number rose to 3.2 million. A federal survey concluded that 90 percent of the nation's citizens participated in outdoor activities during 1960 and estimated that consumer spending for outdoor recreation floated in the "neighborhood of twenty billion annually."[10] The *New York Times* spoke of a "recreation explosion."[11]

Nature increasingly represented a haven from the stresses of hectic modern life, and getting out in the woods or spending a day at the lake or just sitting in a shaded backyard significantly altered the ways in which people judged and perceived the nonhuman world. The sprouting interest in wilderness during the interwar years blossomed into a pervasive sense of both an "intellectual" and an "emotional" bond with the natural environment.[12] In postwar culture, the science of ecology fused with that more spiritual and aesthetic interpretation of the biosphere, a shift that was no more evident than in the works of yet another generation of nature writers. The advertising copy on the dust jacket of *My Wilderness: East to Katahdin,* written by the environmentalist (and Supreme Court justice) William O. Douglas in 1961, best captured this more holistic concept of nature, promising a "remarkable blending of scientific information . . . and a philosophical understanding of the intricate pattern of nature."[13] Other successful works, such as Sally Carrighar's *One Day at Teton Marsh* (1947), Joseph Wood Krutch's *The Desert Year* (1952), and Rachel Carson's early studies *The Sea around Us* (1951) and *The Edge of the Sea* (1955), were at the forefront of society's changing views of animals and nature.[14] Hays's conclusions about the impact of postwar consumption are true: nature and human quality-of-life issues became intimately intertwined, and that swelled the approaching wave of modern environmentalism.

However, such changes equally demonstrated the contradictory forces at work at the time. Cultural attitudes, ecology, and economic prosperity as well as government policies all nurtured a greater understanding and appreciation for nature and animals, but the very same forces also often jeopardized the natural world. For example, the federal government responded to the upsurge of outdoor recreation and nature appreciation by protecting more land under the aegis of the Wilderness Act (1964) and the National Trails Act (1968), which formally designated the Appalachian and Pacific Crest Trails.[15] But in 1956, the National Parks Service also announced an ambitious, ten-year plan to make parks more accessible for the large crowds by building more roads, visitor facilities, parking lots, bathrooms, and campgrounds.[16] This approach was, in theory, a logical response to exploding consumer demands, but the reality created new crises for nature advocates. Asphalt lots surrounded scenic vistas, cars and boats pumped pollutants into air and water, campers sometimes improperly discarded their refuse and sewage, and an occasional careless visitor ignited a forest fire.[17] As Aldo Leopold put it, "Recreation had become a self-destructive process" that forced the "retreat of wilderness under the barrage of motorized tourists."[18] Recreational consumption was, indeed, a paradox, for the nonhuman world had become both revered sanctuary and commodity.

The contradiction becomes more glaring still when one specifically examines the role of science in relation to consumption. Clearly, ecology had matured into an influential and respected discipline, and that discipline facilitated a more compassionate view of nonhumans. But other branches of science generated very different results. Most notably, scientific and medical research handed postwar society a dizzying array of amazing new products that people reveled in and celebrated as yet more evidence of their improving quality of life. If one could travel back as a silent witness and visit a middle-class home in the 1960s, the multiplicity of changes would be evident everywhere. A wife reaches into a medicine cabinet filled with the latest over-the-counter drugs and cosmetics. A patient visits his doctor and receives one of the new wonder drugs, such as cortisone and streptomycin. A parent has her child inoculated against the dreaded polio virus.[19] Dinner is prepared on a new laminated countertop. Sounds from the latest electronics drift from the living room as a child plays on the petroleum-based carpet with her new plastic doll. And plastic is everywhere.[20] The sixties were, in many ways, a brave new world, and Americans loved it. In 1961, *Time* chose "the American Scientist" as its "Man of the Year."[21]

But all this comfort and scientific glory took a toll on animals and nature. Researchers, whether working for manufacturers, universities, or the government, increasingly tested their ideas and products on animals. During the 1960s, several scientific experts estimated that the total number of laboratory animal used each year was between 45 and 60 million. A scientist writing for the *American Journal of Public Health* in 1967 proposed the following numerical breakdown: "40 million mice, 14 million rats, 1 million guinea pigs, 700,000 rabbits, 200,000 monkeys, 350,000 dogs, and 200,000 cats."[22] Moreover, some of those great innovations turned out to be not so great for nonhumans *or* humans. Suburban lawns may have been a green sanctuary, but they were often sprayed with a variety of pesticides such as DDT, herbicides, and chemical fertilizers. By-products of wartime research on chemical warfare, these toxins subsequently saturated the market and the land; after all, wanting to be close to nature did not mean embracing unsightly crabgrass or bothersome mosquitoes.[23] But society's "vogue for poisons," to use the term Rachel Carson employed in *Silent Spring*, also directly or indirectly killed everything from horses to robins to squirrels to pets to eagles to sheep, to name but a few. As Carson so aptly concluded, modern science had armed itself with "terrible weapons" and "turned them against the earth."[24] Science, like the other larger social forces, possessed two faces, one benevolent and one more malevolent.

Equally important, the federal government increasingly funded the scientific experiments that both produced new products and consumed so many animals. In 1945, the NIH issued grant and contract moneys totaling $180,000, but the figure climbed to $139 million by 1955, $1.2 billion by 1965, and $1.75 billion by 1973.[25] Other government branches followed suit; between 1958 and 1970, the Department of Defense and the Atomic Energy Commission budgeted a combined total of more than $100 billion for research and development.[26] But here, too, rested yet another contradiction that presented animal defenders with both challenges and opportunities. Federally funded research killed animals, but the government was also much more willing to regulate the practice. Out of the tragedy of the Great Depression arose the New Deal, which firmly positioned the federal government as society's regulator and watchdog.

Between 1945 and 1975, Congress further enlarged those roles, and animal advocates, heartened by a milieu so conducive to reform, politicized their cause as never before. In addition to forming national coalitions to sway voter and legislator alike, activists launched political action committees to specifically pressure lawmakers. Instead of simply assaulting Congress with bills, professional lobbyists now lunched with politicians and brokered deals. This permanent, more politically savvy presence on Capitol Hill decisively influenced the passage of historic acts, including the Humane Slaughter Act (1958), the Laboratory Animal Welfare Act (LAWA, 1966/1970), the Endangered Species Act (ESA, 1966/1969/1973), and the Marine Mammal Protection Act (MMP, 1972).[27] Animal advocacy would finally rid itself of its most persistent albatross, the failure to attain fundamental federal reforms. And although the laws still reflected the cause's moderation, they also represented its rising power. Not just once or twice but several times during this period, the U.S. government acknowledged and protected the rights of nonhumans. In the wake of the human liberation struggles of the 1960s, it was only a matter of time before the animal advocacy movement would ask society to ponder animal liberation.

Enlivened by postwar changes, animal advocacy enjoyed a period of remarkable organizational growth and activity, akin only to that of the movement's first decades. Elder activists watched as their cause ballooned, with new major groups including Defenders of Furbearers (1947, shortly thereafter renamed Defenders of Wildlife), National Humane Education Society (NHES, 1948), Animal Crusaders (1950), Animal Welfare Institute (1951), Mary Mitchell Humane Fund (1952), WARDS (1953, an acronym for Working for Animals Used in Research, Drugs, and Surgery), National Humane Society (1954, quickly renamed Humane Society of the United States), Society for Animal Protective Legislation (SAPL, 1955, the political arm of the Animal Welfare Institute), Friends of Animals (1957), National Catholic Society for Animal Welfare (1959, later reorganized as the Society for Animal Rights), United Action for Animals (UAA, 1967), Fund for Animals (1967), Animal Protection Institute (API, 1968), United Animal Defenders (1968), United Humanitarians (1968), and International Fund for Animal Welfare

(1969). Building on their movement's historical legacy, most new groups pursued a diverse agenda, stretching from humane education to shelter work to circus protests. But in response to the larger forces discussed previously, they also more explicitly addressed wildlife concerns and prioritized consumer-driven issues. Three campaigns moved to the forefront of post-1945 activism: laboratory animal welfare (including the use of strays), wildlife protection, and meat industry reform. Although earlier activists extensively protested cruelties associated with these issues, their postwar counterparts assailed the problems with fresh vigor and greater determination. Inspired by the ferment within their movement, older groups such as the MSPCA and the AHA set up special departments that specifically coordinated national activism in the priority areas.[28] A new, more potent aggregate of humane organizations stood ready to demand change.

One might suppose that a more imposing voice for the voiceless would express more radical demands. Initially, however, that was not the case. Although postwar groups supplied a new vanguard of activists, many adopted their most recent predecessors' tendency to pursue pragmatic, feasible goals. Few wished to challenge their welcome in mainstream American society. But another force may have also been at work. The so-called red scare of the late 1940s and early 1950s cold war era radiated a political intolerance that infected many Americans, leading them to see Communists lurking behind every tree and believe Senator Joseph McCarthy's tirade against an imaginary list of government traitors. It was a time when consensus and conservatism crushed dissenting views, and radicals or liberals speaking for any cause lived under a constant threat that the Communist witch-hunts would claim them next. In an effort to avoid any kind of public scrutiny that could alienate supporters, many social reform organizations emphasized their more moderate positions and ostracized their radical elements.[29] This ethic also seems to have been adopted by animal advocacy. Even Caroline Earle White's confrontational child, the AAVS, grew somewhat quieter during the red scare years, engaging in fewer direct-action protests.[30]

As McCarthy fell from grace and the red scare slowly waned, the first hint of real rebellion within the movement surfaced when a small group of disillusioned AHA employees—Helen Jones, Larry Andrews, and Fred Myers—openly criticized their organization's conservatism. The AHA leadership branded them troublemakers and ousted them. Together, the three incorporated a significantly more progressive national association, the Humane Society of the United States, in 1954.[31] Just a few years later, however, Jones severed ties with the new group, charging that it had caved in to the conservative pressures surrounding it. In 1959, she created what would quickly evolve into the first truly radical animal advocacy group of the postwar years, the distinctly (but deceptively) conservative-sounding National Catholic Society for Animal Welfare.[32] Together with a smattering of other more militant groups, Jones's organization would not only keep the radical wing of the movement alive but also foster its growth. During the more liberal 1960s, the radicals' position gained greater credibility, and their challenges grew more threatening to conservative humanitarians. Their full power would not be realized until after 1975, but radicals slowly began to push their movement out of its centrist rut.

Whether in conservative associations or small radical societies, women fronted many of the new groups. Of the twenty-seven postwar organizations detailed in a 1963 study of the movement, women founded, cofounded, or led at least twenty societies.[33] Notable figures included Christine Stevens of the Animal Welfare Institute (Rachel Carson served as the group's scientific adviser), Helen Jones of HSUS and NCSAW, Alice Herrington of Friends of Animals, Eleanor Seiling of United Action for Animals, and Anna C. Briggs and Alice Morgan Wright of the National Humane Education Society.[34] Most of these women came from middle- and upper-class families, but a few, such as Briggs, grew up in working-class neighborhoods. Several, including Briggs, Jones, and Seiling, first joined or worked for established humane organizations before founding their own societies. Often, their activism evolved from their lifelong aversion to cruelty or their affection for animals, but sometimes, a specific incident had transformed them.[35] A scene of horror at the local pound spurred Helen Jones to action. While visiting her parents in Pennsylvania during the early 1950s, she and a friend strolled by the exposed kennels of the town shelter and saw rats attacking a litter of puppies. An appalled Jones, joined by her sister, immediately volunteered on a part-time basis at the facility and spearheaded its reform.[36] Whatever their reasons for getting involved, these women established a loyal following in their organizations, and the AWI, NCSAW, and FoA rose to national prominence during several campaigns.

Women had always formed the backbone of animal advocacy, but now they became its primary leaders. The hard work of the woman's

Figure 7.1. Christine Stevens (left), shown here in front of an early Animal Welfare Institute exhibit, played a pivotal role in securing several of the key victories during the era of legislation. *Reproduced with permission of the Animal Welfare Institute.*

rights movement had pried open some new doors of political, economic, and social opportunity, but the road that lay ahead was not entirely smooth. The women's experiences were also rooted in other social forces where paradox again was the theme. Women of the postwar era confronted dilemmas similar to those that complicated the lives of late nineteenth-century women: cultural images and expectations pulled them in one direction, while realities and opportunities pointed them elsewhere. Surrounded by cold war fears and nuclear threats, Americans sought stability through a constructed image of an ideal family, an image that still feels familiar today—the nine-to-five breadwinner husband, a brood of brilliant children, and a thoroughly contented housewife preparing meals and planning PTA meetings in a modern suburban haven. Most important, the ideal dictated that women subordinate their own lives and interests to those of their perfect nuclear family.[37]

Nearly every aspect of culture and politics repeatedly projected that image, but of course, reality rarely conforms so neatly to cultural ideals. Although many middle-class women did sacrifice college educations and jobs to their homemaker careers, they nonetheless chiseled out a public space from their domestic realm. The ideal of a mother selflessly serving her family translated logically and easily to community volunteerism. During the 1950s, PTA moms also organized or contributed time to Young Women's Christian Associations (YWCAs), hospital charities, and more politically active groups such as the League of Women Voters, civil rights organizations, peace coalitions, and animal defense societies. Moreover, before long, the economic realities of increased consumption and the rising standard of living compelled more and more married women to seek employment outside the home. Often, the woman's income furnished the barbecue grill, lawn furniture, and modern appliances that completed the picture of the ideal American home. Workplace and volunteer experiences further politicized women by exposing them to both economic discrimination and greater economic power.[38] Working out of necessity and volunteering out of principle, the women found a cultural and political voice that spoke of societal reforms for others and for themselves.

Activism on behalf of animals meshed perfectly with the rationale behind women's volunteerism. In the nineteenth century, female animal advocates viewed their efforts as an appropriate extension of their prescribed maternal roles. Nearly a century later, postindustrial women still defined their gendered domain to encompass an ethic of caring for both humans and nonhumans. They also continued to connect their activism for animals and nature with the future well-being and, indeed, the very survival of society and families. Animal and nature advocate Rachel Carson exemplified this perspective in her ominous warnings in *Silent Spring.* The biologist cast dark visions of a society that indiscriminately unleashed a barrage of lethal chemicals on the nonhuman world and in doing so doomed itself; it was a vision in which families suffered "much illness" and children "would be stricken suddenly while at play and die within a few hours."[39] In an era when the family was placed on a cultural pedestal, such images touched a nerve. But by using them, Carson and her peers negotiated that fine line between the expectations that relegated women to the home and those that justified public activism. And as could be expected, some opponents turned gender stereotypes against female activists, dismissing their concerns as the rantings of emotional women. After the release of *Silent Spring,* chemical industry representatives hurled many vicious slurs at Carson, but their favorite attack seemed to consist of portraying her as a "hysterical fool" (zoophil-psychosis redux) who "exceeded the bounds of scientific knowledge."[40]

Being the brunt of such gender-based derision was not uncommon for women in the movement. A Washington, D.C., pharmacologist more generally derided all female animal advocates as "the little old lady in sneakers" who embraced emotional, "anti-intellectual," and "fringe causes."[41]

THE KILLING FLOOR

Critics liked to portray female animal advocates as weak or stupid or both, but often, those women led or participated in cruelty investigations that would have rattled the most hardened man. They meticulously documented the conditions they found and collected the evidence of abuse, and they articulated the arguments behind the legislative victories in the movement's priority areas. Helen Jones did just that for the humane slaughter campaign. But even the steely Jones was unprepared for the sights, sounds, and smells that engulfed her during her first investigations of stockyards and killing floors at slaughterhouses. Carefully negotiating the catwalks above the bloody operations, the young and idealistic activist watched as "thousands of animals" went to slaughter in what she described years later as "a vision of hell."[42] The prosperous consumer economy coupled with the baby boom sent demand for meat products soaring after 1945. In terms of beef alone, the average human omnivore ate around 55 pounds annually by the late 1940s; by 1965, the amount climbed to 70 pounds, and by 1970, Americans were adding 80 to 100 pounds of cow to their diets each year.[43] Meat companies kept pace with such demands not through technological innovation but by employing the same primitive method they had always used—speeding up the "killing line." Jones's investigation, along with others, revealed that the only change in the slaughter industry over nearly a century was that the already dismal conditions had further deteriorated.[44]

The time was ripe and the industry vulnerable. In an era increasingly streamlined with efficient, modern technology and governed by protective regulations, meat processing seemed archaic, chaotic, and inhumane. Moreover, the public frequently supported animal advocacy's more conservative initiatives, and humane slaughter was, in some ways, the quintessential moderate reform. Easing the suffering of food animals required no dietary sacrifices or inconveniences for consumers; the balance between human interests and animal needs could be easily achieved through regulation. This, then, would be the modern movement's first national protest. The semblance of a campaign took shape under the guiding hand of the AHA, but initially, the national organization's cozy relationship with the meat industry threatened to undermine even a modest legislative fight. True to its tradition, the AHA shied away from confrontation and urged ongoing cooperation. During the early 1950s, its leaders and meatpacking officials jointly composed vague, voluntary guidelines for a humane meat "seal of approval." The AHA ultimately awarded the seal to nearly every slaughterhouse.[45]

Two events in 1954 prevented the campaign's premature demise. First, at the AHA national convention, delegates representing animal protection groups from across the nation gathered in a darkened auditorium and viewed a documentary film about the slaughter industry. The brutal killing methods that Helen Jones saw firsthand flickered across the screen. When the lights came up, minds had been forever changed. Repulsed attendees immediately resolved to introduce a federal bill to outlaw the poleax as a stunning tool and to mandate proper stunning before hoisting, shackling, and sticking animals.[46] Second, the newly formed HSUS contested the AHA's leadership and complacency and prodded the movement toward more progressive protections for animals. Enthusiasm for an effective federal law steamrolled, and a vast national coalition quickly took shape. Although groups such as the AWI, MSPCA, and HSUS led the charge and captured the headlines, the cause would have surely withered without the aid of innumerable small, local societies such as the Maine State Society for the Protection of Animals.[47]

Politics came next, and coalition leaders asked two of their new political allies to sponsor a bill to rectify the situation. In April 1955, Senator Hubert Humphrey (from Minnesota) introduced the nation's first humane slaughter bill to his colleagues, and in May, Representative Martha Griffiths (of Michigan) repeated the process in the House. While the bills were in committee, USDA secretary Ezra Taft Benson criticized them and countered that the meat industry, not the government, best understood how to slaughter its livestock. The committees tabled the bills. The inaugural effort thus died with barely a whimper, but in the face of stinging defeat, activists set their movement's new political lobbying force, the Society for Animal Protective Legislation, to the task of changing lawmakers' minds. Society lobbyists visited, cajoled, and pressured any politician remotely inclined to support slaughter reform. The tactic worked. Subcommittees considered new bills in 1956, and this time, events favored the campaign. Humphrey now chaired the Senate discussion, while a sympathetic W. R. Poage (Texas) took his House committee on fact-finding tours into slaughterhouses. The trips corroborated humanitarians' allegations and aroused greater public and media interest in the issue. Both committees reported the bills favorably. The year 1957 promised to bring either monumental triumph or monumental loss for the cause.[48]

Even before the debate raged in Congress, animal activists vied with their opponents to win the public's support. Representatives of the American Meat Institute called the bill unnecessary and "premature," arguing that self-regulation could accomplish many of the same reforms. More important, they supplemented that argument with an advertising blitz that hailed meat as the cornerstone of a great American diet.[49] That strategy tapped into cold war fears and suggestions by some social commentators that the amount of meat protein people ingested correlated directly with a nation's "greatness."[50] Groups representing farmers and cattle ranchers warned that federal regulations would unduly burden another American icon, the family farm.[51] Although the proposed legislation addressed corporate abuses and not the behavior of individual farmers, the argument nonetheless conjured up scenes of simple, hardworking Americans stretched to their financial limits by an unnecessary regulation. Moreover, the industry's distinct emphasis on all issues "American" alluded to one of the classic bogeymen—animal advocates as unpatriotic citizens. In that era of hyperpatriotism, such a charge could be damaging.

But humanitarians countered with what one MSPCA official called their most intensive publicity and educational campaign. Small and large groups alike explained and advertised the bill to their respective communities. Lobbyists walked the halls of Congress, and activists walked the streets of their neighborhoods. Graphic field reports of slaughterhouse conditions became weapons of persuasion. Their nineteenth-century predecessors would have been proud; this was their hope and their legacy. But there were sharp contrasts between the two generations. Unlike their forebears, advocates for this initiative rarely injected concerns about human health or moral salvation into the propaganda. Instead, humanitarians increasingly framed their positions around the animals themselves, insisting that they deserved protection and rights regardless of human cost or benefit. They spoke less of tainted meat and more of the perceived interests and needs of nonhumans. Cattle were still food animals, but they had certain rights. The ideological winds within the movement were shifting as modern animal defenders subscribed to less anthropocentric and more ecological notions of activism. As they saw it, humans were a part of nature but not lords over it.[52]

The public response was overwhelmingly sympathetic, and many community and church organizations rallied to the campaign. The General Federation of Women's Clubs and the National Council of Catholic Women also pledged their resources to the fight about to unfold in Congress.[53] New full committee hearings commenced in the House in April 1957. The American Meat Institute reiterated its assertion that reform was unnecessary and reassured legislators that the industry capably regulated itself. The USDA, the National Cattlemen's Association, the Farm Bureau, and the National Grange concurred and further detailed the bill's potentially costly implementation. Meanwhile, animal defenders paraded their own experts. The AWI demonstrated that modern, more humane stunning devices already existed, including the captive bolt pistol, electrical shock equipment, and carbon dioxide chambers.[54] Others testified to the abysmal conditions within the industry, noting that the United States lagged far behind other industrialized countries in enacting reforms. They were all persuasive, but the appearance of one particularly important organization, the Amalgamated Meat Cutters and Butcher Workmen of North America, tipped the scales in favor of the House bill. The workers who dealt with death every day entreated lawmakers to reform the slaughtering process. Their cumulative efforts prevailed, and the bill easily passed the House in February 1958.[55]

In the Senate, however, the initiative faltered. Representatives of the meat lobby had congressional friends too, and they repeatedly tried to weaken the proposed law with amendments. During one session, Senator Humphrey debated the issue nonstop for seven hours, successfully staving off each new assault. But then, a challenge surfaced that even Humphrey's oratory skills could not vanquish. Represented by the Union of Orthodox Rabbis, the Jewish community contested the bill on the grounds that it interfered with the dictates of ritual slaughter, or *shehitah*. Kosher laws pertaining to meat required that an animal be fully conscious and mobile at the time of death, which would be impossible under the bill's provisions for stunning. The thorny issue of religious freedom changed the direction of the debate. Ultimately, the Senate approved the amendment proposed by New Jersey senator Clifford Case and New York senator Jacob Javits, which fully exempted kosher slaughterhouses from any reforms. The revised bill passed. Worried that new debates and additional amendments might permanently kill any reform, supporters in the House agreed to the Senate version.

On August 20, 1958, President Dwight Eisenhower put his pen to the historic Federal Humane Slaughter Act. It took effect in 1960.[56] Enforced by the secretary of agriculture, the law's central provision applied to all meat companies that contracted with the federal government or any of its affiliates (which constituted 80 percent of the industry) and mandated that immediately prior to shackling and hoisting, all large-animal livestock, with the exception of those processed as kosher, be "rendered insensible to pain."[57] Despite the amendment, the law was a landmark victory for animals. Though not by any stretch a radical reform, this measure was not the empty statute of 1877. The American population had deemed that food animals deserved clear and meaningful legal recognition. The movement had won a substantial victory, as well. Animal advocates no longer sat outside the halls of power looking in. As Fred Myers of the HSUS proclaimed, "The organized humane movement has proved that it has political power based on massive public support."[58]

Still, the debate over ritual slaughter cracked the movement and slowly unhinged the national coalition. The more conservative groups such as Christine Stevens's AWI generally endorsed the compromise, praised legislators, and above all staunchly maintained that the federal act effected a "great reduction of needless suffering."[59] Others felt quite differently about both the law and the compromise. For Helen Jones, the incident stoked her nascent radicalism, both personally and politically. Memories of the killing floors lingered in her mind, and she ultimately adopted a vegetarian lifestyle. She also loudly criticized her conservative peers and vowed that her organization, the NCSAW, would bring down Case-Javits. Another leading light of the modern movement, Alice Herrington, echoed Jones's opposition, and during the 1960s, her Friends of Animals locked arms with the NCSAW.[60] Together, the two groups ventured into the difficult and controversial terrain of religious freedom and tradition.

Importantly, radicals disapproved of neither the act of shehitah nor the requirement that the animal be conscious and mobile at the time of execution. They publicly and repeatedly acknowledged the Jews' right to freely practice their religion and agreed with the rabbis that the method used by the *shohet* (ritual slaughter) to cut the animal's carotid arteries brought a humane, quick death. Instead, their objection arose from a procedural dilemma created by the 1906 Pure Food and Drug Act. Responding to the unsanitary conditions of many early twentieth-century packinghouses, Congress stipulated that no cut animal could fall into the blood of previously killed animals. To comply, both Jewish and gentile slaughterhouses began shackling and hoisting animals as they entered the killing floors. In nonkosher facilities, the animals were stunned before being raised; but on the kosher floors, fully conscious animals, some weighing between one and two thousand pounds, hung suspended by a leg, twisting and writhing for several minutes to upwards of half an hour. The frantic, swinging animals also jeopardized the shohet's safety and the crucial accuracy of the one permitted cut. Workers typically restrained the hanging animals by clamping them through their sensitive nostrils.[61]

Jones and her allies opposed the shackling and hoisting, not kosher slaughter. Furthermore, they claimed that regulating the preslaughter handling of kosher meat animals in no way interfered with religious freedom. During the early 1960s, FoA and the NCSAW embarked on a multipronged initiative, calling for the repeal of the Case-Javits amendment as well as new federal and state laws that compelled Jewish meat companies to adopt humane preslaughter handling methods. Other organizations, some quite moderate, enlisted in the cause. In 1964, the ASPCA unveiled a holding pen design that restrained large food animals in an upright position, thus conforming to the requirements of both religion and law. Many subsequently proposed bills requested the mandatory use of the pens in all kosher operations. Similarly, the New York Humane Society, working in conjunction with the NCSAW and FoA, introduced kosher slaughter reform bills into the state legislature nearly every year after 1958. In a state with one of the nation's largest Jewish populations, the legislative assault on ritual slaughter aroused considerable controversy.[62] Fearing allegations of anti-Semitism, the conservative AWI stepped in and proposed a law that required shohets to cut shackled, conscious animals "immediately following total suspension from the floor," but radicals rejected the idea.[63]

But not everyone in the Jewish community opposed the campaign. Some rabbis and organizations agreed with humanitarians that shackling and hoisting were separate from ritual slaughter. Furthermore,

Figure 7.2. In 1964, the ASPCA patented a humane slaughter pen and, in an effort to encourage the industry's participation in slaughter reform, offered it royalty-free to meat packers. *Copyright © 2005 The American Society for the Prevention of Cruelty to Animals (ASPCA). Reprinted with permission of the ASPCA. All rights reserved.*

they insisted that such practices violated the sacred Torah's proscription against inflicting pain on nonhumans.[64] The United Synagogues of America, the Jewish War Veterans, the American Jewish Congress, and a newly formed animal advocacy group known as the Jewish Committee for Humane Slaughter all sanctioned the use of holding pens as an alternative, and at least one kosher packinghouse in New Jersey voluntarily installed the device with the approval of an Orthodox rabbi during the mid-1960s. Unfortunately, the pen was costly, which bolstered opponents' accusations that laws requiring the pen placed unfair and even impossible demands on small kosher slaughterhouses.[65]

But above all, even with some Jewish support, animal advocates could not quell one of the Jewish community's greatest fears: the prospect of legalized anti-Semitism. Historically—and most recently in Germany—countries that limited or banned ritual slaughter usually followed such laws with additional acts that further persecuted Jews.[66] Although humanitarians never intended to impinge on the ritual and publicly stated their aversion to anti-Semitism, the proximity of an era in which a dictator executed six million European Jews haunted the campaign.[67] All efforts at the state and federal levels failed. Conceding that they were pushing a mighty big rock up a bigger hill, the FoA and the NCSAW eventually redirected their attention toward other issues.

Interestingly, just as the slaughter issue had first united and then divided nineteenth-century animal advocacy, it produced a similar effect on the post-1945 movement. The campaign against Case-Javits irritated many moderate leaders who worried that such radicalism over contentious religious issues could erode widespread public support for other movement initiatives.[68] The division soured what otherwise was a sweet victory, and during the ensuing years, the voices of dissension would only grow louder. But despite the bitter aftertaste, the 1958 Humane Slaughter Act was an important postwar precedent and a stimulus for the movement. Inspired by the success represented by that act, many organizations—large and small, radical and conservative—sponsored additional livestock reforms designed, in the words of one leader, to improve "the welfare of all food animals."[69] In the wake of the 1958 law, activists created the Council for Livestock Protection (CLP) to bring regional societies and national groups together in their efforts to revise inadequate existing state livestock laws.[70] The CLP coalition successfully petitioned several states to reform their animal transport regulations.[71] Other organizations, including the ASPCA, commissioned a study in 1968 to explore humane slaughter methods for small animals and birds, two groups of animals that were excluded from the 1958 law.[72] Even the NCSAW stayed in the campaign, annoying its conservative counterparts with its symbolic meat boycotts and pleas on behalf of vegetarianism.[73]

Without the unprecedented legal success in the slaughterhouse, the movement might never have considered tackling what would become the major food animal campaign after 1975—factory farming. (The term was first employed in 1964 by British animal advocate Ruth Harrison.) Factory farms stood apart from traditional farms by focusing solely on "rapid turnover, high-density stocking, a high degree of mechanisation, a low labour requirement, and efficient conversion of food into saleable products."[74] Operators no longer viewed their animals as biological creatures with natural needs but rather as production "units" to be endlessly manipulated and tinkered with in any way that might improve output. Chickens, milk cows, veal calves, and pigs were increasingly crowded and confined, automatically serviced, drugged, and genetically manipulated. When these so-called units vented their frustration with the unnatural conditions through abnormal aggression—pigs often attacked each other's tails, and chickens pecked each other to death—agribusiness simply eliminated the behavior by cutting off the problematic anatomical part.[75] On the human side, this new agribusiness philosophy condemned traditional farmers as "uneconomic and sentimental," and the large and economically powerful businesses inevitably squeezed millions of small cattle, dairy, and chicken farmers out of the market.[76] Moreover, mechanized farms employed fewer human laborers, further contracting the supply of agricultural jobs.[77]

During the 1950s and 1960s, this awesome industrial transformation of agriculture generated a relatively small furor in the United States. Factory farming was a new phenomenon, and consequently, its full ramifications for animals were still unfamiliar to many activists. Moreover, many experts viewed the operations as modern, technological wonders that engineered ever-cheaper foodstuffs for all.[78] But activists were not completely silent on the issue. AWI scientific adviser Rachel Carson penned the forward to Harrison's book, describing modern agribusinesses as one of modern society's "monstrous evils."[79] Other organizations publicized both the book and the issue, but the discussion was still quite limited, and any organized protest was as yet unborn.[80] Even so, with the 1958 mandate, the discussion began to expand, and factory farming was no longer beyond the pale of consideration. Proponents of the federal slaughter initiative had successfully walked a fine line, accomplishing nonthreatening goals that, in turn, would encourage more meaningful reforms and more rights for animals.

THE LABORATORY CAGE

In those postwar years, animal advocates became experts at negotiating fine ideological and legal lines, pushing at the boundary of human dominance and skirting along the border of animal rights. But they always did so with enough caution (too much, radicals would say) to avoid alienating their growing legion of supporters. Moderates would perform the same restrained dance to achieve what some considered one of the greatest victories of the era of legislation—passage of the federal Laboratory Animal Welfare Act of 1966. The old guard of radical antivivisectionism was still there, now joined by younger groups such as NCSAW, but the movement's more powerful and successful conservative wing completely dominated and altered the vivisection controversy between 1945 and 1975. The debate no longer centered strictly on vivisection. Centrists bowed to the cultural ascendancy of scientific and medical research; unlike radicals, they would not level charges of suspect science or question benefits of research. Instead, proponents of the new campaign strove for yet another tenuous balance between deeply entrenched notions of human dominance and burgeoning but ambivalent concerns for the nonhuman world. In doing so, they remodeled two time-honored antivivisection planks: pain alleviation and codified rights for experimental subjects. The goal was not to empty the laboratory cages but rather to ease pain and ensure the comfort of animals sacrificed to science. Dominant humans could experiment on animals, but to do so ethically, they needed to make meaningful concessions for nonhuman well-being.[81] Like the effort to achieve humane slaughter reform, this campaign appeased the mainstream and thereby made the cause at hand more palatable to a very large audience. But moderates also scored points and ultimately secured a win by making the issue quite personal. As the battle over laboratory animals played out, humanitarians resourcefully used one of their most valuable trump cards—the beloved family dog.

Dogs figure prominently in the story of laboratory animal rights, which begins with them and the animal shelters that evolved as a public relations centerpiece for many humane organizations. Scientific and medical research underwent meteoric growth after 1945 as government and corporate interests subsidized an eye-popping array of animal experiments involving everything from hairspray to chemical weapons. This cumulative "force-feeding" of science, as one expert put it, drove the demand for experimental animals rapidly upward, which, in turn, posed a real dilemma for researchers.[82] They desperately needed reliable, affordable supplies of subjects, but breeding companies produced only small numbers of costly specimens. Consequently, private animal dealers filled much of the supply gap. Although these sources charged considerably less for their living goods, many laboratories soon learned that some of them procured their animals from questionable sources (such as the backyards of unsuspecting dog owners) and housed and transported them in substandard conditions. The sometimes questionable health of random source animals, as they were called, compelled many research facilities to purchase more animals than specified in experiment protocols to account for inevitably higher mortality rates. After 1945, frustrated leaders in the research community began discussing the possibility of renewing legal assaults on municipal pounds and private shelters that received some form of government funding.[83] In an era characterized by cold war politics, runaway consumption, and sacred science, the political atmosphere was ripe for victory from the researchers' perspective, but their actions would inadvertently set in motion events that culminated in unprecedented challenges and changes for their professions.

In 1946, a committee of the Association of American Medical Colleges organized a new lobbying force, the National Society for Medical Research (NSMR). The society vowed to achieve several important goals for science, some of which reiterated the mission of its predecessor, the Council on Defense of Medical Research. As before, member groups would oppose any legislation that hindered the freedom of scientific inquiry, while simultaneously educating the public about vivisection's benefits. But above all, the NSMR would fight for pound seizure laws in every state.[84] In making their case to the legislatures, the society's representatives would offer decidedly simple yet potent arguments. First, noting that hundreds of thousands of shelter animals were destined to die anyway, they would ask whether it really mattered if the killing was performed by an organization called a humane society or by a laboratory. Second, they would stress that animals died a pointless death in shelters, whereas in research facilities, their sacrifice served the greater good, helping scientists find new cures and assess the safety of consumer products.[85] And third, the NSMR advocates would assure legislators—and indirectly all nervous pet owners—that mandatory pound seizures would effectively eliminate animal abductions by less reputable dog dealers.[86]

Humane groups initially miscalculated the determination and persuasiveness of the NSMR, and as a result, they were blindsided by the next turn of events. In 1948, without even a whimper of protest from animal advocates, the NSMR pushed a law through the Minnesota legislature that forced all municipal pounds and shelters to surrender strays to science.[87] Jolted from their inertia, humanitarians scrambled to stop the legal precedent from spreading to other states. If they failed, the carefully crafted image of the shelter as a haven for the homeless animal could be destroyed. They knew that the movement's very reputation depended on mounting an effective counterattack. Using the refuge image, activists presented their own simple but distinctly more personal and emotional case. Pound seizure laws, they predicted, would inevitably dissuade people from taking unwanted pets to shelters. Instead, they would simply release their animals in the hope that others would take them in. Equally alarming, good citizens who spotted strays might be more inclined to leave them on the streets rather than turn them over to a shelter. The seizure laws, humanitarians warned, would surely magnify the already dismal problem of strays and further burden taxpayers, since pounds would be forced to hire more agents. But activists also carried the issue beyond the anonymous pound animal and endeavored to make the matter personal for voter and legislator alike, invoking scenarios of a lost Fluffy or Rover recovered by the local shelter only to be shipped to a research institution before the family discovered its whereabouts.[88] If they supported pound seizures, advocates concluded, Americans would knowingly undermine the very purpose of a shelter and condemn the homeless animal and perhaps even their own pet to a painful demise on an operating table.

Their effort was to no avail. In 1949, Wisconsin approved a sweeping statute that forced all municipal *and* charitable shelters to relinquish animals at the request of any scientific institution. Less severe but no less demoralizing losses ensued in Massachusetts, Connecticut, the District of Columbia, New York, South Dakota, Oklahoma, Ohio, and Iowa. Many shelters avoided compliance by voluntarily renouncing their public funds, but during the ensuing years, hundreds of humane societies turned over tens of thousands of dogs and cats to laboratories.[89] Clearly, postwar Americans were inconsistent in their attitudes and actions, both generously supporting shelters and endorsing pound seizure. But their ambivalence must be located within the confluence of larger social forces and the shortcomings of the humanitarian movement. Americans did love dogs and cats and did exhibit a greater appreciation of the nonhuman world, but theirs was an imperfect caring ethic that was sometimes muted by enthusiasm for culturally prized science. Moreover, most pound animals were anonymous entities, and though many people viewed them as pitiable creatures, they were not family pets. And the campaign failed to adequately prove otherwise. In the past, radical antivivisection groups had cited case after lurid case of actual lost or stolen pets that died excruciating deaths at the hands of vivisectors. Conversely, the postwar campaign had thus far presented little evidence that a rescued Rover ended his days in a scientist's lab. Without such evidence, many people felt less personally tied to the issue, doubted the movement, and accepted the NSMR's logic.

After 1975, many of these laws fell before a different confluence of forces, including a more successful and radicalized movement, a stronger caring ethic, and greater public skepticism about biomedicine.[90] But what is important about the pound seizure defeats in the present context is the fire they lit beneath animal advocates. They were roused to action, and during the early 1950s, their organizations initiated a dynamic and protracted national struggle for research animal welfare. Foremost, activists knew that they had to buttress their allegations of mistreatment with hard facts. Led by the AWI, organizations ventured into the world of modern experimentation to uncover the reality. Their members mounted investigations that scrutinized and ultimately exposed even the minutiae of the process leading up to and following experiments. They visited animal dealers and laboratories. They photographed conditions in research kennels. They interviewed facility employees and sympathetic scientists about postoperative care. They verified or negated persistent reports of pet theft. But early on, they carefully avoided attacking the legitimacy or ethics of the actual experiments. The goal was simple: to guarantee animal well-being while respecting scientific inquiry.

Beginning in the early 1950s and continuing over the next decade, the AWI published the findings of several laboratory investigations, revealing an unfathomable litany of inhumane laboratory conditions: a dog so improperly sutured that it entrails fell out; guinea pigs with no water; rabbits in cages so small the animals could not move or lie down; a dog recovering from heart surgery with an eye gouged out; dogs burned over 30 percent of their bodies without any pain relief; and various species of animals that were ill-fed, malnourished, and even emaciated.[91] It was disastrous publicity for the biomedical community, but the bloodletting did not stop there. In 1961, the HSUS released numerous sworn depositions from experimenters that corroborated incidents of pervasive mistreatment, and in 1965, claims of misconduct extended beyond the laboratory when activists unveiled detailed evidence on dog dealers known as "bunchers" who stole pets and then sold them to laboratory dealers.[92]

It was the biomedical community's turn to be blindsided. The evidence was not only damning but hard to refute. The NSMR could not dismiss the reported incidents as exceptional cases, for Christine Stevens's AWI and its allies conclusively demonstrated there was a systemic problem. Nor could they impugn the investigators themselves, for AWI representatives had conducted many of their site inspections with the full knowledge, cooperation, and consent of administrators and scientists.[93] To top off their unfolding nightmare, vivisection advocates discovered that the AWI's president was hardly a wild-eyed, zealous radical. Stevens was a popular and wealthy Washington insider who counted many members of Congress as friends. Her husband, Roger Stevens, exerted considerable influence in the Democratic Party and served as chairman of the National Council on the Arts. As one researcher grudgingly conceded, Christine Stevens commanded "charm, intelligence, money, and connections."[94] For the first time, researchers confronted a highly credible organization that masterfully used shock-value tactics. The AWI was their toughest opponent yet.

For their part, modern centrists such as Stevens deliberately distanced their struggle from the shrill, hostile confrontations that characterized the

Figure 7.3. After AWI investigations uncovered deplorable conditions in many American research facilities, laboratory directors scrambled to repair their image with an outraged public. *Reproduced with permission of the Animal Welfare Institute.*

Figure 7.4. Throughout the movement's history, organizations used powerful and emotional images of suffering to convince Americans to support their campaigns. Many times, the strategy worked. *Reproduced with permission of the Animal Welfare Institute.*

vivisection battles of the past. The new campaign leaders first held out the olive branch to experimenters and suggested voluntary measures. In 1955, to aid researchers, the AWI introduced a manual, appropriately entitled *Comfortable Quarters for Laboratory Animals*, that specifically explained guidelines for the proper housing and care of various species. Distributing the manuals free to any laboratory on request, humanitarians tested one of their oldest strategies on the enemy—the gentle nudging of humane education.[95] But when the provivisection community ignored the gesture, Stevens hardened her position: "It is clear . . . that education alone is totally inadequate to deal with the negligence, callousness, and the sometimes extreme obstinacy which are at the root of most of the worst conditions."[96] She now called for federal legislation.

Between 1960 and 1965, organizations introduced scores of bills to Congress proposing licensure, regulation, and the imposition of minimum standards of care for all dealers and laboratories that housed and/or used animals. The first initiatives foundered, but animal advocates accurately sensed that the rumblings of public outrage over the results of the AWI investigations gave them the momentum necessary to effect national reform.[97]

Biomedical leaders sensed the danger, too, but rather than attack, they circled their new adversary cautiously and opted for their own version of moderation. To stave off restrictive legislation, they desperately needed to mend their tattered reputation and reassure the public of their good and humane intentions. Repeating a strategy from the old vivisection wars, they proffered their own brand of self-regulation. Existing groups such as the Chicago-based Animal Care Panel (ACP, 1950) ratcheted up their efforts to create a community "forum for the subject of care of animals in research."[98] Similarly, in 1952, the National Academy of Sciences, the National Academy of Engineering, and the Institute of Medicine authorized the Institute of Laboratory Animal Resources (ILAR) to promote "high-quality and humane care of laboratory animals." And in 1963, the AMA and NSMR jointly sponsored a task force of leading medical figures to develop a program of voluntary (and announced) inspections and accreditation and devise new uniform guidelines to replace the outdated 1908 code.[99] The process of self-regulation continuously evolved (in 1964, the ACP spawned the American Association for Accreditation of Laboratory Animal Care), but by 1965, researchers engaged in animal experimentation could hardly overlook the barrage of guidelines appearing in numerous scientific books and journals.[100]

Provivisection leaders finessed their public relations makeover in more subtle ways as well. In 1959, two British researchers touted a new ethical vision for animal experimentation, emphasizing the three principles of "refinement, reduction, and replacement." According to these principles, modern researchers should strive for "refinement of techniques to reduce potential suffering, toward reduction in the number of animals needed, and, where possible, toward replacement of animals by non-animal techniques." U.S. scientists swiftly endorsed what became dubbed the "three Rs."[101] Many humane groups applauded the philosophy as a commendable long-term goal but declared it irrelevant to the current need for regulation.[102] But for the defenders of experimentation, the principles irrefutably demonstrated to a suspicious public that researchers had a genuine desire to strike a balance between scientific progress and animal welfare. Experimenters loved animals, too, they insisted, and as proof, scientists and organizations increasingly advertised their affection, admiration, and gratitude for the animal "heroes" of science. Each year and with much fanfare, the NSMR bestowed Research Dog Hero Awards to lucky canines, with names such as Duke and Bozo, that served science and contributed to some notable advance. The award ceremony not only humanized the scientists but also encouraged the public to identify with the dogs. The strategy worked well until 1965, when the highly publicized wrongful death of a family pet at the hands of an experimenter tarnished the idea of personalizing research animals.[103]

The death of a Dalmatian named Pepper reinvigorated the campaign to protect lab animals. In the summer of 1965, the Lackavage family's dog mysteriously disappeared from their Pennsylvania home. The family members frantically searched the neighborhood, but Pepper had seemingly vanished. Then, a very unusual lead gave them an explanation and hope. In the photographs that accompanied a local newspaper's report of a state dog dealer's arrest for the improper overcrowding of animals on his truck, the Lackavages saw Pepper. They immediately departed for the humane society that confiscated the animals, but on arriving, they discovered that the dealer had obtained an acceptable vehicle, retrieved his goods, and driven to a larger New York animal dealer. The family hurried to New York but again faced heartbreak as the second dealer denied them access to his compound. In desperation, the Lackavages appealed to the Animal Rescue League of Berks County, Pennsylvania, which, in turn, asked the AWI for assistance. The AWI immediately telephoned the congressional office of Joseph Resnick, who represented the New York district where the dog dealer resided. The congressman's office agreed to intervene on the family's behalf, but the second dealer still refused to cooperate. Further investigation by Pennsylvania State Police finally revealed the fate of Pepper: the dog had been purchased by the Montefiore Hospital in New York. The director of the Berks County organization contacted the facility, only to discover that scientists had already experimented on Pepper and incinerated her body.[104]

The case generated a publicity windfall for animal advocates. Pepper's story was replete with melodrama, emotion, and tragedy, and magazines and newspapers across the nation told of her demise and described the shady world of dog dealers.[105] Importantly, the movement could now play its trump card, persuasively intertwining the issues of pet abduction and the treatment of laboratory animals. An HSUS official estimated that during the previous year, 1964, bunchers had absconded with nearly one million animals, or approximately 50 percent of all missing pets.[106] Like those pets, Pepper was never meant to be a research dog heroine; she had fallen victim to the unregulated appetite of irresponsible dealers and laboratories. In the view of activists, a federal law just might have saved the dog. Congressman Resnick agreed. Stunned by the dealer's insolence and sickened by the needless death of a family pet, he introduced a House bill to regulate the dog trade and coupled it to laboratory animal legislation. In early 1966, a similar bill was put before the Senate.[107]

Resnick's bill gathered momentum, and prospects for passage looked good, but Stevens and other moderates fretted about the intensifying opposition as well as disunity within their own ranks. Inside the movement, the AAVS, which had always characterized the AWI as provivisection, distributed its own shock literature and redoubled efforts to end all experimentation. The NCSAW more directly criticized the Resnick bill, characterizing it as a sellout, since it did nothing to challenge actual experiments. In the summer of 1966, the group organized a small march on Washington to protest the measure.[108] Radicals were troublesome to the AWI, but the proresearch lobby posed a far greater threat. As legislative maneuvers intensified, the medical lobby abandoned diplomacy and went for the humanitarians' proverbial jugular. Reverting to their predecessors' most inflammatory and vicious indictments, opponents of the bill increasingly lumped all activists under the more assailable rubric of rabid antivivisectionist; an editor for *Science*, for example, accused the AWI of obscuring its radical mission behind "the most positive sounding label, animal welfare."[109] Others simply castigated the campaign's activists as "humaniacs"; dismissed them as "anti-intellectual" and "know-nothing"; or disparaged their efforts as "fringe causes."[110] The NSMR completed the critique by warning that if humanitarians had their way, "an incalculable number of our friends, relatives, and descendants will die soon because discoveries come later."[111] A more strident counteroffensive rapidly amassed its resources, but just as rapidly, it crumbled under the weight of yet another sad tale of canine suffering.

During a cold morning in early 1966, Maryland State Police and Humane Society agents quietly descended on the home of Lester Brown, a dog dealer with a reputation for cruelty. The HSUS had contacted *Life* magazine, and reporters rode along. When photojournalist Stan Wayman hopped out of the vehicle and turned his camera on the scene before him, he unwittingly altered legislative history. Americans who opened the February 4, 1966, edition of the magazine gazed on images of what Wayman and fellow reporter Michel Silva entitled "concentration camps for dogs." In large, black-and-white photographs covering page after page, emaciated, injured, and ill dogs stared back at readers from chicken coops and chains. The brief explanatory article described puppies drenched in their own vomit, dogs forced to lie in their own feces, others gnawing at frozen entrails on the ground, and nearly every animal too weak to stand properly. Lester Brown was charged with twenty-nine counts of cruelty.[112]

The story was nothing short of explosive. Readers deluged the magazine with letters; it was the greatest response in *Life*'s history. Congressional aides were equally swamped as tens of thousands of letters poured in, surpassing the number received on civil rights issues and Vietnam combined.[113] Recognizing defeat, the research lobby shifted its efforts toward limiting the number of species covered under the impending act.[114] In the summer of 1966, the Laboratory Animal Welfare Act passed Congress and was signed by Lyndon Johnson (who initially opposed but then endorsed the bill).[115] As enacted, the law prevented the use of stolen animals for research and established minimum standards of humane care for dogs, cats, primates, rabbits, hamsters, and guinea pigs. Most notably, Congress authorized the USDA to register research facilities, license animal dealers, and periodically perform unannounced inspections of both. To discourage pet theft, the law stipulated that records were to be kept for all protected animals. Failure to strictly comply with these regulations would result in criminal penalties for animal dealers and civil penalties for laboratories.[116] Appropriately, as animal advocacy celebrated the passage of this unprecedented legislation, it also celebrated its centennial. One hundred years earlier, Henry Bergh had started Americans on the road to the ethical consideration of animals.

Like the Humane Slaughter Act, LAWA brought new opportunities for moderates and radicals alike. The law was historic but imperfect, and conservative groups immediately set out to rectify its limitations and close its loopholes. Although LAWA covered many species, it excluded several types of animals that were commonly used in experiments, including marine mammals (such as dolphins), rats, mice, and birds. Furthermore, the humane care requirements safeguarded subjects only prior to the experiment. Once a scientist placed an animal on the operating table, government jurisdiction ended, for moderates had bargained away controls over the infliction of pain during and after experiments. Now, however, they felt emboldened to demand more, and in 1970, they won again. Members of Congress voted to so significantly expand the powers of LAWA that they renamed it the Animal Welfare Act. The new amendments authorized coverage for all warm-blooded animals, as determined by the secretary of the USDA (who, however, took no action to change the list of included animals); extended humane care requirements to an animal's entire stay; and ordered the use of pain-relieving drugs during and after experiments except when anesthetics clearly interfered with experimental protocol. Lastly, the new law expanded standards of care to animals existing in zoos, circuses, carnivals, exhibitions, and wholesale pet businesses (such as so-called puppy mills).[117]

The act also cultivated fertile ground for the more radical activists, and they, unlike their moderate counterparts, ventured unwaveringly into the previously sacrosanct territory of the actual experiment. Specifically, they targeted experiments generated by the larger social forces of cold war militarism and consumerism. By the 1960s, nearly every product that landed in shop or showroom was first tested on the planet's nonhumans. Government regulations required toxicity testing on animals for only some items (pharmaceuticals and food, for example), but they recommended testing more generally as an acceptable way to enhance product safety. In response (and in an effort to reduce their liability for faulty products), manufacturers drizzled everything from floor wax to laundry detergent into the acutely sensitive eyes of albino rabbits and force-fed everything from lipstick to talcum powder and glue to mice or rats.[118] Corporate testing soon spread to another giant industry, automobile manufacturing. General Motors and Ford began testing vehicle safety using animals in the 1950s, and during the 1960s, Ford experimenters strapped conscious, unanesthetized baboons into cars or "impact sleds" and sent them crashing into barriers.[119] Researchers frowned on the use of anesthesia because it interfered with the proper simulation of a human's crash responses. Likewise, most experiments deliberately kept the severely injured animals alive for a specified time following the crashes to observe injury responses; the baboons usually suffered head trauma.[120]

In 1967, the NCSAW and the newly formed United Action for Animals (led by Eleanor Seiling) coordinated a joint protest to publicize and end Ford's tests. The organizations appealed directly to Henry Ford III and asked him to intercede in the name of compassion. When that approach did not work, activists picketed Ford dealerships across the nation. Other organizations rallied to the protests, and the growing outcry caught the attention of the *New York Times.* The paper's subsequent coverage rocketed the protest into the national news, and thousands of letters and phone calls deluged Ford and the National Society for Medical Research. The Federation of Women Shareholders in American Business contacted Ford and registered its objection to the tests. Corporate officials initially defended their studies, but in 1968, the company reversed its position and presented a plan that steadily phased out the tests and explored alternatives, such as the use of human dummies.[121] The crash-test campaign resulted in an unprecedented victory against the very essence and ethics of an experiment, but it also took the debate to another level. Now, both researchers and animal advocates more openly and enthusiastically discussed the notion of alternatives to animal experimentation, and increasingly, groups such as UAA actively promoted research and development that would ultimately halt the use of animal models in scientific experiments.[122]

Advocates next targeted the federal government, and this time, radicals aimed their initiative at the Department of Defense, which extensively used animals to study wounds as well as the effects of chemical, biological, and nuclear weapons.[123] In 1967, the NSCAW tried but failed to halt wound experiments on de-barked dogs (whose vocal chords had been cut) at Fort Bragg; with the subsequent victory in the Ford case, members of the organization became convinced that even the government was vulnerable. In 1973, the NCSAW, now rechristened the Society for Animal Rights, learned of a proposed air force and army experiment that would subject hundreds of beagles with severed vocal chords to lethal poisonous gases. Helen Jones notified other groups, and although lingering animosity over the LAWA fight kept some moderates away, a national coalition formed to challenge the military. Representative Les Aspin (of Wisconsin) also heard of the experiments and threw his support behind the activists. In addition to sponsoring advertisements in several major newspapers, animal advocates marched on the Pentagon. As with the Ford campaign, a sympathetic public rose to the occasion and sent another barrage of letters, directing them to the Armed Services Committee and Congress (this time, the number of letters exceeded those written to protest the bombings of North Vietnam and Cambodia). In 1973, Congress prohibited the use of dogs in the research and development of chemical weapons.[124]

The effects of the Laboratory Animal Welfare Act and these subsequent initiatives rippled through the biomedical community. Statistically, the overall number of animals used in scientific experiments began to noticeably decline after 1968.[125] Animal advocates clearly liked that legacy, but the impact went well beyond any numbers. Science and medicine sustained a sociocultural blow. Before 1945, only a brave few raised their voices to criticize the vivisection practices of the revered and secretive professions. After the war, however, Americans much more readily prodded scientific research out into the glare of public scrutiny and deemed it, at times, unethical. The impetus behind that shift was not some sudden, pervasive disrespect for scientists but rather the cumulative effect of society's evolving respect for the nonhuman world—a respect nurtured by major societal forces, animal advocates, and nature advocates. Whether dealing with a cow in a slaughterhouse, a dog in a laboratory cage, or a harp seal on a remote island, humans increasingly believed in and acted on Aldo Leopold's plea to view the nonhuman world as "a community to which we belong."[126]

THE WILD

For animal advocacy, that community unquestionably and always encompassed wild animals. Bergh detested caged lions. Caroline Earle White boycotted feathered hats. Lucy Furman eschewed furs. And after 1945, many groups endeavored to more explicitly blend their ethical concern for animals with an ecological perspective. But with the rise of an organized and powerful modern environmental movement, animal advocacy often took the back seat in contemporary wildlife campaigns, and at times, environmentalists regarded humanitarians as unwelcome participants. Disagreements over the emphasis to be placed on animal suffering versus biodiversity, particularly in regard to hunting, still drove wedges between the causes and endangered cooperation. Nonetheless, animal defenders insisted on being included, and given their movement's history, their insistence was justified. Wildlife campaigns rounded out their three main priorities (meat industry reform, lab animal welfare, and wildlife protection), and although they conceded the limelight, the valuable historical role they fulfilled on this issue should not be neglected. When they antagonized their sometime allies, animal advocates resolutely persevered alone to change minds. But when the coalition worked, the two sides did more than just change a few minds: they changed legislative history.

During the first decades of the postwar era, one woman perhaps best exemplified the integration of humane and environmental principles. Through her work and activism, Rachel Carson profoundly impacted a nation already poised to embrace her account of a natural world being slowly sickened by humans' overuse of pesticides and chemicals. That account, *Silent Spring*, rode to the top of the *New York Times* best-seller list and stayed there for months. Organizations such as the National Wildlife Federation (NWF) and the Audubon Society honored Carson. The chemical industry spent $250,000 on a smear campaign her editor called "the most bitter and unscrupulous . . . since the publication of Charles Darwin's *Origin of the Species*."[127] The ensuing furor induced President John F. Kennedy to convene the Presidential Scientific Advisory Committee, which issued a report in 1963 that affirmed many of Carson's allegations. Public pressure for reform ultimately led to the Pesticide Control Act of 1972, which finally removed DDT from the market.[128] Above all, *Silent Spring* evoked a response that fanned the already glowing spark of environmentalism.

In part, Carson's message resonated so well with Americans because she made the intellectual mysteries of science approachable and understandable. She sensed the public's growing desire to understand the nonhuman environment and guided her readers painlessly through the basics of chemistry and ecology.[129] But the extraordinary response to her book must also be measured against the backdrop of the sweeping social forces in play. Carson understood the tension in society between forces and behaviors that destroyed nature (such as science and consumption, respectively) and the rising impulse to save it. Her study skillfully connected conclusions about environmental degradation to the growing appreciation of nature and the quality-of-life issues that preoccupied many postwar Americans. A silent spring would mean many things, including a less pleasant life in the suburbs, fewer opportunities to commune with nature, and the suffering and deaths of animals. Disturbing ecological balances threatened both humans and nonhumans alike, she asserted, and Americans could avert disaster for themselves and the environment only by easing human pressure on the nonhuman world. Carson compared the possibilities to Robert Frost's poem about the place "where two roads diverge" and asked Americans to consider traveling a more difficult road but one "that assures the preservation of our earth."[130]

Rachel Carson inspired animal advocates for the same reasons, but they also admired the quiet writer for her consummate ability to connect her belief in the preservation of species with her compassion for individual animals. Like many conservation groups, the AWI bestowed its highest honor on the biologist in 1962, but this award recognized *Silent Spring* for both its ecological message and its "outstanding contribution to animal welfare."[131] For humanitarians, Carson symbolized the possibility of healing the old fractures between themselves and nature advocates. She moved effortlessly between the two movements: serving as scientific adviser at the AWI, working with conservation groups, protesting the cruelties of factory farming, and denouncing the "biocide" caused by pesticides. Perhaps *Silent Spring*'s front pages hold one key to her encompassing activism. Carson dedicated her book to Albert Schweitzer, the philosopher who espoused "a reverence for life." An often-repeated story about Carson confirms that such an ethic undergirded her work. According to friends, when the biologist collected seawater to examine the microscopic creatures contained within, she never tossed it away. Instead, she carefully transported the tiny plankton organisms back to their natural home.[132] Carson's commitment to the nonhuman world was as much spiritual as ecological. If cancer had not prematurely stilled her voice, one wonders what she would have said about later clashes between environmentalists and animal advocates over issues such as hunting and if she could have served as a bridge and a mediator between the two movements.

But by 1964, Carson was gone. Inspired by her legacy and the popularity of environmentalism, animal protection groups sponsored pollution studies and bird and wildlife sanctuaries.[133] Above all, however, they headlined topics they felt best mingled issues of animal suffering and environmental thought, and the broadly construed subject of endangered species held obvious attractions. Hunting, habitat destruction, and other consumer-driven behaviors (such as the wearing of fur) all contributed to the dwindling numbers of certain species. Here was a prime opportunity to both participate in an environmental campaign *and* foreground long-standing animal advocacy issues, including hunting and the use of fur. But that interest in animal welfare was exactly the problem confronting any potential coalition with nature advocates. Even when the two movements found common ground, their commonalities often fell prey to strategic and ideological differences. For environmentalists, the endangered species campaign centered on wildlife and habitat destruction; it was the ecocide of the natural world writ large. But for humanitarians, the initiative also entailed issues of human cruelty and individual suffering. The discord between the groups was most starkly revealed when humane activists attacked hunting. In this arena, prospects for an effective national coalition to save any species looked grim.

Many environmentalists probably groaned quietly every time animal activists raised the issue of hunting. For nature advocates, it was uncomfortable terrain and a political quagmire. Environmentalists and nature organizations had disagreements on this topic even among themselves. Moreover, the politically powerful hunting and gun lobbies sometimes allied with these groups in what was, like the bond with humanitarians, a prickly alliance, and the two sides did not always concur. In 1949, for example, hunting proponents and the National Rifle Association (NRA) successfully lobbied Congress to open as much of 25 percent of wildlife refuges for waterfowl hunting, and in 1958, the percentage was raised to 40 percent. The hunting lobby achieved another notable victory in 1966 when legislators approved the seasonal hunting of some game within the National Wildlife Refuge System. Established as havens for all wildlife, these national refuges became what many environmentalists considered killing fields during the 1950s and 1960s. A government ecologist monitoring one hunt at the Sand Lake refuge in South Dakota in 1969 recounted that "as many as 1,500 hunters surrounded the Lake on some days" and the shooting became so fierce that one sportsman "was wounded in the head when he peered out of the pit to look for geese." Hunters at Sand Lake bagged fifty thousand birds that year.[134]

But sportsmen and sportswomen also counted environmentalists as friends, and they consistently reminded the public that many highly respected nature advocacy groups praised hunting as a legitimate method for maintaining biodiversity. The National Wildlife Federation unequivocally stated: "The management of wildlife, including the establishment of open hunting seasons . . . is both desirable and necessary in order to protect the habitat."[135] Other groups, such as the Izaak Walton League, the World Wildlife Fund, the Sierra Club, and the National Audubon Society, consciously avoided broadcasting their official positions, understanding that whatever their stance, they surely would alienate some members. But when pressed for an opinion, all condoned some form of hunting as a legitimate tool for managing natural systems.[136] Certainly, a number of environmentalists believed in the value of hunting ecologically and scientifically. But there was also another and perhaps more important reason behind the support extended to hunting: in some cases, the political might of the hunting lobby helped save nature. During the early 1960s, for instance, the hunting lobby and the NWF conditioned their support for an unprecedented wilderness protection bill on adding a clause that opened the earmarked lands to hunting. In an attempt to ensure the bill's passage, Howard Zahniser of the Wilderness Society, who was personally opposed to hunting, conceded and rewrote the bill. That bill passed, and the Wilderness Act of 1964 indeed protected vast areas of nature.[137] Consistent with their philosophy, environmentalists emphasized large-scale habitat preservation over the well-being of individual animals, and that approach occasionally meshed with hunting interests.

But for animal advocates, such a position was, to echo the words of Helen Jones, a sellout, and they did not participate in the legislative effort for the Wilderness Act. To counter some environmentalists' charges that they fretted only over animal suffering, humane groups deliberately constructed a modern campaign that painted hunters as both cruel and environmentally destructive. Many animal defense organizations took part in antihunting campaigns, but two groups in particular—Fund for Animals and Friends of Animals—most vociferously denounced those who killed animals for sport. Advocates knew that the hunting lobby worked hard to portray sports shooters as thoughtful environmentalists dedicated to honoring, managing, and thus saving nature for future generations.[138] Moreover, many prohunting groups glorified the predator-prey relationship as the ultimate spiritual bond with nature. One sportsman wrote that hunting is a ritual in which "homage is paid to what is divine, transcendent, in the laws of Nature."[139]

But activists tried to strip away that noble image by methodically and exhaustively documenting how the so-called purveyors of responsible wildlife management had destroyed ecosystems and devastated certain wild animal populations. According to them, prohunting game commissions manipulated nature to swell the populations of desirable game animals, while reducing the unwanted competition—namely, the predators that ate their animated targets.[140] By the mid-1970s, white-tailed deer populations hovered around twelve million, up from an estimated herd of several hundred thousand in 1900.[141] In contrast, wolves, foxes, and other carnivores disappeared in many regions. Based on the imbalances that they artificially manufactured, hunters then justified the need for "harvests" of excess game, such as deer.[142] Humanitarians also contended that the artificial manipulation of habitats to appease hunters decimated large areas of wilderness and inadvertently impacted nontargeted species. Organizations extensively publicized egregious cases, such as Michigan game managers' clear-cutting of 1.2 million acres of forest during the early 1970s to stimulate the deer population, which eliminated "potential roosting and nesting sites for many birds and den sites for many mammals," and a Ducks Unlimited project that flooded over a million acres of land in Canada and drowned an estimated eight million animals.[143] FoA's Alice Herrington summed it up bluntly: the prohunting forces were "creating ecological havoc to please the hunters."[144]

Animal activists did not abandon their oldest concern—preventing cruelty—and their goal in this regard was to culturally shame hunting out of existence. FFA founder Cleveland Amory disparaged the sport for its "mindless savagery and heartless indifference."[145] Amory's group regularly published the kill statistics tallied by state game officials and intentionally highlighted the more provocative numbers, such as the 11,690 fawns that hunters killed in New York in 1970. In his 1974 book, *Man Kind? Our Incredible War on Wildlife*, Amory included a photographic insert that graphically contrasted scenes of majestic animals quite alive in their natural habitats with unflattering hunting images showing piles of wild animal heads, men posing proudly by their animal trophies, a man shooting wolves from a helicopter (with a dead one strapped to the landing bar), raccoon-baiting contests, dozens of dead coyotes crucified on a barbed-wire fence ("to teach other coyotes a lesson"), and a man leisurely shooting animals at a "canned hunt" facility.[146]

The canned hunts, or commercial hunting preserves, were probably among the most vulnerable targets for antihunting efforts, and activists frequently used them to prove the cruelty of hunters. The earliest hunting preserves debuted in this country during the late nineteenth century when a few wealthy families and elite sporting clubs purchased and stocked lands specifically for hunting. After 1945, several shrewd businesspeople converted hunting's popularity and the frustration born of returning empty-handed from depleted woods into a highly profitable venture.[147] These entrepreneurs purchased large tracts of fenced land-stocked them with a variety of often farm-raised "wild" animals, and advertised "action-packed no-limit gunning at reasonable cost."[148] By the 1960s, hundreds of commercial preserves served the more sedentary hunter. On arrival, the visitor selected a desired target from a menu, paid the rate for that animal (most larger animals cost several hundred dollars), and then traveled by jeep out to the range. In some cases, the animal was released from an enclosure, making a tame target. Other preserves tied their animals to stakes to make them even easier marks.[149] Often, customers shot the animals at close range without ever leaving their vehicles. A United Press International reporter described one such hunt: "Ward (an operator) drove straight to one of the several automatic feeders scattered around the ranch and found the buck he was seeking, calmly eating corn from the ground. Ward drove the jeep to within 12 paces of the deer and stopped. The kid rolled down the window, stuck his rifle out and killed the deer."[150] For activists, such evidence confirmed their belief that hunters were not environmental disciples but rather cruel and arrogant executioners of nature.

But did they convince anyone else of this? Apart from the many environmental groups that were less-than-enthusiastic participants in the effort to curtail hunting, how did the public respond to the antihunting initiative? The short answer is, somewhat favorably. In a society already more attuned to the animals and nature around them, activists of the 1960s and 1970s needed only to heighten that sensitivity. Many Americans still accepted some of the justifications for hunting, particularly killing for food, but increasingly, the larger forces of environmentalism, recreation, and affection for the pets at their feet weakened individuals' desire to shoot animals for sport. In addition, influential media, including television, projected and nurtured changing attitudes, and consequently, they, too, sometimes supported the campaign. In 1970, millions of Americans turned on their little glowing boxes and watched as CBS's *Evening News* televised gory footage of a kill at a hunting preserve, and in 1975, the same network produced the highly acclaimed program entitled "Guns of Autumn," which documented both the excesses and the cruelties of sport hunting. One scene chronicled the lingering death of a small deer shot seven times.[151] During an era when the much-watched and much-admired Jacques Cousteau sadly declared that "we are facing a formidable enemy . . . it is the hunters," humanitarians inevitably found a receptive audience and achieved some reforms.[152] Their campaign successfully pressured a number of the more unethical and cruel commercial preserves to close, and in 1971, activists won a congressional ban on the airborne hunting of wolves, birds, and even fish by private citizens.[153]

They achieved cultural victories, too. When ABC aired a new show during the mid-1960s that glorified sport hunting, Amory and the Fund for Animals immediately responded by encouraging viewers to send their criticisms to the network. Thousands did, and the public resoundingly rejected the program. In 1971, ABC announced that *The American Sportsman* would thereafter show only the "rescue and relocation" of wild animals.[154] Moreover, according to every source, hunting in the United States has steadily declined in the postwar era.[155] By no means have hunters retreated or sport hunting disappeared; in fact, they continue to occupy a resilient cultural niche and significantly influence wildlife policies. But as they did with sacred science, animal advocates have persistently and sometimes successfully challenged hunting by probing more deeply into questions about our humanity in relation to the nonhuman world.

The hunting debate strained the relationship between animal and nature advocates, but hostility did not always create impasse. During the late 1960s, the two sides cobbled together a much friendlier alliance on another endangered species issue—fur—and that union encouraged animal advocacy's participation in the fight for federal legislation. Several environmental groups participated in the protests against wearing fur, but one group in particular prominently and vocally represented the cause's position. Disillusioned with more-conservative groups such as the Sierra Club, radical nature advocate David Brower formed Friends of the Earth (FoE) in 1969.[156] A central force in the antifur campaign, FoE applauded animal advocacy's long tradition of activism against fur clothing and embraced some of its strategies. Although many Americans today are familiar with contemporary antifur protests ("I'd Rather Go Naked Than Wear Fur" and "Fur Is Dead"), few know that similar demonstrations captured headlines during the 1960s and 1970s.

Together, humane and environmental activists emphasized the elements of fur production they knew would most appall society, and in post-1945 society, those elements were pain and species destruction. And like their peers in a similar campaign fifty years prior, they persisted in their appeal to consumers, especially women. By convincing shoppers to renounce fur products, organizations hoped to stop cruelty at its source—market demand. To do so, modern activists, again like their predecessors, attracted the public to their cause with celebrity entreaties and then shocked them with astounding statistics and dreadful images. In 1969, FoE orchestrated an impressive gathering of antifur celebrities. At a highly publicized San Francisco news conference, the organization issued a statement calling on the nation and the world to boycott all fur, feather, and exotic-skin products as a way to "assume the responsibility for the world's endangered wildlife."[157] Shortly thereafter, in an FoE advertisement that appeared in both England and the United States, Truman Capote, Johnny Carson, Ossie Davis, Ruby Dee, Pete Seeger, Ali McGraw, Danny Kaye, and nearly one hundred other famous people committed themselves to the organization's boycotts.[158] In 1970, the Fund for Animals partnered with a fake-fur manufacturer to publish a series of advertisements in the *New York Times*, *McCall's*, *Newsweek*, *Look*, and *Esquire*. In these ads, Mary Tyler Moore, Doris Day, Angie Dickinson, Jayne Meadows, and Amanda Blake implored women to boycott real fur. The advertisements also quoted the women's various criticisms about fur fashions, including such lines as "killing animals for vanity I think is a shame" and "a woman gains status when she refuses to see anything killed to put on her back."[159]

These tactics undoubtedly brought new recruits to the antifur ranks, but most organizations understood that celebrities alone would not change minds. The coalition also subsidized a massive awareness campaign to educate people about the ecological and inhumane consequences of using fur. The detriments to the earth were measured in numbers. The United States recorded 9,065,610 animals killed for their fur between 1969 and 1970, with Canadians harvesting 3,540,520 furbearers. Worldwide, the tally approached 40 million animals. FoE estimated that at least 861 species across the globe faced imminent extinction due to consumer demand for fur, skins, and feathers.[160] The pain caused to animals was expressed in photographs. During the late 1960s and early 1970s, another member of the coalition, the Animal Protection Institute, frequently disseminated photographs of dogs, cats, and even a bald eagle "maimed for life . . . in the trapper's quest for pelts to sell."[161] API published perhaps one of most famous advertisements of the fur campaign: a photograph of a dead raccoon that had obviously tried unsuccessfully to free its leg from a trap by chewing it. The caption read, "Because of Their Beauty . . . A Grisly Death."[162] Other organizations used similar tactics. An AWI publication, *Facts about Fur*, interspersed statistical information with arguments about pain, tragic stories with extremely graphic photographs of animals dying in traps, and even a series of frame-by-frame stills of a man beating and slowly stomping a wolf to death on a national wildlife refuge.[163]

It was truly an impressive coalition that persuaded thousands of consumers to rethink their fashion. During the early 1970s, fur sales dipped, and numerous manufacturers declared bankruptcy. In New York State, over one hundred firms closed between 1969 and 1970.[164] As Defenders of Wildlife proclaimed, the "era of environmental awareness" had transformed fur coats from status symbols to "objects of derision and symbols of insensitivity to the environment."[165] When animal and nature advocates traversed the chasm between them and worked together on common goals, they exerted a considerable force, and it was that force that energized the existing legislative campaign to amend and strengthen the 1966 Endangered Species Act (ESA). No broad coalition had existed when Congress approved the original act, and not surprisingly, the final product reflected the lack of concerted activism. Riddled with vague language and lacking any specific plan for implementation, the original statute designated protection for a paltry seventy-eight species.[166]

But by 1969, several important changes had coalesced to improve the prospects for substantive reform. First, the two social movements successfully merged; some of the groups that dedicated resources and staff to the cause included Fund for Animals, Friends of Animals, the Animal Welfare Institute, the Animal Protection Institute, the MSPCA, the Audubon Society, the Sierra Club, Friends of the Earth, Defenders of Wildlife, the Wilderness Society, and Greenpeace.[167] Second, the evidence of the harm being done to animals was irrefutable. Biologists sounded an alarm few could ignore. Innumerable creatures were threatened with extinction. The American bald eagle, perhaps the most glaring example in the United States, languished due to assaults from DDT, hunting, and construction projects; the population dwindled to between four hundred and seven hundred nesting pairs during the late 1960s and the early 1970s.[168] In addition, whooping cranes, alligators, kangaroo rats, falcons, sea otters, and a host of additional creatures were precariously close to disappearing from the earth.[169] Third, environmentalism had heightened the nation's awareness of environmental threats, and many Americans endorsed federal action. Environmentalists spearheaded the lobbying effort, but humanitarians were there, too, and in 1969, a revised statute empowered the secretary of the interior to list endangered species for protection. It also prohibited the importation of such animals or their by-products for any commercial use.[170]

The struggle, however, was not over. Oppositional forces, especially sporting enthusiasts and commercial furriers, diluted the 1969 victory by persuading lawmakers to attach a clause stating no animal would be listed as endangered until it neared "worldwide extinction."[171] In response, activists determined to pursue yet tougher amendments, and this time, an environmental event of international proportions bolstered their position. In 1973, the Convention on International Trade in Endangered Species (CITES) convened in Washington, D.C., with over eighty nations in attendance. Representatives carved out an important agreement to protect animals from extinction worldwide.[172] In the wake of that event and with the coalition's pressure, the U.S. Congress passed the Endangered Species Act of 1973. Using more specific and stronger language, legislators established specific procedures for identifying and protecting endangered and threatened species. Once the U.S. Fish and Wildlife Service registered a species as endangered, humans could not harass, kill, or destroy the habitat of the specified flora or fauna. And in an unprecedented move, the federal government also sanctioned and even encouraged litigation on behalf of wildlife. Environmentalists, animal advocates, and governments could now instigate lawsuits for those species most directly imperiled by human activities.[173]

Federal protection for endangered species certainly pulled numerous animals back from the brink of extinction. The bald eagle rebounded to nearly four thousand nesting pairs by 1995 (also aided by the ban on DDT), and other species such as alligators, sea otters, and falcons slowly recovered as well.[174] However, the 1973 law must also be assessed in terms of its larger sociocultural significance. Although the Humane Slaughter Act and the Laboratory Animal Welfare Act struck some balance between human and animal interests, the Endangered Species Act tipped the scales of ethical consideration slightly in favor of nonhumans. Nature did not necessarily rule the day, but it came closer than it ever had to possessing rights in the judgment of the most dominant species on the planet. The act firmly positioned the nonhuman world within a legal context that offered more than vague assurances of protection. Now, endangered species were guaranteed specific rights within the courts.[175] The ESA was like a cultural comet, foreshadowing yet more radical discussions of nature and animals. The triumph signaled greater possibilities for animal advocates and environmentalists; perhaps the two factions really could unite in the spirit of Rachel Carson. The founding members of the new radical group Greenpeace thought so, and in 1971, they declared their intentions to protect the rights of *all* animals and the earth.[176]

The rights—or violation thereof—of one particular furbearer incensed humanitarians and nature advocates alike and brought them together on one more occasion before 1975. For many years, Canadians and Norwegians had descended on the ice floes of the Gulf of Saint Lawrence with *hakapiks* (spiked clubs) or bats and slaughtered thousands of young harp seals.[177] In the tradition of Caroline Earle White, many animal protection groups had long criticized the hunts, but in 1964, a Canadian film crew inadvertently ignited a new and unprecedented international outcry.[178] Intending to document Canadian culture, the filmmakers recorded part of the annual event. A Canadian journalist viewed the film, and realizing the explosive nature of its content, he wrote an exposé for a Montreal paper. His story created a media chain reaction, as scathing print and video reports circulated the globe. In 1965, the Canadian government responded by sending local SPCA official Brian Davies to inspect the hunts. Davies was so affected by what he witnessed that he formed an organization, the International Fund for Animal Welfare, in 1969 to permanently stop the harvest. In addition, he forged a coalition of environmentalists and humanitarians, including Greenpeace, FFA, FoA, API, and NCSAW, among many others.[179]

In their most ambitious dreams, the activists of both movements could not have manufactured a more powerful symbol for their respective causes and joint concerns than the embattled harp seal. Humanitarians needed to do no more than describe the victims before and after the vicious assault: before, they were small, furry, and defenseless baby seals with large innocent eyes and soft white fur; after, they were no more than bloody, skinned corpses with perforated skulls. Animal activists played to people's emotions, which proved to be a wise strategy. In addition to the victims, they photographed hunters shooting the protective mothers that often charged them and reported stories of surviving mothers returning to sniff the carcasses of their offspring.[180] They also extensively publicized the 1967 findings of a British veterinarian who performed postmortems on the seal carcasses and discovered that the blows of the hakapiks sometimes missed their mark and inflicted only minor skull fractures. The veterinarian calculated that only 64 percent of the animals were conclusively rendered unconscious prior to being skinned.[181] Environmentalists employed a very similar before-and-after approach, but their "after" included biologists' estimates that hunters skinned approximately 200,000 pups each year during the 1960s and 1970s.[182] In addition, population statistics strongly suggested that humans would soon classify the harp seal with so many other lost species. During the 1950s, intensive hunts cut the herds' numbers by more than half, from 3.3 million to 1.25 million. Since 1895, the fur industry had culled over 17 million harp seals.[183]

The fur industry reeled from the assault but responded in kind by forming its own coalition, the Fur Conservation Institute of America, in 1972. The institute mounted an awesome public relations blitz, spending $750,000 during its first year and $900,000 or more in subsequent years. In part, its campaign ridiculed the antifur protests and their celebrities and touted fur as the most natural choice for outerwear. One spokesman derisively suggested that Mary Tyler Moore might stand at deer crossings to ensure the safety of the animals.[184] But most interestingly, even the fur industry tried to exploit the emerging environmental ethic of the time. Representatives publicly expressed resentment over implications that their business trafficked in endangered animals. Foremost, they stressed that the hunts exemplify good conservation practices, since unchecked herds would multiply too quickly and adversely impact the environment and the fishing industry. Moreover, they assured the public that furriers abhorred the excessive slaughter of any species because such environmentally unsound practices would ultimately subvert their own businesses.[185] As one retailer insisted, furriers were "deeply conscious of preservation," and their pelts never originated "from animals endangered by extinction, but from those whose demise helps keep the precious balance of nature."[186]

While the two sides exchanged their barbs, the seal hunts continued. In 1971, activists celebrated a small victory when an international commission established quotas for the hunts, but the kill numbers remained high.[187] As the campaign wore on, activists of both movements decided to more explicitly connect the seal campaign with efforts to help other hunted marine mammals, particularly dolphins and whales. Beginning in the 1960s, tuna boat operators increasingly deployed a new method known as purse seining, which trapped the fish into enclosed nets. The technique was successful for catching tuna but lethal for the dolphins that frequently traveled with the fish; they often became ensnared in the nets and drowned. The U.S. government estimated that during the 1960s, between one hundred thousand and three hundred thousand died in the nets each year.[188] Similarly, the overhunting of whales had so depleted the mammals' numbers that by 1965, scientists located only twenty blue whales in the Antarctic, and some species (such as the Atlantic gray whale) had disappeared.[189] A marine mammal protection bill had already been introduced into Congress, and activists hoped that a multipronged protest would spur its passage.[190]

Thus, the fate of seals, dolphins, and whales became intertwined in a larger marine mammal campaign. During the first years of the 1970s, the coalition resurrected the successful tactic of the feathered-hat campaign—a boycott. Coordinated by the HSUS and the AWI, activists first announced a consumer boycott against tuna.[191] Then, in 1971, twenty environmental and humane groups signed on to another AWI brainchild, the famous "Save the Whales" campaign, which alerted people to both the falling numbers of whales and the industry's use of such tools as grenade-headed harpoons. The campaign also asked consumers to renounce all products derived from whales. Both boycotts impacted the respective industries and the political climate. In 1971, the secretary of the interior listed most whales on the endangered species list.[192] But activists wanted the specific protections that entailed for all three species. And so they persisted. The boycotts continued, and the FoA reenlivened the seal issue by producing a prize-winning documentary of another seal slaughter, the Pribilof hunt. The film aired on national television in United States, and again, letters flowed to Washington, D.C.[193]

In 1972, the persistent efforts of activists culminated in the Marine Mammal Protection Act (MMP), which forbade the killing of seals, whales, dolphins, porpoises, walruses, sea otters, sea lions, and polar bears

Figure 7.5. During the late 1960s and early 1970s, animal advocates and environmentalists joined forces to protect endangered species such as marine mammals. Their sometimes uneasy alliance resulted in the unprecedented Marine Mammal Protection Act of 1972 and the Endangered Species Act of 1973. *Reproduced with permission of the Animal Welfare Institute.*

by any U.S. citizen and banned the importation of products derived from any of the these animals. Passage of the act was yet another historic victory in the era of legislation, but like the others, it was a tempered one. Several conspicuous exemptions weakened the law and angered activists. Specifically, the MMP authorized the taking of some marine mammals, "in accordance with sound principles of resource protection and conservation." Under this conservation stipulation, the government-regulated Pribilof seal hunt continued. Though the importation ban ended the use of harp seal fur in the United States, other nations still desired the commodity. Consequently, each March, sealers continued to turn the white ice of the Gulf of Saint Lawrence pink.[194] Equally troubling, beyond U.S. borders, the International Whaling Commission limited the pursuit of several seriously threatened whales but consistently refused to suspend all whaling. The struggle to save marine mammals would extend into the next decades.[195]

In the wake of these unprecedented environmental laws, API founder Belton Mouras marveled at "the demonstration of power humane and environmental groups can exert by joining forces."[196] Interestingly, however, even though growing numbers of animal advocates called themselves environmentalists, fewer environmentalists considered themselves animal advocates. Obviously, the reason for this derives in part from the historical relationship and ideological differences that have been chronicled in this volume. Humanitarians more easily conflated biocentric concerns with issues of animal sentience; they could envision all animals and one animal, perceiving the interests of both as an interrelated cause. Conversely, environmentalists found that perspective problematic and more strictly adhered to their belief in the natural world as a system. In their view, the fate of an individual animal was not considered unless it affected the health of an ecosystem or the survival of a species. Moreover, few environmentalists lost sleep over the sufferings of domestic animals such as cows or chickens, and they sometimes scoffed at campaigns directed at humane slaughter and similar concerns. There is, however, another possible explanation for the differences between these factions. From the humane movement's beginning in 1866, detractors had painted the animal advocacy movement as a fringe cause dominated by hysterical, primarily female sentimentalists. The stereotype stuck, and it stalked humanitarians into the postwar era. By contrast, most environmentalists grounded their arguments in a strong scientific base, and equally significant, the majority of their organizations were dominated by men. Consequently, the two movements possessed very different images and identities, and though animal activists felt comfortable venturing into the environmental camp, environmentalists did not always respond in kind. Coalitions such as those forged during the ESA and MMP battles were possible, but by 1975, no significant merging of the movements had occurred.[197]

Nonetheless, during the era of legislation, Americans translated their expanding ethical consideration of animals into unprecedented legal recognition. The cultural scales, though still weighted heavily on the side of human interests, tilted perceptibly toward the nonhuman world. Larger social forces helped shift the balance as tensions between science, consumption, and leisure forced Americans to choose between their own interests and the interests of the living world that surrounded them. Certainly, the social and political upheavals of the 1960s encouraged many Americans to make the latter choice. However, a stronger animal advocacy movement was there as well, challenging entrenched notions about human superiority and fostering reforms in laws and attitudes. For animal activists, the postwar period was a time of tremendous successes and enduring divisions. Moderates had led the way to repeated victories for animals and strengthened the movement's social position, but for radicals, the blatant inadequacies of nearly every law begged for new, more defiant forms of activism. Paradoxically, the successes of the conservative activists established the conditions for an internal revolt against them, a revolt that found modern inspiration in the radical ferment of the 1960s.

As the chapters of this volume have shown, the path that brought the movement to that point was a long one. After one hundred years of hardscrabble activism, those who had given a voice to the voiceless arrived at an ideological crossroads. It would be left to the next generation to continue the journey and advance the cause in a new direction. The world of animal liberation beckoned—a world crafted as much in the past as in the present.

Epilogue

> Animal Liberation will require greater altruism on the part of human beings than any other liberation movement. . . . Human beings have the power to continue to oppress other species forever, or until we make this planet unsuitable for living beings. . . . Or will we rise to the challenge and prove our capacity for genuine altruism by ending our ruthless exploitation of the species in our power, not because we are forced to do so . . . but because we recognize that our position is morally indefensible? The way in which we answer this question depends on the way in which each one of us, individually, answers it.
>
> —Peter Singer, *Animal Liberation*

When Peter Singer published *Animal Liberation* in 1975, the sociocultural and even political foundations for his ideas were already in place. Although the historical record may have ignored those voices of the voiceless that echoed over the preceding century, the activism and legacies of the earlier advocates made the developments of 1975 and the years thereafter possible. Thus, it seems appropriate to end this book at that point. But perhaps the greatest significance of the year 1975 is that it marked the moment when Singer's book opened a new door for animal advocacy and for society in general. The publication of *Animal Liberation* propelled animal defenders, even conservative ones, to another level of activism and ideology. But as the movement took off in a new and exciting direction, its evolution would continue to be influenced, for better and for worse, by the past. When post-1975 activists ventured into new campaigns against the wearing of fur or factory farming, they carried with them the movement's historical strengths: diverse strategies (and agendas), adaptability, and determination. But they also inherited their movement's family squabbles and rocky friendships. Exactly where all these new and old forces take animal advocacy or humankind in general, for that matter, is a story yet to be told, but understanding the role of Singer's book is the first crucial step in constructing that tale.

Peter Singer rooted his primary thesis in the long tradition and language of human rights. Just as certain humans experienced racism, sexism, and classism, nonhumans endured speciesism. As he explained, speciesism "is a prejudice or attitude of bias in favor of the interests of members of one's own species and against those of members of other species." Moreover, he continued, "most human beings are speciesists in their readiness to cause pain to animals when they would not cause a similar pain to humans for the same reason."[1] He asserted that, like women, peoples of color, and the poor, animals deserved to be freed from the institutionalized discrimination that oppressed them. To prove his point, the philosopher harkened back to Jeremy Bentham's premise that "the question is not, Can they *reason?* nor Can they *talk?* but, Can they *suffer?*" and he argued that a capacity for suffering and enjoyment meant a creature had legitimate interests that had to be ethically considered. For Singer, the existing social construct of animals, based on speciesism, was as wrong as the social constructs that oppressed fellow humans. The greater difficulty for nonhumans was that they did not share a language with their oppressors and thus could not assert their interests. Change had to emanate solely from the oppressor. To liberate animals, humans had first to liberate themselves of speciesism.

Importantly, Singer did not specifically advocate a doctrine of animal rights. In fact, he denies that animals have rights.[2] Instead, his ideas about speciesism and liberation provided activists with the ideological foundations for their own more radical declarations on behalf of nonhumans. In this way, *Animal Liberation* significantly altered both the larger struggle and individual lives. After 1975, the words *rights* and *liberation* emanated more frequently from diverse animal advocacy organizations. Moreover, when modern activists discuss the motivations behind their involvement in the movement, they might begin by speaking of their lifelong bond with animals or a particular act of cruelty that motivated them to action, but eventually, they come to what they affectionately dub the "bible" of their cause—*Animal Liberation.* Eliot Katz, founder of In Defense of Animals (IDA), credited Singer with providing an ideological structure for "what you believed in your heart." A former labor union activist, Henry Spira became an animal activist after reading Singer and subsequently coordinated several grassroots protests that successfully stopped experiments on cats at the Museum of Natural History in New York City and ended the state's pound seizure law. In assessing Singer's influence, Spira stated, "I felt that animal liberation was the logical extension of what my life was all about—identifying with the powerless and the vulnerable, the victims, dominated and oppressed." Helen Jones judged the book's impact as simply "profound."[3]

Groups that embodied the new philosophy proliferated, and a crusade that increasingly identified itself as the "animal rights movement" set out to correct the shortcomings inherent in the earlier movement's partial victories. Even with state and federal legislation, many problems had not dramatically improved. Fur sales slowly rebounded in the late 1970s, hunters still pursued nearly every animal they desired using almost any method, dolphins still drowned, and millions of nonhumans still felt the experimenter's touch.[4] For the moderates who had dominated the struggle from 1945 to 1975, the writing was on the wall. The new groups that arose reflected the historically diverse agenda but also a liberation ideology. The sheer numbers of new groups and the medley of their names testify to the veritable explosion of this cause. They include, among many others: Animal Advocates, Animal Liberation,

Animal Rights Front, Animal Rights Mobilization, Animal Rights International, Animal Rights America, Animal People, Feminists for Animal Rights, Alley Cat Allies, Pig Sanctuary, United Poultry Concerns, Farm Sanctuary, Farm Animal Reform Movement, Humane Farming Association, Save the Dolphins, Save the Manatee, Reptile Defense Fund, Mission Wolf, Primarily Primates, Jews for Animal Rights, Unitarian Universalists for the Ethical Treatment of Animals, People for the Ethical Treatment of Animals, and Humans against Rabbit Exploitation.

In dramatic fashion, the activists of the 1980s wedded their liberation ideology to the tactics of other radical protest movements. Their aggressive campaigns demanded much more than ever before, and they aimed their actions directly at three targets: the media, the consumer, and profit-minded corporations. They caught the attention of all three. Large crowds of antifur protesters blocked furriers' stores, splashed red paint on fur coats, admonished fur-wearing customers, and displayed heartrending photographs of suffering animals. They also gathered at seal hunts to document atrocities and wave banners, sometimes intervening by spraying paint on the seals' coats or covering the pups' bodies with their own. Greenpeace's Rainbow Warriors sailed out to sea and encircled whaling ships and tuna boats. A new generation of antivivisectionists loudly picketed outside laboratories and flooded the media with photographs of rabbits blinded by bleach and lighter fluid. And farm animal advocates stood outside restaurants and handed customers entering the establishments photographs of calves in tiny veal crates. These protests changed Americans forever. Fur sales dropped to new lows, tuna companies promised "dolphin-safe" tuna, the International Whaling Commission imposed a moratorium, the Canadian government halted the harp seal hunts, companies renounced the practice of testing products on animals, and veal consumption plummeted by 63 percent.[5]

The gains are undeniable. Unlike the moderate campaigns from 1945 to 1975, some of these later protests ended rather than modified cruelties. Furthermore, the 1980s heralded another cultural success, as the concept of animal rights filtered into the social mainstream. In many ways, those were the movement's halcyon days. The children of animal liberation now face disappointments similar to those of their predecessors. Although there is a willingness to expand the realm of ethical consideration once again, society's cultural attitudes toward animals still lag behind those of the movement's activists. Untold numbers of people have stopped eating veal, wearing fur, or buying products tested on animals, but many have not. Similarly, even those who agree with the slogan "Fur Is Dead" balk at the contention that "Meat Is Murder." As in the past, Americans accept some of the movement's ideas and demands but reject others. Yet animal rightists want empty cages, not better cages. They want no traps, not fewer or more humane traps. In short, they want rights for nonhumans, but they cannot seem to completely convince everyone of their ideological truths. They still struggle against the deeply entrenched cultural construct of a human-animal hierarchy. Although weakened, speciesism still prevails.

Animal advocacy struggles with other long-standing problems as well. Although Singer's *Animal Liberation* empowered the radical faction, internal divisions still prevent a more cohesive and powerful movement. Similarly, tensions persist with environmentalists, and the two factions often bicker across that old ideological chasm about such issues as whether Death Valley burros are environmental pests or creatures with rights. Nonetheless, hopeful signs of change glimmer on the horizon. The ascendancy of the "rightists" within animal advocacy and the irrefutable popularity of some of their protests have persuaded many of the more traditional organizations to endorse some of the ideas and campaigns of the radicals. The process remains decidedly incomplete, but as some moderates edge toward a philosophy of animal rights, the rift between the two factions grows smaller. In addition, a new species of activist has appeared: the individual who is neither solely animal advocate nor solely environmentalist. Although few in numbers, those in this vanguard boldly suggest that the barriers between the movements are artificial and that the two causes should strive for a holistic ethic in which "animal liberation and environmental ethics may be . . . united under a common theoretical umbrella."[6] Yet others construct an even broader ethical paradigm. Ecofeminists perceive connections between the oppression of women, animals, and nature and propose that the movements on behalf of each of these sectors should merge into a potent alliance. As one such activist contends, "The liberation of nature is a circular affair" involving "the voices of women and the voice of nature and the voices of all of the Earth's creatures."[7] Whatever the specifics of their views, these new advocates insist that through meaningful coalitions, *all* social justice movements can progress to a new realm of activism grounded in a more encompassing social, political, and cultural context.

Despite calls for unity, environmentalists and animal advocates now stand separately at the same crucial juncture. Each faction has made great strides toward ending some of humans' most egregious assaults on the nonhuman world, but paradox yet again curses their success. In some senses, society's more pervasive acceptance of environmental and animal rights ethics has eroded the two movements' novelty, and as a result, front-page enthusiasm for protests has faded into back-page blurbs. More troubling, success has spawned a powerful oppositional backlash determined to reverse many of the hard-won gains. In recent years, the harp seal hunts have resumed, and the intense debates over small creatures such as snail darters and spotted owls threaten the very law that protects them. Entire habitats still vanish, and animals still perish in traps, await experiments in cages, hover on the verge of extinction, or simply sit alone tied to a tree in some human's backyard. At the dawn of the twenty-first century, the two movements have come to a fork in the road, not unlike the one described in Rachel Carson's closing fable in *Silent Spring.* The "smooth superhighway" is the easier route, where the two movements, resigned to their differences, continue to travel separately. The "other fork in the road" is the rockier, more difficult path, where animal, nature, and all social justice advocates stumble and strive toward "the preservation of our earth." As Carson aptly remarked in 1962, "The choice, after all, is ours to make."[8]

Notes

CHAPTER 1

1. Jim Motavalli, "Rights from Wrongs," *E: The Environmental Magazine* 14 (March–April 2003): 26–33.

2. C. C. Buel, "Henry Bergh and His Work," *Scribner's Monthly* 17 (April 1879): 879.

3. John Loeper, *Crusade for Kindness: Henry Bergh and the ASPCA* (New York: Macmillan, 1991), 94.

4. Gerald Carson, *Men, Beasts, and Gods: A History of Cruelty and Kindness to Animals* (New York: Charles Scribner's Sons, 1972), 116.

5. National Anti-Vivisection Society, "In Defense of the Defenseless," *Expressions* 2 (1994): 28.

6. Amazingly, ASPCA attorneys prosecuted a ship's captain for transporting sea turtles in cruel and inhumane conditions, contending that it was a criminal act to ignore "that the great Creator, in endowing it with life, gave to it feeling and certain rights, as well as to ourselves." For a discussion of the case, see Buel, "Henry Bergh," 879–80.

7. Caroline Earle White, *Silver Festival of the Women's Branch of the Pennsylvania Society for the Prevention of Cruelty to Animals* (Philadelphia: Women's Branch of the Pennsylvania Society for the Prevention of Cruelty to Animals, 1894), 3–4.

8. Helen Jones, president of the International Society for Animal Rights, interview by author, November 28, 1995, tape recording, Clarks Summit, PA.

9. Two notable contributions to the intellectual history genre—Keith Thomas's *Man and the Natural World* (London: Penguin, 1983), and Harriet Ritvo's *The Animal Estate: The English and Other Creatures in the Victorian Age* (New York: Penguin, 1987)—skillfully investigate changing attitudes toward animals in England from 1500 to 1900. More recently on the European front, Kathleen Kete's *The Beast in the Boudoir: Petkeeping in Nineteenth-Century Paris* (Berkeley: University of California Press, 1994), and Moira Ferguson's *Animal Advocacy and Englishwomen, 1780–1900* (Ann Arbor: University of Michigan Press, 1998), explore the social history

of pet-keeping in France and women's activism in England, respectively. In *Reckoning with the Beast: Animals, Pain, and Humanity in the Victorian Mind* (Baltimore, MD: Johns Hopkins University Press, 1980), James Turner describes the intellectual aspects of animal suffering in both the United States and England. Gerald Carson's *Men, Beasts, and Gods* (1972) presents a more expansive history of cruelty to animals beginning with the prehistoric period, but his section on the United States only generally discusses events prior to 1950. On the American front, four of the earliest additions to the historiography of this subject are Sydney Coleman's *Humane Society Leaders in America* (Albany, NY: American Humane Association, 1924), William Shultz's *The Humane Movement in the United States, 1910– 1922* (New York: AMS Press, 1968 [1924]), William Swallow's *Quality of Mercy: History of the Humane Movement in the United* States (Boston: Mary Mitchell Humane Fund, 1963), and Charles Niven's *History of the Humane Movement* (New York: Transatlantic Press, 1967), but all primarily survey the movement without considering larger social forces. More recently, Roderick Nash's *The Rights of Nature* (Madison: University of Wisconsin Press, 1989), and Lisa Mighetto's *Wild Animals and American Environmental Ethics* (Tucson: University of Arizona Press, 1991), have constructed thoughtful explorations of the human-nature relationship, but again, both works concentrate on the development of intellectual thought about animals. Sociologists and scholars of philosophy have also enhanced the discussion with their own studies, including James Jasper and Dorothy Nelkin's *The Animal Rights Crusade: The Growth of a Moral Protest* (New York: Free Press, 1992), and Lawrence and Susan Finsen's *The Animal Rights Movement in America: From Compassion to Respect* (New York: Twayne Publishers, 1994). However, each provides only a cursory description of the pre-1975 movement and lacks a broader historical framework.

10. Based on 1989 statistics from the National Agricultural Statistics Service of the U.S. Department of Agriculture; also see *Vegetarianism* [pamphlet] (Jenkintown, PA: American Anti-Vivisection Society, 1995).

11. Turner, *Reckoning with the Beast*, 22–26; and Jasper and Nelkin, *Animal Rights Crusade*, 58–59.

12. Swallow, *Quality of Mercy*, 74–75.

13. "Humane Society Pioneers," *National Humane Review* 56 (January–February, 1962): 15.

14. Vera Norwood, *Made from This Earth: American Women and Nature* (Chapel Hill: University of North Carolina Press, 1993), pref. and chaps. 1–3.

15. For a discussion of the family during the cold war years and the changing roles of women, see Elaine Tyler May, *Homeward Bound: Ameri-*

can Families in the Cold War Era (New York: Basic Books, 1988), and Eugenia Kaledin, *Mothers and More: American Women in the 1950s* (Boston: Twayne Publishers, 1984).

16. Rachel Carson, *Silent Spring* (Boston: Houghton Mifflin, 1962), 2; Norwood, *Made from This Earth*, 146–47; Kirkpatrick Sale, *The Green Revolution: The American Environmental Movement, 1962–1992* (New York: Hill and Wang, 1993), 4; D. S. Greenberg, "News and Comments," *Science* 140 (May 24, 1963): 878; Frank Graham Jr. *Since Silent Spring* (Boston: Houghton Mifflin, 1970), 48–68; and Robert Gottlieb, *Forcing the Spring: The Transformation of the American Environmental Movement* (Washington, DC: Island Press, 1993), 81–85.

17. "Genesis," *National Humane Review* 56 (January–February 1962): 6; "Early Years," *National Humane Review* 56 (January–February 1962): 20; Coleman, *Humane Society Leaders*, 252 and 255; and Shultz, *Humane Movement in the United States, 1910–1922*, 109.

18. Mary F. Lovell, "Progress or Inertia—Which?" *Journal of Zoophily* 8 (January 1899): 7; and Robert Logan, "Popularity and Progress," *Journal of Zoophily* 26 (November 1917): 163.

19. *AAVS Minutes Books: The Monthly Stated Meeting of the Board of Managers of the AAVS* (Philadelphia, November 27, 1942); "The Paper Curtain," *International Society for Animal Rights Report* (August 1985), 4 (copy available at ISAR headquarters in Clarks Summit, PA); Jones interview; and *Report of the Third Annual Meeting of the NCSAW* (New York, May 26, 1962).

20. Buel, "Henry Bergh," 882.

21. James A Tober, *Who Owns the Wildlife? The Political Economy of Conservation in Nineteenth-Century America* (Westport, CT: Greenwood Press, 1981), 210–12.

22. For the zoophil-psychosis accusation, see Charles L. Dana, "The Zoophil-Psychosis: A Modern Malady," *Medical Record* 75 (March 6, 1909): 381–83.

CHAPTER 2

1. Emily Leavitt and Diane Halverson, "The Evolution of Anti-cruelty Laws in the United States," in *Animals and Their Legal Rights: A Survey of American Laws from 1641 to 1978*, 3d ed., ed. Emily Leavitt (Washington, DC: Animal Welfare Institute, 1978), 11.

2. "Genesis," *National Humane Review* 56 (January–February 1962): 7.

3. Sydney Coleman, *Humane Society Leaders in America* (Albany, NY: American Humane Association, 1924), 18.

4. Jeremy Bentham, *An Introduction to the Principles of Morals and Legislation*, ed. Laurence Lafleur (New York: Hafner Publishing, 1948), 311.

5. Harriet Ritvo, "'Plus Ça Change: Anti-Vivisection Then and Now," *Science, Technology, and Human Values* 9 (Spring 1984): 58.

6. Coleman, *Humane Society Leaders*, 21–22.

7. Roderick Nash, *The Rights of Nature: A History of Environmental Ethics* (Madison: University of Wisconsin Press, 1989), 25; Ritvo, "Plus Ça Change," 58; and *About the RSPCA—History*, 2005, Royal Society for the Prevention of Cruelty to Animals, http://www.rspca.org.uk (July 7, 2005).

8. Henry Salt, *Animals' Rights Considered in Relation to Social Progress* (London: Macmillan, 1894), 6.

9. Coleman, *Humane Society Leaders*, 27–28; and Nash, *Rights of Nature*, 25.

10. Coleman, *Humane Society Leaders*, 29–31.

11. Ibid., 31–32; Lawrence and Susan Finsen, *The Animal Rights Movement in America: From Compassion to Respect* (New York: Twayne Publishers, 1994), 25; James Turner, *Reckoning with the Beast: Animals, Pain, and Humanity in the Victorian Mind* (Baltimore, MD: Johns Hopkins University Press, 1980), 45; and *About the RSPCA—History*.

12. William Swallow, *Quality of Mercy: History of the Humane Movement in the United States* (Boston: Mary Mitchell Humane Fund, 1963), 7; and *About the RSPCA—History*.

13. Ritvo, "Plus Ça Change," 58–59.

14. Cobbe would go on to establish her own organization, the Victoria Street Society, originally chartered in 1875 and renamed the National Anti-Vivisection Society in the early twentieth century. Subsequently, in 1898, she founded one of the most famous and radical antivivisectionist groups, the British Union for the Abolition of Vivisection; it remains an outspoken and active organization today. See Richard French, *Antivivisection and Medical Science in Victorian Society* (Princeton, NJ: Princeton University Press, 1975), 161–63; and Judith Hampson, "Animal Welfare: A Century of Conflict," *New Scientist* 81 (October 25, 1979): 280–81.

15. William Shultz, *The Humane Movement in the United States, 1910–1922* (New York: AMA Press, 1968 [1924]), 12–13, and Leavitt and Halverson, "Evolution of Anti-cruelty Laws," 13–14. Specifically, the states were New York (1828), Massachusetts (1835), Connecticut (1838), New Hampshire (1842), Missouri (1845), Virginia (1848), Iowa (1851), Kentucky (1852), Vermont (1854), Texas (1856), Rhode Island (1857), Tennessee (1858), Pennsylvania (1860), and Oregon (1864). Territories included Wisconsin (1838), Minnesota (1851), Kansas (1859), Washington (1859), Nevada (1861), and Idaho (1864).

16. David Favre and Vivien Tsang, "The Development of Anti-cruelty Laws during the 1800's," *Detroit College of Law Review* 1 (Spring 1993): 6–12; Coleman, *Humane Society Leaders,* 38–42; and Turner, *Reckoning with the Beast,* 45.

17. Turner, *Reckoning with the Beast,* 45.

18. Jane Campbell, "Mrs. Caroline Earle White, Reformer," *Records of the American Catholic Historical Society* 33 (March 1922): 37; and Turner, *Reckoning with the Beast,* 46.

19. Historian Roderick Nash's study of the intellectual roots of modern environmentalism, *The Rights of Nature,* portrays abolitionism as a philosophical ancestor of the twentieth-century concept of the rights of nature. The same assertion has much validity for the evolution of animal advocacy.

20. For a more specific discussion of this topic, see Kenneth M. Stampp, *The Peculiar Institution: Slavery in the Ante-bellum South* (New York: Random House, 1956).

21. Salt, *Animal Rights,* 16–17.

22. C. C. Buel, "Henry Bergh and His Work," *Scribner's Monthly* 17 (April 1879): 879 and 884.

23. Caroline Earle White, "The Practice of Vivisection," *Forum* 9 (March 1890): 15; and Rosa Abbott, "The Higher Civilization versus Vivisection," *Arena* 19 (1898): 127.

24. Marjourie Spiegel, *The Dreaded Comparison* (New York: Mirror Books, 1990); and H. C. Wood, "The Value of Vivisection," *Scribner's Monthly* 20 (September 1880): 766–70.

25. "The Life and Times of George Thorndike Angell," *Animals* 113 (June 1980): 13.

26. Buel, "Henry Bergh," 874.

27. George Angell, *Autobiographical Sketches and Personal Reflections* (Boston: American Humane Education Society, 1892), 13–17; Coleman, *Humane Society Leaders,* 33–64; Caroline Earle White, "Report of the President," *First Annual Report for the Women's Branch of the PSPCA* (Philadelphia, 1870), 4; and *Journal of Zoophily* 8 (December 1899): 136.

28. Mary Lovell, "Progress or Inertia—Which?" *Journal of Zoophily* 8 (January 1899): 7.

29. "South Carolina Resolutions on Abolitionist Propaganda (1835)," in *Documents of American History,* ed. Henry Steele Commager (New York: F. S. Crofts, 1941), 281–82.

30. Writer Jim Mason traces Western culture's justifications for nonhuman servitude to the rise of agriculture and its requisite control of nature as well as Judeo-Christian interpretations of human superiority. See Jim

Mason, *An Unnatural Order: Uncovering the Roots of Our Domination of Nature and Each Other* (New York: Simon and Schuster, 1993).

31. Rupert Hughes, "Animal and Vegetable Rights," *Harper's Monthly Magazine* 103 (November 1901): 853.

32. Turner, *Reckoning with the Beast,* 85–87; Susan Lederer, "The Controversy over Animal Experimentation in America, 1880–1914," in *Vivisection in Historical Perspective,* ed. Nicolas A. Rupke (London: Croom Helm, 1987), 236–42 and 248.

33. Buel, "Henry Bergh," 879 and 882; Coleman, *Humane Society Leaders,* 43–45 and 49; and *The Twentieth Annual Report of the WPSPCA* (Philadelphia, December 1888), 8.

34. William Lloyd Garrison as quoted in Harriet Beecher Stowe, *Men of Our Times* (Hartford, CT: Hartford Publishing, 1868), 166; Coleman, *Humane Society Leaders,* 195; and Ella Wilcox Wheeler as quoted in Jon Wynne-Tyson, ed., *The Extended Circle: A Dictionary of Humane Thought* (Sussex, England: Centaur Press, 1985), 402.

35. Henry Childs Merwin, "Vivisection," *Atlantic Monthly* 89 (March 1902): 321.

36. René Descartes as quoted in Tom Regan and Peter Singer, eds., *Animal Rights and Human Obligations* (Englewood Cliffs, NJ: Prentice-Hall, 1989), 18.

37. Charles Darwin as quoted in Regan and Singer, *Animal Rights and Human Obligations,* 27.

38. J. Howard Moore, "Discovering Darwin," paper presented at the International Anti-Vivisection and Animal Protection Congress, Washington, DC, December 8–11, 1913.

39. Peter Marshall, *Nature's Web: An Exploration of Ecological Thinking* (New York: Simon and Schuster, 1992), 325–26.

40. Charles Darwin as quoted in Jon Wynne-Tyson, ed., *The Extended Circle: A Dictionary of Humane Thought* (Sussex, England: Centaur Press, 1985), 62.

41. Turner, *Reckoning with the Beast,* 66–67.

42. For a good example of an opposing view to animal advocates' interpretation of Darwin, see Burnside Foster, "Results of Animal Experimentation," *Yale Review* 2 (January 1913): 301. For a general discussion of social Darwinism, see Richard Hofstadter, *Social Darwinism in American Thought* (New York: Columbia University Press, 1944); and Robert Wiebe, *The Search for Order* (New York: Hill and Wang, 1967), 40, 136, and 140.

43. Salt, *Animal Rights,* 19–20.

44. Ibid., 20–21.

45. E. P. Evans, "The Nearness of Animals to Man," *Atlantic Monthly* 69 (February 1892): 171–84; Evans, "Mind in Man and Brute," *Unitarian Re-*

view 36 (November 1891): 342–65; Evans, "Progress and Perfectibility in the Lower Animals," *Popular Science Monthly* 40 (December 1891): 170–79; and Allen Pringle, "Reasoning Animals," *Popular Science Monthly* 42 (November 1892): 71–75.

46. Samuel Lockwood, "Animal Humor," *American Naturalist* 10 (May 1876): 257–70.

47. Anna Sewell, *Black Beauty: The Autobiography of a Horse* (Akron, OH: Saalfield Publishing, 1924).

48. Albert Leffingwell, "Vivisection in America," appendix to Salt, *Animal Rights*, 144.

49. Rosa Abbott, "The Higher Civilization versus Vivisection," *Arena* 19 (1898): 127–28.

50. Darwin as quoted in Wynne-Tyson, *Extended Circle*, 62; also see Nash, *Rights of Nature*, 44.

51. Salt, *Animal Rights*, 95.

52. Marshall, *Nature's Web*, 324.

53. According to Darwin's son, he occasionally contacted the RSPCA to report incidents of abuse he witnessed on farms neighboring his estate. In her memoirs, the radical antivivisectionist Frances P. Cobbe recollected how she respected Darwin's gentle nature toward all animals. See Donald A. Dewsbury, "Early Interactions between Animal Psychologists and Animal Activists and the Founding of the APA Committee on Precautions in Animal Experimentation," *American Psychologist* 45 (March 1990): 316–17.

54. Charles Darwin, "Mr. Darwin on Vivisection," *Times* (London), April 18, 1881, reprinted in *Nature* 45 (April 21, 1892): 583.

55. The scholarship on the industrial period is abundant. For this section, I relied primarily on Wiebe, *Search for Order*, chaps. 1 and 2; Donald Nelson, *Managers and Workers: Origins of the New Factory System in the United States* (Madison: University of Wisconsin Press, 1975); Harry Braverman, *Labor and Monopoly Capital: The Degradation of Work in the Twentieth Century* (New York: Monthly Review Press, 1974); Alfred Chandler, *The Visible Hand: The Managerial Revolution in American Business* (Cambridge, MA: Harvard University Press, 1977); and Guy Morrison Walker, "American Debt to Railroads," in *The Making of America*, ed. Robert Marion La Follette (n.p.: John D. Morris, 1906), 408.

56. Arthur Mann, *Yankee Reformers in the Urban Age: Social Reform in Boston, 1880–1900* (New York: Harper and Row, 1954), 1–2.

57. Wiebe, *Search for Order*, chap. 2; Alan Dawley, *Struggle for Justice* (Cambridge, MA: Harvard University Press, 1991); Olivier Zunz, *The Changing Face of Inequality: Urbanization, Industrial Development and*

Immigrants in Detroit, 1880–1920 (Chicago: University of Chicago Press, 1982); Stephen Thernstrom, *The Other Bostonians: Poverty and Progress in the American Metropolis* (Cambridge, MA: Harvard University Press, 1973); David Brody, *Steelworkers in America: The Nonunion Era* (Cambridge, MA: Harvard University Press, 1960); and Harold Underwood Faulkner, *The Quest for Social Justice, 1898–1914* (New York: Macmillan, 1931), chap. 1.

58. Faulkner, *Quest*, 7–9; and Marshall, *Nature's Web*, 262–63.

59. Henry Salt's biography helped to resurrect Thoreau and his ideas. See Lisa Mighetto, *Wild Animals and American Environmental Ethics* (Tucson: University of Arizona Press, 1991), 55–56.

60. Henry David Thoreau, *Walden and Other Writings* (New York: Bantam Books, 1854 [1989]), 190–91.

61. Robert Engberg, ed., *John Muir: Summering in the Sierra* (Madison: University of Wisconsin Press, 1984); Susan Fenimore Cooper, *Rural Hours* (New York: G. P. Putnam, 1850); and Mary Austin, *From the Land of Little Rain* (Boston: Houghton Mifflin, 1950 [1903]). For a more lengthy discussion of the back-to-nature movement, see Peter Schmitt, *Back to Nature: The Arcadian Myth in Urban America* (New York: Oxford University Press, 1969).

62. Frederick Law Olmstead, "The Yosemite Valley and the Mariposa Big Trees," *Landscape Architecture* 43 (1952): 17–21; quoted is from Carolyn Merchant, ed., *Major Problems in American Environmental History* (Lexington, MA: D. C. Heath, 1993), 384; and Faulkner, *Quest*, 281–83.

63. Susan Porter Benson, *Counter Cultures: Saleswomen, Managers, and Customers in American Department Stores, 1890–1940* (Chicago: University of Illinois Press, 1986), intro. and chaps. 1 and 3.

64. Salt, *Animal Rights*, 68.

65. Ibid., 63, 70.

66. Greta Nilsson, "The Fur Trade, a Short History," in *Facts about Furs* (Washington, DC: Animal Welfare Institute, 1980), 9.

67. James R. Barrett, *Work and Community in the Jungle: Chicago's Packinghouse Workers, 1894–1922* (Chicago: University of Illinois Press, 1990), chap. 1.

68. Roberta Kalechofsky, *Autobiography of a Revolutionary* (Marblehead, MA: Micah Publications, 1991), 72.

69. Barrett, *Work and Community*, 18.

70. Ibid., 22–23.

71. Ibid., 14–15; and Chandler, *Visible Hand*, 299–302.

72. Barrett, *Work and Community*,19.

73. Animal and Plant Health Inspection Service of the U.S. Department of Agriculture, "First Federal Law to Prevent Cruelty to Animals," in *Ani-*

mals and Their Legal Rights: A Survey of American Laws from 1641 to 1978, 3d ed., ed. Emily Leavitt (Washington, DC: Animal Welfare Institute, 1978), 33.

74. Turner, *Reckoning with the Beast*, 37.

CHAPTER 3

1. "Early Years," *National Humane Review* 56 (January–February 1962): 20; and William Swallow, *Quality of Mercy: History of the Humane Movement in the United States* (Boston: Mary Mitchell Humane Fund, 1963), 10–30.

2. *Brief History of the Movement for the Protection of Animals in the State of Pennsylvania* (n.p.: n.d. [Philadelphia, c. 1905–1909]), 1–3; Jane Campbell, "Mrs. Caroline Earle White, Reformer," *Records of the American Catholic Historical Society* 33 (March 1922): 37; and *AAVS Minutes Books: Special Meeting of the Board of Managers, American Anti-Vivisection Society* (September 22, 1916), 189–90.

3. James Turner, *Reckoning with the Beast: Animals, Pain, and Humanity in the Victorian Mind* (Baltimore, MD: Johns Hopkins University Press, 1980), 46; and Sydney Coleman, *Humane Society Leaders in America* (Albany, NY: American Humane Association, 1924), 144–47.

4. George T. Angell, *Autobiographical Sketches and Personal Reflections* (Boston: American Humane Education Society, 1892), 1–5; Coleman, *Humane Society Leaders*, 92; and Swallow, *Quality of Mercy*, 9.

5. *Henry Bergh: Founder of the ASPCA* [pamphlet] (New York: ASPCA, n.d.). In addition, many sources mistakenly record Bergh's year of birth as 1823, including Coleman, *Humane Society Leaders*, 34–35; and C. C. Buel, "Henry Bergh and His Work," *Scribner's Monthly* 17 (April 1879): 876.

6. Buel, "Henry Bergh," 877–78; and Coleman, *Humane Society Leaders*, 61.

7. Coleman, *Humane Society Leaders*, 35–36.

8. *Henry Bergh* [pamphlet]; Coleman, *Humane Society Leaders*, 33–37; and Buel, "Henry Bergh," 878.

9. Buel, "Henry Bergh," 879.

10. Both Buel, "Henry Bergh," and Zulma Steele, *Angel in Top Hat: A Biography of Henry Bergh, Founder of American Society for the Prevention of Cruelty to Animals* (New York: Harper and Brothers, 1942), add elements of the melodrama to Bergh's life.

11. Swallow, *Quality of Mercy*, 11.

12. Steele, *Angel in Top Hat*, 36–37; and Roswell McCrea, *The Humane Movement: A Descriptive Survey* (New York: Columbia University Press, 1910), 32–35.

13. Buel, "Henry Bergh," 879; McCrea, *Humane Movement,* 200; *Henry Bergh,* [pamphlet]; and Coleman, *Humane Society Leaders,* 37.

14. Buel, "Henry Bergh" 879; and Coleman, *Humane Society Leaders,* 37.

15. In particular, James Gordon Bennett's *New York Herald* initially satirized Bergh. See Buel, "Henry Bergh," 880; and Coleman, *Humane Society Leaders,* 42–43.

For Bergh's philosophy of animal rights, see Clara Morris, "Riddle of the Nineteenth Century: Mr. Henry Bergh," *McClure's Magazine* 18 (March 1902): 416–18; and Peggy Robbins, "Henry Bergh, Founder of the ASPCA," *American History Illustrated* 16 (April 1981): 8.

16. Coleman, *Humane Society Leaders,* 37.

17. Steele, *Angel in Top Hat,* 36–37.

18. McCrea, *Humane Movement,* 200–201.

19. David Favre and Vivien Tsang, "The Development of Anti-cruelty Laws during the 1800's," *Detroit College of Law Review* 1 (Spring 1993): 14; and Richard Simmonds, *Abbreviated History of the Animal Welfare/Antivivisection/Rights Movements* (Bethesda, MD: Uniformed Services University of the Health Sciences, 1986), 4.

20. Coleman, *Humane Society Leaders,* 39–40.

21. Buel, "Henry Bergh," 875 and 879.

22. Some of the best sources on White's early life are *Brief History of the Movement,* 2–3; Campbell, "Mrs. Caroline Earle White," 29–31; "History of Caroline Earle White," undated photocopied information provided by Janice Mininberg of the Women's Humane Society (Philadelphia); and Coleman, *Humane Society Leaders,* 178–80. Campbell sets the date of marriage as 1854, whereas both Coleman and the biographical information provided by the Women's Humane Society note the date as 1856.

23. Coleman, *Humane Society Leaders,* 185; and Campbell, "Mrs. Caroline Earle White," 47.

24. "Extracts from the Ninth Annual Report of the Department of Mercy of the National WCTU," *Journal of Zoophily* 8 (December 1899): 136; "Thirteenth Annual Report for the Year Ending November 15, 1903, of the Department of Mercy of the National WCTU," *Journal of Zoophily* 13 (March 1904): 28; and Campbell, "Mrs. Caroline Earle White," 36 and 41.

25. Campbell, "Mrs. Caroline Earle White," 29.

26. "History of Caroline Earle White," 1–2; Campbell, "Mrs. Caroline Earle White," 37, 52; and Coleman, *Humane Society Leaders,* 178–79.

27. Caroline Earle White, *Silver Festival of the Women's Branch of the Pennsylvania Society for the Prevention of Cruelty to Animals* (Philadelphia: Women's Branch of the PSPCA, 1894), 4.

28. The records and publications of White's organizations definitively illustrate her shifting views. See *Journal of Zoophily* 2 (January 1893): 9; *First*

Annual Report of the American Anti-Vivisection Society (Philadelphia, 1883); *Fifth Annual Report of the American Anti-Vivisection Society* (Philadelphia, 1888); *Second Annual Report of the Women's Branch of the PSPCA* (Philadelphia, 1871), 12–13; *Eighteenth Annual Report of the Women's Branch of the PSPCA* (Philadelphia, 1886), 7; *Journal of Zoophily* 12 (June 1903): 71; and "History of Caroline Earle White." For Bergh's proclivity for well-done meat, which probably stemmed more from a fear of tainted meat than from any association between steak and an animal, see Steele, *Angel in Top Hat*, 94.

29. Campbell, "Mrs. Caroline Earle White," 38.

30. *Brief History of the Movement*, 1–5; Coleman, *Humane Society Leaders*, 144–47; and Campbell, "Mrs. Caroline Earle White," 38.

31. *Brief History of the Movement*, 1–5; Coleman, *Humane Society Leaders*, 144–47; and Campbell, "Mrs. Caroline Earle White," 38.

32. Turner, *Reckoning with the Beast*, 49.

33. Nearly all reliable information on Angell's life derives from his autobiography; see Angell, *Autobiographical Sketches*, 1–6. For other sources, most of which rely on the autobiography, see Coleman, *Humane Society Leaders*, chap. 4; and "Humane Educator," *National Humane Review* 56 (January–February 1962): 13–14.

34. Turner, *Reckoning with the Beast*, 49.

35. Unfortunately, much of what is known about Appleton's animal advocacy comes from Angell; see Angell, *Autobiographical Sketches*, 8–10.

36. Ibid., 7–11. Eventually, Angell convinced the society's officials to elect her as a "lady director" in 1871; see "The Life and Times of George Thorndike Angell," *Animals* 113 (June 1980): 13.

37. Angell, *Autobiographical Sketches*, 12–13; and Coleman, *Humane Society Leaders*, 98.

38. Although most historians acknowledge links between the social reforms of the period, several studies specifically allude to reformers' interest in animal issues. See Coleman, *Humane Society Leaders*, chaps. 1, 3, and 7; Roberta Kalechofsky, *Autobiography of a Revolutionary* (Marblehead, MA: Micah Publications, 1991), 97–122; and Lawrence Finsen and Susan Finsen, *The Animal Rights Movement in America: From Compassion to Respect* (New York: Twayne Publishers, 1994), chap. 2.

39. John Loeper, *Crusade for Kindness: Henry Bergh and the ASPCA* (New York: Macmillan, 1991), 62, 80, and 84.

40. Buel, "Henry Bergh," 883–84.

41. Ibid., 879.

42. Steele, *Angel in Top Hat*, 286–90.

43. Notably, White's father, Thomas Earle, ran as the vice-presidential candidate for the Liberty Party in 1840. The party platform included an

antislavery plank. See Campbell, "Mrs. Caroline Earle White," 29–30 and 43–44.

44. Angell, *Autobiographical Sketches*, 1–5; and Coleman, *Humane Society Leaders*, 107–8 and 177–202.

45. *Animals, People, and the MSPCA: 125 Years of Progress* [booklet] (Boston: MSPCA, 1993), 3.

46. McCrea, *Humane Movement*, 10–15; Swallow, *Quality of Mercy*, 22; and Coleman, *Humane Society Leaders*, 150.

47. Only the Tennessee society prospered and operated without an ongoing deficit in moneys and membership. See Swallow, *Quality of Mercy*, 42, 52–53, and 58.

48. William Shultz, *The Humane Movement in the United States, 1910–1922* (New York: AMS Press, 1968 [1924]), 26–28.

49. McCrea, *Humane Movement*, 25–26.

50. Angell, *Autobiographical Sketches*, 12–14; *Animals, People, and the MSPCA*, 2; Turner, *Reckoning with the Beast*, 47; and Simmonds, *Abbreviated History*, 4.

51. Turner, *Reckoning with the Beast*, 47.

52. McCrea, *Humane Movement*, 25–26.

53. "The Negro in His Relations to the Lower Animals," *Journal of Zoophily* 12 (April 1903): 50–51.

54. Turner, *Reckoning with the Beast*, 47, 51, and 53.

55. Coleman, *Humane Society Leaders*, 177.

56. Ibid.

57. For a more detailed discussion of the various elements of the separate spheres interpretation of history as well as the gendered division of space, see Robyn Muncy, *Creating a Female Dominion in American Reform, 1890–1935* (New York: Oxford University Press, 1991); Linda Kerber, "Separate Spheres, Female Worlds, Woman's Place: The Rhetoric of Women's History," *Journal of American History* 75 (June 1988): 9–39; Barbara Welter, "The Cult of True Womanhood: 1820–1860," *American Quarterly* 18 (Summer 1966): 151–74; Carroll Smith-Rosenberg, "The Female World of Love and Ritual: Relations between Women in Nineteenth-Century America," *Signs* 1 (Autumn 1975): 1–29; Ellen DuBois, Mari Jo Buhle, Temma Kaplan, Gerda Lerner, and Carroll Smith-Rosenberg, "Politics and Culture in Women's History: A Symposium," *Feminist Studies* 6 (Spring 1980): 26–64; Estelle Freedman, "Separatism as Strategy: Female Institution Building and American Feminism, 1870–1930," *Feminist Studies* 5 (Fall 1979): 512–29; Mary Ryan, *Women in Public: Between Banners and Ballots, 1825–1880* (Baltimore, MD: Johns Hopkins University Press, 1990); and Nancy Cott, *The Bonds of Womanhood: "Woman's Sphere" in New England, 1780–1835* (New Haven, CT: Yale University Press, 1977).

58. Shultz, *Humane Movement*, 69.

59. Buel, "Henry Bergh," 875; and Coleman, *Humane Society Leaders*, 177–78.

60. Shultz, *Humane Movement*, 69–70 and 126.

61. Specific examples include the WPSPCA secretary Mary Lovell, Alva C. Blaffer of the Louisiana SPCA, and Ruth Ewing of the Illinois Humane Society. Notably, the Illinois society permitted Ewing to serve only as an honorary member. See Coleman, *Humane Society Leaders*, 186–90 and 196–97.

62. Shultz, *Humane Movement*, 70 and 126.

63. Mary Lovell, *Outline of the History of the WPSPCA: From Its Foundation April 14, 1869 to January 1908* (Philadelphia: WPSPCA), 57. The PSPCA did not reinstitute its Women's Branch until 1917, and thereafter, it strictly supervised the branch and limited its tasks to watering stations and parades for horses. See Shultz, *Humane Movement*, 71.

64. Coleman, *Humane Society Leaders*, 208; Lovell, *Outline of the History*, 37; *Journal of Zoophily* 13 (August 1904): 92; and Swallow, *Quality of Mercy*, 39.

65. Coleman, *Humane Society Leaders*, 187, 211, and 216.

66. Shultz, *Humane Movement*, 65–66; Coleman, *Humane Society Leaders*, 196 and 217; and *About Bide-a-Wee*, 2002, Bide-a-Wee, http://www.bideawee.org/about.asp (July 10, 2005).

67. "Where We Came From," *The Anti-Cruelty Society: 75th Anniversary Annual Report* (Chicago: Anti-Cruelty Society, 1975), 1–2.

68. Notably, White sought the guidance of Frances Power Cobbe. See *Fifteenth Annual Report of the Women's Branch of the PSPCA* (Philadelphia, December 31, 1883), 3–4; Campbell, "Mrs. Caroline Earle White," 42–43; and Coleman, *Humane Society Leaders*, 204–5.

69. Examples of female-led antivivisection societies include the Illinois Anti-Vivisection Society (1892, Mrs. Fairchild Allen), the New York Anti-Vivisection Society (1910, Mrs. Diana Belais), and the Vivisection Investigation League of New York (1908–1909?), Mrs. Clinton Pinckney Farrel and Mrs. Maude R. Ingersoll Probasco). See *Journal of Zoophily* 1 (1892): 67–68 and 99–100; *Journal of Zoophily* 2 (March 1893): 1; Coleman, *Humane Society Leaders*, 207; and Shultz, *Humane Movement*, 147, 148, and 152. Women also played an integral role in the founding of other notable antivivisection groups, such as NEAVS and NAVS. See Margaret Moreland Stathos, "The History of the New England Anti-Vivisection Society," *NEAVS* 80 (1995 centennial issue): 4–5; *Expressions* (National Anti-Vivisection Society) 2 (1994): 3 and 28–29; and *Journal of Zoophily* 4 (1895): 51.

70. *Journal of Zoophily* 1 (1892): 67–68 and 99–100; *Journal of Zoophily* 8 (December 1899): 136; *Journal of Zoophily* 13 (March 1904): 28; and

Coleman, *Humane Society Leaders,* 186. Mary Lovell also served as secretary to the WPSPCA and president of the Montgomery County SPCA. See Coleman, *Humane Society Leaders,* 186; and Lovell, *Outline of the History,* 1.

71. *First Annual Report of the Women's Branch of the PSPCA* (Philadelphia, 1870), 9.

72. Ibid., 4; *Fifteenth Annual Report of the Women's Branch of the PSPCA* (Philadelphia, 1883), 8; White, *Silver Festival,* 18; and *Forty-first Annual Report of the WPSPCA* (Philadelphia, 1909), 3.

73. WPSPCA Minute Book No. 1, April 28 and June 16, 1869 (Philadelphia); *First Annual Report of the Women's Branch,* 4–5; and Lovell, *Outline of the History,* 1–2.

74. *Eighteenth Annual Report of the Women's Branch,* 4.

75. *First Annual Report of the Women's Branch,* 2–4; and Coleman, *Humane Society Leaders,* 180.

76. *First Annual Report of the Women's Branch,* 5–7.

77. *AAVS Minutes Book: Special Meeting of the Board of Managers of the American Anti-Vivisection Society* (September 22, 1916), 190.

78. Coleman, *Humane Society Leaders,* 185; and Campbell, "Mrs. Caroline Earle White," 48.

CHAPTER 4

1. C. C. Buel, "Henry Bergh and His Work," *Scribner's Monthly* 17 (April 1879): 879; Sydney Coleman, *Humane Society Leaders in America* (Albany, NY: American Humane Association, 1924), 40; and "Henry Bergh," *National Humane Review,* 56 (January–February 1962): 11.

2. *First Annual Report of the Women's Branch of the PSPCA* (Philadelphia, 1870), 3–4.

3. David Favre and Vivien Tsang, "The Development of Anti-cruelty Laws during the 1800's," *Detroit College of Law Review* 1 (Spring 1993): 19; Coleman, *Humane Society Leaders,* 42 and 47; and Buel, "Henry Bergh," 879.

4. Elbridge Gerry, grandson of a Declaration of Independence signer, was also instrumental in the founding of the Society for the Prevention of Cruelty to Children in 1874. See Coleman, *Humane Society Leaders,* 68.

5. Buel, "Henry Bergh," 884; and Coleman, *Humane Society Leaders,* 61.

6. Coleman, *Humane Society Leaders,* 149.

7. *Second Annual Report of the Women's Branch of the PSPCA* (Philadelphia, 1871), 7.

8. *Animals, People, and the MSPCA: 125 Years of Progress* (Boston: MSPCA, 1993), 4.

9. Ibid., 9; *Fifteenth Annual Report of the Women's Branch of the PSPCA* (Philadelphia, 1883), 4.

10. Buel, "Henry Bergh," 872 and 880; and "Henry Bergh," *National Humane Review*, 11.

11. "The Other SPCA," *Penn Monthly Magazine* 12 (January 1881): 53–71.

12. *First Annual Report of the Women's Branch*, 5–6.

13. Buel, "Henry Bergh," 879–81; Coleman, *Humane Society Leaders*, 42–44; Zulma Steele, *Angel in Top Hat: A Biography of Henry Bergh, Founder of American Society for the Prevention of Cruelty to Animals* (New York: Harper and Brothers, 1942), 44–45; and Peggy Robbins, "Henry Bergh, Founder of the ASPCA," *American History Illustrated* 16 (April 1981): 8.

14. Henry Bergh, "The Cost of Cruelty," *North American Review* 133 (July 1881): 81.

15. *Philadelphia Evening Ledger*, January 27, 1917, 10; Caroline Earle White, *Silver Festival of the Women's Branch of the Pennsylvania Society for the Prevention of Cruelty to Animals* (Philadelphia: Women's Branch of the Pennsylvania Society for the Prevention of Cruelty to Animals, 1894), 4; Buel, "Henry Bergh," 872–73, 880, and 884; and Coleman, *Humane Society Leaders*, 49 and 56.

16. *Fourth Annual Report of the Women's Branch of the PSPCA* (Philadelphia, 1873), 12–13; and *Seventy-first Annual Report of the WPSPCA* (Philadelphia, 1939), 14.

17. Buel, "Henry Bergh," 880; Coleman, *Humane Society Leaders*, 43; and James Turner, *Reckoning with the Beast: Animals, Pain, and Humanity in the Victorian Mind* (Baltimore, MD: Johns Hopkins University Press, 1980), 156n35. For information on rising convictions, see *First Annual Report of the Women's Branch*, 4; *Fourth Annual Report of the Women's Branch*, 12–13; and Coleman, *Humane Society Leaders*, 46, 51, 61, and 149.

18. Coleman, *Humane Society Leaders*, 206.

19. Bergh, "Cost of Cruelty," 76.

20. "Henry Bergh," 11.

21. Jane Campbell, "Mrs. Caroline Earle White, Reformer," *Records of the American Catholic Historical Society* 33 (March 1922): 40.

22. Gerald Carson, *Men, Beasts, and Gods: A History of Cruelty and Kindness to Animals* (New York: Charles Scribner's Sons, 1972), 93.

23. *First Annual Report of the Women's Branch*, 3; and Coleman, *Humane Society Leaders*, 44.

24. Buel, "Henry Bergh," 881 and 884.

25. *Second Annual Report of the Women's Branch*, 9.

26. *First Annual Report of the Women's Branch*, 8.

27. Coleman, *Humane Society Leaders*, 111; and *Fourth Annual Report of the Women's Branch*, 12.

28. *Forty-first Annual Report of the WPSPCA* (Philadelphia, 1909), 8.

29. Coleman, *Humane Society Leaders*, 111.

30. Buel, "Henry Bergh," 872–75; and *First Annual Report of the Women's Branch*, 3.

31. Coleman, *Humane Society Leaders*, 43; Bergh, "Cost of Cruelty," 77; and Buel, "Henry Bergh," 881.

32. Buel, "Henry Bergh," 882.

33. William Swallow, *Quality of Mercy: History of the Humane Movement in the United States* (Boston: Mary Mitchell Humane Fund, 1963), 14.

34. *Animals, People, and the MSPCA*, 2; Buel, "Henry Bergh," 880; and *Journal of Zoophily* 12 (June 1903): 93–94. Ultimately, the WPSPCA established a permanent department to administer the erection of fountains. See *Operatic Scenes and Costume Songs under the Direction of Perley Dunn Aldrich for the Benefit of the Horse Watering Stations Department of the Women's PSPCA* [pamphlet] (Philadelphia: WPSPCA, March 6, 1914).

35. Sources dispute whether the WPSPCA or the ASPCA first devised the horse ambulance. See Coleman, *Humane Society Leaders*, 50 and 211–19; *Animals, People, and the MSPCA*, 4; *Angell: 75 Years of Veterinary Excellence, Dedication to Animals, and Humane Care* (Boston: MSPCA, 1990), 6–10; William Shultz, *The Humane Movement in the United States, 1910–1922* (New York: AMS Press, 1968 [1924]), 37; Buel, "Henry Bergh," 884; "History of Caroline Earle White," undated photocopied information provided by Janice Mininberg of the Women's Humane Society (Philadelphia); and *Forty-first Annual Report of the WPSPCA*, 7. Ambulance services and rest farms proved crucial in 1902 when a protracted nationwide coal strike idled mines and left thousands of workhorses without regular care. See Mary Lovell, *Outline of the History of the WPSPCA: From Its Foundation April 14, 1869 to January 1908* (Philadelphia: WPSPCA, 1908), 68.

36. Animal advocate Henry Childs Merwin brought the idea of a parade to the United States from England. Boston held the first workhorse celebration in 1903. See Coleman, *Humane Society Leaders*, 214–15 and 150; and Shultz, *Humane Movement*, 72–74.

37. The Animal and Plant Health Inspection Service of the U.S. Department of Agriculture, "First Federal Law to Prevent Cruelty to Animals," in *Animals and Their Legal Rights: A Survey of American Laws from 1641 to 1978*, 3d ed., ed. Emily Leavitt (Washington, DC: Animal Welfare Institute, 1978), 33.

38. Bergh, "Cost of Cruelty," 80.

39. *Animals into Meat: A Report on the Pre-slaughter Handling of Livestock* (New York: Argus Archives, 1971), 10; Shultz, *Humane Movement*, 112–16; Coleman, *Humane Society Leaders*, 53 and 58; Animal and Plant Health Inspection Service, "First Federal Law," 33; Emily Leavitt, "Humane Slaughter Laws," in *Animals and Their Legal Rights: A Survey of American Laws from 1641 to 1978*, 3d ed., ed. Emily Leavitt (Washington, DC: Animal Welfare Institute, 1978), 36; and James R. Barrett, *Work and Community in the Jungle: Chicago's Packinghouse Workers, 1894–1922* (Chicago: University of Illinois Press, 1990), 24–25.

40. *American Humane Association, 44th Annual Report* (Albany, NY, 1920), 33.

41. Buel, "Henry Bergh," 875; and Leavitt, "Humane Slaughter Laws," 36.

42. Francis H. Rowley, "Slaughter House Reform," paper presented at the International Anti-Vivisection and Animal Protection Congress, Washington, DC, December 8–11, 1913.

43. Bergh, "Cost of Cruelty," 79.

44. Bergh actually argued that the roughshod push for profit blinded industrialists to the economic waste generated by their own cruelty. Incorporating a statistical analysis, he calculated financial losses due to livestock shrinkage at seven locations during 1872 and arrived at the astronomical figure of $44,374,712. See Bergh, "Cost of Cruelty," 78.

45. Coleman, *Humane Society Leaders*, 251–52; Bergh, "Cost of Cruelty," 81; and *Fourth Annual Report of the Women's Branch*, 5–7.

46. Bergh, "Cost of Cruelty," 80–81; Coleman, *Humane Society Leaders*, chaps. 2 and 10; "Early Years," *National Humane Review* 56 (January–February 1962): 20–23; Swallow, *Quality of Mercy*, 11–30; Animal and Plant Health Inspection Service, "First Federal Law," 33–35; *Fourth Annual Report of the Women's Branch*, 5–7; and Mary Lovell, *Outline of the History*, 6–8.

47. Animal and Plant Health Inspection Service, "First Federal Law," 34.

48. Mary Lovell, *Outline of the History*, 54.

49. Animal and Plant Health Inspection Service, "First Federal Law," 34; Shultz, *Humane Movement*, 111; Bergh, "Cost of Cruelty," 79; and U.S. Department of Agriculture, *Animal Health Delivery Systems in the United States* (Washington, DC: USDA, 1984–1985), 2–3, 9, and 14.

50. *American Humane Association, 45th Annual Report* (Albany, NY, 1921), 10.

51. Shultz, *Humane Movement*, 110.

52. Bergh, "Cost of Cruelty," 81.

53. The federal government disbanded the BAI in 1953; its duties currently fall within the jurisdiction of the Food Safety and Inspection Service

(FSIS) and the Animal and Plant Health Inspection Service (APHIS), both agencies within the USDA. See Shultz, *Humane Movement*, 109–13; Animal and Plant Health Inspection Service, "First Federal Law," 34; U.S. Department of Agriculture, *Animal Health Delivery Systems*, 2–3, 9, and 14; and *Animals into Meat*, 15.

54. During the inaugural meeting in Cleveland, delegates voted to name the new association the International Humane Society, but the designation was changed to the AHA the next year. See "Genesis," *National Humane Review* 56 (January–February 1962): 6; and "Early Years," 20.

55. Coleman, *Humane Society Leaders*, 252; and "Early Years," 21–22.

56. Swallow, *Quality of Mercy*, 14; and Campbell, "Mrs. Caroline Earle White," 40.

57. *American Humane Association, 45th Annual Report*, 10.

58. Shultz, *Humane Movement*, 109.

59. Ibid., 117; and Coleman, *Humane Society Leaders*, 255.

60. Mary Lovell, "Progress or Inertia—Which?" *Journal of Zoophily* 8 (January 1899): 7.

61. Ibid.; *Journal of Zoophily* 26 (November 1917): 163; "Early Years," 22; and Turner, *Reckoning with the Beast*, 117–18.

62. Coleman, *Humane Society Leaders*, 252; and "Early Years," 22.

63. In particular, several leaders and organizations publicly discussed and endorsed vegetarianism. See Mary Lovell, "Anti-Vivisection Work in America," paper presented at the International Anti-Vivisection and Animal Protection Congress, Philadelphia, October 17–20, 1926; Rowley, "Slaughter House Reform," 52–53; and Mrs. Fairchild Allen, "The Vivisector's Defense," *Anti-Vivisection* (Journal of the Illinois A-V Society) 3 (January 1896): 2.

64. Coleman, *Humane Society Leaders*, 250–52; and "Early Years," 22.

65. Turner, *Reckoning with the Beast*, 117–18; Lovell, "Progress or Inertia," 7; and Robert Logan, "Popularity and Progress," *Journal of Zoophily* 26 (November 1917): 163.

66. *Journal of Zoophily* 12 (February 1903): 21.

67. Shultz, *Humane Movement*, 35–36.

68. Buel, "Henry Bergh," 882.

69. Coleman, *Humane Society Leaders*, 47–48.

70. Ibid.; Buel, "Henry Bergh," 882; and "Henry Bergh," *National Humane Review*, 12.

71. Swallow, *Quality of Mercy*, 14.

72. *Animal Control in New York City: Past, Present, and Future* [pamphlet] (New York: United Action for Animals, n.d.); *First Annual Report of the Women's Branch*, 5; and Swallow, *Quality of Mercy*, 74.

73. Buel, "Henry Bergh," 880; and John F. Kullberg, "Henry Bergh's Legacy 100 Years Later," Spring 1988, photocopy provided by Kullberg.

74. *First Annual Report of the Women's Branch*, 5.

75. Ibid.; Campbell, "Mrs. Caroline Earle White," 39 and 45; Coleman, *Humane Society Leaders*, 181; Lovell, *Outline of the History*, 37; and *Journal of Zoophily* 13 (August 1904): 92. In 1907, the Morris shelter was renamed Morris Refuge Association, but it was also referred to as the Morris Animal Refuge.

76. Coleman, *Humane Society Leaders*, 209 and 267; Swallow, *Quality of Mercy*, 23, 31, and 39; and *Animals, People, and the MSPCA*, 6.

77. By 1924, Smith's shelter had amassed "large sums of money," and it handled thousands of animals each year. See Coleman, *Humane Society Leaders*, 209; and Swallow, *Quality of Mercy*, 74–76.

78. Coleman, *Humane Society Leaders*, 62 and 267; Shultz, *Humane Movement*, 29, 64, and 68; and *The Anti-Cruelty Society: 75th Anniversary Annual Report* (Chicago: Anti-Cruelty Society, 1974), 1–2. Swallow, in *Quality of Mercy*, discusses early SPCAs and their shelters through much of the first half of his study.

79. *Third Annual Report of the Women's Branch of the PSPCA* (Philadelphia, 1872), 18; and White, *Silver Festival*, 20.

80. Shultz, *Humane Movement*, 65–66.

81. *First Annual Report of the Women's Branch*, 5.

82. Ibid.; *Journal of Zoophily* 13 (August 1904): 92; Coleman, *Humane Society Leaders*, 209; *Anti-Cruelty Society*, 3; and *Bide-a-Wee Newsletter*, Summer 1973, 1.

83. Carbonic acid gas is an archaic term for carbon dioxide. Coleman, *Humane Society Leaders*, 164, 181, and 208; *First Annual Report of the Women's Branch*, 5; *Second Annual Report of the Women's Branch*, 4; *Fifteenth Annual Report of the Women's Branch*, 13; and *Forty-eighth Annual Report of the* WPSPCA (December 1916): 8.

84. Swallow, *Quality of Mercy*, 85; and *Bide-a-Wee Newsletter*, 1.

85. Coleman, *Humane Society Leaders*, 48–49; and A. H. Saxon, *P. T. Barnum: The Legend and the Man* (New York: Columbia University Press, 1989), 391n43.

86. *First Annual Report of the Women's Branch*, 4; Coleman, *Humane Society Leaders*, 48; *Animals, People, and the MSPCA*, 8; and Swallow, *Quality of Mercy*, 22–23 and 29.

87. Buel, "Henry Bergh," 882; and Coleman, *Humane Society Leaders*, 48–49.

88. The seven states were Arizona, Kansas, Louisiana, Maryland, New Mexico, Oregon, and Vermont. See Shultz, *Humane Movement*, 101–2 and 248–52.

89. Coleman, *Humane Society Leaders*, 256.

90. Henry Salt, *Animals' Rights Considered in Relation to Social Progress* (London: Macmillan, 1894), 59.

91. *First Annual Report of the Women's Branch*, 4. In addition, shortly after its formation, the WCTU's Department of Mercy initiated a campaign to end rabbit coursing. See *Journal of Zoophily* 8 (December 1899): 136.

92. Lovell, *Outline of the History*, 39–40.

93. Swallow, *Quality of Mercy*, 29; and Coleman, *Humane Society Leaders*, 104.

94. Many of the state's rural counties weathered the legal fray, and pigeon shoots retained their legality and popularity. Only in Philadelphia County, where White's group enjoyed considerable support, did the contests eventually disappear. See Campbell, "Mrs. Caroline Earle White," 45; *Fifteenth Annual Report of the Women's Branch*, 6; *Journal of Zoophily* 12 (February 1903): 22; and Lovell, *Outline of the History*, 53.

95. John Kullberg, former president and executive director of the ASPCA, interview by author, December 15, 1995, tape recording, Gaithersburg, MD.

96. Coleman, *Humane Society Leaders*, 50–51; and Buel, "Henry Bergh," 882.

97. For Bergh's views, see Buel, "Henry Bergh," 880 and 882. White is quoted in the *Fifteenth Annual Report of the Women's Branch of the PSPCA*, 6.

98. Lisa Mighetto, *Wild Animals and American Environmental Ethics* (Tucson: University of Arizona Press, 1991), 48; James A Tober, *Who Owns the Wildlife? The Political Economy of Conservation in Nineteenth-Century America* (Westport, CT: Greenwood Press, 1981), 210–12; and Coleman, *Humane Society Leaders*, 50–51 and 104.

99. Coleman, *Humane Society Leaders*, 51.

100. Salt, *Animals' Rights*, 53.

101. Robert Engberg, ed., *John Muir: Summering in the Sierra* (Madison: University of Wisconsin Press, 1984), 38–39; and Mighetto, *Wild Animals*, 55–56.

102. Ernest Thompson Seton, *Lives of the Hunted* (New York: Charles Scribner's Sons, 1901); and Seton, "Cruel Methods of Trapping," paper presented at the International Anti-Vivisection and Animal Protection Congress, Washington, DC, December 8–11, 1913.

103. Shultz, *Humane Movement*, 19.

104. Teddy Roosevelt, one of the most notable conservationists of the period, along with Grinnell, who founded the Audubon Society, created the Boone and Crockett Club to conserve game. See Peggy Morrison and

Susan Hagood, *Changing U.S. Trapping Policy: A Handbook for Activists* (Washington, DC: Defenders of Wildlife, 1984), 2–3; and Coleman, *Humane Society Leaders*, 105.

105. For a detailed discussion of his view of hunting and its spiritual and physical benefits, see Theodore Roosevelt, *The Wilderness Hunter* (New York: P. F. Collier and Son, 1893).

106. Stephen Kellert and Miriam Westervelt, "Historical Trends in American Animal Use and Perception," *International Journal for the Study of Animal Problems* 4 (1983): 137 and 145.

107. The AHA and the Colorado State Bureau of Child and Animal Protection initiated campaigns to "modify the evils" of rodeos and Wild West shows and achieved some success. See Coleman, *Humane Society Leaders*, 172 and 256. Notably, however, organization publications and records before the twentieth century mention few serious protests over any of these events, which further indicates that the early movement did not make much progress on this issue.

108. Philip B. Kunhardt Jr., Philip B. Kunhardt III, and Peter Kunhardt, *P. T. Barnum: America's Greatest Showman* (New York: Alfred A. Knopf, 1995), 269.

109. Ibid.

110. Saxon, *P. T. Barnum*, 235–38; Salt, *Animals' Rights*, chap. 3 and esp. p. 39; E. B. Nicholson, *The Rights of Animal: A New Essay in Ethics* (London: Kegan Paul, 1879); and Alexander Pope, "Animal Life in a Zoo: The Modern Way of Keeping Animals," *Scientific American* 112 (April 24, 1915): 390.

111. Martin Kaufman and Herbert Kaufman, "Salamander the Fire Horse," *American History Illustrated* 15 (October 1980): 36.

112. Steele, *Angel in Top Hat*, 236–37.

113. Ibid.

114. The entire exchange appeared in the *New York World*, March 19, 1867.

115. Steele, *Angel in Top Hat*, 236–37.

116. Kaufman and Kaufman, "Salamander the Fire Horse," 36–38; and Saxon, *P. T. Barnum*, 236–37.

117. Although their primary thesis involves perceptions of woodlands, Thomas Cox, Robert Maxwell, Phillip Thomas, and Joseph Malone briefly discuss settlers' antagonistic perceptions of wild animals in *This Well-Wooded Land: Americans and Their Forests from Colonial Times to the Present* (Lincoln: University of Nebraska Press, 1985), chap. 1. Also see Roderick Nash, *The Rights of Nature: A History of Environmental Ethics* (Madison: University of Wisconsin Press, 1989), 35.

118. *Journal of Zoophily* 2 (January 1893): 6; and *Journal of Zoophily* 3 (January 1894): 7.

119. Several thorny political issues complicated federal intervention on behalf of the bison. President Ulysses S. Grant, as well as many members of Congress, expressed reservations about any policy that potentially impeded the expansion of the railroads, western settlement, or even the rights of sport hunters. Equally important, the government viewed the buffalo's destruction as a weapon in breaking the resistance of the more stubborn Plains tribes. See Greta Nilsson, "The Fur Trade, a Short History," in *Facts about Furs* (Washington, DC: Animal Welfare Institute, 1980), 5; and Philip Weeks, *Farewell, My Nation: The American Indian and the United States, 1820–1890* (Arlington Heights, IL: Harlan Davis, 1990), 47, 163–64, and 169–73. For the congressional report, see U.S. Congress, Senate, Committee on Territories, *Reports of Committees*, 43rd Cong., 1st sess., June 9, 1874, *Congressional Record*, 4705. For general involvement on this issue, see Coleman, *Humane Society Leaders*, 256; "Early Years," 22; Clara Morris, "Riddle of the Nineteenth Century: Mr. Henry Bergh," *McClure's Magazine* 18 (March 1902): 422; *Third Annual Report of the Women's Branch*, 14; and Lovell, *Outline of the History*, 7.

120. Nilsson, "Fur Trade," 5.

121. Morrison and Hagood, *Changing U.S. Trapping*, 2.

122. Seward Newhouse invented the trap, and by 1867, his factory manufactured 750,000 of the devices each year. See ibid., 2; and *Furs and Fashion: Traps and Trapping* (New York: Argus Archives, 1971), 4 and 5.

123. Nilsson, "Fur Trade," 3, 7, and 11.

124. *Journal of Zoophily*, 2 (November 1893): 1; *Journal of Zoophily* 9 (February 1900): 18; *Journal of Zoophily* 12 (June 1903): 71; and *Journal of Zoophily* 25 (January 1916): 12.

125. Nilsson, "Fur Trade," 10; and William T. Hornaday, *Our Vanishing Wildlife: Its Extermination and Preservation* (New York: Zoological Society, 1913).

126. Nilsson, "Fur Trade," 7.

127. Shultz, *Humane Movement*, 250.

128. Lovell, *Outline of the History*, 33–34.

129. *Journal of Zoophily* 13 (March 1904): 28.

130. According to Coleman, White championed the cause of bird preservation before the advent of Audubon societies, but I could find nothing in any records to confirm his statement. See Coleman, *Humane Society Leaders*, 183.

131. *Florence Merriam Bailey: Pioneer Naturalist*, n.d., Saint Lawrence County, NY, Branch of the American Association of University Women,

www.northnet.org/stlawrenceaauw/bailey.htm (July 17, 2005). Also see H. Kofalk, *No Woman Tenderfoot: Florence Merriam Bailey* (College Station: Texas A&M Press, 1989); Cynthia Parsons, *George Bird Grinnell: A Biographical Sketch* (Lanham, MD: University Press of America, 1992); Morrison and Hagood, *Changing U.S. Trapping*, 3; and Rosewell McCrea, *The Humane Movement: A Descriptive Survey* (New York: Columbia University Press, 1910), 127–34 and 247–55.

132. *Animals, People, and the MSPCA*, 9; and *Eighteenth Annual Report of the Women's Branch of the PSPCA* (Philadelphia, 1886), 7.

133. *First Annual Report of the Women's Branch*, 9–10; and *Proceedings of the Fourth Conservation Congress* (Indianapolis, IN: National Conservation Congress, 1912), 258–62; quote is from Carolyn Merchant, ed., *Major Problems in American Environmental History* (Lexington, MA: D. C. Heath, 1993), 355.

134. *Journal of Zoophily* 8 (January 1899): 8; and Carolyn Merchant, "The Women of the Progressive Conservation Crusade, 1900–1915," in *Environmental History: Critical Issues in Comparative Perspective*, ed. Kendall E. Bailes (Lanham, MD: University Press of America, 1985), 153–70.

135. Coleman, *Humane Society Leaders*, 221–22.

136. Lovell, *Outline of the History*, 33–34.

137. Morrison and Hagood, *Changing U.S. Trapping*, 3; and Dona Finnley, "Laws to Protect Wildlife," in *Animals and Their Legal Rights: A Survey of American Laws from 1641 to 1978*, 3d ed., ed. Emily Leavitt (Washington, DC: Animal Welfare Institute, 1978), 175–76.

138. *Animals, People, and the MSPCA*, 8; Finnley, "Laws to Protect Wildlife"; and Coleman, *Humane Society Leaders*, 221–22.

139. Merchant, "Women," 157–64.

140. *Animals, People, and the MSPCA*, 8; Finnley, "Laws to Protect Wildlife"; and Coleman, *Humane Society Leaders*, 221–22.

141. Coleman, *Humane Society Leaders*, 222.

142. *Animals, People, and the MSPCA*, 3; and George T. Angell, *Autobiographical Sketches and Personal Reflections* (Boston: American Humane Education Society, 1892), app. and 5.

143. *First Annual Report of the Women's Branch*, 10.

144. Campbell, "Mrs. Caroline Earle White," 41–42.

145. *First Annual Report of the Women's Branch*, 5; and Lovell, *Outline of the History*, 62. An example of a prize-winning essay was Elizabeth Wright's 1900 entry, "What Patience and Kindness Will Accomplish with Animals." See *Journal of Zoophily* 9 (January 1900): 3–4; *Fourth Annual Report of the Women's Branch*, 13; and *Sixth Annual Report of the Women's Branch of the PSPCA* (Philadelphia, 1875): 19–20.

146. *Journal of Zoophily* 8 (December 1899): 136.

147. Mary Lovell, "Humane Education," paper presented at the International Anti-Vivisection and Animal Protection Congress (1913); and *American Humane Association, 39th Annual Report* (Albany, NY, 1915).

148. Wyoming (1901), Pennsylvania (1905), North Dakota (1905), Texas (1907), and Illinois (1909) all mandated compulsory instruction in kindness. See *Journal of Zoophily* 8 (December 1899): 136; Shultz, *Humane Movement,* 264 and 304; and Coleman, *Humane Society Leaders,* 190.

149. Coleman, *Humane Society Leaders,* 91 and 103; Swallow, *Quality of Mercy,* 18; *Animals, People, and the MSPCA,* 2; "Humane Educator," *National Humane Review* 56 (January–February 1962): 13; "The Life and Times of George Thorndike Angell," *Animals* (June 1980): 13; and Angell, *Autobiographical Sketches,* 82–86.

150. *Fourth Annual Report of the Women's Branch,* 13; *Sixth Annual Report of the Women's Branch,* 19–20; *Fifteenth Annual Report of the Women's Branch,* 6–7; and *Journal of Zoophily* 12 (August 1903): 97. The only book that even suggests that White initiated the first club is Coleman's *Humane Society Leaders,* 181–82.

151. Angell, *Autobiographical Sketches,* 78–98; Shultz, *Humane Movement,* 38, 69, and chap. 8; and *Journal of Zoophily* 8 (December 1899): 136.

152. Louis Harlan, ed., *The Booker T. Washington Papers,* vol. 2, *1860–1889* (Chicago: University of Illinois, 1972), 242–43.

153. Coleman, *Humane Society Leaders,* 263; "That Special Week," *National Humane Review* 56 (January–February 1962): 48–50; Swallow, *Quality of Mercy,* 174; and *American Humane Association, 38th Annual Report* (Albany, NY, 1914), 14.

154. Castle lectured on behalf of the AAVS and financed the construction of a shelter for strays, Orphans of the Storm, in Illinois. Fiske joined various groups and frequently addressed large gatherings of women on issues ranging from trapping to slaughter reform. See *Starry Cross* 29 (January 1920): 9 (from 1920 to 1939, the *Journal of Zoophily* was renamed the *Starry Cross,* and it became the A-V in 1940); *AAVS Minutes Book: The Monthly Stated Meeting of the Board of Managers of the AAVS* (Philadelphia, April 30, 1941); Carson, *Men, Beasts, and Gods,* 122–23; Coleman, *Humane Society Leaders,* 193; and *1883–1983: 100 Years against Cruelty* [pamphlet] (Jenkintown, PA: American Anti-Vivisection Society, 1983).

155. *Journal of Zoophily* 9 (January 1900): 7.

CHAPTER 5

1. For the scholars who perceive a decline in the general movement, see Lawrence Finsen and Susan Finsen, *The Animal Rights Movement in Amer-*

ica: From Compassion to Respect (New York: Twayne Publishers, 1994), 50; Andrew Rowan, "The Development of the Animal Protection Movement," *Journal of NIH Research* 1 (November–December 1989): 97; James Turner, *Reckoning with the Beast: Animals, Pain, and Humanity in the Victorian Mind* (Baltimore, MD: Johns Hopkins University Press, 1980), 122–23; Laurence Pringle, *The Animal Rights Controversy* (New York: Harcourt Brace Jovanovich, 1989), 9–11; James Jasper and Dorothy Nelkin, *The Animal Rights Crusade: The Growth of a Moral Protest* (New York: Free Press, 1992), 60; and Charles Niven, *History of the Humane Movement* (New York: Transatlantic Press, 1967), 100–114.

2. Turner, *Reckoning with the Beast*, 122–23.

3. For general studies on the Progressive movement, see Paul Boyer, *Urban Masses and Moral Order in America, 1820–1920* (Cambridge, MA: Harvard University Press, 1992); Steven Diner, *A Very Different Age: America in the Progressive Era* (New York: Hill and Wang, 1998); and Allen F. Davis, *Spearheads for Reform: The Social Settlements and the Progressive Movement* (New York: Oxford University Press, 1967). Linda Gordon's pathbreaking study of the history of domestic abuse demonstrates that Progressives believed wife battering and child battering contributed to a general weakening of the family. See Linda Gordon, *Heroes of Their Own Lives: The Politics and History of Family Violence* (New York: Viking Penguin, 1988), 21, 61, and 73–74; Robyn Muncy, *Creating a Female Dominion in American Reform, 1890–1935* (New York: Oxford University Press, 1991); *The PETA Guide to Animal Liberation* (Washington, DC: PETA, n.d., 1993?), 8; and Sidney Coleman, *Humane Society Leaders in America* (Albany, NY: American Humane Association, 1924), 188.

4. The ASPCA prosecuted New York City's first child abuse case in 1874, and in 1885, the AHA began investigating child cruelty cases. In smaller or rural communities, typically one officer administered both animal and child cases. A few societies, such as the Chattanooga Humane Education Society, added the protection of both children and battered women to their animal advocacy agenda in the 1920s. See William Shultz, *The Humane Movement in the United States, 1910–1922* (New York: AMS Press, 1968 [1924]), 11, 124–25, and 184–88; Coleman, *Humane Society Leaders*, 225 and 257; *American Humane Association, 46th Annual Report* (Albany, NY, 1922), 62; and *The Anti-Cruelty Society: 75th Anniversary Annual Report* (Chicago: Anti-Cruelty Society), 1–2.

5. During 1918, the tiny Western Pennsylvania Humane Society netted $4,150 from direct mailings. See Shultz, *Humane Movement*, 89. For evidence of mainstream acceptance and celebrity support, see Coleman, *Humane Society Leaders*, 193 and 269–70; Albert Schweitzer, *Part II: Civilization and Ethics*, trans. John Naish (London: A. and C. Black, 1923); Ann

Cottrell Free, ed., *Animals, Nature, and Albert Schweitzer* (Washington, DC: Flying Fox Press, 1988); *Great Minds Think Alike* [pamphlet] (Mill Valley, CA: In Defense of Animals, n.d.); *Anti-Cruelty Society: 75th Anniversary Annual Report,* 3; and Gerald Carson, *Men, Beasts, and Gods: A History of Cruelty and Kindness to Animals* (New York: Charles Scribner's Sons, 1972), 123.

6. *First Annual Report of the Women's Branch of the PSPCA* (Philadelphia, 1870); 5–7; William Swallow, *Quality of Mercy: History of the Humane Movement in the United States* (Boston: Mary Mitchell Humane Fund, 1963), 23; and Coleman, *Humane Society Leaders,* 267.

7. Coleman, *Humane Society Leaders,* 267; John F. Kullberg, "Henry Bergh's Legacy 100 Years Later" (Spring 1988), copy provided by Kullberg; Shultz, *Humane Movement,* 30 and 56; and Swallow, *Quality of Mercy,* 10–157.

8. *Anti-Cruelty Society: 75th Anniversary Annual Report,* 1–3; Swallow, *Quality of Mercy,* 10–157; and *Animals, People, and the MSPCA: 125 Years of Progress* (Boston: MSPCA, 1993).

9. *Anti-Cruelty Society: 75th Anniversary Annual Report,* 3; Swallow, *Quality of Mercy,* 76 and 99; Shultz, *Humane Movement,* 66–68; Coleman, *Humane Society Leaders,* 123–24; and Elliot Evans, "A Historic Perspective: The Early Years," in *The Latham Foundation: First in Humane Education—Since 1918* (Alameda, CA: Latham Foundation, n.d.), 3–4.

10. Swallow, *Quality of Mercy,* 113–14; Coleman, *Humane Society Leaders,* 213; *The Anti-Cruelty Society: 75th Anniversary Annual Report,* 2–3; *Forty-first Annual Report of the WPSPCA* (Philadelphia, 1909), 7; and *Sixty-eighth Annual Report of the WPSPCA* (Philadelphia, 1936), 3, 5, and 8.

11. Since just one of the ASPCA hospitals cost an estimated $200,000 to build, it seems unlikely that the city pound duties completely drained the organization's finances. See Coleman, *Humane Society Leaders,* 211–13. Also see *Angell: 75 Years of Veterinary Excellence, Dedication to Animals, and Humane Care* (Boston: MSPCA, 1990), 8; Swallow, *Quality of Mercy,* 15, 18, 23, and 26; and Shultz, *Humane Movement,* 30 and 36.

12. Swallow, *Quality of Mercy,* 178; and Evans, "Historic Perspective," 3–4.

13. Here again, I would suggest some of the general studies on the Progressive movement, as mentioned earlier. See Boyer, *Urban Masses*; Diner, *Very Different Age*; and Davis, *Spearheads for Reform.*

14. Shultz, *Humane Movement,* 23, 99, 124–25, and 140; and *American Humane Association, 46th Annual Report*: 64.

15. Coleman, *Humane Society Leaders,* 264; and Evans, "Historic Perspective," 3–4.

16. Coleman, *Humane Society Leaders*, 191 and 262; *American Humane Association, 39th Annual Report* (Albany, NY, 1915), 1–10; *American Humane Association, 45th Annual Report* (Albany, NY, 1921), 18; and Shultz, *Humane Movement*, 263–64.

17. *Anti-Cruelty Society: 75th Anniversary Annual Report*, 3; and Shultz, *Humane Movement*, 127–29.

18. *Anti-Cruelty Society: 75th Anniversary Annual Report*, 3; Evans, "Historic Perspective," 3–4; and Swallow, *Quality of Mercy*, 76 and 99. Interestingly, for a Boy Scout to receive a badge for first aid, he had to pass a test in which he could, among other ministrations, treat a horse for colic. See Shultz, *Humane Movement*, 130–32.

19. *American Humane Association, 44th Annual Report* (Albany, NY, 1920), 15; Coleman, *Humane Society Leaders*, 263–64; and *Seventy-first Annual Report of the WPSPCA* (Philadelphia, 1939), 9.

20. Coleman, *Humane Society Leaders*, 264.

21. *Anti-Cruelty Society: 75th Anniversary Annual Report*, 4; Swallow, *Quality of Mercy*, 15; Evans, "Historic Perspective," 3–4; Shultz, *Humane Movement*, 123; *1883–1983: 100 Years against Cruelty* [pamphlet] (Jenkintown, PA: American Anti-Vivisection Society, 1983), 6; and *Starry Cross* 41 (June 1933): 71.

22. Coleman, *Humane Society Leaders*, 133–34; Shultz, *Humane Movement*, 122–23; and Swallow, *Quality of Mercy*, 102–9.

23. *Fiftieth Annual Report of the WPSPCA* (Philadelphia, 1918), 5–6; and Shultz, *Humane Movement*, 56–60.

24. The English organization was called the English Red Star and was sponsored by the RSPCA. See Coleman, *Humane Society Leaders*, 129–30.

25. Ibid.; and Shultz, *Humane Movement*, 60–61.

26. *Forty-sixth Annual Report of the WPSPCA* (Philadelphia, 1914), 4; *Fiftieth Annual Report of the WPSPCA*, 30; and Coleman, *Humane Society Leaders*, 195.

27. Coleman, *Humane Society Leaders*, 131; and Shultz, *Humane Movement*, 31.

28. Coleman, *Humane Society Leaders*, 132; *Fiftieth Annual Report of the WPSPCA*, 30; and Shultz, *Humane Movement*, 62. Red Star was ultimately renamed Emergency Animal Relief after World War II. See Swallow, *Quality of Mercy*, 163; and *1994 Annual Report of the American Humane Association* (Englewood, CO, 1994), 7.

29. *Anti-Cruelty Society: 75th Anniversary Annual Report*, 4; and *A-V* 50 (February 1942): 18.

30. Richard Dempewolff, *Animal Reveille* (New York: Doubleday, Doran, 1945); *A-V* 50 (February 1942): 18; and *A-V* 50 (October 1942): 129–30.

31. During the 1920s and 1930s, estimates of the mortality rates among range stock varied, but studies by humane groups indicated that between one and two million animals died from starvation, thirst, and exposure each year. See Shultz, *Humane Movement*, 118; and Coleman, *Humane Society Leaders*, 132 and 254.

32. Coleman, *Humane Society Leaders*, 132–33, 163, 172, and 255; *American Humane Association, 43rd Annual Report* (Albany, NY, 1919), 15; and *Fiftieth Annual Report of the WPSPCA*, 30.

33. *American Humane Association, 41st Annual Report* (Albany, NY, 1917).

34. Shultz, *Humane Movement*, 107.

35. *American Humane Association, 44th Annual Report*; and Shultz, *Humane Movement*, 117.

36. Shultz, *Humane Movement*, 117; Coleman, *Humane Society Leaders*, 255–57; *American Humane Association, 46th Annual Report*; and Swallow, *Quality of Mercy*, 76.

37. *Film Monitoring*, 2005, American Humane Association, http://www.americanhumane.org/site/PageServer?pagename=pa_film (July 7, 2005); Sian Lawson, "Digital Horses: Ending Cruelty in Film," International Fund for Horses, http://www.fund4horses.org/info.php?id=128 (July 10, 2005); Karen O'Connor, *Sharing the Kingdom: Animals and Their Rights* (New York: Dodd, Mead, 1984), 40–41; Shultz, *Humane Movement*, 102; and Jill Donner, "Lassie Stay Home," WGAW (April 1989): 23.

38. Donner, "Lassie Stay Home," 23, and Swallow, *Quality of Mercy*, 163.

39. *Starry Cross* 29 (February 1920): 27.

40. Jack London, *Michael, Brother of Jerry* (New York: Macmillan, 1917), vi.

41. *PETA Guide to Animal Liberation*, 27; London, *Michael*, 234, 245, 299, and 304.

42. George Chindahl, *A History of the Circus in America* (Caldwell, ID: Caxton Printers, 1959), 122–23.

43. London, *Michael*; and Jack London, *Jerry of the Islands* (New York: Macmillan, 1916).

44. London, *Michael*, 304.

45. Ibid., vi.

46. Ibid., vi–vii.

47. Ibid., vii–viii.

48. *Animals, People, and the MSPCA*, 6 and 10; and Shultz, *Humane Movement*, 133–34.

49. Although the club had no official membership roster, organizers kept track of supporters through pledges, mailings, and the press. See Swallow, *Quality of Mercy*, 64; and Shultz, *Humane Movement*, 123 and 133–34.

50. As quoted in Chindahl, *History of the Circus*, 209.

51. Ibid., 168.

52. Ibid., 230–31.

53. *Sixty-eighth Annual Report of the WPSPCA*, 8; and "Rules and Regulations on Zoos," in *Animals and Their Legal Rights*, 3d ed., ed. Emily Leavitt (Washington, DC: Animal Welfare Institute, 1978), app., xxxix.

54. I would urge those interested in this subject to read Lisa Mighetto's fine study on such shifting attitudes, *Wild Animals and American Environmental Ethics* (Tucson: University of Arizona Press, 1991), 24, 25, 69, and 86–90. Also see James Oliver Curwood, *The Grizzly King* (New York: Cosmopolitan Books, 1918); Mary Austin, *Land of Little Rain* (Boston: Houghton Mifflin, 1903); Ernest Thompson Seton, *Lives of the Hunted* (New York: Charles Scribners' Sons, 1901); Seton, *Animal Heroes* (New York: Charles Scribners' Sons, 1905); and Seton, *The Arctic Prairies* (New York: Charles Scribners' Sons, 1911).

55. Some of the best studies of conservation include Samuel Hays, *Conservation and the "Gospel of Efficiency": The Progressive Conservation Movement, 1890–1920* (Cambridge, MA: Harvard University Press, 1959); Roderick Nash, *The Rights of Nature: A History of Environmental Ethics* (Madison: University of Wisconsin Press, 1989), chap. 3; and Donald Worster, *Nature's Economy: A History of Ecological Ideas* (New York: Cambridge University Press, 1991), chaps. 13 and 14. Lisa Mighetto's study of environmental ethics includes a particularly interesting discussion of the changing views of predators; see Mighetto, *Wild Animals*, chap. 5.

56. Women also played a key role in these conservation efforts. See Glenda Riley, *Women and Nature: Saving the Wild West* (Lincoln: University of Nebraska Press, 1999); Carolyn Merchant, "The Women of the Progressive Conservation Crusade, 1900–1915," in *Environmental History: Critical Issues in Comparative Perspective*, ed. Kendall E. Bailes (Lanham, MD: University Press of America, 1985), 153–70; and Vera Norwood, *Made from This Earth: American Women and Nature* (Chapel Hill: University of North Carolina Press, 1993).

57. Peggy Morrison and Susan Hagood, *Changing U.S. Trapping Policy: A Handbook for Activists* (Washington, DC: Defenders of Wildlife, 1984), 42.

58. Worster, *Nature's Economy*, 263–64; Morrison and Hagood, *Changing U.S. Trapping*, 45; and Christine Stevens, "From Fur Bearer to Fur Wearer: The Agony of the Transition," in *Facts about Furs* (Washington, DC: Animal Welfare Institute, 1980), 116–17.

59. Worster, *Nature's Economy*, 259; and Morrison and Hagood, *Changing U.S. Trapping*, 45.

60. Thomas Dunlap, *Saving America's Wildlife* (Princeton, NJ: Princeton University Press, 1988), 111–24.

61. Worster, *Nature's Economy*, 270; and Mighetto, *Wild Animals*, 95.

62. Liberty Hyde Bailey, *The Holy Earth* (New York: Charles Scribner's Sons, 1915), 30–31.

63. Worster, *Nature's Economy*, 275 and 279; and Nash, *Rights of Nature*, 57.

64. Arthur Tansley, "The Use and Abuse of Vegetational Concepts and Terms," *Ecology* 16 (1935): 284–306.

65. Worster, *Nature's Economy*, 284; Aldo Leopold, "The Conservation Ethic," *Journal of Forestry* 31 (October 1933): 634–43; and Leopold, *A Sand County Almanac and Sketches Here and There* (New York: Oxford University Press, 1968), vii, 129, and 201–6.

66. Worster, *Nature's Economy*, 277 and 284; and Nash, *Rights of Nature*, 57–59.

67. Berg Bengt, *The Motherless* (New York: Doubleday, 1924); Henry Williamson, *Tarka the Otter* (New York: E. P. Dutton, 1928); Rachel Carson, *Under the Sea Wind: A Naturalist's Picture of Ocean Life* (New York: Simon and Schuster, 1941); Donald C. Peattie, *An Almanac for Moderns* (New York: G. P. Putnam's Sons, 1935); and Cherry Keaton, *The Island of Penguins* (New York: Viking Press, 1931).

68. Stephen Kellert and Miriam Westervelt, "Historical Trends in American Animal Use and Perception," *International Journal for the Study of Animal Problems* 4 (1983): 137–38 and 144–45.

69. The figure for automobiles on the road is from Alan Brinkley and Ellen Fitzpatrick, *America in Modern Times since 1890* (New York: McGraw-Hill, 1997), 196.

70. Schweitzer, *Part II: Civilization and Ethics*; *Animals, People, and the MSPCA*, 8; and Free, *Animals, Nature, and Albert Schweitzer.*

71. Coleman, *Humane Society Leaders*, 133; *A-V* 47 (January 1939): 82–83; and *Animals, People, and the MSPCA*, 8.

72. Henry Osborn and Harold Anthony, "Can We Save the Mammals?" *Natural History* 22 (1922): 389–415.

73. From 1919 to 1920, a warden with the BBS surveyed a section of Alaska once heavily populated with arctic fox and found the "tracks of but one fox." See E. W. Nelson, "Decrease of Fur-Bearing Animals in Alaska," *Natural History* 22 (1922): 83.

74. Greta Nilsson, "The Fur Trade, a Short History," in *Facts about Furs* (Washington, DC: Animal Welfare Institute, 1980), 11–12.

75. Osborn and Anthony, "Can We Save the Mammals?" 410–15; Morrison and Hagood, *Changing U.S. Trapping*, 4; and Nilsson, "Fur Trade," 15–16.

76. Cleveland Amory, *Man Kind? Our Incredible War on Wildlife* (New York: Harper and Row, 1974), 207; and Morrison and Hagood, *Changing U.S. Trapping*, 4.

77. Niven, *History of the Humane Movement*, 114–15. Also see Amory, *Man Kind?* 207–9; Morrison and Hagood, *Changing U.S. Trapping*, 4; Coleman, *Humane Society Leaders*, 264–65; and *1883–1983: 100 Years against Cruelty*, 8.

78. Lucy Furman, "The Price of Furs," *Atlantic Monthly* 141 (February 1928): 206–9.

79. Ibid.; Coleman, *Humane Society Leaders*, 264–65; Morrison and Hagood, *Changing U.S. Trapping*, chap. 4; *PETA Guide to Animal Liberation*, 25; *Furs and Fashion: Traps and Trapping* (New York: Argus Archives, 1971), 5–11; Ernest Thompson Seton, "Cruel Methods of Trapping," paper presented at the International Anti-Vivisection and Animal Protection Congress, Washington, DC, December 8–11, 1913; and *Journal of Zoophily* 25 (January 1916): 12.

80. Weldon B. Robinson, "The 'Humane Coyote-Getter' vs. the Steel Trap in Control of Predatory Animals," *Journal of Wildlife Management* 7 (1943): 179–89.

81. Furman, "Price of Furs," 206–9.

82. Amory, *Man Kind?* 208.

83. Charlotte Perkins Gilman, "A Study in Ethics," Schlesinger Library, Radcliffe College, Cambridge, MA, 1933; quote is from Josephine Donovan, "Animal Rights and Feminist Theory," in *Beyond Animal Rights: A Feminist Caring Ethic for the Treatment of Animals*, ed. Josephine Donovan and Carol Adams (New York: Continuum, 1996), 36.

84. Amory, *Man Kind?* 207–9; Furman, "Price of Furs," 206–9; Sally Ranney, "Heroines and Hierarchy: Female Leadership in the Conservation Movement," in *Voices from the Environmental Movement: Perspectives for a New Era*, ed. Donald Snow (Covelo, CA: Island Press, 1992), 117–23; and Norwood, *Made from This Earth*, pref., 157.

85. *Starry Cross* 29 (January 1920): 9; *Furs and Fashion: Traps and Trapping*, 20–26; and Amory, *Man Kind?* 212–14.

86. I found it interesting that fake furs even existed in the 1930s. Perhaps they emerged to satisfy the smaller consumer budgets of the Depression. See *1883–1983: 100 Years against Cruelty*, 8; *Journal of Zoophily* 25 (January 1916): 12; *Starry Cross* 29 (January 1920): 9; and *A-V* 47 (January 1939): 82–83.

87. Furman, "Price of Furs," 206–9; Coleman, *Humane Society Leaders*, 264–65; Stevens, "From Fur Bearer to Fur Wearer," 114; Morrison and Hagood, *Changing U.S. Trapping*, 4; and Mighetto, *Wild Animals*, 58.

88. Dunlap, *Saving America's Wildlife*, 93.

89. Shultz, *Humane Movement*, 102; Morrison and Hagood, *Changing U.S. Trapping*, 4; and Nilsson, "Fur Trade," 16.

90. As quoted in *Animals, People, and the MSPCA*, 10.

91. In 1974, the MSPCA successfully lobbied for a new trap bill, and in 1996, yet another tougher law went into effect, banning leghold and body-gripping traps and prohibiting the use of dogs to hunt. The 1996 referendum passed overwhelmingly, by 64 to 36 percent. See *Animals, People, and the MSPCA*, 10; and "We Won! Wildlife Protection Act Is a Historic Victory for Animals," *Animal Action*, Fall 1996, 1.

92. Morrison and Hagood, *Changing U.S. Trapping*, 4.

93. Nelson, "Decrease of Fur-Bearing Animals," 83; and Robinson, "'Humane Coyote-Getter,'" 179–89.

94. Shultz, *Humane Movement*, 98.

CHAPTER 6

1. In 1869, the Medical Society of the State of Pennsylvania resolved that "the profession is competent to declare . . . what shall be the standard of attainments for those to be recognized and admitted to its ranks." See *Twentieth Annual Meeting of the Medical Society of the State of Pennsylvania* (Erie, PA, June 1869), in Howard Petry, ed., A *Century of Medicine, 1848–1948: The History of the Medical Society of the State of Pennsylvania* (Harrisburg: Medical Society of the State of Pennsylvania, 1952), 48. Also see Albert Leffingwell, "The Future of Vivisection," paper presented at the International Anti-Vivisection and Animal Protection Congress, Washington, DC, December 8–11, 1913; and Frances Power Cobbe and Benjamin Bryan, *Vivisection in America* (London: Swan Sonnenschein and Co., 1890), 5. For one of the best general discussions of how the biomedical profession has historically defined and perpetuated itself, see Thomas Kuhn, *The Structure of Scientific Revolutions* (Chicago: University of Chicago Press, 1970).

2. Albert Leffingwell, "Vivisection in America," appendix to Henry Salt, *Animals' Rights Considered in Relation to Social Progress* (London: Macmillan, 1894), 140.

3. James Turner, *Reckoning with the Beast: Animals, Pain, and Humanity in the Victorian Mind* (Baltimore, MD: Johns Hopkins University Press, 1980), 115–19.

4. The Marine Hygienic Laboratory later evolved into the National Institutes of Health. See Edward Shorter, *The Health Century* (New York: Doubleday, 1987), 7, 19, and 23–25.

5. Ibid., 17; and Louis Galambos and Merck, *Values and Visions: A Merck Century* (Rahway, NJ: Merck, 1991), 15, 20, and 185.

6. Some, such as the Rockefeller Institute, bypassed private breeding companies and built their own facilities; the institute built a farm in New Jersey in 1907. See Leffingwell, "Future of Vivisection," 105–10; and "The Antivivisection Agitation in N.Y.," *Journal of the American Medical Association* 54 (1910): 1062–63.

7. Mary Ann Elston, "Women and Anti-vivisection in Victorian England, 1870–1900," in *Vivisection in Historical Perspective*, ed. Nicolas A. Rupke (London: Croom Helm, 1987), 272–73; and Roberta Kalechofsky, *Autobiography of a Revolutionary* (Marblehead, MA: Micah Publications, 1991), 108.

8. For a discussion of the rise of pet-keeping, see Harriet Ritvo, *The Animal Estate: The English and Other Creatures in the Victorian Age* (Cambridge, MA: Harvard University Press, 1987); and Kathleen Kete, *The Beast in the Boudoir: Petkeeping in Nineteenth-Century Paris* (Los Angeles: University of California Press, 1994).

9. Henry Salt, *Animals' Rights Considered in Relation to Social Progress* (London: Macmillan, 1894), 33.

10. Robert Sharpe, *Consenting Guinea Pigs: The Human Participants Who Advance Medicine* (Jenkintown, PA: American Anti-Vivisection Society [1991?]), 12–13; and Richard French, *Antivivisection and Medical Science in Victorian Society* (Princeton, NJ: Princeton University Press, 1975), 20–33, 55–56, and 126.

11. Richard Simmonds, *Abbreviated History of the Animal Welfare/Antivivisection/Rights Movements* (Bethesda, MD: Uniformed Services University of the Health Sciences, 1986), 4; and Albert Leffingwell, "Does Vivisection Pay?" *Scribner's Monthly* 20 (July 1880): 391.

12. Margaret Moreland Stathos, "The History of the New England Anti-Vivisection Society," *NEAVS* 80 (centennial issue): 4–5.

13. Leffingwell, "Does Vivisection Pay?" 391; and Henry Childs Merwin, "Vivisection," *Atlantic Monthly* 89 (March 1902): 325.

14. Leffingwell, "Does Vivisection Pay?" 398.

15. Studies that describe Bergh as opposing all vivisection include Sydney Coleman, *Humane Society Leaders in America* (Albany, NY: American Humane Association, 1924), 204; Lisa Mighetto, *Wild Animals and American Environmental Ethics* (Tucson: University of Arizona Press, 1991), 59; and Turner, *Reckoning with the Beast*, 87. An alternative perspective appears in a magazine interview with Bergh; see C. C. Buel, "Henry Bergh and His Work," *Scribner's Monthly* 17 (April 1879): 881.

16. *Second Annual Report of the Women's Branch of the PSPCA* (Philadelphia, 1871), 12–13.

17. Coleman, *Humane Society Leaders*, 204.

18. *1883–1983: 100 Years against Cruelty* [pamphlet] (Jenkintown, PA: American Anti-Vivisection Society, 1983); *Fifteenth Annual Report of the Women's Branch of the PSPCA* (Philadelphia, 1883), 3; Jane Campbell, "Mrs. Caroline Earle White, Reformer," *Records of the Catholic Historical Society* 33 (March 1922): 43; *Journal of Zoophily* 2 (January 1893): 9.

19. Coleman, *Humane Society Leaders*, 186, 207; *The Man from Rochester Protests Too Much* [pamphlet] (Philadelphia: American Anti-Vivisection Society, 1965), 7–11; *Journal of Zoophily* 2 (March 1893): 1; *Journal of Zoophily* 1 (1892): 67–68 and 99–100; *Journal of Zoophily* 8 (December 1899): 136; and *Journal of Zoophily* 13 (March 1904): 28. One of the founders of the NEAVS, Abbey Morton Diaz, was also a member of Brook Farm, a transcendental utopian community. See Stathos, "History of the NEAVS," 5.

20. For example, of thirty-seven members in 1893, twenty-seven were women. See *Journal of Zoophily* 2 (February 1893): 21; *AAVS Minutes Books: Monthly Statement of the Treasurer of the AAVS* (April 29, 1919); *AAVS Minutes Books: Monthly Statement of the Treasurer of the AAVS* (February 27, 1923); and *AAVS Minutes Books: Statement of the Treasurer of the AAVS* (1912), 19.

21. For one of the best studies, see Cynthia Eagle Russett, *Sexual Science: The Victorian Construction of Womanhood* (Cambridge, MA: Harvard University Press, 1989), 190. Other related works include Ludmilla Jordanova, *Sexual Visions: Images of Gender in Science between the Eighteenth and Twentieth Centuries* (Madison: University of Wisconsin Press, 1989); and Wendy Mitchison, *The Nature of Their Bodies: Women and Their Doctors in Victorian Canada* (Toronto: University of Toronto Press, 1991).

22. Coral Lansbury, *The Old Brown Dog: Women, Workers, and Vivisection in Edwardian England* (Madison: University of Wisconsin Press, 1985), pref., 11–12, and 86–87.

23. Merwin, "Vivisection," 325.

24. Leffingwell, "Vivisection in America," 166.

25. Noah Davis, "The Moral Aspects of Vivisection," *North American Review* 140 (March 1885): 205.

26. Leffingwell, "Vivisection in America," 143.

27. Several orphans suffered permanent loss of vision. See *1883–1983: 100 Years against Cruelty*, 5–6.

28. Details of experiments can be found throughout the literature. A few representative examples include Bernard Unti, "The Birth of Animal Rights in America: Caroline Earle White and AAVS," *AV Magazine* (Fall

2000): 8–10; Albert Leffingwell, *An Ethical Problem or Sidelights upon Scientific Experimentation on Man and Animals*, 2d ed. (New York: G. Bell and Sons, 1916), 172–73; and Merwin, "Vivisection," 323.

29. *Journal of Zoophily* 2 (January 1893): 2. University of Pennsylvania was the likely target, since the WPSPCA and the AAVS singled out and protested against the institution on numerous occasions. See Mary Lovell, *Outline of the History of the WPSPCA: From Its Foundation April 14, 1869 to January 1908* (Philadelphia: WPSPCA, 1908).

30. Caroline Earle White, "The Practice of Vivisection," *Forum* 9 (March 1890): 115. White's accusation contained much truth, particularly after the American antivivisectionist campaign attracted greater publicity. In an intriguing article, Susan Lederer explores the social construction of twentieth-century biomedical research; see Lederer, "Political Animals: The Shaping of Biomedical Research Literature in Twentieth-Century America," *Isis* 83 (1992): 61–79.

31. White, "Practice of Vivisection," 109–11 and 114.

32. Robert Sharpe, "Temples of the Future," *Liberator* (November–December 1987): 24, and Robert Sharpe, *Basic Mistakes: The Unreliability of Animal Models in Research and Testing* (Jenkintown, PA: AAVS [1991?], 3.

33. As quoted in White, "Practice of Vivisection," 112.

34. Leffingwell, "Does Vivisection Pay?" 395–96; and White, "Practice of Vivisection," 107–13.

35. William Shultz, *The Humane Movement in the United States, 1910–1922* (New York: AMS Press, 1968 [1924]), 144–45; Coleman, *Humane Society Leaders*, 107; and *Journal of Zoophily* 12 (May 1903): 56.

36. White, "Practice of Vivisection," 109; and W. W. Keen, "Vivisection and Brain Surgery," *Harper's New Monthly Magazine* 87 (June 1893): 128–39.

37. H. C. Wood, "The Value of Vivisection," *Scribner's Monthly* 20 (September 1880): 769; and Susan Lederer, "The Controversy over Animal Experimentation in America, 1880–1914," in *Vivisection in Historical Perspective*, ed. Nicolas A. Rupke (London: Croom Helm, 1987), 249–51. The quote is from "Ammunition against the Anti-vivisectionists," *Science* 29 (February 26, 1909): 342.

38. Henry Bowditch, "Vivisection Justifiable," *Sanitarian* 38 (1896): 230–31.

39. Wood, "Value of Vivisection," 766; Davis, "Moral Aspects," 204, 211; Burnside Foster, "Results of Animal Experimentation," *Yale Review* 2 (January 1913): 311; W. W. Keen, *Animal Experimentation and Medical Progress* (Boston: Houghton Mifflin, 1914), 108; and Keen, "Vivisection and Brain Surgery," 139.

40. Davis, "Moral Aspects," 220; and Wood, "Value of Vivisection," 770.

41. Quoted in Shultz, *Humane Movement*, 150.

42. Nearly every provivisection commentary chastises antivivisectionists for attacking legitimate scientific endeavors. For a few examples, see Davis, "Moral Aspects," 210 and 217; Foster, "Results of Animal Experimentation," 302–3; Leffingwell, "Does Vivisection Pay?" 399; and Wood, "Value of Vivisection," 770.

43. Davis, "Moral Aspects," 207.

44. W. B. Cannon, "Animal Experimentation and Its Benefits to Mankind," *Journal of the American Medical Association* 58 (1912): 1829–37; W. H. Welch, "Fields of Usefulness of the American Medical Association: President's Address at the 61st Annual Session of the American Medical Association," *Journal of the American Medical Association* 54 (1910): 2011–17; Foster, "Results of Animal Experimentation," 306–7; Keen, "Vivisection and Brain Surgery," 128–30; and Keen, *Animal Experimentation*, 282–85.

45. Wood, "Value of Vivisection," 767.

46. Ibid., 769; Foster, "Results of Animal Experimentation," 313–14; and Keen, "Vivisection and Brain Surgery," 128–30.

47. Stathos, "History of the NEAVS," 5; Keen, "Vivisection and Brain Surgery," 131–38; Wood, "Value of Vivisection," 768; Foster, "Results of Animal Experimentation," 307–8; and Davis, "Moral Aspects," 220.

48. Keen, *Animal Experimentation*, 234–85.

49. Welch, "Fields of Usefulness."

50. Charles L. Dana, "The Zoophil-Psychosis: A Modern Malady," *Medical Record* 75 (March 6, 1909): 381–83.

51. Ibid., 381. *Zoophily* seems to have been a common term within the animal advocacy movement. Indeed, as indicated in the primary sources of this research, the joint publication of the WPSPCA and the AAVS was entitled the *Journal of Zoophily*.

52. Dana, "Zoophil-Psychosis," 381–82.

53. Ibid. For a relevant discussion of the misogyny of Victorian medicine, see Russett, *Sexual Science*, 190.

54. *Journal of Zoophily* 18 (June 1909): 60–61.

55. For a representative statement of support, see James Warbasse, *The Conquest of Disease through Animal Experimentation* (New York: Appleton, 1910), 158–61; and "The Antivivisectionists," *Science* 33 (March 17, 1911): 429–30.

56. For a more thorough discussion of the provivisectionist response to Dana's article, see Craig Beuttinger, "Antivivisection and the Charge of Zoophil-Psychosis in the Early Twentieth Century," *Historian* 15 (Winter 1993): 277–89.

57. William Jennings Bryan delivered the keynote address at the 1913 International Anti-Vivisection and Animal Protection Congress, praising delegates' efforts as a "benefit to the world." Bryan, keynote speech delivered at the International Anti-Vivisection and Animal Protection Congress, Washington, DC, December 8–11, 1913. Also see Coleman, *Humane Society Leaders*, 193–94; Stathos, "History of the NEAVS," 7; and Lederer, "Controversy," 248.

58. *1883–1983: 100 Years against Cruelty*, 3–5; *Second Annual Report of the Women's Branch*, 12–13; and *Journal of Zoophily* 13 (March 1904): 28.

59. Kalechofsky, *Autobiography of a Revolutionary*, 126 and 133; Keen, "Vivisection and Brain Surgery," 139; Donald Dewsbury, "Early Interactions between Animal Psychologists and Animal Activists and the Founding of the APA Committee on Precautions in Animal Experimentation," *American Psychologist* 45 (March 1990): 317–18; and White, "Practice of Vivisection," 112–13.

60. "Little Vivisection Here: Authorities However Decry Publicity as Hampering Research," *New York Times*, December 31, 1906, 5.

61. Unti, "The Birth of Animal Rights," 9; Shultz, *Humane Movement*, 153; *1883–1983: 100 Years against Cruelty*, 4; *Journal of Zoophily* 13 (February 1904): 14; *Journal of Zoophily* 2 (August 1893): 1; and *Journal of Zoophily* 2 (September 1893): 1.

62. The puppy incident was also discussed in the April 18, 1908, edition of the *New York Herald*. On the topics of pet theft and kennel conditions, see *1883–1983: 100 Years against Cruelty*, 5; *Journal of Zoophily* 12 (March 1903): 35; *AAVS Minutes Books: The Monthly Stated Meeting of the Board of Managers of the AAVS* (Philadelphia, February 24, 1942); Katharine Stanley Nicholson, "Sources of Supply to Vivisection Laboratories," paper presented at the International Anti-Vivisection and Animal Protection Congress (1913); and *Journal of Zoophily* 2 (January 1893): 1–4.

63. Stathos, "History of the NEAVS," 5.

64. Leffingwell, *An Ethical Problem*, 172–73.

65. Shultz, *Humane Movement*, 148 and 154; and Dewsbury, "Early Interactions," 316.

66. Merwin, "Vivisection," 323.

67. *1883–1983: 100 Years against Cruelty*, 5; *Journal of Zoophily* 12 (March 1903): 35; *AAVS Minutes Books* (February 24, 1942); Katharine Stanley Nicholson, "Sources of Supply to Vivisection Laboratories," paper presented at the International Anti-Vivisection and Animal Protection Congress (1913); and *Journal of Zoophily* 2 (January 1893): 1–4.

68. Carol Farley Kessler, *Elizabeth Stuart Phelps* (Boston: Twayne Publishers, 1982), pref. and chrono. When Phelps died, she bequeathed $2,000

to the AAVS. See Mary Angela Bennett, *Elizabeth Stuart Phelps* (Philadelphia: University of Pennsylvania Press, 1939), 126.

69. Kessler, *Elizabeth Stuart Phelps*, 111.

70. Elizabeth Stuart Phelps, *Chapters from a Life* (New York: Houghton Mifflin, 1896), 250–52.

71. Kessler, *Elizabeth Stuart Phelps*, 110–12.

72. According to Bennett, "Tammyshanty" was "so obviously propaganda that it was reprinted by the American Anti-Vivisection Society for distribution as a tract." See Bennett, *Elizabeth Stuart Phelps*, 124–26. Also see Kessler, *Elizabeth Stuart Phelps*, 110–12 and 118.

73. Mark Twain, Vienna, to Sidney G. Trist, Esq., London, May 26, 1899, in Charles Neider, ed., *Mark Twain: Life as I Find It* (Garden City, NY: Hanover House, 1961), 238. Notably, Twain wrote another short story about animal cruelty issues, "A Horse's Tale," at the behest of actress Minnie Maddern Fiske. Fiske, desirous of publicizing the cruelty of Spanish bullfights to both horses and bulls, contacted Twain shortly after reading "A Dog's Tale." Twain obliged, but the second story never achieved the acclaim of the first. See James D. Wilson, *A Reader's Guide to the Short Stories of Mark Twain* (Boston: G. K. Hall, 1987), 45–47.

74. Mark Twain, "A Dog's Tale," *Harper's Monthly Magazine* 108 (December 1903): 11–19. The work appeared in later editions, including Twain, *A Dog's Tale*, with illustrations by W. T. Smedley (New York: Harper and Brothers, 1904); and Twain, "A Dog's Tale," in *The $30,000 Bequest* (New York: Harper and Brothers, 1917).

75. Twain, "Dog's Tale," 14 (*Harper's Monthly*).

76. Ibid., 19.

77. Ibid.

78. Merwin, "Vivisection," 325.

79. *Background Note: Walter B. Cannon Papers*, February 2003, American Philosophical Society, http://www.amphilsoc.org/library/mole/c/cannon/htm (July 17, 2005).

80. Roswell McCrea, *The Humane Movement: A Descriptive Survey* (New York: Columbia University Press, 1910), 123; "Report of the Council on Defense of Medical Research," *Journal of the American Medical Association* 52 (1909): 2073–74; and W. B. Cannon, "Report of the Committee for the Protection of Medical Research," *Journal of the American Medical Association* 86 (1926): 862–63.

81. Dewsbury, "Early Interactions," 318.

82. Cannon, "Report of the Committee," and *The First Public Declaration of the Open Door in Laboratories for Animal Experimentation* (Springfield, MA: Blue Cross Society, 1922).

83. *Background Note.*

84. Lederer, "Controversy," 250–51; "Report of the Council"; and "Report of the Council on Defense of Medical Research," *Journal of the American Medical Association* 54 (1910): 2079.

85. Two of the most famous undercover investigations occurred at the Rockefeller Institute in 1910 and the University of Pennsylvania between 1913 and 1914. See Lederer, "Political Animals," 67; Lovell, *Outline of the History*, 20; *AAVS Minutes Books: Meeting of the Committee of the American Anti-Vivisection Society* (January 2, 1914); and "University of Pennsylvania Professor Defends Vivisection," *Public Ledger*, December 21, 1913, 6.

86. Lederer, "Political Animals," 69–75.

87. Simmonds, *Abbreviated History*, 4; Leffingwell, "Does Vivisection Pay?" 391–92; and Shultz, *Humane Movement*, 141–42.

88. Simmonds, *Abbreviated History*, 4; Shultz, *Humane Movement*, 141–41; and Buel, "Henry Bergh," 881.

89. Elizabeth Stuart Phelps, *A Plea for the Helpless* [pamphlet] (New York: American Humane Association, 1901); Phelps, *Vivisection and Legislation in Massachusetts* [pamphlet] (Philadelphia: American Anti-Vivisection Society, 1902); Stathos, "History of the NEAVS," 5; Turner, *Reckoning with the Beast*, 94; and Dewsbury, "Early Interactions," 316.

90. Lederer, "Controversy," 239 and 241; Andrew Rowan, *Of Mice, Models, and Men: A Critical Evaluation of Animal Research* (Albany: State University of New York, 1984), 50; S. Flexner and J. T. Flexner, *William Henry Welch and the Heroic Age of American Medicine* (New York: Viking Press, 1941), 254–65; and W. W. Keen, "Editorial," *Journal of the American Medical Association* 33 (1899): 1618.

91. Lederer, "Controversy," 240–41; Flexner and Flexner, *William Henry Welch*, 254–65; and Keen, "Editorial," 1618.

92. *1883–1983: 100 Years against Cruelty*, 3.

93. "Philadelphia County Medical Society," in Howard Petry, ed., *A Century of Medicine, 1848–1948: The History of the Medical Society of the State of Pennsylvania* (Harrisburg: Medical Society of the State of Pennsylvania, 1952), 283; *1883–1983: 100 Years against Cruelty*, 6; and Shultz, *Humane Movement*, 157.

94. One of the biggest early legislative battles over pound seizures took place in 1913. See Unti, "Birth of Animal Rights," 9; *1883–1983: 100 Years against Cruelty*, 6; and Shultz, *Humane Movement*, 157.

95. In 1880, the WPSPCA initiated the dispute and protests that led to the prosecution. See Lovell, *Outline of the History*, 20; *AAVS Minutes Books* (Philadelphia, January 2, 1914); and "University of Pennsylvania Professor Defends Vivisection."

96. *Journal of Zoophily* 4 (1895): 27 and 37; and *Journal of Zoophily* 6 (1897): 39–40. When Shultz published his book in 1924, he listed the Washington law as still active; see Shultz, *Humane Movement*, 256.

97. Pound seizure seems to have arisen as a bigger issue during the 1920s and 1930s. See Lederer, "Political Animals," and *1883–1983: 100 Years against Cruelty*.

98. Studies that neglect these bans include: Lawrence Finsen and Susan Finsen, *The Animal Rights Movement in America: From Compassion to Respect* (New York: Twayne Publishers, 1994), 47–54; Steven Smith, Mark Evans, Micaela Sullivan-Fowler, and William Hendee, "Use of Animals in Biomedical Research: Historical Role of the American Medical Association and the American Physician," *Archives of Internal Medicine* 148 (August 1988): 1849–53; and Dewsbury, "Early Interactions," 315–25. Turner mentions the Massachusetts law only briefly; see Turner, *Reckoning with the Beast*, 94.

99. White's opinions on vivisection and animal rights in general have been thoroughly documented throughout this book. For her willingness to be flexible, see Unti, "Birth of Animal Rights," 8. For Leffingwell's position, see his articles "Vivisection in America," "Does Vivisection Pay?" and "Future of Vivisection"; also see, Shultz, *Humane Movement*, 146.

100. Phelps, *Plea for the Helpless*; Phelps, *Vivisection and Legislation in Massachusetts*; Leffingwell, "Future of Vivisection," 105–10; *Journal of Zoophily* 8 (January 1899): 4; Salt, *Animals' Rights*, app. b, 175–76; and *Journal of Zoophily* 1 (1892): 37–38, 45–47, and 71–72.

101. In 1906, for example, John Shortall, president of the Illinois Humane Society and one of the founders of the AHA, stated to the *New York Times* that an operation on an anesthetized animal "in the interest of science" did not constitute cruelty. Shortall is quoted in Dewsbury, "Early Interactions," 320. Also see Shultz, *Humane Movement*, 154 and 157; and Finsen and Finsen, *Animal Rights Movement*, 51.

102. The quotes are from Turner, *Reckoning with the Beast*, 117–18; Dewsbury, "Early Interactions," 324; and Finsen and Finsen, *Animal Rights Movement*, 52. Other scholars who perceive a decline of antivivisection include Andrew Rowan, "The Development of the Animal Protection Movement," *Journal of NIH Research* 1 (November–December, 1989): 97; Laurence Pringle, *The Animal Rights Controversy* (New York: Harcourt Brace Jovanovich, 1989), 9–11; and James Jasper and Dorothy Nelkin, *The Animal Rights Crusade: The Growth of a Moral Protest* (New York: Free Press, 1992), 60–61. The only dissenting voices that I located are Lederer, "Political Animals," 62; and Smith, Evans, Sullivan-Fowler, and Hendee, "Use of Animals in Biomedical Research," 1850–51. Lederer convincingly

argues that historians have overestimated "the invulnerability of biomedical research" and underestimated "the durability of opposition to animal experimentation."

103. Turner, *Reckoning with the Beast*,117–18; Finsen and Finsen, *Animal Rights Movement*, 50–53; Jasper and Nelkin, *Animal Rights Crusade*, 59–60; and Pringle, *Animal Rights Controversy*, 9–11.

104. Coleman, *Humane Society Leaders*, 207.

105. Shultz, *Humane Movement*, 148, 159, and 161.

106. As quoted in Stathos, "History of the NEAVS," 8.

107. Shultz, *Humane Movement*, 156; and National Anti-Vivisection Society, "In Defense of the Defenseless," *Expressions* 2 (1994): 29.

108. Stathos, "History of the NEAVS," 9; and *American Anti-Vivisection Society Audit* (Philadelphia, 1945).

109. Shultz, *Humane Movement*, 156; Coleman, *Humane Society Leaders*, 207; Mary F. Lovell, "Anti-vivisection Work in America," paper presented at the International Anti-Vivisection and Animal Protection Congress, Philadelphia, October 17–20, 1926; various papers presented at the International Anti-Vivisection and Animal Protection Congress (1913); and *1883–1983: 100 Years against Cruelty*.

110. Various papers presented at the International Anti-Vivisection and Animal Protection Congresses (1913, 1926); and *1883–1983: 100 Years against Cruelty*.

111. Lederer, "Political Animals," 66.

112. *Journal of Zoophily* 25 (January 1916). See *Starry Cross* 29 (January 1920): 9; *A-V* 47 (June 1939): 83; various papers presented at the International Anti-Vivisection and Animal Protection Congress (1913); Stathos, "History of the NEAVS," 7; and *1883–1983: 100 Years against Cruelty*, 8.

113. Hearst specifically assigned reporters to investigate and expose incidents of lab abuses, pet theft, or grisly experiments. See Shultz, *Humane Movement*, 154; Stathos, "History of the NEAVS," 6 and 9; Lederer, "Political Animals," 63; and Dewsbury, "Early Interactions," 316 and 323.

114. Turner, *Reckoning with the Beast*, 117; Stathos, "History of the NEAVS," 7; and *1883–1983: 100 Years against Cruelty*, 7.

115. *AAVS Minutes Books: The Monthly Stated Meeting of the Board of Managers of the AAVS* (Philadelphia, April 30, 1941); *AAVS Minutes Books: The Monthly Stated Meeting of the Board of Managers of the AAVS* (Philadelphia, May 29, 1941); Stathos, "History of the NEAVS," 8; and *1883–1983: 100 Years against Cruelty*, 9.

116. In 1915, the AAVS sent a questionnaire to a large sampling of physicians and received replies of both support and rejection. The questions included: "Have you ever practised vivisection?" and "Have you found the

practice of it essential in your own education?" See AAVS *Minutes Books: The Monthly Stated Meeting of the Board of Managers of the* AAVS (Philadelphia, February 23, 1915), 134–35. For the entire questionnaire, see AAVS *Minutes Books: Questionnaire Sent to Area Physicians* (Philadelphia, February 1915). Also see Nina Halvey, "Fiftieth Anniversary: The AAVS Radio Broadcast," *Starry Cross* 41 (June 1933): 71, and Carol Hackbarth, "Experiments on Humans Hit by Foe of Practice: Woman Quotes Doctors in Arguments against Such Research Activities," *Columbus (OH) Citizen*, 1933, photocopy provided by the PETA library.

117. AAVS *Minutes Book: Suggestions for Exhibit* (Philadelphia, n.d., 1917?).

118. Ida Clyde Clarke, *American Women and the World War* (New York: D. Appleton, 1918), 62–63; Stathos, "History of the NEAVS," 8; *Starry Cross* 29 (October 1920): 155; *A-V* 50 (January 1942): 16; and *A-V* 50 (October 1942): 130.

119. AAVS *Minutes Books* (April 30, 1941); AAVS *Minutes Books* (May 29, 1941); Stathos, "History of the NEAVS," 8; and *1883–1983: 100 Years against Cruelty*, 9.

120. AAVS *Minutes Books* (February 24, 1942); and *1883–1983: 100 Years against Cruelty*, 8–9.

121. For various discussion on the California battles, see Shultz, *Humane Movement*, 153, 159, and 254; Smith, Evans, Sullivan-Fowler, and Hendee, "Use of Animals in Biomedical Research," 1850; AAVS *Minutes Books: An Act before the Legislature of Pennsylvania, No. 1130, Session of 1919* (Philadelphia, March 1919); Stathos, "History of the NEAVS," 7–8; George Hoyt Whipple, "Value of Animal Experimentation to Mankind," *American Journal of Public Health* 11 (February 1921): 105; and Lederer, "Political Animals," 62.

122. Shultz, *Humane Movement*, 153 and 254; Smith, Evans, Sullivan-Fowler, and Hendee, "Use of Animals in Biomedical Research," 1850; AAVS *Minutes Books* (March 1919); Stathos, "History of the NEAVS," 8; and Lederer, "Political Animals," 62.

123. Shultz, *Humane Movement*, 158; Dewsbury, "Early Interactions," 324; and Lederer, "Political Animals," 62n5, and 64.

124. Lederer, "Political Animals," 65–66. It is unclear whether this law stood the test of appeal. Similarly, Lederer notes that other states forced shelters to sell animals, but I have not located any significant evidence to support her findings. Christine Stevens suggests that the first such law to stand was enacted in Minnesota in 1948. Undoubtedly, a historical study of this legal issue would be most beneficial. See Stevens, "Laboratory Animal Welfare," in *Animals and Their Legal Rights: A Survey of American Laws*

from 1641–1978, 3d ed., ed. Emily Leavitt (Washington, DC: Animal Welfare Institute, 1978), 51 and 56.

125. Shultz, *Humane Movement*, 157; *AAVS Minutes Books: Leaflet in Opposition to Senate Bill No. 325* (Philadelphia, 1917); *1883–1983: 100 Years against Cruelty*, 5–9; Stathos, "History of the NEAVS," 8; and Dewsbury, "Early Interactions," 324.

126. Ernest Harold Baynes, "The Truth about Vivisection," *Woman's Home Companion* 48 (July 1921): 9–10.

127. Many of the Depression era issues contained in the AAVS archives are noticeably shorter than previous or subsequent editions. For example, see *Starry Cross* 41 (June 1933); and *A-V* 47 (January 1939). Also see Stathos, "History of the NEAVS," 7 and 8; and *Fiftieth Annual Report of the Women's PSPCA* (Philadelphia, December 31, 1918).

128. Only the donations of older, wealthier siblings such as the AAVS, which contributed $200 per month for a year, saved the fledgling Midwest organization from perishing in hard times. See Stathos, "History of the NEAVS," 8; and *AAVS Minutes Books: The Monthly Stated Meeting of the Board of Managers of the AAVS* (Philadelphia, November 30, 1943).

129. Whipple, "Value of Animal Experimentation," 107; Robert Logan, "After 50 Years," *Starry Cross* 41 (June 1933): 6; Shorter, *Health Century*, 18; Galambos and Merck, *Values and Visions*, 72–73; and Lederer, "Political Animals," 65.

130. Shorter, *Health Century*, 19–20 and 55; and Galambos and Merck, *Values and Visions*, 72–73.

CHAPTER 7

1. I was struck by how an obituary for a member and director of the National Catholic Society for Animal Welfare specifically noted the deceased's childhood membership in a Band of Mercy group. I would speculate that other postwar activists were similarly influenced as children by humane education programs, but few records or personal papers are available to document my theory. The obituary of Frances Coleman appeared in the *NCSAW Report*, September 1967, 5.

2. Roderick Nash, *The Rights of Nature: A History of Environmental Ethics* (Madison: University of Wisconsin Press, 1989), 48, 73, and 137–38. Other environmental and animal rights scholars agree that any understanding of the modern animal advocacy movement must be placed within the context of the 1960s. See Robert Gottlieb, *Forcing the Spring: The Transformation of the American Environmental Movement* (Washington, DC: Island Press, 1993), 196; and Andrew Rowan, "The Development of the Animal

Protection Movement," *Journal of NIH Research* 1 (November–December 1989): 99.

3. Samuel P. Hays, *Beauty, Health, and Permanence: Environmental Politics in the U.S., 1955–85* (New York: Cambridge University Press, 1987), chap. 1, 54 and 117.

4. *Welcome to the Fund for Animals* [pamphlet] (New York: Fund for Animals, n.d.); Cleveland Amory, *The Cat and the Curmudgeon* (Boston: Little, Brown, 1990), 222; Helen Jones, president of the International Society for Animal Rights, interview by author, November 28, 1995, tape recording, Clarks Summit, PA; and "NCSAW's New Name: Society for Animal Rights, Inc.," *NCSAW Report*, September 1972, 1.

5. Elaine Tyler May, *Homeward Bound: American Families in the Cold War Era* (New York: Basic Books, 1988), 165–67; Lawrence A. Mayer, "The Diverse $10,000-and-Over Masses," *Fortune* 76 (December 1967): 114; William Chafe, *The Unfinished Journey: America since World War II* (New York: Oxford University Press, 1991), 111 and 117–18; and *Outdoor Recreation for America: A Report to the President and to the Congress by the Outdoor Recreation Resources Review Commission*, Superintendent of Documents, Washington, DC, 1962, 1–10.

6. Kenneth Jackson, *The Crabgrass Frontier: The Suburbanization of the United States* (New York: Oxford University Press, 1985), 23–32, 231–32, and 235; Jon Teaford, *The Rough Road to Renaissance: Urban Revitalization in America, 1940–1985* (Baltimore, MD: Johns Hopkins University Press, 1985), 93–94; and Chafe, *Unfinished Journey*, 119.

7. James Miller, "Conservation Is Everybody's Battle," *Reader's Digest* 85 (August 1964): 161–62.

8. Estimates suggest that the average workweek declined from 60 or 70 hours in 1850 to a mere 40 by 1960. Factoring a paid vacation into a 52-week equation, the number of laboring hours per workweek fell to 32.5. See "Spare Time? What Spare Time?" *Changing Times* 18 (May 1964): 18–19.

9. In 1959, approximately thirty-two million people went fishing and sixteen million hunted. In 1964, consumers spent over $100 million on hunting and fishing licenses and at least $3 billion on related accessories. Boating enthusiasts paid out nearly $2.1 billion in 1958 to purchase and outfit their rigs. See Max Kaplan, *Leisure in America: A Social Inquiry* (New York: Wiley, 1960); quote is from Bruce Bliven, "Using Our Leisure Is No Easy Job," *New York Times Magazine* (April 26, 1964): 18–19; also see *Outdoor Recreation for America*, 78–79.

10. *Outdoor Recreation for America*, 74, 79–80, and 81–82.

11. *New York Times*, May 7, 1961, 31.

12. The Kellert and Westervelt study found a steadily rising trend in the public's interest in both ecology and wild animals after World War II. See Stephen Kellert and Miriam Westervelt, "Historical Trends in American Animal Use and Perception," *International Journal for the Study of Animal Problems* 4 (1983): 138 and 141–43.

13. William O. Douglas, *My Wilderness: East to Katahdin* (Garden City, NY: Doubleday, 1961), dust jacket.

14. Sally Carrighar, *One Day at Teton Marsh* (New York: Alfred A. Knopf, 1947); Joseph W. Krutch, *The Desert Year* (New York: William Sloane Associates, 1952); Rachel Carson, *The Sea around Us* (New York: Oxford University Press, 1951); and Carson, *The Edge of the Sea* (Boston: Houghton Mifflin, 1955).

15. Dona Finnley, "Laws to Protect Wildlife," in *Animals and Their Legal Rights: A Survey of American Laws from 1641–1978*, 3d ed., ed. Emily Leavitt (Washington, DC: Animal Welfare Institute, 1978), 177; Hays, *Beauty, Health, and Permanence*, 54, 57, 117, and 471; and Gottlieb, *Forcing the Spring*, 43.

16. Shortly after the Parks Service announced its plan, the Forest Service formulated a similar strategy, and the Fish and Wildlife Act of 1956 authorized a new agency (the Fish and Wildlife Service) to manage natural resources specifically for public consumption. See Gottlieb, *Forcing the Spring*, 43; Hays, *Beauty, Health, and Permanence*, 117 and 386; *Outdoor Recreation for America*, 175–78; and Finnley, "Laws to Protect Wildlife," 177.

17. Aldo Leopold discusses the destructive aspects of recreation in some detail in the final section of *A Sand County Almanac*; entitled "The Upshot," the section includes the articles "The Conservation Esthetic," "Wildlife in American Culture," "Wilderness," and "The Land Ethic." Leopold, *A Sand County Almanac: And Sketches Here and There* (New York: Oxford University Press, 1949), 165–226.

18. Ibid., 166 and 172.

19. Loren Winterscheid, "Animal Experimentation Leading to the Development of Advanced Surgical Technics," *American Journal of Public Health* 57 (September 1967): 1606–10; Louis Galambos and Merck, *Values and Visions: A Merck Century* (Rahway, NJ: Merck, 1991), 81; *Use of Animals in Biomedical Research: Understanding the Issues* (Cordova, TN: American Association for Laboratory Science, n.d.), 1; and U.S. Congress, Office of Technology Assessment, *Alternatives to Animal Use in Research, Testing, and Education*, OTA-BA-273 (Washington, DC: Government Printing Office, February 1986), 90–91.

20. Notably, a poultry industry publication devoted an entire section to such novel innovations as television dinners. See Leslie Card and Malden

Nesheim, *Poultry Production* (Philadelphia: Lea and Febiger, 1971), chap. 13. For an insightful discussion of the rise and public perception of consumer plastics, see Jeffrey L. Meikle, "Material Doubts: The Consequences of Plastic," *Environmental History* 2 (July 1997): 278–300.

21. Alan Brinkley and Ellen Fitzpatrick, *America in Modern Times since 1890* (New York: McGraw-Hill, 1997), 421.

22. The quote is from Orland A. Soave, "Animal Experimentation Leading to Better Care of Laboratory and Pet Animals," *American Journal of Public Health* 57 (September 1967): 1621. Also see Elinor Langer, "Animal Care: The Humane Movement Is Pulling Ahead," *Science* 151 (March 25 1966): 1518; and Peter Singer, *Animal Liberation*, rev. ed. (New York: Avon Books, 1990), 37.

23. Production of pesticides rose from 124,259,000 pounds in 1947 to 637,666,000 pounds in 1960. See Rachel Carson, *Silent Spring* (Boston: Houghton Mifflin, 1962), 16–17.

24. Ibid., 297, chapter 7, 109, 118–20, 158, and 161.

25. Edward Shorter, *The Health Century* (New York: Doubleday, 1987), 56–57; Dallas Pratt, *Painful Experiments on Animals* (New York: Argus Archives, 1976), 18; and Margaret Moreland Stathos, "The History of the New England Anti-Vivisection Society," *NEAVS* 80 (centennial issue): 12.

26. Ralph Lapp, *Arms beyond Doubt* (n.p.: Cowles, 1970), 144–45.

27. Two of the most prominent were the Animal Welfare Institute's Society for Animal Protective Legislation and the Friends of Animals's Committee for Humane Legislation. See *The Work of the Society of Animal Protective Legislation from 1955* [pamphlet] (Washington, DC: Society for Animal Protective Legislation, 1993); Harry Minetree, "Animal Rights—and Wrongs," *Town & Country* (May 1988): 160–61; and "Alice Herrington, 75, Founder of Friends of Animals, Is Dead," *New York Times*, April 28, 1994, photocopy provided by the PETA library, Washington, DC, and Rockville, MD.

28. *Animals, People, and the MSPCA: 125 Years of Progress* (Boston: MSPCA, 1993), 7–8; *Furs and Fashion, Traps and Trapping* (New York: Argus Archives, 1971), 16; and William Swallow, *Quality of Mercy: History of the Humane Movement in the United States* (Boston: Mary Mitchell Humane Fund, 1963), 15, 21, and 31.

29. There are many fine books on the cold war and the red scare. For a few examples, see John L. Gaddis, *We Know Now: Rethinking Cold War History* (New York: Oxford University Press, 1998); Ralph B. Levering, *The Cold War: A Post–Cold War History* (Arlington Heights, IL: Harlan Davidson, 1994); Lisle A. Rose, *The Cold War Comes to Main Street: America in 1950* (Lawrence: University Press of Kansas, 1999); Ellen Schrecker, *Many*

Are the Crimes: McCarthyism in America (Princeton, NJ: Princeton University Press, 1998); and Victor Navasky, *Naming Names* (New York: Viking Press, 1980).

30. *A-V* seems to indicate there was a more subdued radicalism between 1948 and 1952 than during previous or subsequent periods. Although a few articles retain the group's characteristic aggressive approach and perspective, many discuss relatively tame topics, such as the "How to Answer" section on responding to questions about vivisection and "Vegetarian Suggestions for a Cool Supper." See *A-V*, vols. 56–60 (1948–1952). Also see the *AAVS Minutes Book for November 1946–1961* (Philadelphia). In addition, large public protest campaigns occurred less frequently. In a 1983 retrospective of the group's work, only two events are highlighted between 1948 and 1954—the retirement of President Logan and the International Conference on Animal Welfare in Switzerland. See *1883–1983: 100 Years against Cruelty* (Jenkintown, PA: American Anti-Vivisection Society, 1983), 9–10.

31. Belton Mouras, *I Care about Animals: Moving from Emotion to Action* (New York: A. S. Barnes, 1977), 119–20; Swallow, *Quality of Mercy*, 16–66; and Helen Jones interview.

32. Helen Jones interview.

33. Of the remaining seven biographies, two mention neither origins nor officers. Five appear to have been clearly controlled by men but again are lacking specific details. See Swallow, *Quality of Mercy*, 126–57.

34. Alice Morgan Wright was also an heiress, sculptor, and one of the organizers of the United Nations Educational, Scientific, and Cultural Organization (UNESCO). See Anna Briggs, *For the Love of Animals* (n.p.: Potomac Publishing, 1990), 73–74.

35. Helen Jones interview; "First Anniversary Marked," *NCSAW Report*, June 1960, 8; *Report of the Third Annual Meeting of the NCSAW* (New York, May 26, 1962); Briggs, *For the Love of Animals*, chap. 3, 47–48; "Eleanor E. Seiling," *International Society for Animal Rights Report*, November 1985, 2; Swallow, *Quality of Mercy*, 142–43; Minetree, "Animal Rights—and Wrongs," 160; and Langer, "Animal Care," 1516.

36. Helen Jones interview.

37. For a thoughtful examination of cold war families, see May, *Homeward Bound*. This discussion also benefited from Eugenia Kaledin, *Mothers and More: American Women in the 1950s* (Boston: Twayne Publishers, 1984).

38. Kaledin, *Mothers and More*, 11, 33, 40, 88, and chap. 4.

39. The quote is from Carson, *Silent Spring*, 2. Also see Vera Norwood, *Made from this Earth: American Women and Nature* (Chapel Hill: University of North Carolina Press, 1993), 146–47.

40. The quotes are from Kirkpatrick Sale, *The Green Revolution: The American Environmental Movement, 1962–1992* (New York: Hill and Wang, 1993), 4; and D. S. Greenberg, "News and Comments," *Science* 140 (May 24, 1963): 878. For other works that discuss attacks on Carson, see Frank Graham Jr., *Since Silent Spring* (Boston: Houghton Mifflin, 1970), 48–68; Gottlieb, *Forcing the Spring,* 81–86; and Norwood, *Made from this Earth,* pref., and 146–47.

41. Frederick Sperling, "Letters," *Science* 151 (February 18, 1966): 778. Helen Jones also spoke of similar attitudes directed toward her; see Helen Jones interview.

42. Helen Jones interview.

43. Total per capita meat consumption—including beef, pork, lamb, mutton, veal, turkey, and chicken—jumped from 140 pounds in 1960 to between 166 and 196 pounds in 1970. One expert factored consumption another way: "Every minute of the day throughout the year we kill 67 beef cattle, 159 hogs, 8 calves and twenty sheep." *Animals into Meat: A Report on the Pre-slaughter Handling of Livestock* (New York: Argus Archives, 1971), 2. See also *Feedstuffs,* November 23, 1992, 22; L. S. Pope, "Commercial Beef Production in the United States," in *Commercial Beef Cattle Production,* ed. C. C. O'Mary and Irwin Dyer (Philadelphia: Lea and Febiger, 1972), 1; and Card and Nesheim, *Poultry Production,* 317.

44. *Animals into Meat,* 3; Emily Stewart Leavitt, "Humane Slaughter Laws," in *Animals and Their Legal Rights: A Survey of American Laws from 1641–1978,* 3d ed., ed. Emily Leavitt (Washington, DC: Animal Welfare Institute, 1978), 36.

45. Swallow, *Quality of Mercy,* 163–64; and *The Anti-Cruelty Society: 75th Anniversary Annual Report* (Chicago: Anti-Cruelty Society, 1974), 5.

46. Leavitt, "Humane Slaughter Laws," 37; and Swallow, *Quality of Mercy,* 163–64.

47. Helen Jones interview; Swallow, *Quality of Mercy,* 31–32, 143, and 163–65; Ingrid Newkirk, *Save the Animals! 101 Easy Things You Can Do* (New York: Warner Books, 1990), 100; *Animals, People, and the MSPCA,* 7; and Leavitt, "Humane Slaughter Laws," 37–38.

48. Leavitt, "Humane Slaughter Laws," 37; and *Work of the Society of Animal Protective Legislation.*

49. Newkirk, *Save the Animals,* 100; and John Robbins, *Diet for a New America* (Walpole, NH: Stillpoint Publishing, 1987), 170–220.

50. F. J. Schling and M. C. Phillips, *Meat Three Times a Day* (New York: Richard R. Smith, 1946), 54.

51. Mouras, *I Care about Animals,* 137.

52. Swallow, *Quality of Mercy,* 21, 31–32, 138, 142–43, 163–65, and 166; Fred Myers, "Humane Legislation Marches On," *A-V* 67 (October 1959):

129–30; Helen Jones interview; *Anti-Cruelty Society: 75th Anniversary Annual Report*, 5; and Leavitt, "Humane Slaughter Laws," 37–38.

53. Charles Niven, *History of the Humane Movement* (New York: Transatlantic Press, 1967), 121; and "Women's Convention Exhibit Planned," *NCSAW Report*, October 1962, 2.

54. Leavitt, "Humane Slaughter Laws," 38–40; and *Animals into Meat*, 10–12.

55. Animal advocacy groups possessed considerable ammunition when countering meat industry claims that the law was premature. Many industrialized nations had already implemented national humane slaughter laws, including Switzerland (1874), the Netherlands (1920), Norway (1924), Scotland (1928), Ireland (1932), England (1933), Finland (1934), Sweden (1937), New Zealand (1951), and Denmark (1953). See Leavitt, "Humane Slaughter Laws," 36–38.

56. Ibid., 38; and *Animals into Meat*, 18–20.

57. The quote from the law is in Henry Cohen, "Federal Animal Protection Statutes," *Animal Law* 1 (1995): 153–54. Also see *Work of the Society of Animal Protective Legislation*; Mouras, *I Care about Animals*, 24 and 137; Leavitt, "Humane Slaughter Laws," 42; Swallow, *Quality of Mercy*, 23; and *Animals into Meat*, 19.

58. *A-V* 67 (October 1959): 129–30.

59. Swallow, *Quality of Mercy*, 144 and 163.

60. Helen Jones interview; "Slaughter Campaign Pamphlet Planned," *NCSAW Report*, June 1960, 8; *NCSAW Report*, June 1961, 2; *Report of the Third Annual Meeting of the N.C.S. for A.W.* (New York, May 1962), 7–10; *NCSAW Report*, June 1964, 10; and "In Memoriam: Alice Herrington," *International Society for Animal Rights Report*, Spring 1994, 6.

61. *Animals into Meat*, 16–17; and "In Memoriam: Alice Herrington."

62. "In Memoriam: Alice Herrington"; "Alice Herrington, 75, Founder of Friends of Animals, Is Dead"; *Animals into Meat*, 15–17 and 33–36; *NCSAW Report*, June 1960, 8; *NCSAW Report*, June 1961, 2; *Report of the Third Annual Meeting of the N.C.S. for A.W.*; *NCSAW Report*, June 1964, 7–11; and Jacques V. Sichel to Jo Morgan, February 16, 1971, Argus Archives, Garrison, NY.

63. Leavitt, "Humane Slaughter Laws," 41; and *Report of the Third Annual Meeting of the N.C.S. for A.W.*, 11.

64. *Animals into Meat*, 26–27.

65. Ibid., 20–21, 27, 34, and 36.

66. Morris Laub, "Why the Fuss over Humane Slaughter Legislation?" *Women's League Outlook* 36 (March 1966): 8–9.

67. In recent years, the biomedical community has resurrected attempts to connect animal advocates to anti-Semitism by suggesting that the Nazis

passed an antivivisection law in 1933 because they preferred to experiment on humans, thus insinuating that those who struggle for animals hate humans. However, as Roberta Kalechofsky points out in her study, the Nazi law was like the British law, a weak statute that did not prevent animal experimentation. Equally important, much of the Nazi experimentation on humans in the death camps was first performed on animals. See Roberta Kalechofsky, *Autobiography of a Revolutionary: Essays on Animal and Human Rights* (Marblehead, MA: Micah Publications, 1991), 137.

68. *Animals into Meat*, 33–36; Sichel to Morgan, February 16, 1971; NCSAW *Report*, June 1960, 8; NCSAW *Report*, June 1961, 2; *Report of the Third Annual Meeting of the* N.C.S. *for* A.W., 7–11; and NCSAW *Report*, June 1964, 10.

69. *Testimony on a Bill for Humane Treatment of Livestock* [pamphlet] (Council for Livestock Protection, 1974).

70. Ibid.; and Sichel to Morgan, February 16, 1971.

71. *Report of the Council's Activities from June 6 thru November 30, 1973* (Council for Livestock Protection, 1973), photocopy provided by Ron Scott, Argus Archives, Garrison, NY; Emily Leavitt, ed., *Animals and Their Legal Rights: A Survey of American Laws from 1641–1978*, 3d ed. (Washington, DC: Animal Welfare Institute, 1978), app., i–vi.

72. "ASPCA Commissions Humane Slaughter Study," *Animal Protection* (Spring 1968): 6–7; "H.R. 264, Humane Methods of Poultry Slaughter Act of 1995," *Poultry Press* 5 (Summer–Fall 1995): 4; Cohen, "Federal Animal Protection Statutes," 154.

73. NCSAW *Report*, February 1972, 4.

74. Ruth Harrison, *Animal Machines* (London: Vincent Stuart, 1964); quote is in W. Ray Stricklin and Janice Swanson, "Technology and Animal Agriculture," *Journal of Agricultural and Environmental Ethics* 6 (1993): 72.

75. Holland's veal producers first devised veal confinement crates, and the crates were introduced into the United States in 1962. See Singer, *Animal Liberation*, 129–31. Also see Artturi Virtanen, "Milk Production of Cows on Protein-Free Feed," *Science* 153 (September 30, 1966): 1603–14; and Singer and Mason, *Animal Factories*, chaps. 1–3.

76. By 1970, according to a trade publication, large industrial feedlots handled more cattle than the entire meat industry had produced just twenty years earlier. Corporate farms similarly infiltrated milk production, causing the number of small dairy farms to fall from over 1 million in 1964 to just over 500,000 in 1969. And a 1971 study of poultry production noted that many "small" operations had "gone out of business." Between 1954 and 1959, 1.3 million family-operated chicken farms disappeared from the industry. See Pope, "Commercial Beef Production in the United States," 1–3;

Card and Nesheim, *Poultry Production*, 7, 131, and 317; *Special Report: Turning Cows into Biotech Milk Machines* (San Rafael, CA: Humane Farming Association, 1994); and Ruth Harrison, "Animals in Factory Farms," in *Animals and Their Legal Rights: A Survey of American Laws from 1641–1978*, 3d ed., ed. Emily Leavitt (Washington, DC: Animal Welfare Institute, 1978), 69.

77. One industry report stated that only twelve employees were needed to fully operate a feedlot holding thirty thousand cattle. See Pope, "Commercial Beef Cattle Production," 6. Also see Card and Nesheim, *Poultry Production*, 357 and 359; and Mason and Singer, *Animal Factories*, 102–3.

78. Robbins, *Diet for a New America*, 170–220.

79. Rachel Carson, foreword to Ruth Harrison's *Animal Machines*, quoted in Stricklin and Swanson, "Technology and Animal Agriculture," 72.

80. *NCSAW Report*, February 1972, 4; and *Report of the Council's Activities*.

81. For a few examples of the new approach, see Animal Welfare Institute, *Comfortable Quarters for Laboratory Animals* (New York: Animal Welfare Institute, 1955); C. W. Hume, "The Ethics of Experiments on Animals," *Nature* 167 (February 10, 1951): 213; Langer, "Animal Care," 1516; and Swallow, *Quality of Mercy*, 143.

82. Alvin Weinberg, *Reflections on Big Science* (Cambridge, MA: MIT Press, 1967), 106; quote is in Joseph Ben-David, *The Scientist's Role in Society* (Chicago: University of Chicago Press, 1984), 166.

83. Herman Kretschmer, "Address of the President," *Journal of the American Medical Association* 129 (1945): 1107–9; and Christine Stevens, "Laboratory Animal Welfare," in *Animals and Their Legal Rights: A Survey of American Laws from 1641–1978*, 3d ed., ed. Emily Leavitt (Washington, DC: Animal Welfare Institute, 1978), 51.

84. In 1984, the NSMR was merged with another proresearch organization, the Association for Biomedical Research (1979), to form the National Association for Biomedical Research. See Steven Smith, Mark Evans, Micaela Sullivan-Fowler, and William Hendee, "Use of Animals in Biomedical Research: Historical Role of the American Medical Association and the American Physician," *Archives of Internal Medicine* 148 (August 1988): 1852. Also see T. S. Grafton, "The Founding and Early History of the National Society for Medical Research," *Laboratory Animal Science* 30 (1980): 759–64; Howard Petry, ed., *A Century of Medicine, 1848–1948: The History of the Medical Society of the State of Pennsylvania* (Harrisburg: Medical Society of the State of Pennsylvania, 1952), 324; Pratt, *Painful Experiments on Animals*, 149; Stevens, "Laboratory Animal Welfare," 51; and *Organizational History—National Society for Medical Research*, June 25, 2005, United States

National Library of Medicine, http://www.nlm.nih.gov/hmd/manuscripts/ead/nsmr.html (July 7, 2005).

85. Pratt, *Painful Experiments on Animals,* 94; and "Use of Animals in Biomedical Research: The Challenge and Response," *An American Medical Association White Paper* (Chicago: AMA, 1989, rev. 1992), 21–22.

86. Stevens, "Laboratory Animal Welfare," 54; "Women's Clubs in the News," A-V 56 (September 1948): 123; Susan Lederer, "Political Animals: The Shaping of Biomedical Research Literature in Twentieth-Century America," *Isis* 83 (1992): 73.

87. Stevens, "Laboratory Animal Welfare," 51.

88. Pratt, *Painful Experiments on Animals,* 100–101; and Stevens, "Laboratory Animal Welfare," 54 and 56.

89. Patrick Nace, "WARDS and the Animal Welfare Act," *Our Animal WARDS* (Winter 1994): 4–5; "Legislature Repeals Metcalf-Hatch," *ASPCA Bulletin* 3 (Fall 1979): 1; Stevens, "Laboratory Animal Welfare," 51 and 53–54; "Pet Theft: Can We Stop It?" *Animals' Agenda* 12 (April 1992): 13; "Connecticut Seizure Law Repealed," *Society for Animal Rights Report,* May 1980, 1; Pratt, *Painful Experiments on Animals,* 101 and 147–51; "Metcalf-Hatch Repealed," *Society for Animal Rights Report,* September 1979, 1; *Coalition to Abolish Metcalf-Hatch* [circular] (New York: Coalition to Abolish Metcalf-Hatch, 1979); and "Los Angeles Seizure Ordinance Repealed," *Society for Animal Right Report,* August 1981, 1.

90. For information on repeals, see "Legislature Repeals Metcalf-Hatch"; "Connecticut Seizure Law Repealed"; "Los Angeles Seizure Ordinance Repealed"; "Metcalf-Hatch Repealed"; *Coalition to Abolish Metcalf-Hatch*; and U.S. Congress, Office of Technology Assessment, *Alternatives to Animal Use.*

91. "Visits to Laboratories Show Need for H.R. 1937," *AWI Information Report* 11 (January–February 1962): 1; Stevens, "Laboratory Animal Welfare," 53; and "Burning," *AWI Information Report* 11 (March–April 1962): 3.

92. The force behind the investigation of dog bunchers was Lucille Aaron Moses, who amassed an impressive report on the practice between 1957 and 1965. See Pratt, *Painful Experiments on Animals,* 1; and "Pet Theft: Can We Stop It?"

93. Stevens, "Laboratory Animal Welfare," 53.

94. Langer, "Animal Care," 1516; and Minetree, "Animal Rights—and Wrongs," 160.

95. Animal Welfare Institute, *Comfortable Quarters.*

96. "Visits to Laboratories."

97. Stevens, "Laboratory Animal Welfare," 54.

98. The Animal Care Panel was renamed the American Association for Laboratory Animal Science (AALAS) in 1967. See *AALAS Timeline:* 1946–

Present, 1999, American Association for Laboratory Animal Science, http://aalas.org (July 10, 2005); *Our Animal WARDS*, April 1987, cover page; Smith, Evans, Sullivan-Fowler, and Hendee, "Use of Animals in Biomedical Research," 1852–53; and Pratt, *Painful Experiments on Animals*, 105.

99. *Principles and Guidelines for the Use of Animals in Pre-college Education* [pamphlet] (Washington, DC: Institute of Laboratory Animal Resources, 1989); "Concerned Authorities Reveal Facts," *Our Animal WARDS*, November 1980, 4; Smith, Evans, Sullivan-Fowler, and Hendee, "Use of Animals in Biomedical Research," 1853; Pratt, *Painful Experiments on Animals*, 105; "Use of Animals in Biomedical Research: The Challenge and Response," 20; and *Report of the Animal Alternatives Study Task Force* (Berkeley: University of California Press, 1988), app. iv-a, 1.

100. Norman Bleicher, "Care of Animals during Surgical Experiments," in *Methods of Animal Experimentation*, ed. William I. Gay, vol. 1 (New York: Academic Press, 1965), 103–50; and *AALAS Timeline*.

101. "Use of Animals in Biomedical Research: The Challenge and Response," 18; Deborah Rudacille, "Alternatives Called New Branch of Science," *Center for Alternatives to Animal Testing* 11 (Winter 1994): 1–3; and "Words and Their Meaning," *International Society for Animal Rights Report* (June 1985): 3.

102. "Words and Their Meaning" and *Aims and Programs of the Animal Welfare Institute* [pamphlet] (Washington, DC: Animal Welfare Institute, n.d.).

103. The award was first given in 1946. See *Organizational History*; W. Lane-Petter, "Science, Animals, and Humanity," *Nature* 174 (September 18, 1954): 534; and Lederer, "Political Animals," 73.

104. Cole Phinizy, "The Lost Pets That Stray to the Labs," *Sports Illustrated* 29 (November 29, 1965): 38 and 41; and Stevens, "Laboratory Animal Welfare," 46.

105. Phinizy, "Lost Pets," 38 and 41; Langer, "Animal Care, 1515–17; "Pet Theft: Can We Stop It?" 14; and Lawrence Finsen and Susan Finsen, *The Animal Rights Movement in America: From Compassion to Respect* (New York: Twayne Publishers, 1994), 56–57.

106. "Pet Theft: Can We Stop It?" 14; and Stan Wayman and Michel Silva, "Concentration Camps for Dogs," *Life* 60 (February 4, 1966): 22–29.

107. Langer, "Animal Care," 1515–16; and Stevens, "Laboratory Animal Welfare," 46.

108. One of the most shocking photographs the AAVS advertised depicted an experiment in which a living puppy's severed head and forelegs were surgically attached to an adult dog's neck until it died. See *Death of a Vivisectionist* [pamphlet] (Philadelphia: American Anti-Vivisection Society,

n.d.). Also see *Vivisection Is Cruel, Brutal, and Futile* [pamphlet] (Philadelphia: American Anti-Vivisection Society, n.d.); *AAVS Minutes Books: The Monthly Stated Meeting of the Board of Managers of the AAVS* (Philadelphia, November 27, 1952); *AAVS Minutes Books: The Monthly Stated Meeting of the Board of Managers of the AAVS* (Philadelphia, November 24, 1959); *A-V* 75 (January 1967): 2 and 8; Stathos, "History of the NEAVS," 9; *1883–1983: 100 Years against Cruelty*, 10–11; *Report of the Third Annual Meeting of the NCSAW*; Stevens, "Laboratory Animal Welfare," 54 and 57; Helen Jones interview; "The Paper Curtain," *International Society for Animal Rights Report*, August 1985, 4; *Washington March for the Animals* [pamphlet] (n.p.: National Catholic Society for Animal Welfare, n.d.); "Some Groups Support Pets in Research," *International Society for Animal Rights Report*, December 1988, 1 and 4; and "White House Pickets Assail Bills on Treatment of Lab Animals," *Washington Post*, July 11, 1966, A3.

109. Dael Wolfe, "Animal Care Legislation," *Science* 153 (September 2, 1966): 1.

110. For various comments by the biomedical community, see Lowell Greenbaum, "Animal-Care Laws: The Mood of Congress," *Science* 151 (March 18, 1966): 1329; *The Man from Rochester Protests Too Much* [pamphlet] (Philadelphia: American Anti-Vivisection Society, 1965), 1; Stevens, "Laboratory Animal Welfare," 54; and Frederick Sperling, "Animal Care in the Laboratory: Who Should Regulate It?" *Science* 151 (February 18, 1966): 776–77.

111. Sperling, "Animal Care in the Laboratory," 777.

112. Wayman and Silva, "Concentration Camps for Dogs," 22–29.

113. One Maryland man wrote to the magazine to identify one of the dying dogs as his missing collie, Reddy. See "Letters to the Editor," *Life* 60 (February 25, 1966): 25. Also see Langer, "Animal Care," 1515; Stevens, "Laboratory Animal Welfare," 47; Nace, "WARDS and the Animal Welfare Act," 8; and "Pet Theft: Can We Stop It?" 14.

114. Patrick Nace, "WARDS and the Animal Welfare Act (Part 2)," *Our Animal WARDS* (Spring 1994): 6.

115. Ann Church, "Understanding the Animal Welfare Act," *Humane Society News* (Winter 1989): 17–18.

116. There are abundant sources explaining this act; some of the better ones include U.S. Congress, Office of Technology Assessment, *Alternatives to Animal Use*, 276–80; Church, "Understanding the Animal Welfare Act," 17–21; W. C. Stewart, "Legal Standards for Humane Care: The Animal Welfare Act," *Lab Animal* 13 (September 1984): 33–41; and Cohen, "Federal Animal Protection Statutes," 146–47.

117. Standards for marine mammals were established in 1979. See Church, "Understanding the Animal Welfare Act," 17–21; Maurice Viss-

cher, "The Animal Welfare Act of 1970," *Science* 172 (May 28, 1971): 916–17; Marc Leepson, "Animal Rights," *CQ Researcher* 1 (May 24, 1991): 309. Congress again amended the Animal Welfare Act and expanded its powers in 1976, 1985, and 1990. Some of the more recent provisions include protection for hunting, security, and breeding dogs; a ban on the interstate commerce of fighting animals; broadened transportation regulations for nonfood animals; exercise for dogs; and the mandatory establishment of animal care committees at every federally funded research center, to name a few. See U.S. Congress, Office of Technology Assessment, *Alternatives to Animal Use*, 276–80; Church, "Understanding the Animal Welfare Act," 17–21; Stewart, "Legal Standards for Humane Care," 33–41; and Cohen, "Federal Animal Protection Statutes," 146–47.

118. Rudy Baum, "Biomedical Researchers Work to Counter Animal Rights Agenda," *Chemical and Engineering News* 68 (May 7, 1990): 11–12; Lauren Nethery and John McArdle, *Animals in Product Development and Safety Testing: A Survey* (Washington, DC: Institute for the Study of Animal Problems, 1985), 2–6; *Consumer Product Safety: Why We Need It, How We Achieve It* (Washington, DC: Join Hands Health and Safety Educational Alliance, n.d.); Rick Weiss, "Inventing the Skin You Love to Test," *Washington Post*, February 21, 1988, B3; U.S. Congress, Office of Technology Assessment, *Alternatives to Animal Use*, 8–9 and 153–62; D. W. Swanston, "Eye Irritancy Testing," in *Animals and Alternatives in Toxicity Testing*, ed. M. Balls, R. J. Riddell, and A. N. Worden (London: Academic Press, 1983), 337–66; Pratt, *Painful Experiments on Animals*, 29–46; "Draize Unreliable," *Our Animal WARDS*, November 1989, 9 and 14; *Facts on the Draize Eye and Skin Irritancy Tests* (Chicago: National Anti-Vivisection Society, n.d.); D. W. Parke, "Regulatory Aspects," in *Animals and Alternatives in Toxicity Testing*, ed. M. Balls, R. J. Riddell, and A. N. Worden (London: Academic Press, 1983), 445–56; V. K. H. Brown, "Acute Toxicity Testing," in *Animals and Alternatives in Toxicity Testing*, ed. M. Balls, R. J. Riddell, and A. N. Worden (London: Academic Press, 1983), 1–16; and Michael Kreger, *The LD50 (Median Lethal Dose) and LC50 (Median Lethal Concentration) Toxicity Tests, January 1980–March 1992*, Special Reference Briefs, 92–12 (Beltsville, MD: National Agricultural Library, 1992), i.

119. *NCSAW Report*, November 1967, 1; "Protest Mail Pours in on Ford," *NCSAW Report*, February 1968, 1; Dallas Pratt, typed comment on the founding of United Action for Animals, 1969, Argus Archives, Garrison, NY; Pratt, *Painful Experiments on Animals*, 168–69; "VFA (Voices for Animals of Central Florida) Demonstrates against GM, 'The Heartbreak of America,'" *Vocalizations* 2 (December–January 1992): 1.

120. Interestingly, one of the researchers who conducted car crash tests on baboons was Thomas A. Gennarelli. In 1984, an undercover videotape

of Gennarelli's head injury laboratory at the University of Pennsylvania initiated a new era of successful attacks on painful experiments and rocketed the group People for the Ethical Treatment of Animals to the forefront of the movement. The sixty hours of videotape not only showed the actual infliction of head wounds on baboons but also captured experimenters laughing at the severely injured primates. The experiments were suspended. See T. A. Gennarelli, L. E. Thibault, and A. K. Ommaya, "Comparison of Translational and Rotational Head Motions in Experimental Cerebral Concussion," in *Proceedings of the Fifteenth Annual Stapp Car Crash Conference, Held in Coronado, California, November 17–19, 1971* (New York: Society of Automotive Engineers, 1971), 800. Also A. K. Ommaya, A. E. Hirsch, E. S. Flamm, and R. H. Mahone, "Cerebral Concussion in the Monkey: An Experimental Model," *Science* 153 (July 1966): 211–12; Pratt, *Painful Experiments on Animals*, 168–69; and Richard Willing, "20,000 Animals Killed in Decade of GM Safety Tests," *Detroit News*, September 27, 1991, A1, A5.

121. *Proceedings of the Fifteenth Stapp Car Crash Conference*, 797–802. Also see "Urgent!" *NCSAW Report*, November 1967, 1; "Protest Mail Pours in On Ford; Dealer Seeks Picketing Injunction," *NCSAW Report*, February 1968, 1; "Ford Phasing Out Cruelty to Animals," *NCSAW Report*, June 1968, 1; Pratt, typed comment; and Pratt, *Painful Experiments on Animals*, 160.

122. "Eleanor E. Seiling," 2; and "United Action for Animals," *NCSAW Report*, October 1968, 5.

123. The year after Japan's surrender, scientists loaded approximately forty-five hundred animals into navy ships, anchored them near Bikini Atoll, and detonated an atomic bomb. Between 1957 and 1958, monkeys were placed variable distances from ground zero in nuclear weapons tests, and throughout the 1960s, the Atomic Energy Commission and Department of Defense authorized the irradiation of millions of rats, mice, monkeys, dogs, and other animals annually. For a discussion of those and other experiments, see U.S. Congress, Office of Technology Assessment, *Alternatives to Animal Use*, 294; U.S. Congress, General Accounting Office, *Use of Dogs in Experiments at Edgewood Arsenal, Maryland: Department of the Army*, GAO Rep. No. PSAD-76-80 (Washington, DC: March 12, 1976); "Who Needs Enemies?" *NCSAW Report*, March 1967, 3; Suzanne Roy, "'Exposed': The Military's War on Animals," in *A Report to the Armed Services Committee, Subcommittee on Research and Development* (San Francisco: In Defense of Animals, n.d.); Phillip W. D. Martin, *The Animal Rights Movement in the United States: Its Composition, Funding Sources, Goals, Strategies, and Potential Impact on Research* (Cambridge, MA: Harvard University's Office of Government and Community Affairs, Septem-

ber, 1982), 3; Robert Sharpe, *The Cruel Deception: The Use of Animals in Medical Research* (Northamptonshire and London: Thorsons Publishers, 1988), 220–25; "The Pentagon's Secret War on Animals," *Animals' Agenda* 7 (June 1987): 29, 48; "Animals in the Laboratory: . . . In the Name of Defense," *Unicorn* 2 (November 1981): 3; Dallas Pratt, *Alternatives to Pain in Experiments on Animals* (New York: Argus Archives, 1980), 114–15; Pratt, *Painful Experiments on Animals*, 63–65; and Singer, *Animal Liberation*, 25–28 and 30–31.

124. U.S. Congress, Office of Technology Assessment, *Alternatives to Animal Use*, 294; Martin, *Animal Rights Movement*, 5; "Who Needs Enemies," 3; and Singer, *Animal Liberation*, 29. For a discussion of the NCSAW name change, see "NCSAW's New Name," 1.

125. Institute of Laboratory Animal Resources, *Fiscal Year 1978 National Survey of Laboratory Animal Facilities and Resources*, NIH Publication No. 80-2091 (Washington, DC: U.S. Department of Health and Human Services, March 1980), 21; and Philip J. Hilts, "Use of Animals Falls 50% since 1968," *New York Times*, March 3, 1994, A18.

126. Leopold, *Sand County Almanac*, viii.

127. Paul Brooks, foreword to Rachel Carson, *Silent Spring*, 25th anniversary ed. (Boston: Houghton Mifflin, 1987), xii.

128. Ibid., xiii; and Sale, *Green Revolution*, 4.

129. Carson's view of science for the public is discussed in Gottlieb, *Forcing the Spring*, 82.

130. Carson, *Silent Spring*, 277.

131. "The Albert Schweitzer Medal of the Animal Welfare Institute," in *Animals and Their Legal Rights: A Survey of American Laws from 1641–1978*, 3d ed., ed. Emily Leavitt (Washington, DC: Animal Welfare Institute, 1978), app., lxxii.

132. One source for the story is Jonathan Weiner, "Animal Liberation," *Cosmopolitan*, June 1980, 146. Photocopy provided by the Animal Welfare Information Center, Beltsville, MD.

133. Swallow, *Quality of Mercy*, 169; *Animals, People, and the MSPCA: 125 Years of Progress*, 4 and 8; "Group Profile," *Animal Rights Reporter* 1 (September 1989): 8; and *Work of the Society of Animal Protective Legislation*.

134. *Refuge Report* [circular] (Washington, DC: Wildlife Refuge Reform Coalition, n.d., 1995?); Cleveland Amory, *Man Kind? Our Incredible War on Wildlife* (New York: Harper and Row, 1974), 56 and 78–81; Wayne Pacelle, "Flying the Unfriendly Skies," *Animals' Agenda* 8 (November 1988): 15; and Alice Herrington, *Some Things You're Not Supposed to Know about Hunters, Hunting and "Wildlife Management"* [pamphlet] (Neptune, NJ: Friends of Animals, 1976), 4.

135. Wayne Pacelle, "Saviors or Sellouts? How 'Wildlife' Groups Lend Support to Sport Hunting," *Animals' Agenda* 8 (July–August 1988): 7.

136. For statistics on rising membership, see Sale, *Green Revolution*, 23. Also see Pacelle, "Saviors or Sellouts?" 7–8; Amory, *Man Kind?* 69–73 and 77; and Mouras, *I Care about Animals*, 130.

137. Gottlieb, *Forcing the Spring*, 42–46 and 158; Pacelle, "Saviors or Sellouts?" 8; and Finnley, "Laws to Protect Wildlife," 177.

138. G. Snyder, *Turtle Island* (New York: New Directions, 1974), 98; Ron Baker, *The American Hunting Myth* (New York: Vantage, 1985), 70–82; and Herrington, *Some Things You're Not Supposed to Know*," 4. For more discussion on this topic, see L. L. Rue, *The Deer of North America* (Los Angeles: Times-Mirror, 1978).

139. Jose Ortega y Gassett, *Meditations on Hunting*, trans. H. B. Wescott (New York: Scribner's, 1972), 112. For another "meditation" on hunting, see N. Woodcock, *Fifty Years a Hunter and Trapper* (Columbus, OH: Fur-Fish-Game, 1972).

140. Baker, *American Hunting Myth*, 70–82; Peter Gwynne, "Hunting under Fire," *National Wildlife* 12 (October–November 1974): 38–41; *Friends of Animals: Who We Are, What We Do and How to Join* [pamphlet] (Darien, CT: Friends of Animals, n.d.), 5–6; Mouras, *I Care about Animals*, 26 and 132; and Amory, *Man Kind?* 15 and 57.

141. Herrington, *Some Things You're Not Supposed to Know*, 5.

142. The statistics on coyotes and a discussion of declining numbers of predators are found in Donald Worster, *Nature's Economy: A History of Ecological Ideas* (New York: Cambridge University Press, 1977), 259 and 258–90. Also see Baker, *American Hunting Myth*, 70–82; Herrington, *Some Things You're Not Supposed to Know*, 4–7; and Amory, *Man Kind?* 107.

143. Herrington, *Some Things You're Not Supposed to Know*, 5 and 7; Peggy Morrison and Susan Hagood, *Changing U.S. Trapping Policy* (Washington, DC: Defenders of Wildlife, 1984), 9.

144. Herrington, *Some Things You're Not Supposed to Know*, 4.

145. Amory, *Man Kind?* 17.

146. Ibid., 113 and 140. The photographs appear between pp. 180 and 181.

147. *Game Animals: Animated Targets for Hunters* [pamphlet], reprinted from *Humane Society News* (Winter 1981).

148. Amory, *Man Kind?* 151.

149. These descriptions are taken variously from *Game Animals: Animated Targets*; and Amory, *Man Kind?* 150–60.

150. *Game Animals: Animated Targets*.

151. John O'Connor, "'The Guns of Autumn': Hunted and the Hunters," *New York Times*, September 14, 1975, D25; and *Game Animals: Animated Targets*.

152. The quote is from Herrington, *Some Things You're Not Supposed to Know*, 1.

153. The 1971 act excluded federal and state officials from its stipulations, and consequently, the government's predator control programs continued. See ibid., 160; "Cruel Pursuit of Wolves by Airplane," *AWI Information Report* 18 (October–December 1969): 3; *Work of the Society of Animal Protective Legislation*; *Welcome to the Fund for Animals*, back page; and Finnley, "Laws to Protect Wildlife," 177.

154. As retold in Amory, *Man Kind?* 117–20.

155. For a few of the abundant sources discussing the slipping percentage of hunters, see Matt Cartmill, *A View to a Death in the Morning: Hunting and Nature through History* (Cambridge, MA: Harvard University Press, 1993), 230; Jim Mason, *An Unnatural Order: Uncovering the Roots of Our Domination of Nature and Each Other* (New York: Simon and Schuster, 1993), 288; and James Jasper and Dorothy Nelkin, *The Animal Rights Crusade: The Growth of a Moral Protest* (New York: Free Press, 1992), 83. Amory also cites several studies noting a decline; see his *Man Kind?* 56, 89–90, 117, and 186–88.

156. Gottlieb, *Forcing the Spring*, 42–46 and 144–45; and *Who We Are*, no date, Friends of the Earth, www.foe.org/about/whoweare.html (July 7, 2005).

157. Amory, *Man Kind?* 227.

158. Ibid., 229.

159. Ibid., 230–31; and *Furs and Fashion*, 40.

160. Greta Nilsson, "Animals Killed for the Fur Trade," in *Facts about Furs* (Washington, DC: Animal Welfare Institute, 1980), 31, 40, and 75; and Amory, *Man Kind?* 228.

161. *Condemned to Die! Why?* [flyer] (Sacramento, CA: Animal Protection Institute, n.d.).

162. Mouras, *I Care about Animals*, 37 and 149.

163. The stomping of the wolf appears on pp. 24–25, and additional photographs are found on pp. 4, 32, 33, 35, 48, 86, 88, 91, 93, 96, 97, 134–37, etc.

164. "The Fur Furor," *Gentlemen's Quarterly* 40 (November 1970): 151; *Furs and Fashion*, 39–40; Amory, *Man Kind?* 237; Morrison and Hagood, *Changing U.S. Trapping Policy*, 5; Nilsson, "The Fur Trade, a Short History," in *Facts about Furs* (Washington, DC: Animal Welfare Institute, 1980); Nilsson, "Animals Killed for the Fur Trade," 20 and 72; and *Condemned to Die!*.

165. Morrison and Hagood, *Changing U.S. Trapping Policy*, 5.

166. Nash, *Rights of Nature*, 172; and Adam Roberts, "The Endangered Species Act: A Commitment Worth Keeping," *Animal Guardian* 8 (1995): 5.

167. *Furs and Fashion*, 39; *Endangered Species* [pamphlet] (Sacramento, CA: Animal Protection Institute, 1990); *Welcome to the Fund for Animals*; *The Work of the Society of Animal Protective Legislation*; *Aims and Programs of the Animal Welfare Institute*; *Animals, People, and the MSPCA*, 4; *What Is Greenpeace?* [pamphlet] (Washington, DC: Greenpeace, 1995); Hays, *Beauty, Health, and Permanence*, 112; and Nash, *Rights of Nature*, 175–77.

168. Roberts, "Endangered Species Act," 5–8; and Herrington, *Some Things You're Not Supposed to Know*, 7.

169. Roberts, "Endangered Species Act," 5–8; *Endangered Species*; and *World Wildlife Fund 1993 Annual Report* (Washington, DC: World Wildlife Fund, 1994), 31–35.

170. "Endangered Species Bill Becomes Law," *AWI Information Report* 18 (October–December 1969): 3; *Work of the Society of Animal Protective Legislation*; and Finnley, "Laws to Protect Wildlife," 178.

171. Finnley, "Laws to Protect Wildlife," 178; "Endangered Species Bill Becomes Law"; *Furs and Fashion*, 39; *Endangered Species*; *Welcome to the Fund for Animals*; *Work of the Society of Animal Protective Legislation*; *Aims and Programs of the Animal Welfare Institute*; *Animals, People, and the MSPCA*, 4; *What Is Greenpeace?*; Hays, *Beauty, Health, and Permanence*, 112; and Nash, *Rights of Nature*, 175–77.

172. Elizabeth Layne, "Eighty Nations Write Magna Carta for Wildlife," *Audubon* 75 (May 1973): 99–102; "The World's 'Most Wanted' Species," *Focus* 15 (May–June 1993): 4–5.

173. For a detailed history of the act, see Brian Czech and Paul Krausman, *The Endangered Species Act: History, Conservation Biology, and Public Policy* (Baltimore, MD: Johns Hopkins University Press, 2001); Cohen, "Federal Animal Protection Statutes," 151; Nash, *Rights of Nature*, 177; Hays, *Beauty, Health, and Permanence*, 112–13; and *Refuge Report*.

174. *World Wildlife Fund 1993 Annual Report*, 34; and Roberts, "Endangered Species Act," 5–8.

175. Roderick Nash offers greater thought on the law's ramifications for the legal rights of nature. See Nash, *Rights of Nature*, 176–77.

176. Robert Hunter, *Warriors of the Rainbow: A Chronicle of the Greenpeace Movement* (New York: Holt, Rinehart and Winston, 1979), intro.

177. For a description of the hunt, see David Lavigne, "Life or Death for the Harp Seal," *National Geographic* 149 (January 1976): 129–42; and William McCloskey, "Bitter Fight Still Rages over the Seal Killing in Canada," *Smithsonian* 10 (November 1979): 54–65.

178. Niven, *History of the Humane Movement*, 121.

179. Brian Davies, *Savage Luxury* (New York: Ballantine Books, 1970), 12 and 20–21; Richard Ryder, *Animal Revolution: Changing Attitudes towards*

Speciesism (Oxford: Basil Blackwell, 1989), 226–30; "Seal Slaughter for Fashion," *NCSAW Report*, June 1968, 2; "Seals," *NCSAW Report*, February 1972, 1; "And the Hunt Goes On," *One World: The Newsletter of Transpecies Unlimited* 1 (Spring 1982): 6; *Imprisoned and Tortured to Make "Oriental Folk Medicines!"* [flyer] (Yarmouth Port, MA: International Fund for Animal Welfare, 1994); "In Memoriam: Alice Herrington"; *Animal Advocacy and You* [pamphlet] (Sacramento, CA: Animal Protection Institute, n.d.); and "Alice Herrington, 75, Founder of Friends of Animals, Is Dead."

180. Nilsson, "Animals Killed for the Fur Trade," 68 and 70; Mouras, *I Care about Animals*, 19, 26, and 31; "Seal Slaughter for Fashion"; Amory, *Man Kind?* 285–309; and Jasper and Nelkin, *Animal Rights Crusade*, 72.

181. Nilsson, "Animals Killed for the Fur Trade," 70.

182. "And the Hunt Goes On"; Nilsson, "Animals Killed for the Fur Trade," 67, 69, and 70; and Nilsson, "Alternatives to Fur," in *Facts about Fur* (Washington, DC: Animal Welfare Institute, 1980), 175.

183. Lavigne, "Life or Death for the Harp Seal"; Mouras, *I Care about Animals*, 28; Nilsson, "Animals Killed for the Fur Trade," 67, 69, and 70; and Nilsson, "Alternatives to Fur."

184. Nilsson, "Fur Trade," 21; and Amory, *Man Kind?* 242 and 249–53.

185. Nilsson, "Fur Trade," 21; Nilsson, "Animals Killed for the Fur Trade," 71; *Furs and Fashion*, 30–31; and Amory, *Man Kind?* 243–44.

186. "Fur Furor," 151.

187. Nilsson, "Animals Killed for the Fur Trade," 68.

188. Mouras, *I Care about Animals*, 28, 50, chap. 3.

189. Christine Stevens, "Marine Mammals," in *Animals and Their Legal Rights: A Survey of American Laws from 1641–1978*, 3d ed., ed. Emily Leavitt (Washington, DC: Animal Welfare Institute, 1978), 169; and Lewis Regenstein, "Animal Rights, Endangered Species, and Human Survival," in *In Defense of Animals*, ed. Peter Singer (New York: Harper and Row, 1985), 125.

190. Stevens, "Marine Mammals," 168.

191. "Dolphins Still Drowning in Tuna Purse Seines," *AWI Information Report* 22 (April–June 1973): 1; Jasper and Nelkin, *Animal Rights Crusade*, 77.

192. "AWI Urges Moratorium on Killing of Whales," *AWI Information Report* 20 (January–March 1971): 1; Stevens, "Marine Mammals," 169–70; Mouras, *I Care about Animals*, 28 and 134.

193. "Group Profile"; and Minetree "Animal Rights—and Wrongs," 160–61.

194. The quote is from Cohen, "Federal Animal Protection Statutes," 154. Also see *Work of the Society of Animal Protective Legislation*; Mouras, *I Care about Animals*, 55; and Stevens, "Marine Mammals," 168.

195. Stevens, "Marine Mammals," 168–73.

196. Mouras, *I Care about Animals,* 133–34.

197. Two historians discuss the ideological differences between the movements at length. See Nash, *Rights of Nature;* and Lisa Mighetto, *Wild Animals and American Environmental Ethics* (Tucson: University of Arizona Press, 1991).

EPILOGUE

1. Peter Singer, *Animal Liberation,* rev. ed. (New York: Avon Books, 1990), 6 and 17.

2. Peter Singer, "The Fable of the Fox and the Unliberated Animals," *Ethics* 88, no. 2 (January 1978): 122.

3. The quotes are from Elliot Katz of San Rafael, CA, telephone interview by author, September 12, 1995; Henry Spira, "Fighting to Win," in *In Defense of Animals,* ed. Peter Singer (New York: Harper and Row, 1985), 195; and Helen Jones, "Animal Rights: A View and Comment," *Society for Animal Rights Report,* October 1981, 1. Two additional activists interviewed by the author also cited Singer as a pivotal figure for their activism. See Esther Mechler of Port Washington, NY, telephone interview by author, September 27, 1995; and Virginia Woolf, president of Lehigh Animal Rights Coalition, interview by author, September 26, 1995, tape recording, Allentown, PA. For two books that more generally discuss Singer's impact, see Lawrence Finsen and Susan Finsen, *The Animal Rights Movement in America: From Compassion to Respect* (New York: Twayne Publishers, 1994); and James Jasper and Dorothy Nelkin, *The Animal Rights Crusade: The Growth of a Moral Protest* (New York: Free Press, 1992).

4. For a discussion of rising fur sales, see Greta Nilsson, "The Fur Trade, a Short History," in *Facts about Furs* (Washington, DC: Animal Welfare Institute, 1980), 21–23, 27.

5. Finsen and Finsen, *Animal Rights Movement,* 115–16, 134–41; Jasper and Nelkin, *Animal Rights Crusade,* 76–78; "Unfinished Business: Renewing the Fight for Canada's Seals, Africa's Elephants, and the World's Whales," *Animals' Agenda* 17 (September–October 1997): 22–26; *Veal Production in the United States* [pamphlet] (San Francisco: Humane Farming Association, 1992); and "News from the Dying Industry," *Farm Report,* Fall 1994, 8.

6. J. Baird Callicott, "Animal Liberation and Environmental Ethics: Back Together Again," in *Earth Ethics: Environmental Ethics, Animal Rights, and Practical Applications,* ed. James Sterba (Englewood Cliffs, NJ: Prentice-Hall, 1995), 197.

7. Marti Kheel, "If Women and Nature Were Heard," *Feminists for Animal Rights*, Spring–Summer 1995, 10, and Kheel "The Liberation of Nature: A Circular Affair," in *Beyond Animal Rights: A Feminist Caring Ethic for the Treatment of Animals*, ed. Josephine Donovan and Carol Adams (New York: Continuum, 1996), 26.

8. Rachel Carson, *Silent Spring*, 25th anniversary ed. (Boston: Houghton Mifflin, 1987), 277.

Bibliography

In addition to the specific works listed below, the author consulted the following sources:

A-V (1939–67)

Journal of Zoophily (1892–1917)

NCSAW Report (1960–72)

Starry Cross (1920–33)

1883–1983: 100 *Years against Cruelty*. Pamphlet. Jenkintown, PA: American Anti-Vivisection Society, 1983.

1994 *Annual Report of the Animal Welfare League of Alexandria, Inc.* Alexandria, VA: Animal Welfare League of Alexandria, 1994.

AALAS Timeline: 1946–Present. 1999. American Association for Laboratory Animal Science. http://aalas.org.

AAVS Minutes Books. Philadelphia: American Anti-Vivisection Society, 1912–1959. The American Anti-Vivisection Society holdings, Jenkintown, PA.

Abbott, Rosa. "The Higher Civilization versus Vivisection." *Arena* 19 (1898): 127–30.

About Bide-a-Wee. 2002. Bide-a-Wee. http://www.bideawee.org/about.asp.

About the RSPCA—History. 2005. Royal Society for the Prevention of Cruelty To Animals. http://www.rspca.org.uk.

"AHA Visits Seal Harvests." *National Humane Newsletter* 17 (September 1971): 1.

Aims and Programs of the Animal Welfare Institute. Pamphlet. Washington, DC: Animal Welfare Institute, n.d.

"Alice Herrington, 75, Founder of Friends of Animals, Is Dead." *New York Times*, April 28, 1994. Photocopy provided by the library of PETA, Washington, DC, and Rockville, MD.

Allen, Mrs. Fairchild. "The Vivisector's Defense." *Anti-Vivisection* 3 (January 1896): 2.

American Anti-Vivisection Society. *Annual Reports*, 1st (1883), 5th (1888).

———. *American Anti-Vivisection Society Audit*. Philadelphia: AAVS, 1945.

American Humane Association. *Annual Reports*, 38th (1914), 39th (1915), 41st (1917) 43rd (1919), 44th (1920), 45th (1921), 46th (1922), Albany, NY; and 1994 *Annual Report of the American Humane Association*, Englewood, CO, 1994.

"Ammunition against the Anti-vivisectionists." *Science* 29 (February 26, 1909): 342.

Amory, Cleveland. *The Cat and the Curmudgeon*. Boston: Little, Brown, 1990.

——. *Man Kind? Our Incredible War on Wildlife*. New York: Harper and Row, 1974.

"And the Hunt Goes On." *One World: The Newsletter of Transpecies Unlimited* 1 (Spring 1982): 6.

Angell: 75 Years of Veterinary Excellence, Dedication to Animals, and Humane Care. Boston: MSPCA, 1990.

Angell, George. *Autobiographical Sketches and Personal Reflections*. Boston: American Humane Education Society, 1892.

Animal Advocacy and You. Pamphlet. Sacramento, CA: Animal Protection Institute, n.d.

Animal and Plant Health Inspection Service of the U.S. Department of Agriculture. "First Federal Law to Prevent Cruelty to Animals." In *Animals and Their Legal Rights: A Survey of American Law from 1641–1978*, 3d ed., ed. Emily Leavitt, 33–35. Washington, DC: Animal Welfare Institute, 1978.

Animal Behavior 17 (1969): 208.

Animal Control in New York City: Past, Present, and Future. Pamphlet. New York: United Action for Animals, n.d.

Animal Welfare Institute. *Comfortable Quarters for Laboratory Animals*. New York: Animal Welfare Institute, 1955.

——. *Humane Biology Projects*. New York: Animal Welfare Institute, 1960.

Animals' Agenda 10 (January–February): 40.

Animals into Meat: A Report of the Pre-slaughter Handling of Livestock. New York: Argus Archives, 1971.

"Animals in the Laboratory: . . . In the Name of Defense." *Unicorn* 2 (November 1981): 3.

Animals, People, and the MSPCA: 125 Years of Progress. Booklet. Boston: MSPCA, 1993.

Anthony, Harold, and Henry Osborn. "Can We Save the Mammals?" *Natural History* 22 (1922): 389–415.

The Anti-Cruelty Society: 75th Anniversary Annual Report. Chicago: Anti-Cruelty Society, 1975.

"The Antivivisection Agitation in N.Y." *Journal of the American Medical Association* 54 (1910): 1062–63.

"The Antivivisectionists." *Science* 33 (March 17, 1911): 429–30.
"ASPCA Commissions Humane Slaughter Study." *Animal Protection* (Spring 1988), 6–7.
Austin, Mary. *From the Land of Little Rain*. Boston: Houghton Mifflin, 1950 [1903].
AWI Information Report 18 (April–June 1969): 1–3.
"AWI Urges Moratorium on Killing of Whales." *AWI Information Report* 20 (January–March 1971): 1.
Background Note: Walter B. Cannon Papers. February 2003. American Philosophical Society. http://www.amphilsoc.org/library/mole/c/cannon.htm.
Bailey, Liberty Hyde. *The Holy Earth*. New York: Charles Scribner's Sons, 1915.
Baker, Ron. *The American Hunting Myth*. New York: Vantage, 1985.
Barrett, James. *Work and Community in the Jungle: Chicago's Packinghouse Workers, 1894–1922*. Chicago: University of Chicago Press, 1990.
Baum, Rudy. "Biomedical Researchers Work to Counter Animal Rights Agenda." *Chemical and Engineering News* 68 (May 7, 1990): 9–24.
Baynes, Earnest Harold. "The Truth about Vivisection." *Woman's Home Companion* 48 (July 1921): 9–10.
Ben-David, Joseph. *The Scientist's Role in Society*. Chicago: University of Chicago Press, 1984.
Bengt, Berg. *The Motherless*. New York: Doubleday, 1924.
Bennett, Mary Angela. *Elizabeth Stuart Phelps*. Philadelphia: University of Pennsylvania Press, 1939.
Benson, Susan Porter. *Counter Cultures: Saleswomen, Managers, and Customers in American Department Stores, 1890–1940*. Chicago: University of Illinois Press, 1986.
Bentham, Jeremy. *An Introduction to the Principles of Morals and Legislation*. Ed. Laurence Lafleur. New York: Hafner, 1948.
Bergh, Henry. "The Cost of Cruelty." *North American Review* 133 (July 1881): 75–81.
Beuttinger, Craig. "Antivivisection and the Charge of Zoophil-Psychosis in the Early Twentieth Century." *Historian* 15 (Winter 1993): 277–89.
Bide-a-Wee Newsletter, Summer 1973.
Bleicher, Norman. "Care of Animals during Surgical Experiments." In *Methods of Animal Experimentation*, ed. William Gay, vol. 1, 103–50. New York: Academic Press, 1965.
Bliven, Bruce. "Using Our Leisure Is No Easy Job." *New York Times Magazine*, April 26, 1964, 18–19.
Blum, John M. *V Was for Victory: Politics and American Culture during World War II*. New York: Harcourt Brace Jovanovich, 1976.

Boorstin, Daniel J. "Welcome to the Consumption Community." *Fortune* 76 (September 1, 1967): 118–21.

Bowditch, Henry. "Vivisection Justifiable." *Sanitarian* 38 (1896): 230–31.

Boyer, Paul. *Urban Masses and Moral Order in America, 1820–1920*. Cambridge, MA: Harvard University Press, 1992.

Braverman, Harry. *Labor and Monopoly Capital: The Degradation of Work in the Twentieth Century*. New York: Monthly Review Press, 1974.

Brewster, William. *October Farm*. Cambridge, MA: Harvard University Press, 1936.

Brief History of the Movement for the Protection of Animals in the State of Pennsylvania. n.p.: n.d. [Philadelphia, c. 1905–1909].

Briggs, Anna C. *Because We Love Them: A Handbook for Animal Lovers*. Leesburg, VA: National Humane Education Society, 1994.

———. *For the Love of Animals: The Story of the National Humane Education Society*. n.p.: Potomac Publishing, 1990.

Brinkley, Alan, and Ellen Fitzpatrick. *America in Modern Times since 1890*. New York: McGraw-Hill, 1997.

Brisk, Fay. "Dog Owners vs. Dognappers." *Pure Bred Dogs/American Kennel Gazette* (August 1977). Reprinted with permission of the American Kennel Club. Photocopy provided by Argus Archives, Garrison, NY.

Brody, David. *Steelworkers in America: The Nonunion Era*. Cambridge, MA: Harvard University Press, 1960.

Brooks, Paul. Foreword to *Silent Spring*, 25th anniversary ed., by Rachel Carson. Boston: Houghton Mifflin, 1993.

Brown, V. K. H. "Acute Toxicity Testing." In *Animals and Alternatives in Toxicity Testing*, ed. M. Balls, R. J. Riddell, and A. N. Worden, 1–16. London: Academic Press, 1983.

Buel, C. C. "Henry Bergh and His Work." *Scribner's Monthly* 17 (April 1879): 872–84.

"Burning." *AWI Information Report* 11 (March–April 1962): 3.

"Business Bulletin." *Wall Street Journal*, March 26, 1970, 1.

Callicott, J. Baird. "Animal Liberation and Environmental Ethics: Back Together Again." In *Earth Ethics: Environmental Ethics, Animal Rights, and Practical Applications*, ed. James Sterba, 190–98. Englewood Cliffs, NJ: Prentice-Hall, 1995.

"Campaign to Repeal Metcalf-Hatch Opens." *NCSAW Report*, October 1968, 1.

Campbell, Jane. "Mrs. Caroline Earle White, Reformer." *Records of the American Catholic Historical Society* 33 (March 1922): 29–53.

Cannon, W. B. "Animal Experimentation and Its Benefits to Mankind." *Journal of the American Medical Association* 58 (1912): 1829–37.

———. "Report of Committee for the Protection of Medical Research." *Journal of the American Medical Association* 86 (1926): 862–63.

Card, Leslie, and Malden Nesheim. *Poultry Production.* Philadelphia: Lea and Febiger, 1971.

Carrighar, Sally. *One Day at Teton Marsh.* New York: Alfred A. Knopf, 1947.

Carson, Gerald. *Men, Beasts, and Gods: A History of Cruelty and Kindness to Animals.* New York: Charles Scribner's Sons, 1972.

Carson, Rachel. *The Edge of the Sea.* Boston: Houghton Mifflin, 1955.

———. *The Sea around Us.* New York: Oxford University Press, 1951.

———. *Silent Spring.* Boston: Houghton Mifflin, 1962.

———. *Under the Sea Wind: A Naturalist's Picture of Ocean Life.* New York: Simon and Schuster, 1941

Cartmill, Matt. *A View to a Death in the Morning: Hunting and Nature through History.* Cambridge, MA: Harvard University Press, 1993.

"Cat Protest Continues." *East Side Express* (New York), August 19, 1976, 8.

Chafe, William. *The Unfinished Journey: America since World War II.* New York: Oxford University Press, 1991.

Chandler, Alfred. *The Visible Hand: The Managerial Revolution in American Business.* Cambridge, MA: Harvard University Press, 1977.

Chindahl, George. *A History of the Circus in America.* Caldwell, ID: Caxton Printers, 1959.

Church, Ann. "Understanding the Animal Welfare Act." *Humane Society News,* Winter 1989, 17–21.

Clarke, Ida Clyde. *American Women and the World War.* New York: D. Appleton, 1918.

Clifton, Merritt. "Fur Farms: Where the Sun Doesn't Shine." *Animals' Agenda* 11 (November 1991): 12–15.

———. "Pet Theft: Can We Stop It? *Animals' Agenda* 12 (April 1992): 12–18.

Coalition to Abolish Metcalf-Hatch. Circular. New York: Coalition to Abolish Metcalf-Hatch, 1979.

Cobbe, Frances Power, and Benjamin Bryan. *Vivisection in America.* London: Swan Sonnenschein and Co., 1890.

Cohen, Henry. "Federal Animal Protection Statutes." *Animal Law* 1 (1995): 143–61.

Coleman, Sydney. *Humane Society Leaders in America.* Albany, NY: American Humane Association, 1924.

"Concerned Authorities Reveal Facts." *Our Animal WARDS,* November 1980, 4.

Condemned to Die! Why? Flyer. Sacrament, CA: Animal Protection Institute, n.d.

"Connecticut Seizure Law Repealed." *Society for Animal Rights Report*, May 1980, 1.
Consumer Product Safety: Why We Need It, How We Achieve It. Washington, DC: Join Hands Health and Safety Educational Alliance, n.d.
Cooper, Susan Fenimore. *Rural Hours*. New York: G. P. Putnam, 1850.
"The Cost of a Set of Furs." *Journal of Zoophily* 25 (January 1916): 12.
Cott, Nancy. *The Bonds of Womanhood: "Woman's Sphere" in New England, 1780–1835*. New Haven, CT: Yale University Press, 1977.
Cox, Thomas, Robert Maxwell, Phillip Thomas, and Joseph Malone. *This Well-Wooded Land: Americans and Their Forests from Colonial Times to the Present*. Lincoln: University of Nebraska Press, 1985.
"Crucial Test for Laboratory Animals." *Medical World News* (February 11, 1966): 84. Photocopy provided by the International Society for Animal Rights, Clarks Summit, PA.
"Cruel Pursuit of Wolves by Airplane." *AWI Information Report* 18 (October–December 1969): 3.
Curwood, James Oliver. *The Grizzly King*. New York: Cosmopolitan Books, 1918.
Czech, Brian, and Paul Krausman. *The Endangered Species Act: History, Conservation Biology, and Public Policy*. Baltimore, MD: Johns Hopkins University Press, 2001.
Dana, Charles L. "The Zoophil-Psychosis: A Modern Malady." *Medical Record* 75 (March 6, 1909): 381–83.
Daniel, Pete. "Technology and Ethics in Agriculture." *Journal of Agricultural and Environmental Ethics* 6 (1993): 52–59.
Darwin, Charles. "Mr. Darwin on Vivisection." *Times* (London), April 18, 1881. Reprinted in *Nature* 45 (April 21, 1892): 583.
Davies, Brian. *Savage Luxury*. New York: Ballantine Books, 1970.
Davis, Allen. *Spearheads for Reform: The Social Settlements and the Progressive Movement*. New York: Oxford University Press, 1967.
Davis, Karen. "The Plight of Poultry." *Poultry Press* 6 (Summer 1996): 4–5.
Davis, Noah. "The Moral Aspects of Vivisection." *North American Review* 140 (March 1885): 203–20.
Dawley, Alan. *Struggle for Justice*. Cambridge, MA: Harvard University Press, 1991.
Death of a Vivisectionist. Pamphlet. Philadelphia: American Anti-Vivisection Society, n.d.
Dempewolff, Richard. *Animal Reveille*. New York: Doubleday, Doran, 1945.
Dewey, John. "The Ethics of Animal Experimentation." *Atlantic Monthly* 138 (1926): 343.

Dewsbury, Donald. "Early Interactions between Animal Psychologists and Animal Activists and the Founding of the APA Committee on Precautions in Animal Experimentation." *American Psychologist* 45 (March 1990): 315–27.

Diner, Steven. *A Very Different Age: American in the Progressive Era.* New York: Hill and Wang, 1998.

"Dolphins Still Drowning in Tuna Purse Seines." *AWI Information Report* 22 (April–June 1973): 1.

Donner, Jill. "Lassie Stay Home." *WGAW* (April 1989): 23.

Donovan, Josephine. "Animal Rights and Feminist Theory." In *Beyond Animal Rights: A Feminist Caring Ethic for the Treatment of Animals,* ed. Josephine Donovan and Carol Adams, 34–59. New York: Continuum, 1996.

Douglas, William O. *My Wilderness: East to Katahdin.* Garden City, NY: Doubleday, 1961.

"Draize Unreliable." *Our Animal WARDS,* November 1989, 9, 14.

Dubois, Ellen, Mari Jo Buhle, Temma Kaplan, Gerda Lerner, and Caroll Smith-Rosenberg. "Politics and Culture in Women's History: A Symposium." *Feminist Studies* 6 (Spring 1980): 26–64.

Dunlap, Thomas. *Saving America's Wildlife.* Princeton, NJ: Princeton University Press, 1988.

"Early Years." *National Humane Review* 56 (January–February 1962): 20–23.

"Eleanor E. Seiling." *International Society for Animal Rights Report,* November 1985, 2.

Elston, Mary Ann. "Women and Anti-vivisection in Victorian England, 1870–1900." In *Vivisection in Historical Perspective,* ed. Nicolas A. Rupke, 259–94. London: Croom Helm, 1987.

Endangered Species. Pamphlet. Sacramento, CA: Animal Protection Institute, 1990.

"Endangered Species Bill Becomes Law." *AWI Information Report* 18 (October–December 1969): 3.

Engberg, Robert, ed. *John Muir: Summering in the Sierra.* Madison: University of Wisconsin Press, 1984.

Evans, E. P. "Mind in Man and Brute." *Unitarian Review* 36 (November 1891): 342–65.

———. "The Nearness of Animals to Man." *Atlantic Monthly* 69 (1892): 171–84.

———. "Progress and Perfectibility in the Lower Animals." *Popular Science Monthly* 40 (December 1891): 170–79.

Evans, Elliot. "A Historic Perspective: The Early Years." In *The Latham Foundation First in Humane Education—Since 1918.* Alameda, CA: Latham Foundation, n.d.

"Extracts from the Ninth Annual Report of the Department of Mercy of the National WCTU." *Journal of Zoophily* 8 (December 1899): 136.

Facts on the Draize Eye and Skin Irritancy Tests. Chicago: National Anti-Vivisection Society, n.d.

"The Fashion in Furs." *Journal of Zoophily* 9 (February 1900): 18.

Faulkner, Harold Underwood. *The Quest for Social Justice, 1898–1914.* New York: Macmillan, 1931.

Favre, David, and Vivien Tsang. "The Development of Anti-cruelty Laws during the 1800's." *Detroit College of Law Review* 1 (Spring 1993): 1–35.

Feedstuffs, November 23, 1992.

Ferguson, Moira. *Animal Advocacy and Englishwomen, 1780–1900.* Ann Arbor: University of Michigan Press, 1998.

Film Monitoring. 2005. American Humane Association. http://www.americanhumane.org/site/PageServer?pagename=pa_film.

Finnley, Dona. "Laws to Protect Wildlife." In *Animals and Their Legal Rights: A Survey of American Law, 1641–1978,* 3d ed., ed. Emily Leavitt, 175–204. Washington, DC: Animal Welfare Institute, 1978.

Finsen, Lawrence, and Susan Finsen. *The Animal Rights Movement in America: From Compassion to Respect.* New York: Twayne Publishers, 1994.

"First Anniversary Marked." *NCSAW Report,* June 1960, 8.

The First Public Declaration of the Open Door in Laboratories for Animal Experimentation. Springfield, MA: Blue Cross Society, 1922.

Flexner, S., and J. T. Flexner. *William Henry Welch and the Heroic Age of American Medicine.* New York: Viking Press, 1941.

Florence Merriam Bailey: Pioneer Naturalist. No date. Saint Lawrence County, NY, Branch of the American Association of University Women. http://northnet.org/stlawrenceaauw/bailey.htm.

"Ford Phasing Out Cruelty to Animals." *NCSAW Report,* June 1968, 1.

Foster, Burnside. "Results of Animal Experimentation." *Yale Review* 2 (January 1913): 301–14.

Fox, M. W. "Use of the Dog in Behavioral Research." In *Methods of Animal Experimentation,* ed. William Gay, vol. 3, 27–80. New York: Academic Press, 1968.

Free, Ann Cottrell, ed. *Animals, Nature, and Albert Schweitzer.* Washington, DC: Flying Fox Press, 1988.

Freedman, Estelle. "Separatism as Strategy: Female Institution Building and American Feminism, 1870–1930." *Feminist Studies* 5 (Fall 1979): 512–29.

French, Richard. *Antivivisection and Medical Science in Victorian Society.* Princeton, NJ: Princeton University Press, 1975.

Friends of Animals: Who We Are, What We Do and How to Join. Pamphlet. Darien, CT: Friends of Animals, n.d.
"The Fur Furor." *Gentlemen's Quarterly* 40 (November 1970): 151.
Furman, Lucy. "The Price of Furs." *Atlantic Monthly* 141 (February 1928): 206–9.
Furs and Fashion: Traps and Trapping. New York: Argus Archives, 1971.
Gaddis, John. *We Know Now: Rethinking Cold War History*. New York: Oxford University Press, 1998.
Galambos, Louis, and Merck. *Values and Visions: A Merck Century*. Rahway, NJ: Merck, 1991.
Game Animals: Animated Targets for Hunters. Pamphlet. Reprinted from *Humane Society News* (Winter 1981).
"Genesis." *National Humane Review* 56 (January–February 1962): 6–8.
Gennarelli, T. A., L. E. Thibault, and A. K. Ommaya. "Comparison of Translational and Rotation Head Motions in Experimental Cerebral Concussion." *Proceedings of the Fifteenth Annual Stapp Car Crash Conference Held in Coronado, California, November 17–19, 1971*. New York: Society of Automotive Engineers, 1971.
Gordon, Linda. *Heroes of Their Own Lives: The Politics and History of Family Violence*. New York: Viking Penguin, 1988.
Gottlieb, Robert. *Forcing the Spring: The Transformation of the American Environmental Movement*. Washington, DC: Island Press, 1993.
Grafton, T. S. "The Founding and Early History of the National Society for Medical Research." *Laboratory Animal Science* 30 (1980): 759–64.
Graham, Frank, Jr. *Since Silent Spring*. Boston: Houghton Mifflin, 1970.
Great Minds Think Alike. Pamphlet. Mill Valley, CA: In Defense of Animals, n.d.
Greenbaum, Lowell. "Animal-Care Laws: The Mood of Congress." *Science* 151 (March 18, 1966): 1329.
Greenberg, D. S. "Basic Research: The Tides Are Shifting." *Science* 152 (June 24, 1966): 1724–26.
———. "News and Comments." *Science* 140 (May 24, 1963): 878.
"Group Profile." *Animal Rights Report* 1 (September 1989): 8.
Guerrini, Anita. *Experimenting with Humans and Animals: From Galen to Animal Rights*. Baltimore, MD: Johns Hopkins University Press, 2003.
Gwynne, Peter. "Hunting under Fire." *National Wildlife* 12 (October–November 1974): 38–41.
Hackbarth, Carol. "Experiments on Humans Hit by Foe of Practice: Woman Quotes Doctors in Arguments against Such Research Activities." *Columbus (OH) Citizen*, 1933. Photocopy provided by PETA, Washington, DC, and Rockville, MD.

Halvey, Nina. "Fiftieth Anniversary: The AAVS Radio Broadcast." *Starry Cross* 41 (June 1933): 71.

Hampson, Judith. "Animal Welfare: A Century of Conflict." *New Scientist* 81 (October 25, 1979): 280–82.

Harlan, Louis, ed. *The Booker T. Washington Papers*, vol. 2, *1860–1889*. Chicago: University of Illinois Press, 1972.

Harlow, Harry F., and M. K. Harlow. "Social Deprivation in Monkeys." *Scientific American* 207 (1962): 136–46.

Harrison, Ruth. *Animal Machines.* London: Vincent Stuart, 1964.

Hays, Samuel P. *Beauty, Health, and Permanence: Environmental Politics in the U.S., 1955–85.* New York: Cambridge University Press, 1987.

———. *Conservation and the "Gospel of Efficiency": The Progressive Conservation Movement, 1890–1920.* Cambridge, MA: Harvard University Press, 1959.

"Henry Bergh." *National Humane Review* 56 (January–February 1962): 10–12.

Henry Bergh: Founder of the ASPCA. Pamphlet. New York: ASPCA, n.d.

Herrington, Alice. *Some Things You're Not Supposed to Know about Hunters, Hunting and "Wildlife Management."* Pamphlet. Neptune, NJ: Friends of Animals, 1976.

Hershel, Matt. "Why Keep Kosher?" *Women's League Outlook* 36 (March 1966): 10 and 21.

Hilts, Philip J. "Use of Animals Falls 50% since 1968." *New York Times*, March 3, 1994, A18.

"History of Caroline Earle White." Undated photocopied information provided by Janice Mininberg of the Women's Humane Society, Philadelphia.

Hofstadter, Richard. *Social Darwinism in American Thought.* New York: Columbia University Press, 1944.

Hornaday, William T. *Our Vanishing Wildlife: Its Extermination and Preservation.* New York: Zoological Society, 1913.

"H.R. 264, Humane Methods of Poultry Slaughter Act of 1995." *Poultry Press* 5 (Summer–Fall 1995): 4.

Hughes, Rupert. "Animal and Vegetable Rights." *Harper's Monthly Magazine* 103 (November 1901): 852–53.

"Humane Education in the 20th Century." *NCSAW Report*, June 1961, 11.

"Humane Educator." *National Humane Review* 56 (January–February 1962): 13–14.

"Humane Society Pioneers." *National Humane Review* 56 (January–February 1962): 15.

Hume, C. W. "The Ethics of Experiments on Animals." *Nature* 167 (February 10, 1951): 213–15.

Hunter, Robert. *Warriors of the Rainbow: A Chronicle of the Greenpeace Movement.* New York: Holt, Rinehart and Winston, 1979.

Imprisoned and Tortured to Make "Oriental Folk Medicines"! Flyer. Yarmouth Port, MA: International Fund for Animal Welfare, 1994.

"In Memoriam: Alice Herrington." *International Society for Animal Rights Report,* Spring 1994, 6.

Institute of Laboratory Animal Resources. *Fiscal Year 1978 National Survey of Laboratory Animal Facilities and Resources.* NIH Publication No. 80-2091. Washington, DC: U.S. Department of Health and Human Services, March 1980.

Jackson, Christine. "Dissection: Science or Violence?" *Mothering Magazine* (Spring 1991): 91–94.

Jackson, Kenneth. *The Crabgrass Frontier: The Suburbanization of the United States.* New York: Oxford University Press, 1985.

Jasper, James, and Dorothy Nelkin. *The Animal Rights Crusade: The Growth of a Moral Protest.* New York: Free Press, 1992.

Jemski, Joseph, and G. Briggs Phillips. "Aerosol Challenge of Animals." In *Methods of Animal Experimentation,* ed. William Gay, vol. 1, 274–342. New York: Academic Press, 1965.

Jones, David. "A Family's Needs Found 50% Higher." *New York Times,* October 25, 1967, 1.

Jones, Helen. "Animal Rights: A View and Comment." *Society for Animal Rights Report,* October 1981, 1–4.

———. President of the International Society for Animal Rights. Interview by author, November 28, 1995. Taped recording. Clarks Summit, PA.

Jordanova, Ludmilla. *Sexual Visions: Images of Gender in Science between the Eighteenth and Twentieth Centuries.* Madison: University of Wisconsin Press, 1989.

Kalechofsky, Roberta. *Autobiography of a Revolutionary.* Marblehead, MA: Micah Publications, 1991.

Kaledin, Eugenia. *Mothers and More: American Women in the 1950s.* Boston: Twayne, 1984.

Katz, Elliot. President of In Defense of Animals of San Rafael, CA. Telephone interview by author, September 12, 1995.

Kaufman, Martin, and Herbert Kaufman. "Salamander the Fire Horse." *American History Illustrated* 15 (October 1980): 36–38.

Keaton, Cherry. *The Island of Penguins.* New York: Viking Press, 1931.

Keen, W. W. *Animal Experimentation and Medical Progress.* Boston: Houghton Mifflin, 1914.

———. "Editorial." *Journal of the American Medical Association* 33 (1899): 1618.

———. "Vivisection and Brain Surgery." *Harper's New Monthly Magazine* 87 (June 1893): 128–39.

Kellert, Stephen, and Miriam Westervelt. "Historical Trends in American Animal Use and Perception." *International Journal for the Study of Animal Problems* 4 (1983): 133–46.

Kerber, Linda. "Separate Spheres, Female Worlds, Woman's Place: The Rhetoric of Women's History." *Journal of American History* 75 (June 1988): 9–39.

Kessler, Carol Farley. *Elizabeth Stuart Phelps*. Boston: Twayne Publishers, 1982.

Kete, Kathleen. *The Beast in the Boudoir: Petkeeping in Nineteenth-Century Paris*. Los Angeles: University of California Press, 1994.

Kheel, Marti. "If Women and Nature Were Heard." *Feminists for Animal Rights*, Spring–Summer 1995, 10.

———. "The Liberation of Nature: A Circular Affair." In *Beyond Animal Rights: A Feminist Caring Ethic for the Treatment of Animals*, ed. Josephine Donovan and Carol J. Adams, 17–33. New York: Continuum, 1996.

Kofalk, H. *No Woman Tenderfoot: Florence Merriam Bailey*. College Station: Texas A&M Press, 1989.

Kreger, Michael. *The LD50 (Median Lethal Dose) and LC50 (Median Lethal Concentration) Toxicity Test, January 1980–March 1992*. Special Reference Briefs, 92-12. Beltsville, MD: National Agricultural Library, 1992.

Kretschmer, Herman. "Address of the President." *Journal of the American Medical Association* 129 (1945): 1107–9.

Krutch, Joseph W. *The Desert Year*. New York: William Sloane Associates, 1952.

Kuhn, Thomas. *The Structure of Scientific Revolutions*. Chicago: University of Chicago Press, 1970.

Kuker-Reines, Brandon. *Psychology Experiments on Animals: A Critique of Animal Models of Human Psychopathology*. Boston: New England Anti-Vivisection Society, 1982.

Kullberg, John F. "America's Endangered Symbol." *ASPCA Report*, Winter 1984, 2. Photocopy provided by John Kullberg.

———. "Henry Bergh's Legacy 100 Years Later." Spring 1988. Photocopy provided by John Kullberg.

———. Former president and executive director of the ASPCA. Interview by author, December 15, 1995. Taped recording. Gaithersburg, MD.

Kunhardt, Philip Jr., Philip B. Kunhardt III, and Peter Kunhardt. *P. T. Barnum: America's Greatest Showman*. New York: Alfred A. Knopf, 1995.

Lamont, Gil. "Banking on Animal Organs." *Mainstream* 26 (Summer 1995): 9–12.

Lane-Petter, W. "Science, Animals, and Humanity." *Nature* 174 (September 18, 1954): 532–34.

Langer, Elinor. "Animal Care: The Humane Movement Is Pulling Ahead." *Science* 151 (March 25, 1966): 1515–18.

———. "Dogs and Cats: Humane Treatment Legislation Nears Passage." *Science* 153 (August 19, 1966): 846.

Lansbury, Coral. *The Old Brown Dog: Women, Workers, and Vivisection in Edwardian England.* Madison: University of Wisconsin Press, 1985.

Lapp, Ralph. *Arms beyond Doubt.* N.p.: Cowles, 1970.

Laub, Morris. "Why the Fuss over Humane Slaughter Legislation?" *Women's League Outlook* 36 (March 1966): 8–9.

Lavigne, David. "Life or Death for the Harp Seal." *National Geographic* 149 (January 1976): 129–42.

Lawson, Sian. "Digital Horses: Ending Cruelty in Film." February 15, 2005. International Fund for Horses. http://www.fund4horses.org.

Layne, Elizabeth. "Eighty Nations Write Magna Carta for Wildlife." *Audubon* 75 (May 1973): 99–102.

Leavitt, Emily. "Humane Slaughter Laws." In *Animals and Their Legal Rights: A Survey of American Laws from 1641–1978*, 3d ed., ed. Emily Leavitt, 36–45. Washington, DC: Animal Welfare Institute, 1978.

Leavitt, Emily, and Diane Halverson. "The Evolution of Anti-cruelty Laws in the United States." In *Animals and Their Legal Rights: A Survey of American Laws from 1641–1978*, 3d ed., ed. Emily Leavitt, 11–32. Washington, DC: Animal Welfare Institute, 1978.

Lederer, Susan. "The Controversy over Animal Experimentation in America, 1880–1914." In *Vivisection in Historical Perspective*, ed. Nicolas A. Rupke, 236–58. London: Croom Helm, 1987.

———. "Political Animals: The Shaping of Biomedical Research Literature in Twentieth-Century America." *Isis* 83 (1992): 61–78.

Lee, Susan Previant, and Peter Passell. *A New Economic View of American History.* New York: W. W. Norton, 1979.

Leepson, Marc. "Animal Rights." *CQ Researcher* 1 (May 24, 1991): 301–24.

Leffingwell, Albert. "Does Vivisection Pay?" *Scribner's Monthly* 20 (July 1880): 391–99.

———. *An Ethical Problem or Sidelights upon Scientific Experimentation on Man and Animals.* 2d ed. New York: G. Bell and Sons, 1916.

———. "The Future of Vivisection." Paper presented at the International Anti-Vivisection and Animal Protection Congress, Washington, DC, December 8–11, 1913.

———. "Vivisection in America." Appendix to Henry Salt, *Animals' Rights Considered in Relation to Social Progress*, 133–74. London: Macmillan, 1894.
"Legislature Repeals Metcalf-Hatch." ASPCA *Bulletin* 3 (Fall 1979): 1.
Leopold, Aldo. "The Conservation Ethic." *Journal of Forestry* 31 (October 1933): 634–43.
———. *A Sand County Almanac and Sketches Here and There*. New York: Oxford University Press, 1968.
"Letters." *Science* 150 (December 17, 1965): 1536.
"Letters to the Editor." *Life* 60 (February 25, 1966): 25.
Levering, Ralph. *The Cold War: A Post–Cold War History*. Arlington Heights, IL: Harlan Davidson, 1994.
"The Life and Times of George Thorndike Angell." *Animals* 113 (June 1980): 12–13.
"Little Vivisection Here: Authorities However Decry Publicity as Hampering Research." *New York Times*, December 31, 1906, 5.
Lockwood, Samuel. "Animal Humor." *American Naturalist* 10 (May 1876): 257–70.
Loeper, John. *Crusade for Kindness: Henry Bergh and the ASPCA*. New York: Macmillan, 1991.
Loercher, Diane. "Anti-vivisection Battle Shifts to New York Museum." *Christian Science Monitor*, September 20, 1976. Photocopy provided by Argus Archives, Garrison, NY.
Logan, Robert. "Address of the President." A-V 50 (February 1942): 17.
———. "After 50 Years." *Starry Cross* 41 (June 1933): 6.
———. "The Enemy." *Journal of Zoophily* 26 (May 1917): 67–68.
———. "A New Year's Message from the Editor." *Journal of Zoophily* 26 (January 1917): 1.
———. "Popularity and Progress." *Journal of Zoophily* 26 (November 1917): 163.
———. "The Symbol of the Cross." *Journal of Zoophily* 26 (December 1917): 180.
London, Jack. *Jerry of the Islands*. New York: Macmillan, 1916.
———. *Michael, Brother of Jerry*. New York: Macmillan, 1917.
"Los Angeles Seizure Ordinance Repealed." *Society for Animal Rights Report*, August 1981, 1.
Lovell, Mary. "Anti-vivisection Work in America." Paper presented at the International Anti-Vivisection and Animal Protection Congress, Philadelphia October 17–20, 1926.
———. "Humane Education." Paper presented at the International Anti-Vivisection and Animal Protection Congress, Washington, DC, December 8–11, 1913.

———. *Outline of the History of the WPSPCA: From Its Foundation April 14, 1869 to January 1908.* Philadelphia: WPSPCA, 1908.

———. "Progress or Inertia—Which?" *Journal of Zoophily* 8 (January 1899): 7

Maggitti, Phil. "Is Fur Really Dead?" *Animals' Agenda* 15 (1995): 24–28.

The Man from Rochester Protests Too Much. Pamphlet. Philadelphia: American Anti-Vivisection Society, 1965.

Mann, Arthur. *Yankee Reformers in the Urban Age: Social Reform in Boston, 1880–1900.* New York: Harper and Row, 1954.

Marshall, Peter. *Nature's Web: An Exploration of Ecological Thinking.* New York: Simon and Schuster, 1992.

Martin, Phillip. *The Animal Rights Movement in the United States: Its Composition, Funding Sources, Goals, Strategies, and Potential Impact on Research.* Cambridge, MA: Harvard University's Office of Government and Community Affairs, 1982.

Mason, Jim. "Never on Sunday." *Animals' Agenda* 15 (1995): 20–24.

———. *An Unnatural Order: Uncovering the Roots of Our Domination of Nature and Each Other.* New York: Simon and Schuster, 1993.

Mason, Jim, and Peter Singer. *Animal Factories.* New York: Crown Publishers, 1980.

May, Elaine Tyler. *Homeward Bound: American Families in the Cold War Era.* New York: Basic Books, 1988.

Mayer, Lawrence A. "The Diverse $10,000-and-Over Masses." *Fortune* 76 (December 1967): 114–17.

McCann, Mary, and Frederick Stare. "The Contribution of Animal Studies to Nutritional Discoveries That Have Benefited Both Animals and Man." *American Journal of Public Health* 57 (September 1967): 1597–603.

McCloskey, William. "Bitter Fight Still Rages over the Seal Killing in Canada." *Smithsonian* 10 (November 1979): 54–65.

McCrea, Roswell. *The Humane Movement: A Descriptive Survey.* New York: Columbia University Press, 1910.

Mechler, Esther. Spay/USA of Port Washington, NY. Telephone interview by author, September 27, 1995.

Meikle, Jeffrey L. "Material Doubts: The Consequences of Plastic." *Environmental History* 2 (July 1997): 278–300.

Meir, Gilbert. "Use of Cats in Behavioral Research." In *Methods of Animal Experimentation,* ed. William Gay, vol. 3, 125–74. New York: Academic Press, 1968.

Merchant, Carolyn, ed. *Major Problems in American Environmental History.* Lexington, MA: D. C. Heath, 1993.

———. "The Women of the Progressive Conservation Crusade, 1900–1915." In *Environmental History: Critical Issues in Comparative Perspectives,* ed. Kendall E. Bailes, 153–70. Lanham, MD: University Press of America, 1985.

Merwin, Henry Childs. "Vivisection." *Atlantic Monthly* 89 (March 1902): 320–25.

"Metcalf-Hatch Repealed." *Society for Animal Rights Report*, September 1979, 1.

Midgley, Mary. *Animals and Why They Matter*. Athens: University of Georgia Press, 1983.

Mighetto, Lisa. *Wild Animals and American Environmental Ethics*. Tucson: University of Arizona Press, 1991.

Miller, James. "Conservation Is Everybody's Battle." *Reader's Digest* 85 (August 1964): 161–66.

Minetree, Harry. "Animal Rights—and Wrongs." *Town & Country*, May 1988, 158–61, 230, 232, 235–36, and 238.

Mitchison, Wendy. *The Nature of Their Bodies: Women and Their Doctors in Victorian Canada*. Toronto, Canada: University of Toronto Press, 1991.

Moore, J. Howard. "Discovering Darwin." Paper presented at the International Anti-Vivisection and Animal Protection Congress, Washington, DC, December 8–11, 1913.

Morris, Clara. "Riddle of the Nineteenth Century: Mr. Henry Bergh." *McClure's Magazine* 18 (March 1902): 416–18.

Morrison, Peggy, and Susan Hagood. *Changing U.S. Trapping Policy: A Handbook for Activists*. Washington, DC: Defenders of Wildlife, 1984.

Motavalli, Jon. "Rights from Wrongs." *E: The Environmental Magazine* 14 (March–April 2003): 26–33.

Mouras, Belton. *I Care about Animals*. New York: A. S. Barnes, 1977.

Muncy, Robyn. *Creating a Female Dominion in American Reform, 1890–1935*. New York: Oxford University Press, 1991.

Myers, Fred. "Humane Legislation Marches On." A-V 67 (October 1959): 129–30.

Nace, Patrick. "WARDS and the Animal Welfare Act (Part 1)." *Our Animal WARDS*, Winter 1994, 4–5.

———. "WARDS and the Animal Welfare Act (Part 2)." *Our Animal WARDS*, Spring 1994, 6.

Nash, Roderick. *The Rights of Nature: A History of Environmental Ethics*. Madison: University of Wisconsin Press, 1989.

National Anti-Vivisection Society. "In Defense of the Defenseless." *Expressions* 2 (1994): 28–29.

Navasky, Victor. *Naming Names*. New York: Viking Press, 1980.

"NCSAW's New Name: Society for Animal Rights, Inc.," *NCSAW Report*, September 1972, 1.
"The Negro in His Relations to the Lower Animals." *Journal of Zoophily* 12 (April 1903): 50–51.
Neider, Charles, ed. *Mark Twain: Life as I Find It*. Garden City, NY: Hanover House, 1961.
Nelson, Donald. *Managers and Workers: Origins of the New Factory System in the United States*. Madison: University of Wisconsin Press, 1975.
Nelson, E. W. "Decrease of Fur-Bearing Animals in Alaska." *Natural History* 22 (1922): 83.
Nethery, Lauren, and John McArdle. *Animals in Product Development and Safety Testing: A Survey*. Washington, DC: Institute for the Study of Animal Problems, 1985.
Newkirk, Ingrid. *Save the Animals! 101 Easy Things You Can Do*. New York: Warner Books, 1990.
"News from the Dying Industry." *Farm Report*, Fall 1994, 8.
Nicholson, E. B. *The Rights of an Animal: A New Essay in Ethics*. London: Kegan Paul, 1879.
Nicholson, Katharine Stanley. "Sources of Supply to Vivisection." Paper presented at the International Anti-Vivisection and Animal Protection Congress, Washington, DC, December 8–11, 1913.
Nilsson, Greta. "Animals Killed for the Fur Trade." In *Facts about Furs*, 30–85. Washington, DC: Animal Welfare Institute, 1980.
———. "The Fur Trade, a Short History." In *Facts about Furs*, 1–29. Washington, DC: Animal Welfare Institute, 1980.
———. "The Fur Trade and Endangered Species." In *Facts about Furs*, 162–74. Washington, DC: Animal Welfare Institute, 1980.
———. "Legislation Regulating the Taking of Furbearers." In *Facts about Furs*, 141–61. Washington, DC: Animal Welfare Institute, 1980.
Niven, Charles. *History of the Humane Movement*. New York: Transatlantic Press, 1967.
Norwood, Vera. *Made from this Earth: American Women and Nature*. Chapel Hill: University of North Carolina Press, 1993.
O'Connor, John. "'The Guns of Autumn': Hunted and the Hunters." *New York Times*, September 14, 1975, D25.
O'Connor, Karen. *Sharing the Kingdom: Animals and Their Rights*. New York: Dodd, Mead, 1984.
Olmstead, Frederick. "The Yosemite Valley and the Mariposa Big Trees." *Landscape Architecture* 43 (1952): 17–21.

Ommaya, A. K., A. E. Hirsch, E. S. Flamm, and R. H. Mahone. "Cerebral Concussion in the Monkey: An Experimental Model." *Science* 153 (July 1966): 211–12.

Operatic Scenes and Costume Songs under the Direction of Perley Dunn Aldrich for the Benefit of the Horse Watering Stations Department of the Women's PSPCA. Pamphlet. Philadelphia: WPSPCA, March 6, 1914.

Organizational History—National Society for Medical Research. June 25, 2005. U.S. National Library of Medicine. http://nlm.nih.gov/hmd/manuscripts/ead/nsmr.html.

Orlans, F. Barbara. *In the Name of Science: Issues in Responsible Animal Experimentation.* New York: Oxford University Press, 1993.

Ortega y Gassett, Jose. *Meditations on Hunting.* Trans. H. B. Wescott. New York: Scribner's, 1972.

"The Other SPCA." *Penn Monthly Magazine* 12 (January 1881): 53–71.

Outdoor Recreation for America: A Report to the President and to the Congress by the Congress by the Outdoor Recreation Resources Review Commission. Superintendent of Documents. Washington, DC, 1962.

"PA Animal Dealers Found Big Supporters of NY Vivisection." *A-V* 56 (July 1948): 101.

Pacelle, Wayne. "Flying the Unfriendly Skies." *Animals' Agenda* 8 (November 1988): 12–15, 17, and 19–20.

———. "Saviors or Sellouts? How 'Wildlife' Groups Lend Support to Sport Hunting." *Animals' Agenda* 8 (July–August 1988): 7–9.

"The Paper Curtain." *International Society for Animal Rights Report,* August 1985, 4.

Parke, D. W. "Regulatory Aspects." *In Animals and Alternatives in Toxicity Testing,* ed. M. Balls, R. J. Riddell, and A. N. Worden, 445–56. London: Academic Press, 1983.

Parsons, Cynthia. *George Bird Grinnell: A Biographical Sketch.* Lanham, MD: University Press of America, 1992.

Peattie, Donald. *An Almanac for Moderns.* New York: G. P. Putnam's Sons, 1935.

"The Pentagon's Secret War on Animals." *Animals' Agenda* 7 (June 1987): 29 and 48.

The PETA Guide to Animal Liberation. Washington, DC: PETA, n.d.

Petry, Howard, ed. A *Century of Medicine, 1848–1948: The History of the Medical Society of the State of Pennsylvania.* Harrisburg: Medical Society of the State of Pennsylvania, 1952.

Phelps, Elizabeth Stuart. *Chapters from a Life.* New York: Houghton Mifflin, 1896.

——. A *Plea for the Helpless.* Pamphlet. New York: American Humane Association, 1901.

——. *Vivisection and Legislation in Massachusetts.* Pamphlet. Philadelphia: American Anti-Vivisection Society, 1902.

Philadelphia Evening Ledger, January 27, 1917, 10.

Phinizy, Cole. "The Lost Pets That Stray to Labs." *Sports Illustrated* 29 (November 29, 1965): 38 and 41.

Physiological Behavior 12 (1974): 93.

Pope, Alexander. "Animal Life in a Zoo: The Modern Way of Keeping Animals." *Scientific American* 112 (April 24, 1915): 390.

Pope, L. S. "Commercial Beef Production in the United States." In *Commercial Beef Cattle Production*, ed. C. C. O'Mary and Irwin Dyer, 1–7. Philadelphia: Lea and Febiger, 1972.

Pratt, Dallas. *Alternatives to Pain in Experiments on Animals.* New York: Argus Archives, 1980.

——. *Painful Experiments on Animals.* New York: Argus Archives, 1976.

——. Typed comment/notes of two-hour discussion with Jacques Sichel, March 6, 1968. Argus Archives, Garrison, NY.

——. Typed comment on the founding of United Action for Animals, 1969. Argus Archives, Garrison, NY.

Prentice, Arthur. A *Candid View of the Fur Industry.* Ontario, Canada: Clay Publishing, 1976.

Principles and Guidelines for the Use of Animals in Pre-college Education. Pamphlet. Washington, DC: Institute of Laboratory Animal Resources, 1989.

Pringle, Allen. "Reasoning Animals." *Popular Science Monthly* 42 (November 1892): 71–75.

Pringle, Laurence. *The Animal Rights Controversy.* New York: Harcourt Brace Jovanovich, 1989.

Problems in Preventing the Marketing of Raw Meat and Poultry Containing Potentially Harmful Residues. Washington, DC: Comptroller General of the United States, April 17, 1979.

Proceedings of the Fifteenth Annual Stapp Car Crash Conference Held in Coronado, California, November 17–19, 1971. New York: Society of Automotive Engineers, 1971.

Proceedings of the Fourth Conservation Congress. Indianapolis, IN: National Conservation Congress, 1912.

Profiles and Parameters: Harlan Canine Models. Indianapolis, IN: Harlan Sprague Dawley, n.d.

"Protest Mail Pours in on Ford." *NSCAW Report*, February 1968, 1.

Ranney, Sally. "Heroines and Hierarchy: Female Leadership in the Conservation Movement." In *Voices from the Environmental Movement:*

Perspectives for a New Era, ed. Donald Snow, 117–23. Covelo, CA: Island Press, 1992.

Reece, Kathleen A. *Animal Organizations and Services Directory*. Manhattan Beach, CA: Animal Stories, 1991.

Refuge Report. Circular. Washington, DC: Wildlife Refuge Reform Coalition, n.d.

Regan, Tom. *The Case for Animal Rights*. Berkeley: University of California Press, 1983.

Regan, Tom, and Peter Singer, eds. *Animal Rights and Human Obligations*. Englewood Cliffs, NJ: Prentice-Hall, 1989.

Regenstein, Lewis. "Animal Rights, Endangered Species, and Human Survival." In *In Defense of Animals*, ed. Peter Singer, 118–34. New York: Harper and Row, 1985.

Reid, Edward. "Trappers Want a Fair Deal." *Fur-Fish-Game* 67 (April 1971): 44.

Report of the Animal Alternatives Study Task Force. Berkeley: University of California Press, 1988.

"Report of the Council on Defense of Medical Research." *Journal of the American Medical Association* 52 (1909): 2073–74.

"Report of the Council on Defense of Medical Research." *Journal of the American Medical Association* 54 (1910): 2079.

Report of the Council's Activities from June 6 thru November 30, 1973 (Council for Livestock Protection, Inc.). Photocopy provided by Ron Scott, Argus Archives, Garrison, NY.

Report of the Third Annual Meeting of the N.C.S. for A.W. New York: National Catholic Society for Animal Welfare, May 26, 1962.

Riley, Glenda. *Women and Nature: Saving the "Wild" West*. Lincoln: University of Nebraska Press, 1999.

Riopelle, Arthur, and Curtis Thomsen. "The Use of Primates as Behavioral Subjects." In *Methods of Animal Experimentation*, ed. William Gay, vol. 3, 81–124. New York: Academic Press, 1968.

Ritvo, Harriet. *The Animal Estate: The English and Other Creatures in the Victorian Age*. Cambridge, MA: Harvard University Press, 1987.

———. "Plus Ça Change: Anti-vivisection Then and Now." *Science, Technology, and Human Values* 9 (Spring 1984): 57–66.

Robbins, John. *Diet for a New America*. Walpole, NH: Stillpoint Publishing, 1987.

Robbins, Peggy. "Henry Bergh, Founder of the ASPCA." *American History Illustrated* 16 (April 1981): 8.

Roberts, Adam. "The Endangered Species Act: A Commitment Worth Keeping." *Animal Guardian* 8 (1995): 5–8.

Robinson, Harry. "Animal Experimentation Leading to the Development of Drugs Benefiting Human Beings and Animals." *American Journal of Public Health* 57 (September 1967): 1615–20.
Robinson, Weldon B. "The 'Humane Coyote-Getter' vs. the Steel Trap in Control of Predatory Animals." *Journal of Wildlife Management* 7 (1943): 179–89.
Rollin, Bernard E. *Animal Rights and Human Morality.* Rev. ed. Buffalo, NY: Prometheus Books, 1992.
Roosevelt, Theodore. *The Wilderness Hunter.* New York: P. F. Collier and Son, 1893.
Rose, Lisle. *The Cold War Comes to Main Street: America in 1950.* Lawrence: University Press of Kansas, 1999.
Rovner, Julie. "Puppy Mill Misery." *Humane Society News.* Reprinted circular. Washington, DC: Humane Society of the United States, 1981.
Rowan, Andrew. "The Development of the Animal Protection Movement." *Journal of NIH Research* 1 (November–December 1989): 97–100.
———. *Of Mice, Models, and Men: A Critical Evaluation of Animal Research.* Albany: State University of New York, 1984.
Rowley, Francis. "Slaughter House Reform." Paper presented at the International Anti-Vivisection and Animal Protection Congress, Washington, DC, December 8–11, 1913.
Roy, Suzanne. "'Exposed': The Military's War on Animals." A *Report to the Armed Services Committee, Subcommittee on Research and Development.* San Francisco: In Defense of Animals, n.d.
Rudacille, Deborah. "Alternatives Called New Branch of Science." *Center for Alternatives to Animal Testing* 11 (Winter 1994): 1–3.
Rue, L. L. *The Deer of North America.* Los Angeles: Times-Mirror, 1978.
"Rules and Regulations on Zoos." In *Animals and Their Legal Rights: A Survey of American Laws from 1641–1978,* 3d ed., ed. Emily Leavitt, app., xxxix. Washington, DC: Animal Welfare Institute, 1978.
Russett, Cynthia Eagle. *Sexual Science: The Victorian Construction of Womanhood.* Cambridge, MA: Harvard University Press, 1989.
Ryan, Mary. *Women in Public: Between Banners and Ballots, 1825–1880.* Baltimore, MD: Johns Hopkins University Press, 1990.
Ryder, Richard. *Animal Revolution: Changing Attitudes towards Speciesism.* Oxford: Basil Blackwell, 1989.
Sale, Kirkpatrick. *The Green Revolution: The American Environmental Movement, 1962–1992.* New York: Hill and Wang, 1993.
Salt, Henry S. *Animals' Rights Considered in Relation to Social Progress.* London: Macmillan, 1894.

Saxon, A. H. *P. T. Barnum: The Legend and the Man.* New York: Columbia University Press, 1989.

Schmitt, Peter. *Back to Nature: The Arcadian Myth in Urban America.* New York: Oxford University Press, 1969.

Schrecker, Ellen. *Many Are the Crimes: McCarthyism in America.* Princeton, NJ: Princeton University Press, 1998.

Schweitzer, Albert. *Part II: Civilization and Ethics.* Trans. John Naish. London: A and C Black, 1923.

Scott, Martha. "Trapping and Poisoning." In *Animals and Their Legal Rights: A Survey of American Laws from 1641–1978,* 3d ed., ed. Emily Leavitt, 159–67. Washington, DC: Animal Welfare Institute, 1978.

"Seal Slaughter for Fashion." *NCSAW Report,* June 1968, 2.

"Seals." *NCSAW Report,* February 1972, 1.

Seton, Ernest Thompson. *Animal Heroes.* New York: Charles Scribner's Sons, 1905.

———. *The Arctic Prairies.* New York: Charles Scribner's Sons, 1911.

———. "Cruel Methods of Trapping." Paper presented at the International Anti-Vivisection and Animal Protection Congress, Washington, DC, December 8–11, 1913.

———. *Lives of the Hunted.* New York: Charles Scribner's Sons, 1901.

Sewell, Anna. *Black Beauty: The Autobiography of a Horse.* Akron, OH: Saalfield Publishing, 1924.

Sharpe, Robert. *Basic Mistakes: The Unreliability of Animal Models in Research and Testing.* Jenkintown, PA: AAVS [1991?].

———. *Consenting Guinea Pigs: The Human Participants Who Advance Medicine.* Jenkintown, PA: American Anti-Vivisection Society [1991?]

———. *The Cruel Deception: The Use of Animals in Medical Research.* Northamptonshire and London: Thorsons Publishers, 1988.

———. "Temples of the Future." *The Liberator,* November–December 1987, 24.

Shorter, Edward. *The Health Century.* New York: Doubleday, 1987.

Shultz, William. *The Humane Movement in the United States, 1910–1922.* New York: AMA Press, 1968 [1924].

Sichel, Jacques, to Jo Morgan, February 16, 1971. Argus Archives, Garrison, NY.

Simmonds, Richard. *Abbreviated History of the Animal Welfare/Antivivisection/Rights Movements.* Bethesda, MD: Uniformed Services University of the Health Sciences, 1986.

Singer, Peter. *Animal Liberation.* Rev. ed. New York: Avon Books, 1990.

"Slaughter Campaign Pamphlet Planned." *NCSAW Report,* June 1960, 8.

Smith, Dietrich. "Methods of Euthanasia and Disposal." In *Methods of Animal Experimentation*, ed. William Gay, vol. 1, 167–96. New York: Academic Press, 1965.

Smith, Steve, Mark Evans, Micaela Sullivan-Fowler, and William Hendee. "Use of Animals in Biomedical Research: Historical Role of the American Medical Association and the American Physician." *Archives of Internal Medicine* 148 (August 1988): 1849–53.

Smith-Rosenberg, Carol. "The Female World of Love and Ritual: Relations between Women in Nineteenth-Century America." *Signs* 1 (Autumn 1975): 1–29.

Snyder, G. *Turtle Island.* New York: New Directions, 1974.

Soave, Orland A. "Animal Experimentation Leading to Better Care of Laboratory and Pet Animals." *American Journal of Public Health* 57 (September 1967): 1621–26.

"Some Groups Support Pets in Research." *International Society for Animal Rights Report*, December 1988, 1, 4.

Soos, Troy. "Charles River Breeding Laboratories: Turning Out Animals from an Assembly Line." *Cease Synopsis*, no. 4 (Fall 1986): 4–5.

"South Carolina Resolutions on Abolitionist Propaganda (1835)." In *Documents of American History*, ed. Henry Steele Commager, 281–82. New York: F. S. Crofts, 1941.

"Spare Time? What Spare Time?" *Changing Times* 18 (May 1964): 18–20.

"Spaying Survey of Shelters Completed." NCSAW *Report*, June 1964, 4.

Special Report: Turning Cows into Biotech Milk Machines. San Rafael, CA: Humane Farming Association, 1994.

Sperling, Frederick. "Animal Care in the Laboratory: Who Should Regulate It?" *Science* 151 (February 18, 1966): 776–77.

———. "Letters." *Science* 151 (February 18, 1966): 778.

Spiegal, Majourie. *The Dreaded Comparison.* New York: Mirror Books, 1990.

Spira, Henry. "Fighting to Win." In *In Defense of Animals*, ed. Peter Singer, 194–208. New York: Harper and Row, 1985.

Stampp, Kenneth M. *The Peculiar Institution: Slavery in the Ante-bellum South.* New York: Random House, 1956.

Stathos, Margaret Moreland. "The History of the New England Antivivisection Society." *NEAVS* 80 (centennial issue): 4–13.

Steele, Zulma. *Angel in Top Hat: A Biography of Henry Bergh, Founder of American Society for the Prevention of Cruelty to Animals.* New York: Harper and Brothers, 1942.

Stephens, Martin. *Alternatives to Current Uses of Animals in Research, Safety Testing, and Education: A Layman's Guide.* Washington, DC: Humane Society of the United States, 1986.

———. *Maternal Deprivation Experiments in Psychology: A Critique of Animal Models.* N.p.: American Anti-Vivisection Society, National Anti-Vivisection Society, and the New England Anti-Vivisection Society, 1986.

Stevens, Christine. "From Fur Bearer to Fur Wearer." In *Facts about Furs,* 86–119. Washington, DC: Animal Welfare Institute, 1980.

———. "Laboratory Animal Welfare" and "Marine Mammals." In *Animals and Their Legal Rights: A Survey of American Laws from 1641–1978,* 3d ed., ed. Emily Leavitt, 46–68 and 168–74. Washington, DC: Animal Welfare Institute, 1978.

Stewart, W. C. "Legal Standards for Humane Care: The Animal Welfare Act." *Lab Animal* 13 (September 1984): 33–41.

Stowe, Harriet Beecher. *Men of Our Times.* Hartford, CT: Hartford Publishing, 1868.

Stricklin, W. Ray, and Janice Swanson. "Technology and Animal Agriculture." *Journal of Agricultural and Environmental Ethics* 6 (1993): 67–80.

Swallow, William. *Quality of Mercy: History of the Humane Movement in the United States.* Boston: Mary Mitchell Humane Fund, 1963.

Swanston, D. W. "Eye Irritancy Testing." In *Animals and Alternatives in Toxicity Testing,* ed. M. Balls, R. J. Riddell, and A. N. Worden, 337–66. London: Academic Press, 1983.

Tansley, Arthur. "The Use and Abuse of Vegetational Concepts and Terms." *Ecology* 16 (1935): 284–306.

Teaford, Jon. *The Rough Road to Renaissance: Urban Revitalization in America, 1940–1985.* Baltimore, MD: Johns Hopkins University Press, 1985.

Teale, Edwin Way, ed. *Green Treasury.* New York: Dodd, Mead, 1952.

Terres, John, ed. *The Audubon Book of True Nature Stories.* New York: Thomas Y. Crowell, 1958.

Testimony on a Bill for Humane Treatment of Livestock. Pamphlet. N.p.: Council for Livestock Protection, 1974.

"That Special Week." *National Humane Review* 56 (January–February 1962): 48–50.

Thernstrom, Stephen. *The Other Bostonians: Poverty and Progress in the American Metropolis.* Cambridge, MA: Harvard University Press, 1973.

"Thirteenth Annual Report for the Year Ending November 15, 1903, of the Department of Mercy of the National WCTU." *Journal of Zoophily* 13 (March 1904): 28.

Thoreau, Henry David. *Walden and Other Writings.* New York: Bantam Books, 1989 [1854].

Time, August 18, 1952, cover.

"Timeline." *Meat and Poultry* (August 1989). Photocopy provided by the library of PETA, Washington, DC, and Rockville, MD.

Titus, Harry W. *The Scientific Feeding of Chickens.* Danville, IL: The Interstate, 1949.

Tober, James. *Who Owns the Wildlife? The Political Economy of Conservation in Nineteenth-Century America.* Westport, CT: Greenwood Press, 1981.

Transcript of Proceedings, 96th Annual Meeting of the AHA. American Humane Association, Denver, October 8–11, 1972.

Turner, James. *Reckoning with the Beast: Animals, Pain, and Humanity in the Victorian Mind.* Baltimore, MD: Johns Hopkins University Press, 1980.

Twain, Mark. "A Dog's Tale." *Harper's Monthly Magazine* 108 (December 1903): 11–19.

"Twelve Dogs Develop Lung Cancer in Group of 86 Taught to Smoke." *New York Times,* February 6, 1970, 1.

Tyson, Jon Wynne, ed. *The Extended Circle: A Dictionary of Humane Thought.* Sussex, England: Centaur Press, 1985.

"Unfinished Business: Renewing the Fight for Canada's Seals, Africa's Elephants, and the World's Whales." *Animals' Agenda* 17 (September–October 1997): 22–26.

"United Action for Animals." NCSAW *Report,* October 1968, 5.

"University of Pennsylvania Professor Defends Vivisection." *Public Ledger,* December 21, 1913, 6.

Unti, Bernard. "The Birth of Animal Rights in America: Caroline Earle White and AAVS." *AV Magazine* (Fall 2000): 8–10.

———. "Using Animals in the Classroom." *Animals' Agenda* 6 (July–August 1986): 10.

"Urgent!" NCSAW *Report,* November 1967, 1.

U.S. Congress. General Accounting Office. *Use of Dogs in Experiments at Edgewood Arsenal, Maryland: Department of the Army.* GAO Rep. No. PSAD-76–80. Washington, DC, March 12, 1976.

———. Office of Technology Assessment. *Alternatives to Animal Use in Research, Testing, and Education.* OTA-BA-273. Washington, DC: Government Printing Office, February 1986.

———. Senate. Committee on Territories. *Reports of Committees.* 43d Cong., 1st sess., June 9, 1874.

U.S. Department of Agriculture. *Animal Health Delivery Systems in the United States.* Washington, DC: USDA, 1984–1985.

"Use of Animals in Biomedical Research: The Challenge and Response." *An American Medical Association White Paper.* Chicago: AMA, 1989, rev. 1992.

Use of Animals in Biomedical Research: Understanding the Issues. Cordova, TN: American Association for Laboratory Science, n.d.

Veal Production in the United States. Pamphlet. San Francisco: Humane Farming Association, 1992.

Vegetarianism. Pamphlet. Jenkintown, PA: American Anti-Vivisection Society, 1995.

"VFA Demonstrates against GM, 'The Heartbreak of America.'" *Vocalizations* 2 (December–January 1992): 1.

Virtanen, Artturi. "Milk Production of Cows on Protein-Free Feed." *Science* 153 (September 30, 1966): 1603–14.

"Visits to Laboratories Show Need for H.R. 1937." *AWI Information Report* 11 (January–February 1962): 1.

Visscher, Maurice. "Animal Care Legislation: Why Scientists Do Object." *Science* 151 (February 18, 1966): 636.

———. "The Animal Welfare Act of 1970." *Science* 172 (May 28, 1971): 916–17.

Vivisection Is Cruel, Brutal, and Futile. Pamphlet. Philadelphia: American Anti-Vivisection Society, n.d.

Walker, Guy Morrison. "American Debt to Railroads." In *The Making of America,* ed. Robert Marion La Follette, 408–17. N.p.: John D. Morris, 1906.

Warbasse, James. *The Conquest of Disease through Animal Experimentation.* New York: D. Appleton, 1910.

Washington March for the Animals. Pamphlet. N.p.: National Catholic Society for Animal Welfare, n.d.

Wayman, Stan, and Michel Silva. "Concentration Camps for Dogs." *Life* 60 (February 4, 1966): 22–29.

Weeks, Philip. *Farewell, My Nation: The American Indian and the United States, 1820–1890.* Arlington Heights, IL: Harlan Davis, 1990.

Weinberg, Alvin. *Reflections on Big Science.* Cambridge, MA: MIT Press, 1967.

Weiner, Jonathan. "Animal Liberation." *Cosmopolitan,* June 1980, 146. Photocopy provided by the Animal Welfare Information Center, Beltsville, MD.

Weiss, Rick. "Inventing the Skin You Love to Test." *Washington Post,* February 21, 1988, B3.

Welch, W. H. "Fields of Usefulness of the American Medical Association: President's Address at the 61st Annual Session of the American Medical Association." *Journal of the American Medical Association* 54 (1910): 2011–7.

Welcome to the Fund for Animals. Pamphlet. New York: Fund for Animals, n.d.

Welter, Barbara. "The Cult of True Womanhood: 1820–1860." *American Quarterly* 18 (Summer 1966): 151–74.
"We Won! Wildlife Protection Act Is a Historic Victory for Animals." *Animal Action*, Fall 1996, 1.
What Is Greenpeace? Pamphlet. Washington, DC: Greenpeace, 1995.
"Where We Came From." *The Anti-Cruelty Society: 75th Annual Report.* Chicago: Anti-Cruelty Society, 1975, 1–2.
Whipple, George Hoyt. "Value of Animal Experimentation to Mankind." *American Journal of Public Health* 11 (February 1921): 105–7.
White, Caroline Earle. "Comments and Reflections." *Journal of Zoophily* 3 (August 1894): 114.
———. "The Practice of Vivisection." *Forum* 9 (March 1890): 106–16.
———. *Silver Festival of the Women's Branch of the Pennsylvania Society for the Prevention of Cruelty to Animals.* Philadelphia: Women's Branch of the Pennsylvania Society for the Prevention of Cruelty to Animals, 1894.
"White House Pickets Assail Bills on Treatment of Lab Animals." *Washington Post*, July 11, 1966, A3.
"Who Needs Enemies?" *NCSAW Report*, March 1967, 3.
Who We Are. No date. Friends of the Earth. http://www.foe.org/about/whoweare/html.
Wiebe, Robert. *The Search for Order.* New York: Hill and Wang, 1967.
Williamson, Henry. *Tarka the Otter.* New York: E. P. Dutton, 1928.
Willing, Richard. "20,000 Animals Killed in Decade of GM Safety Tests." *Detroit News*, September 27, 1991, A1, A5.
Wilson, James D. *A Reader's Guide to the Short Stories of Mark Twain.* Boston: G. K. Hall, 1987.
Winterscheid, Loren. "Animal Experimentation Leading to the Development of Advanced Surgical Technics." *American Journal of Public Health* 57 (September 1967): 1604–12.
Wolfe, Dael. "Animal Care Legislation." *Science* 151 (September 2, 1966): 1.
Women's Branch of the PSPCA. *Annual Reports*, 1st (1870), 2d (1871), 3d (1872), 4th (1873), 6th (1875), 15th (1883), 18th (1886), 20th (1888), 41st (1909), 46th (1914), 48th (1916), 50th (1918), 68th (1936), 71st (1939), 82d (1950). Philadelphia.
"Women's Clubs in the News." *A-V* 56 (September 1948): 123.
"Women's Convention Exhibit Planned." *NCSAW Report*, October 1962, 2.
Women's SPCA of Pennsylvania. Booklet. Philadelphia: Women's SPCA, 1959.
Wood, H. C. "The Value of Vivisection." *Scribner's Monthly* 20 (September 1880): 766–70.
Woodcock, N. *Fifty Years a Hunter and Trapper.* Columbus, OH: Fur-Fish-Game, 1972.

Woolf, Virginia. President, Lehigh Animal Rights Coalition. Interview by author, September 26, 1995. Taped recording. Allentown, PA.

"Words and Their Meaning." *International Society for Animal Rights Report*, June 1985, 3.

The Work of the Society of Animal Protective Legislation from 1955. Pamphlet. Washington, DC: Society for Animal Protective Legislation, 1993.

"The World's 'Most Wanted' Species." *Focus* 15 (May–June 1993): 4–5.

World Wildlife Fund 1993 Annual Report. Washington, DC: World Wildlife Fund, 1994.

Worster, Donald. *Nature's Economy: A History of Ecological Ideas*. New York: Cambridge University Press, 1991.

WPSPCA Minute Book No. 1. Philadelphia: WPSPCA, April 28 and June 16, 1869.

Wright, Gordon. *The Ordeal of Total War, 1939–1945*. New York: Harper and Row, 1968.

Written Testimony for Hearings on Military Animal Research Convened by the Armed Services Committee Subcommittee on Research and Technology. Submitted by Suzanne Roy, April 13, 1994.

Zbinden, Gerhard. "Current Concepts of Acute Toxicity Testing." In *Touch . . . New Methods in Toxicology* 1 (November 1982): 5–6.

Zunz, Olivier. *The Changing Face of Inequality: Urbanization, Industrial Development, and Immigrants in Detroit, 1880–1920*. Chicago: University of Chicago Press, 1982.

Index